PROFESSIONAL PSYCHOLOGY HANDBOOK

THE BRITISH
PSYCHOLOGICAL
SOCIETY

First published in 1995 by BPS Books (The British Psychological Society), St Andrews House, 48 Princess Road East, Leicester LE1 7DR, UK

A catalogue record for this book is available from the British Library.

ISBN 1 85433 124 8

Co-ordinated by Susan Pacitti and Rochelle Serwator.
Typeset by Fakenham Photosetting Limited, Norfolk.
Printed in Great Britain by BPC Wheatons Ltd, Exeter.

CONTENTS

Foreword

The concept of a professional psychology handbook is a good one. Everyone who was consulted welcomed the idea of putting together into a single reference book many statements and other bits of information about psychology that had, hitherto, existed in isolated and, thus, relatively inaccessible form. Professional psychologists, especially those early in their careers, should benefit from having information about the Society and the practice of psychology in the United Kingdom all in one place. Those contemplating a career in psychology should also find a volume of this sort useful. Sections of the book cover topics, such as examining and doing research, which are relevant to psychologists whose profession is that of lecturer or teacher of psychology.

Translating a good idea into a published book proved more difficult and took longer than originally hoped. Deciding what to include and what to leave out was difficult and readers often have to be referred to other publications for more detail. Finding experts with the time to prepare relevant chapters was not always easy. Moreover, the world about which the authors were writing keeps changing. New legislation can alter the environment in which psychological services are delivered. Topical information, such as salary levels, gets out-of-date. Whilst every effort has been made to give factual, accurate information up to the time of going to press, errors and omissions must be accepted. Similarly, rules and regulations of the Society itself are described, but such material is published to give general guidance and cannot replace or diminish the Statutes, Rules and Regulations of the Society to which they refer and which may evolve and change over time.

To what extent the aims of the book have been achieved will be for others to judge. Constructive criticisms will be welcome and it will be useful to learn if a reference book of this type has met the needs of its readers and thus, whether revised editions in years to come would be welcomed. All the authors must be thanked for their contributions which have been made so willingly and for scant reward. The true measure of their success will be the extent to which those who have made psychology their profession are better informed having read this book.

COLIN V. NEWMAN
Executive Secretary
The British Psychological Society

Acknowledgements

We would like to thank all those people who helped with the compilation of the *Handbook*. Those who wrote sections are credited within the text but there are a number of other people who advised, checked, provided extra information, and wrote supplementary material, often at very short notice, and they deserve to be recognized too. We are very grateful to all those who have helped, both by writing, and behind the scenes.

Thanks to: the Committees of the Divisions and Special Groups, the Training Committees of the Divisions, the Steering Committee on Test Standards, the Journals Committee, Irene Aggus, John Allen, Bob Archer, Liz Baikie, Amanda Biggs, Derek Blackman, Valerie Bull, Carol Shillito-Clark, Joyce Collins, Graham Davey, Hilton Davis, Pete Dingwall, Pat Frankish, Nicky Hayes, Libby Irvine, Stuart Lewis, Pat Lindley, Geoff Lindsay, Bob Logie, David Marks, Jenny Marks, Bernard Marriott, Cynthia McDougall, Donald McLeod, Colin Newman, Steve Newstead, Marion Newton, Susan Pacitti, John Richardson, Muriel Russell, Allan Sakne, Rochelle Serwator, John Sloboda, Ann Smith, Sheelagh Strawbridge, Fraser Watts, Mark Williams, Tom Williams, Jenifer Elton Wilson, Valerie Young.

Copyright acknowledgements

The following have been reprinted with permission:

Sections 4.5.1 and 4.5.2 originally appeared in Parry and Watts: *Behavioural and Mental Health Research: A Handbook of Skills and Methods*, © 1989. Reprinted by permission of Lawrence Erlbaum Associates Ltd, Hove, UK. 2nd edition currently in preparation. *Section 5.3* originally appeared in *Teaching Psychology: Information and Resources*, 3rd edition © 1993. Published by BPS Books (The British Psychological Society). *Appendices A* and *B* reproduced by permission from the *Directory of Chartered Psychologists*, © 1995, published by The British Psychological Society. *Appendix C* originally appeared in Vol. 8, No. 2 of *The Psychologist*, © 1995, reprinted by permission.

SECTION I
AREAS OF PROFESSIONAL PRACTICE

Contributors:

Bruce Napier
Head of Psychology Services (Mental Health), Gwynedd Community Health Trust

John Sheppard
Chartered Educational Psychologist and Past Chair of the Division of Educational and Child Psychology

Martin Crawshaw
Department of Psychology, University of Hull

Mary McMurran
Honorary Secretary, Division of Criminological and Legal Psychology, and Director of Psychological Services, Rampton Hospital

Hugh Foot
Head of Department of Psychology, University of Strathclyde

Anthony Gale
Director of Research and Development, Department of Psychology, University of Portsmouth

Mary Watts
Senior Lecturer in Health and Counselling Psychology, and Director of Modular Health Scheme, City University, London

Robert Bor
Chartered Clinical and Counselling Psychologist, Reader in Counselling Psychology, City University, London

Marie Johnston
Professor of Psychology, University of St Andrews

John Weinman
Professor of Psychology as Applied to Medicine, Psychology Unit, United Medical and Dental Schools of Guys and St Thomas' Hospitals

1.1   CLINICAL PSYCHOLOGY

Bruce Napier

ORGANIZATION AND STRUCTURE OF THE PROFESSION

CLINICAL psychology has its roots in the use of psychological techniques to assist battle-fatigued personnel during World War II, working alongside psychiatrists in the Mill Hill Emergency Hospital. There is thus a sense in which what is now called Post Traumatic Stress Disorder was the first problem with which clinical psychologists were called to deal. The profession was recognized as part of the National Health Service from its inception in 1948, when it was grouped with Medical Physics and Clinical Biochemistry as a clinical science for wage bargaining purposes.

Originally, the distinction between clinical and educational psychology was blurred (a situation which continues today in some European countries), and the early role of psychology in the NHS was as a diagnostic profession. In 1966 the Division of Clinical Psychology (DCP) formed by separation from the English and Scottish Divisions of Professional Psychologists, with those remaining becoming the Division of Educational and Child Psychology (DECP) and the Scottish Division of Educational and Child Psychology (SDECP). At about the same time, the Society established the Diploma of Clinical Psychology as a qualification which could be taken by any probationer clinical psychologist.

The majority of clinical psychologists are employed in the NHS. In 1994, the DCP had 2840 members, and 2236 had chosen to Register as Chartered Psychologists.

Who employs clinical psychologists?

Most clinical psychologists in the UK are employed by Health Authorities in England and Wales, Health Boards in Scotland and NHS Trusts. There is a small number working exclusively in private practice or for local authorities, and rather more in academic and research settings such as universities or MRC (Medical Research Council) Research Units.

Many clinical psychologists do undertake some private work part-time, mainly associated with the preparation of court reports and the like. There is an Association of Chartered Clinical Psychologists in Private Practice which provides professional support to all those undertaking private work (see also Section 2.4 on Private Practice).

With whom does the clinical psychologist work?

Much of the work of clinical psychology is undertaken in the context of a multidisciplinary team of healthcare professionals. Such a team will often include medical practitioners, nurses, social workers, occupational and speech therapists and physiotherapists. Increasingly, voluntary agencies, carers and service users themselves are involved in both the planning and delivery of care. In fields such as learning disabilities, where the service user may have only a limited understanding of issues such as consent or strategic planning, there may be an advocacy service to provide representation of the users' interests.

Clinical psychologists will also work with a range of other professions, depending on the exact nature of the client group. Section 1.4 on Criminological and Legal Psychology indicates the range of others involved in the care and control of people whose problems include offending behaviour, and Section 1.2 on Educational Psychology discusses those working with children.

Who are the service users?

Most people coming into contact with a clinical psychologist will have originally gone to their GP and been referred either directly to the psychology service, or to some part of the health service which uses psychology. In addition, many mental health teams and psychology services accept self-referrals, especially from former users seeking further help and advice.

Direct work with users may involve diagnostic assessment of cognitive function or mood, or analysis of problem behaviours, but is also very likely to include therapy, counselling or advice. A very wide range of psychological difficulties may be involved, including anxiety, depression, relationship problems, learning disability, child behaviour problems and so on. In addition to these direct clinical interventions, an important part of the clinical psychologist's role is advice, supervision or consultancy to other members of the team, and input to the local and strategic planning processes.

All of the work described may also be undertaken by other members of the team; the psychologist's special contribution is to approach the tasks from a psychological perspective. A further, more distinct, role is that of the scientist–practitioner innovator and evaluator. Of all the professions involved in healthcare, psychology is the one whose practitioners are trained to think critically and creatively, and to be prepared to bring a research-based evaluative approach to bear on the work.

ETHICAL AND PROFESSIONAL ISSUES

Like the other types of psychologist described in this book, the clinical psychologist is bound by the *Code of Conduct* of the Society as the recognized standard of professional practice (see Section 3.4). The DCP also publishes a set of *Guidelines for Professional Practice*, which addresses those matters particular to clinical work. Since most clinical psychologists are employed professionals, they may find themselves caught in conflicts of responsibility to the client, the employer and society at large.

For example, clients are entitled to both confidentiality and privacy in their dealings with their clinical psychologist, but the psychologist will often need to share some of the information gained with other members of the team. Furthermore, if the client indicates that he or she has or is about to commit a serious crime such as child abuse, then the psychologist's duty to the potential or actual victims may override the duty of confidentiality.

Clinical psychologists have a responsibility to try to ensure the proper use of psychological techniques which they have taught to other team members, to offer appropriate supervision, and to seek it for themselves when they feel in need of it because of the issues raised by a particular case.

REGISTRATION, QUALIFICATIONS AND TRAINING

Like all professional psychologists, training as a clinical psychologist requires a degree in psychology which gives the Graduate Basis for Registration (GBR) (see Section 3.2), followed by a minimum period of three years' academic, practical and research training leading to a postgraduate qualification which confers eligibility to register as a Chartered Psychologist. At the time of writing, this qualification may be an M.Sc., M.Phil. or a Doctorate in Clinical Psychology.

In practice, many more people apply for professional training every year than there are training places, and so relevant experience in a caring profession, or in clinical research is essential. Many psychology graduates choose to work for between one and three years as an assistant psychologist in a clinical psychology service. Assistant psychologists undertake routine assessment and therapy work, for which they receive on the job training; it is an excellent way of sampling the work whilst acquiring the necessary experience, although concerns are often raised about the assistant's vulnerability to exploitation as a clinician 'on the cheap'.

Once qualified, a Chartered Clinical Psychologist is expected to undertake continuing professional development via attendance at courses, reading journals and going to scientific meetings.

Clinical psychologists who trained overseas may apply to the Committee for Scrutiny of Individual Clinical Qualifications for a decision as to whether they are eligible to Register and practise immediately in the UK, or if not, to have specified what additional training or experience they require (see Section 2.2).

PAY, PROSPECTS AND CONDITIONS

With very few exceptions, posts for qualified clinical psychologists are advertised in the BPS *Appointments Memorandum*. Some assistant psychologist posts are also advertised there, but more commonly they are only advertised locally, as removal expenses would not normally be payable for such a post. The training bottleneck means that many qualified posts are vacant at any one time, and some heads of service list their names in the back of *Clinical Psychology Forum*, the house journal of the DCP, to indicate that they are willing to be approached by job seekers at any time.

Most training places are funded as trainee psychologists, although some courses now offer bursaries, rather than salaried posts. This is an unpopular move, because of the loss of various benefits such a superannuation credits. Assistant psychologists are paid between £9,400 and £10,995, whilst trainees receive £11,437 to £12,865.

After qualification, most clinical psychologists will be offered a post on Grade A of the Whitley Council Scales, usually between spine point 25 and 30, worth £15,651 to £19,042. NHS Trusts are not obliged to pay Whitley Council scales, and of course the private sector can pay on whatever basis it chooses, but in practice most salaries are still described with reference to the national scales. Appointment at higher spine points follows as, with increasing experience, the psychologist undertakes work involving input at higher levels of the service, and of greater autonomy. Posts involving responsibilities for a Regional service, or for a training scheme, or with managerial responsibilities are paid on Grade B, which presently ranges from £28,187 to £46,934.

Clinical psychology shares the dilemma of other branches of professional psychology. There is a commitment amongst its practitioners to equal opportunities for women and for those from ethnic minority groups, but in practice there are comparatively few black members of the profession, and women are underrepresented at the higher grades. The DCP has a standing subcommittee to advise it on ways of moving forward on these matters.

Opportunities to work abroad vary. Training and professional structures in Australia, New Zealand and South Africa are fairly similar to the UK, but migration to those countries is no longer easy. UK trained psychologists have rights of establishment under EC law in an ever-increasing number of European countries, but there are substantial language and structural barriers.

Clinical psychologists from overseas

Owing to the large number of clinical psychologists moving to the UK and seeking registration, the Society has agreed a special procedure for the scrutiny of their qualifications.

The largest employer of clinical psychologists within the UK is the National Health Service, although some clinical psychologists do work in private practice. Those wishing to work as clinical psychologists in the National Health Service in any grade must be eligible for the Graduate Basis for Registration (see p. 163) and must hold a postgraduate qualification in clinical psychology approved by The British Psychological Society. Owing to the number of psychologists wishing to enter the United Kingdom and work in the National Health Service, the Society has a special procedure which is designed to enable psychologists from overseas to establish as rapidly as is possible whether they are eligible to work in the Health Service as unsupervised clinical psychologists.

Such psychologists are required to submit an application to the Committee for Scrutiny of Individual Clinical Qualifications for a Statement of Equivalence in Clinical Psychology. Applicants are required to provide details, in a supplementary application form, of their undergraduate and postgraduate training in psychology. This training is compared to the Society's Qualifying Examination (see p. 165) in order to establish whether or not the applicant has met the requirements of the Graduate Basis for Registration. If these requirements have been met, the remainder of the applicant's training is compared to the Society's Qualification in Clinical Psychology. The Committee will also collect reports from two referees nominated by the applicant who are able to comment on the applicant's professional training and professional practice as a clinical psychologist.

Those applicants whose training and experience is judged to be equivalent to the Society's Qualifying Examination and the Society's Qualification in Clinical Psychology, are issued with a Statement of Equivalence which is proof of eligibility to work in unsupervised posts in the National Health Service. The grading of the post which the applicant may undertake remains a matter for local negotiation and is usually determined once a Health Authority has decided to employ the person concerned.

When the Committee is able to agree that the applicant has met the requirements for the Graduate Basis for Registration, but that the further professional training does not meet the requirements of the Society's Qualification in Clinical Psychology then the Committee will specify what further training needs to be undertaken before a Statement of Equivalence can be issued. The psychologist concerned may then sit the specified parts of the Society's Qualification in Clinical Psychology and work within the National Health Service as a clinical psychologist in the meantime. In some cases further training requirements will be substantial, including written examinations, research work and several placements with various client groups. In other cases, the training requirements may be rather less and the Committee may specify only one or two placements with particular client groups that need be undertaken. Usually, whilst the psychologist is completing these requirements, they may be appointed at any point on Grade A of the clinical psychologists' salary scales. However, it is imperative that the training should be supervised. The psychologist will be required to make special arrangements for these further training experiences, and the necessary information and documentation will be provided when the applicant's training requirements are specified.

In some cases, the applicant's qualifications may not meet the criteria for eligibility for the Graduate Basis for Registration with the Society. These people will be advised to undertake a UK psychology degree, or a qualification such as a conversion course, or to sit the Society's Qualifying Examination. Those who are not eligible for the Graduate Basis for Registration with The British Psychological Society cannot be employed in the Health Service as a clinical psychologist in either a trainee or qualified grade.

Those who wish to apply for a Statement of Equivalence should contact the Society's office and request application forms for a Statement of Equivalence in Clinical Psychology for psychologists who have trained overseas.

THE FUTURE

It is probably more difficult to predict the future of clinical psychology now than it has been for the past 20 years. Change follows change in the structure of the NHS as the Department of Health struggles to square the circle of rising expectations, increasingly costly hi-tech medicine and an ageing population. Within psychology there is the challenge of the newly-emerging disciplines of health psychology, counselling psychology and clinical neuropsychology. Nonetheless, clinical psychology still has unique contributions to make to healthcare in the UK. It has grown at a phenomenal rate since 1948, and although the rate of growth is likely to be slower in the future, there is no reason to be pessimistic about the viability of the profession.

FURTHER READING

Guidelines for the Professional Practice of Clinical Psychology (1990). Leicester: The British Psychological Society, Division of Clinical Psychology.
How to Get a Psychology Assistant Post. Leicester: National Graduate Psychologists' Group, c/o The British Psychological Society.

1.2 EDUCATIONAL PSYCHOLOGY

John Sheppard

ORGANIZATION AND STRUCTURE OF THE PROFESSION

EDUCATIONAL psychologists have existed in Britain since one was employed part-time by the London County Council in 1913. Their number has grown particularly since the Summerfield Report in 1968 (*Psychologists in Education Services*, the report of a Government committee chaired by Professor Arthur Summerfield). Formal training of psychologists for work with children and in education has similarly largely been established as such since the 1960s. Since that time, training courses and thus formal qualifications have been distinct from those for clinical psychologists, though some would argue that this distinction does not reflect any great differences in real skills, but only in employment base and job titles.

The terms 'educational psychologist' and 'child psychologist' are often used synonymously. 'Child psychologist' is sometimes the term used to refer to an educational psychologist who works with children but is not LEA-based, and sometimes to refer to a clinical psychologist who specializes in work with children.

There are now about 1500 educational psychologists employed by local authorities within England and Wales. In Scotland there are about 300, and in Northern Ireland there are about 60. About 1100 belong to the Division of Educational and Child Psychology of The British Psychological Society (DECP), of whom some are resident and work outside Britain. About 150 belong to the Society's Scottish Division of Educational and Child Psychology (SDECP). About 75 per cent of full members of the DECP and about 78 per cent of full members of the SDECP choose to register as Chartered Psychologists and may use the title Chartered Educational Psychologist.

Who employs educational psychologists?

In England and Wales the most common employer of educational psychologists is the local education authority (LEA) of the county council or, in metropolitan areas, the district council or London Borough council. Local government re-organization is likely to bring many or all counties into the metropolitan pattern. In Scotland the equivalent employer is the Regional Council. In Northern Ireland the government structures are slightly different and the education authorities are the Education and Library Boards. In the Isle of Man the Government employs educational psychologists directly. In the Channel Islands, the States of Jersey and of Guernsey employ educational psychologists. The British Services Children's Education Authority also employs a small number of educational psychologists in Europe.

A few local authorities employ educational and child psychologists within their Social Services departments. Many others have arrangements whereby part or all of the time of some educational psychologists is bought from or otherwise provided by the LEA.

Several of the larger voluntary agencies concerned with child care and education employ full- or part-time educational psychologists to work in their own organizations. Some others pay psychologists as consultants, regularly or sessionally.

Increasingly, educational psychologists are working at least part-time independently. There is at present no national register and it is difficult to estimate the number, but it is thought that outside London and the Home Counties few educational psychologists make a full-time living out of private practice.

It remains the case that the overwhelming proportion of educational psychologists are employed by LEAs, but changes in national education policies may lead to a different balance in the future.

With whom does the educational psychologist work?

Typically within the LEA, educational psychologists are grouped together in what may be called an Educational Psychology Service or a School Psychological Service or simply a Psychological Service. That Psychological Service may be organizationally part of a department known as Special Services or Pupil Support Services or some similar name. Within the Psychological Service as well as psychologists there may be social workers, counsellors, specialist teachers, Portage home advisors, or others – this varies between LEAs. Learning support and advisory teachers, behaviour support teachers, specialist teachers of the sensorily disabled, bilingual and language support teachers, education welfare officers and home tutors may be in separate or closely related teams, and in either case will be common contacts of the psychologists. Also within the LEA, psychologists may have frequent contact with youth and community workers, careers officers, advisors and inspectors, and other officers of the authority. School governors will sometimes seek professional advice or receive training from educational psychologists. Outside the Education Department, but still within the local authority, the most common contacts are probably social workers, but there are many others – housing, community relations, and librarians, for example. Psychologists may be in direct contact with the elected members – the councillors – though in some authorities this is frowned upon. The most common contacts of all are teachers and other staff in schools, mainstream and special, all age ranges, and to a lesser extent in Sixth Form and FE colleges and in nurseries.

Educational psychologists are not normally hospital-based, but may occasionally undertake some work in a hospital setting, for example with a child who is ill or has suffered an accident, and work with the hospital teaching staff. Child Development Units attached to hospital paediatric departments may have educational or clinical psychologists, or both, working as part of their staff team.

It was once common for educational psychologists to work in Child Guidance Clinics with psychiatrists and social workers. This is now rarely the case, but these colleagues are often in frequent contact and cross-referral may take place. Similarly, there may well be close contact with clinical psychologists working with children from a health base.

Law enforcement and related agencies such as the NSPCC, the probation service and intermediate treatment teams will work with educational psychologists in particular cases where there is a mutual interest. Some educational psychologists, working from an LEA or a Social Services base, may specialize in work with abused children or with children and young people offending or at risk, and will devote an accordingly greater proportion of their time to such areas. Many educational psychologists will be involved at least sometimes with social services assessment centres and residential homes.

As part of paid LEA responsibilities, or independently, or on a voluntary basis, an educational psychologist may be involved with organizations outside the local authority structure, such as parents groups, youth organizations, groups for people with disabilities, children's rights organizations, the Independent Panel for Special Education Advice, and the Children's Legal Centre.

To whom does the educational psychologist offer a service?

A service is offered to any or all of those mentioned in the preceding paragraphs. Educational psychologists are largely concerned with ensuring that children and young people generally and individually are enabled to benefit as much as possible from their education and upbringing, giving due regard to their individual needs; that parents and teachers and others concerned with their development are advised as to how best to help them; and that systems and organizations are developed to enable optimal benefit. LEA psychological services are commonly involved with children and young people aged 0–19, but may also be interested in others, particularly those involved in further or adult education. Educational psychologists not working from an LEA base will probably be largely concerned with roughly the same age range, or a part of it.

A common conception is that educational psychologists work with children. Certainly this is part of the job and one of the essential skills is to be able easily to develop a working relationship with a child or a young person. In practice, however, educational psychologists probably work more with adults than with children themselves, though some observation of and interaction with the child in question may well be part of a process of consultation. Such observation or direct work with the child may on occasion take place at the psychologist's office but is more likely to be in school or home or another setting where the child is usually or temporarily based.

Work with families in depth or at length has become less common than was once the case, due to other pressures on the LEA educational psychologist. The psychologist will nevertheless often be asked for advice and provide some brief intervention, particularly where family circumstances are having an adverse effect on a child's behaviour or learning in school. In some instances the educational psychologist will be able to offer a longer-term relationship, and this is sometimes inevitably the case regarding a child who has special educational needs.

LEA educational psychologists are frequently asked to provide advice on children who appear to have special educational needs. Where an LEA is formally assessing these needs with a view to making a written Statement of them, in accordance with Part 3 of the Education Act 1993 (see pp. 105–108), or in Scotland a Record, in accordance with the Education (Scotland) Act 1981, it requires the written advice of an educational psychologist. A Statement or Record, once issued, needs to be operationalized with detailed plans and programmes. It then requires annual review and a full reconsideration during secondary school. Some LEA psychologists are currently finding that work on formal advice forms an increasingly large part of their work. A few have said they now find time for little else.

The Children Act of 1989 (see pp. 80–86), applying to England, Wales and Northern Ireland (with some minor differences in application), requires that children's needs be assessed in various circumstances, but does not require that an educational psychologist be involved in this assessment. Nevertheless as a matter of good practice, in some cases the local authority will choose to involve an educational or child psychologist, and in some authorities this will be routine under certain circumstances. In Scotland there is a statutory role with respect to the Children's Hearing system.

Solicitors and guardians *ad litem* may ask educational and child psychologists to advise on a child or young person's needs. This may be in the context of family proceedings or of a case for compensation arising out of an accident, or in a case pertaining to alleged unmet special educational needs. An educational psychologist working for a local authority is likely to be strictly limited in the input possible to such cases, but one operating independently may be employed by any of the parties to a case.

What does an educational psychologist do?

Like all applied psychologists, an educational psychologist uses a knowledge of the principles and techniques of psychology, applying them in a particular context. The context in this case is that described in preceding paragraphs.

Work is sometimes conceived of as being at three levels: the individual (for example, a child); the organization (for example, a school); and the system (for example, the LEA). So it will vary in form from, for example, individual assessment of needs, through work such as in-service training of teachers, to considering such questions as why reading standards are slipping or how best to reorganize surplus school provision.

A common preconception is that educational psychologists administer intelligence tests. All educational psychologists are trained and qualified to use intelligence and other restricted normative tests. Many, but not all, choose to do so but only where they consider that appropriate, which would certainly not be in every case. Criterion-referenced testing may be more appropriate. Tests as such may not be what is required in an assessment, but rather assessment through teaching, or structured/semi-structured/natural observation, or examination of materials already produced by the child. Individual assessment of a child's skills or abilities in any way may not be directly relevant to the questions which are to be answered. Part of the educational psychologist's skills must be to determine what questions are actually being asked, what questions *need* to be asked and what are the most appropriate ways of approaching the answers. Intelligence tests are one comparatively minor part of the battery available.

Some educational psychologists have special skills such as hypnotherapy or family group therapy, but it cannot be assumed that all educational psychologists will have such skills or wish to employ them.

ETHICAL DILEMMAS

An educational psychologist employed by an LEA or any other body or person occasionally finds that difficult questions arise as to who is the client, what exactly are the professional's responsibilities, and what can be demanded. While arguably the one who pays is the client, this payment is often being made for advice to be given to another – for example an LEA-employed psychologist who is advising a parent. Indeed, this advice may be used against some of the perceived interests of the one who is paying, as when advising parents of their rights to appeal against an LEA decision. Sometimes the wishes of one client will be in direct conflict with the wishes of another – for example parent v. teacher or parent v. child – and one may want the psychologist to take their side against the other. Sometimes simultaneous clients will be at different system levels – for example the child, the school, the LEA – and the different levels of client will require different levels of response. Sometimes what would seem to be the correct advice is politically unacceptable or temporarily inexpedient for some or all of the parties involved. Most LEAs and other employing bodies would recognize that there must be a degree of professional autonomy. The legal situation is clear, and Eric Forth, Minister of State, in October 1994 clarified in answer to a parliamentary question that the educational psychologist must give an independent opinion. In practice dilemmas do arise to which the correct solutions are not always so clear.

The educational psychologist working independently is not free of such questions. The paying client may have fixed ideas as to outcome, and it is incumbent on the psychologist to point out sometimes that what is desired is not in accordance with reality, or possibility, or legal constraints, or the best interests of a child. The professional will try to meet the client's needs and, as far as possible, wishes, but only within the bounds of ethical codes.

Normally an educational psychologist is working with shared and open information; reports written will usually be available to all involved. However, information provided in the course of an educational psychologist's work can be regarded as confidential where that is desirable and desired. Where confidentiality is not in the best interests of a client, it may be possible to negotiate a different arrangement. It is important that expectations regarding confidentiality are clear. Occasionally an unthinking employer or line manager will ask for access to inappropriate information, but normally such a demand can be resisted. Very

occasionally it is not possible legally to withold information, for example regarding a serious crime or personal
danger, in which case the educational psychologist has no
more privilege than anyone else. However, sometimes it
may be possible to negotiate an agreed position, before
disclosure, with those affected.

REGISTRATION, QUALIFICATION, SUPERVISION AND FURTHER TRAINING

To practise as an educational psychologist requires a psychology degree, which gives the Graduate Basis for Registration (GBR) of The British Psychological Society (see
Section 3.2), plus a postgraduate qualification in educational psychology. Postgraduate training courses in educational psychology, accredited by the Society, are run at
fourteen university locations in England, Wales, Northern
Ireland and Scotland. Except in the case of the Scottish
courses, they are twelve or thirteen months in length and
entry normally requires not only the Graduate Basis for
Registration, but also teacher training and experience. In
Scotland, the two year courses require the Graduate Basis
for Registration. Entry to all training courses is stiffly competitive.

Funding for postgraduate training in educational psychology is available under the teacher in-service training
programme. However, this is very difficult to access, and
the current trend is for increasing numbers of trainees to
self-fund, a very expensive undertaking. The Society is
unhappy about the difficulty and confusion inherent in the
present system, and has made repeated and continuing
representations on this matter.

Employment by an LEA as an educational psychologist,
except in Scotland, is unlikely to be achieved without a
history of at least two years' successful experience as a
teacher. More than two years' experience, or other work
with children and young people, is likely to be regarded as
advantageous.

To qualify for full membership of the Division of Educational and Child Psychology or the Scottish Division of
Educational and Child Psychology, and to qualify for the
status of Chartered Educational Psychologist, requires after
postgraduate training the completion of a year of successful
supervised practice as an educational psychologist. The
Divisions issue some guidance as to what is expected from
this initial year.

Fieldwork placements from the postgraduate course of
initial training are supervised by practising educational
psychologists, and a working group of the DECP Training
Committee has issued a report on what is expected of each

party in these circumstances. In the initial year of experience leading to Chartered status, the DECP has ruled that a programme of induction and at least fortnightly supervision of the initiate is to be expected. Beyond that year, no expectation of supervision exists. In some Psychological Services the Principal or a Senior exercises managerial oversight and in some Services there is an established system of appraisal. In some an informal network of peer-appraisal or peer-supervision operates. In many cases the educational psychologist is a lone operator, at the centre of many working networks and relating professionally to many colleagues, but professionally unsupervised. (This issue is discussed more fully in *Educational and Child Psychology, 10(2), Supervision and Professional Psychologists.*)

A chartered educational psychologist who applies for an annual practising certificate is expected to have undertaken continuing professional development. There is at present no system for enforcing this expectation. The important annual residential courses for educational psychologists are those organized by the DECP, SDECP, AEP (Association of Educational Psychologists) and the Education Section of the Society.

In other countries there are systems of qualification which are different from those in Britain. This reflects not only differing academic structures but also different professional expectations. Those qualified abroad and wishing to work in Britain as educational psychologists may well have to satisfy a potential employer that they are sufficiently qualified according to the Society's standards. The Society has recently reintroduced its own Diploma in Educational Psychology. This provides a standard by which other patterns of training can be judged. If necessary, an applicant will be advised what aspect of training is still to be covered, or will be required to undergo a year of supervised practice in Britain.

PAY, PROSPECTS AND CONDITIONS

Most advertisements for educational psychologists appear in the weekly *Appointments Broadsheet* of the Association of Educational Psychologists. Some also appear in the national press and in the Society's *Appointments Memorandum.*

Within LEAs there are normally three career grades of educational psychologist post: maingrade, senior and principal. Senior posts may include responsibility within a Psychological Service for a geographical or a specialist professional area or may reflect senior practitioner status. A Principal is normally the head of a Psychological Service.

LEAs normally offer salaries on the Soulbury scales, negotiated nationally. 1994–95 scales are taken from the ranges £20,460–£29,793 (maingrade) and £26,642–£37,689 (senior/principal). They will normally offer starting salary above the minimum, and in some cases have agreed individual salaries above the scales. Educational psychologists employed by Social Services or by other agencies may be on Soulbury related scales or another salary structure.

Standard LEA conditions for educational psychologists are nationally defined as not worse than those for other local government officers, and vary according to local conditions. Working hours are normally considerably longer than the school day, and holidays are shorter than schools'. Some Psychological Services prefer that educational psychologists take their leave during school holidays.

LEAs have traditionally taken responsibility for funding the continuing professional development (CPD) of educational psychologists. With the decreasing budgets of LEAs, such funds are becoming scarce. It seems that if educational psychologists are to fulfil their professional obligations to undertake CPD, they will increasingly have to fund this themselves, whether or not they are LEA-employed.

At present not many black or multilingual psychologists are working in Britain. The number of educational psychologists with sensory or physical disabilities is also small. There has been a preponderance of male educational psychologists, and this tends to be reflected in senior positions within the profession, but in recent times most entrants have been female.

There is some scope for British-trained educational psychologists to work abroad, although the different professional structures mean that careful consideration is required as to the most appropriate settings.

The most appropriate trade union for educational psychologists, except in Scotland, is the Association of Educational Psychologists (AEP). While the AEP operates primarily for those working in LEAs, some other educational psychologists also find membership offers them legal, insurance or peer-network benefits. In Scotland the Educational Institute of Scotland (EIS) is generally considered the most appropriate union.

Those working independently should consider how to gain the legal and insurance benefits of union membership. Whether or not working for a local authority, and whether or not belonging to a trade union, educational psychologists have a personal interest in cover, and their clients also deserve protection (see also *Appendix C: Professional liability insurance*). Those working independently, whether full-time or part-time, and whether solely or in conjunction with other employment, must of course also inform the Inland Revenue of their earnings and must pay all relevant classes of national insurance. AEP or EIS, BPS, and fees for being chartered should all be claimed as expenses against tax. A local authority car allowance is taxable and there is no special clothing allowance for an educational psychologist.

The future for educational psychologists is a little unclear at present. The main employers, LEAs, are not guaranteed to survive the effects of recent legislation. Social Services departments have not universally rushed to employ psychologists. Other agencies employ comparatively small numbers. Nevertheless there is much agreement that there is a continuing great need and some degree of demand which educational psychologists can meet. (The position is different in Scotland, where virtually the whole range of educational and clinical work carried out by educational psychologists is statutory – see Section 2.3.) It may be that the independent sector will increase from its present modest proportions. It may be that statutory work will be taken over by another local or central government department or agency. It may be that expert witnesses will become *de rigueur* in every case involving a child or young person. It may be that educational and child and other applied psychologists will reform their work structures to form local or regional teams of psychologists. All this is at present a matter of speculation and planning.

REFERENCES

Education (Scotland) Act 1981. London: HMSO.

Children Act 1989. London: HMSO.

Education Act 1993. London: HMSO.

Department of Education and Science (1968). *Psychologists in Education Services; the Report of a working party appointed by the Secretary of State for Education and Science (The Summerfield Report)*. London: HMSO.

LUNT, I. and POMERANTZ, M. (Eds) (1993). Supervision and Psychologists' Professional Work. *Educational and Child Psychology, 10(2)*. Leicester: The British Psychological Society.

FURTHER READING

Guidelines for the Practice of Professional Educational Psychologists (1993). Leicester: Division of Educational and Child Psychology, The British Psychological Society.

1.3 OCCUPATIONAL PSYCHOLOGY

Martin Crawshaw

ORGANIZATION AND STRUCTURE OF THE PROFESSION

OCCUPATIONAL psychology is that part of psychology which deals with work. Work – or the lack of it – has a very central role in people's lives and occupational psychology has a substantial contribution to make to the protection, satisfaction and efficiency of workers. It concerns the design of the workplace and of the work organization, the selection of the workers, their training, their motivation and their interactions with each other.

The eight areas recognized for training purposes show how varied occupational psychology is. The areas are:

- human–machine interaction
- design of environments and work; health and safety
- personnel selection and assessment, including test and exercise design
- performance appraisal and career development
- counselling and personal development
- training (identification of needs, training design, and evaluation)
- employee relations and motivation
- organizational development and change

Occupational psychology started life as 'industrial' psychology just after the end of the First World War. It had originally been assumed that increasing the number of hours which factory workers worked would increase the output of munitions proportionally. However, the expected gain was not realized and a committee was formed to investigate and to make recommendations. The findings of the committee lead to the realization that conditions of work had a powerful influence on output and productivity and, after the war was over, the National Institute of Industrial Psychology (NIIP) was set up with moral support from all the political parties and the TUC, and with financial support from the Rowntree family.

Between the wars the NIIP was active in what would now be called industrial relations and in organizational development, and also in the provision of career guidance to individuals. The Second World War saw psychologists involved in selecting large numbers of men for the Forces. Results of this involvement included the development of objective aptitude tests for pilots and technicians, and the introduction of relatively lengthy, diverse assessment programmes for selecting agents and saboteurs. Other psychologists worked on the optimum design of displays – radar was the secret weapon – and of controls.

After the war, these developments were transferred to the ordinary world of work and led to the now everyday use of psychometric testing, assessment centres and ergonomics.

The Division of Occupational Psychology (DOP) currently has around 750 members, with the number increasing by about 10 per cent every year. Not every psychologist working in one or other of the eight areas of occupational psychology (see p. 19) is a member of the Division, so the number of people concerned is difficult to calculate. An estimate might be another 350 or so Chartered Psychologists giving, say, 1,100 altogether. On top of that, of course, are many more psychology graduates who are involved professionally with one or other of the eight areas, but who do not qualify for the title of Chartered Psychologists.

Who employs occupational psychologists?

Occupational psychologists have never been employed under a unified set of conditions, as their clinical and educational colleagues have been; on the contrary, the range of employers has been particularly diverse.

Occupational psychologists are spread thin; their ratio to the working population is around 1:30,000 and this helps to explain the structure of the profession. Few organizations have 30,000 staff to justify the employment of a psychologist and rarer still are organizations with enough employees to justify a team of psychologists, if we are working on this ratio. (Government service is the obvious exception to this.) A few large firms do have small teams of psychologists; there are more who have one or two psychologists as employees. In this last case, however, there may not have been a deliberate decision to employ a psychologist at all. Perhaps a need was identified to improve some aspect of training or development within the company, and an advertisement placed to recruit someone with the necessary skills. Among the applicants with a training, personnel or general management background, there may be an occupational psychologist who has those skills. This is not a particularly rare happening, and of course it is most likely to happen where the traditional skills of training (in this case) are not in themselves adequate. And so it happens that psychologists are found in posts which could have been filled by trainers, ergonomists or maybe human relations specialists, and with a job title which does not necessarily contain the word 'psychologist'.

The Government employs about 80 Chartered Occupational Psychologists, many of whom work in the employment services. At the time of writing, these services have been undergoing considerable change, and the changes are far from finished; it may yet come about that these services are privatized or semi-privatized. Another significant proportion are employed by the Ministry of Defence, through the Defence Research Agency and the like. Although their employment has so far not been subject to quite as much change as that of those in the employment services, the reductions in defence spending raise the question of whether their situation can stay as it now is. A very small number work in the National Health Service.

Around 140 Chartered Occupational Psychologists work in universities. Naturally a large part of their work is teaching students – either on courses giving a qualification in occupational psychology, or on general undergraduate psychology degree courses which often have an optional occupational psychology component – but they also carry out basic research in the field and many undertake consultancy work as well.

The number of Chartered Occupational Psychologists in the commercial world is about 300. This includes those who are in small independent consultancies as well as those in large multinationals. Although it is known that there are substantial numbers of occupational psychologists employed in all categories, no breakdown of employers is kept, so the relative proportions are unknown.

A certain amount of flux exists between state and private employment, but there is much more transfer from state to private than in the opposite direction. Government agencies tend to hire people who are near the beginning of their careers, and later these people often switch to commercial employment.

ETHICAL ISSUES IN THE WORKPLACE

Most commonly, occupational psychologists' services are paid for by a relatively large organization rather than by an individual. (Exceptions include some career counselling.) Yet individuals are involved, and ethical conflicts can easily arise. Some of these individuals, who are members of the organization, will have been asked to provide information to the occupational psychologist. They may have been asked to demonstrate their jobs so that a selection scheme can be designed to appoint additional staff. If they are informed of the true situation, they will generally co-operate, and if the selection scheme will be a fair one, ethical problems are few. But what of the situation where an occupational psychologist needs to seek the co-operation of workers, in order to improve efficiency which will result in some of the workers being made redundant? The psychologist's client is the organization, but doesn't the psychologist also owe a duty to those individuals?

Ethical problems can be especially difficult for the psychologist working alone, as so many occupational psychologists do. The Society's *Code of Conduct*, which is backed by disciplinary procedures, and the DOP's *Code of Professional Conduct*, (and the Society's *Ethical Principles of Conducting Research with Human Participants* in some instances) can give vital guidance, but even so some problems can be very vexing to resolve.

TRAINING

A long-standing principle of the DOP is that although it would be impractical to expect everyone to be an expert in every possible field of practice, occupational psychologists should all have familiarity with the full scope of the specialty, at least at the level of 'book-learning'. A common experience of occupational psychologists is to have a client ask for help with, say, a problem in selection. The client may explain that new employees are not as satisfactory as their predecessors were – can a better system of selection be devised? Now, if the person consulted is an expert in selection, then a 'selection' solution will be forthcoming, but if that is their only area of expertise, then an inadequate or even·inappropriate service may have been provided. An occupational psychologist should at the very least be aware of alternatives to the client's diagnosis of the problem. Jobs change over time and it may be that the training has not changed to accommodate this. Perhaps the changes in the job consist of new equipment or procedures which no longer fit the original pattern of the job. Selection may still be an issue, but training and job design would clearly be areas requiring attention. So, a professional must be in a position to recognize areas in need of attention and, if he or she cannot personally provide it, to suggest someone who can.

As already mentioned, the situation of a psychologist being in a post which is not reserved for psychologists is quite common. It is especially common, however, for those near the start of their career – new M.Sc. graduates leave their Occupational Psychology courses needing work as much as any other graduates. In particular, however, they need work which will afford them the experience necessary to complete their training. There are few opportunities in explicitly occupational psychology posts, so they have to look further. There is great demand for personnel management posts; occupational psychology graduates have some particularly relevant expertise and they are sometimes offered such posts. In fact, their knowledge of selection methods, for example, is greater than that of most people in personnel and they may quite quickly find themselves using their psychological skills to devise or develop new methods for their employers. To their employers they are personnel officers and that is what their pay slips say; to the Division of Occupational Psychology they may be gaining experience in occupational psychology which will count towards the requirements to become Chartered. Meeting these requirements can be quite intricate, as one personnel officer may be gaining experience which will be accepted, while another personnel officer is not. This is why all decisions on recognition of experience are made on an individual basis; job title carries no weight – it is the actual content, nature, context and extent of work which is the issue.

A Chartered Psychologist who is a Full Member of the Division of Occupational Psychology (DOP) may expand his or her description to 'Chartered Occupational Psychologist'. (There is also a class of Affiliate Member of the DOP, the trainee grade, which is open to people who are en route to becoming Full Members.)

There have essentially been two routes to Full Membership. The first, which still continues, applies to people who have a specialist occupational psychology qualification approved by the DOP Training Committee, and the second was by experience alone. The Committee accredits courses which cover the necessary breadth of knowledge in the field of occupational psychology, and provide some opportunities for practical experience, project work and so on. There are also requirements concerning staff qualifications and institutional facilities. The qualification is usually an M.Sc. and a course prerequisite is that the student holds the Graduate Basis for Registration (GBR) of The British Psychological Society; that is, that at least 50 per cent of their undergraduate course was devoted to psychology and it contained particular elements such as practical work, research methods and statistics. Certain undergraduate degrees at Cardiff, Hull and Nottingham are accredited for GBR and also by the Training Committee as a specialist occupational psychology qualification. A total of three years' training is required (in addition to the basic, first-degree general psychology), and the M.Sc. counts as one of these years. The rest of the time must be spent in supervised practice of occupational psychology, and there are requirements governing, in particular, the breadth of experience necessary to satisfy the DOP Training Committee.

Until recently, the number of universities offering an approved M.Sc. was quite limited and the second method existed for people who had not had the opportunity to study for an approved qualification. The same requirements for broad, supervised experience applied as for the first method, but the lack of a formal qualification in the subject was compensated for to some extent by a requirement for greater experience, to be of five years in total.

Extending experience to make up for the lack of an assurance that people's basic knowledge is sound is not a very satisfactory solution, even to an admittedly difficult problem. Accordingly, the Society has created a Postgraduate Certificate in Occupational Psychology (PCOP), awarded to those who are successful in a set of examinations testing knowledge and understanding across the range of eight occupational psychology topics (listed on p. 19). Four papers are taken over two successive days. In keeping with the principle that occupational psychologists must have knowledge of all parts of the subject, all papers must be successfully completed in order for the candidate to pass. There are no prerequisites to taking the PCOP examination except that the individual has the Graduate Basis for Registration. PCOP may become a useful qualification for people wishing to enter the specialism, as it is a way of demonstrating to potential employers the possession of basic theoretical knowledge underpinning practice.

The lack of a unified set of conditions of employment has had a very marked effect on the pattern of career. This lack, and also a lack of large employers, has led to a lack of standardized training schemes. Small employers (individuals or partnerships of two or three people) have not usually been able to support a trainee. Furthermore, because these small concerns tend to specialize, they do not provide opportunities for trainees to gain experience across a range of different aspects of occupational psychology.

The DOP's requirement for breadth of experience, coupled with relatively poor opportunities for widening experience which many individuals find in their everyday jobs, means that it not surprising that there is a substantial body of practitioners within the area of occupational psychology who are not members of the Division. This state of affairs is not really desirable from anyone's point of view; the Division is denied members, the individuals are denied full recognition. Though the situation has come to be accepted (not without complaint) and will continue, there have been developments which will help to ameliorate this.

First, the argument that professionals should have an acquaintance with areas which impinge upon their own area of expertise has generality. The DOP's rules do not apply to non-members, but the PCOP is a Society qualification, not a Division qualification, and the Society's Membership and Qualifications Board has decided that in future people wishing to become registered in the general field of occupational psychology will have to gain the Certificate or an exemption, whether or not they become members of the Division.

Second, there has been a change in the Division's rules which will permit a certain amount of trade-off between breadth and depth of professional experience. Previously people had to show that they have substantial experience at practitioner level in two areas of occupational psychology. In future, provided they can demonstrate comprehensive experience, one area may be acceptable.

The third development is an improvement in the clarity of the DOP's requirements. The rules for admission were changed a few years ago and expressed the intentions of the Division. However, it must be said that the interpretation of the rules was a difficult task. One had to be a lawyer to become a Chartered Occupational Psychologist! There is no doubt that potential members have been deterred purely because of this. Now that the rules have been changed again the same mistake will not be repeated. It is not easy to write rules which achieve their purpose but which are more lucid than before, but much more is being done through presentation, articles in *The Occupational Psychologist* and in literature for applicants to explain the way things work.

An important new development is the BPS *Register of Competence in Occupational Testing*. This is not exclusively for occupational psychologists, nor is it relevant for all occupational psychologists, but for many of them qualifications in testing form a significant part of their training. More details are given in Section 2.5 on Psychometrics.

Supervision

Occupational psychologists who are not in an organization which recognizes their profession are effectively independent as far as their psychological work is concerned. People who have not yet become Chartered but who are progressing towards that goal must be supervised, and the proper person to do this is a Chartered Occupational Psychologist. The supervision need not be by the trainee's work manager, or indeed by any other member of the work organization. Provided the supervisor is in a position to oversee the trainee's pyschological practice by means of regular visits and other appropriate means, this may be acceptable.

Part-time and freelance work

Reference has already been made to academics undertaking consultancy work. Some employers in other areas may permit this also, but it is often forbidden as conflicts of interest can easily arise. Freelance work is common, and there are many single-person consultancies (see also Section 2.4 on Private Practice).

There are some opportunities for part-time work, which may take the form of independent consultancy work, or as permanent, or, more commonly, temporary staff in a larger organization. Occasionally there are part-time jobs available, usually of short duration, for occupational psychology students or others without full qualifications. These are prized for the experience as much as for the pay.

Few Chartered Occupational Psychologists seem to emigrate, perhaps because of the lack of opportunities in what is a rather underdeveloped profession in most countries. On the other hand, it does seem to be quite common for people working for multinationals to work temporarily abroad, perhaps for the very same reason.

With the major exception of the United States, few other countries have any significant number of people who correspond at all closely to the British occupational psychologist. Along with the small scale of occupational psychology in these countries goes the fact that few of them have as well-developed training and qualification schemes as has the UK. There is a procedure to allow holders of overseas qualifications to submit these to scrutiny by the Admissions Committee of the BPS in order to become appropriately recognized. Indeed, for citizens of the EC wishing to move to Britain, the Society is obliged to have such a procedure and to ensure that it operates without undue delay. However, numbers of applicants are rather small.

At the present time, there are developments taking place in the EC which suggest that occupational psychology – often well-named in Europe 'work psychology' – will expand and become more of a recognized profession. These developments are being watched carefully but it seems that they are likely to be quite compatible with the British provisions for training and qualification.

Equal opportunities

Approximately 25 per cent of Chartered Occupational Psychologists are women. There are no data on ethnic minorities or people with disabilities.

PAY, PROSPECTS AND CONDITIONS

Jobs in the Civil Service are advertised in the monthly BPS *Appointments Memorandum*. Jobs for qualified, and fairly senior, people with other employers are also commonly advertised there. However, with the exception of the Civil

Service, junior-level jobs tend not to appear; at least, not under the Occupational Psychology section. They do sometimes appear under 'Research', when university research assistantships and the like in areas of occupational psychology are advertised. As a rule *The Ergonomist* has one or two jobs for those with interests in that quarter. For those jobs which are not exclusively aimed at occupational psychologists, the appropriate newspaper or journal is the best source. A certain number of opportunities come up at conferences and workshops. Circulars are sometimes sent round known centres of occupational psychology. For those who are already in the field, there is quite an active grapevine, and personal contact is an important factor.

There are no nationally-agreed pay scales or conditions of service except in government employment, and in practice people often change their employers or their duties or both, so there is no such thing as a typical career pattern. The fact is, people have to construct their own future in occupational psychology, taking – or making – opportunities to extend their expertise as they may. It can be rather daunting to embark on a career with so little structure and certainty, but the plus side is that there are no artificial barriers to success such as time limits or quotas. Lack of opportunities may sometimes delay one's progress in the profession, but only delay – there is nothing to prevent a capable and determined person from succeeding.

1.4 CRIMINOLOGICAL AND LEGAL PSYCHOLOGY

Mary McMurran

ORGANIZATION AND STRUCTURE OF THE PROFESSION

THERE is a diversity in the professional roles of the forensic psychologist, although it is true to say that clinical psychologists working in special hospitals, regional secure units, and youth treatment centres, and prison psychologists form the two largest professional groups. Many university-based researchers whose areas of inquiry cover psycho-legal studies, policing, and court procedures also adopt a professional role in consultancy and training.

The title 'Criminological and Legal' was originally chosen for the Division to represent the various areas of practice amongst its members. Whilst accurate, this title is somewhat cumbersome, and because of this, the Division proposed the adoption of the specialist term 'Chartered Forensic Psychologist' to describe its members. The term 'forensic' is acceptable to the majority of the Division's membership as the best term to describe our work, which is related – directly or indirectly – to the courts and their functioning. Full members of the Division are entitled to call themselves 'Chartered Forensic Psychologists'; however some members may prefer to denote their specific area of expertise and call themselves 'Chartered Psychologist (Criminological)' or 'Chartered Psychologist (Legal)'.

The DCLP has just over 300 members, 200 of whom are full members of the Division. The majority of forensic psychologists are employed by Health Authorities, NHS Trusts, the Prison Service, and universities. Private practice is becoming more common as a way of life, and there are independent organizations which offer consultancy, training, and research in the field (see also Section 2.4 on setting up in private practice). It is, however, rather more common for members employed in the public sector to contract private work in their own time, particular examples being the provision of offender assessment reports for solicitors or barristers, the training of police officers in investigative interviewing, and the construction of offender profiles for police forces.

Many members of the Division work in closed institutions with offenders (patients and prisoners). Here, assessment, treatment, and rehabilitation are major aspects of the psychologist's work. Clinical psychologists working in hospitals typically work closely with the multidisciplinary team, which includes the patient's Responsible Medical Officer, key nurse, and social worker. Prison psychologists work closely with an equivalent group, including the prisoner's responsible governor grade, key prison officer, and probation officer/social worker. Clinical psychologists working in youth treatment centres liaise with the detainee's key care staff. Together, the team devises a treatment plan or sentence plan for the individual concerned. Relevant contributions are made by each discipline, including psychologists, to the implementation of this plan.

Psychologists working in community forensic teams and regional secure units contribute to a regional forensic service, where individuals are seen on an out-patient basis, often in liaison with probation officers or social workers.

Psychologists contribute to the *assessment* of offenders to address various issues, for example fitness to plead, levels of dangerousness, treatability, and where the offender might be appropriately placed. Psychologists also *treat* offenders to reduce their likelihood of reoffending. When working with offenders, issues relating to confidentiality of information disclosed in interview are salient. Psychologists typically do not offer complete confidentiality, particularly where there are implications for security within an institution, the safety of other persons, and where other serious offences come to light.

Psychologists do not, however, work entirely with offenders. There are many other aspects to their work, including staff training, service development, and research.

All psychologists work to the Society's *Code of Conduct* (see Section 3.4). Psychologists in training are supervised by qualified psychologists, and most departments have mechanisms for peer review of qualified psychologists' work.

REGISTRATION, QUALIFICATION AND FURTHER TRAINING

Full membership of the DCLP requires, in addition to the Graduate Basis for Registration (GBR), *either* an approved postgraduate qualification along with supervised experience in a relevant setting, the total training period being three years full-time or equivalent; *or* other postgraduate training and experience which the DCLP Committee judges to be equivalent. There is no single route to full membership.

A number of relevant postgraduate training courses are available, including: M.Sc. in Applied Criminological Psychology (Home Office/Birkbeck College), which forms the in-service training for prison psychologists; M.Sc. in Investigative Psychology (University of Liverpool); Diploma in Behavioural Forensic Psychology (University of Liverpool); Diploma in Clinical Criminology (University of Birmingham).

The Division has a mechanism for accrediting both University courses and other short courses (one day up to nine months). Developments in the standards for Continuing Professional Development (CPD) may mean that completion of accredited courses will become important requirements for full membership of the Division.

PAY, PROSPECTS AND CONDITIONS

Vacancies are normally advertised in the BPS *Appointments Memorandum* and sometimes also in the quality national press. Advertisements for assistant psychologist posts may appear in local newspapers.

Psychologists working in special hospitals and regional secure units are employed by the NHS and have the same terms and conditions as do other qualified clinical psychologists and assistant psychologists (see p. 5). In addition, working in a secure environment attracts an Environmental Allowance of £1,887 per annum. The career structure is also identical to that for other NHS-employed psychologists. In fact, clinical psychologists working in forensic settings are almost always members of the Division of Clinical Psychology (DCP) in addition to being members of the DCLP.

Many psychology departments are flexible in their recruitment strategies, offering, for example, split-post arrangements. Where budget control has been delegated to the psychology department, psychologists may be bought in as consultants to conduct specific tasks.

A psychologist who sells his or her services on a consultancy basis may do so as a freelance agent. Where a psychologist accepts paid work during work time, this is usually done by arrangement with the head of department and may count towards income generation; that is, any earnings are retained by the department.

Psychologists employed by the Prison Service and the Department of Social Services are civil servants with a pay scale and career structure which is different to that of Health Service psychologists. Appointment as a prison psychologist is normally at Basic Grade, although appointment at Higher Grade is possible where the appointee has a minimum of two years' experience. In exceptional circumstances, appointment at Senior Grade may be possible, where the appointee has a minimum of four years' relevant experience, and is also eligible for Chartered Psychologist status.

Salaries for prison psychologists (as at 1 August 1994) are as follows:

Psychologist	£12,644–£20,062
Higher Psychologist	£15,207–£23,469
Senior Psychologist	£19,289–£29,699
Principal Psychologist	£24,724–£38,290
Senior Principal Psychologist	£28,313–£47,044

Salaries in London attract a Recruitment and Retention Allowance, and prison-based posts attract an environmental allowance of £929 per annum.

1.5 PSYCHOLOGY TEACHING AND RESEARCH

1.5.1 PRE-DEGREE TEACHING

Hugh Foot

THE popularity of psychology as a degree course is matched by the growing pool of examination centres and candidates for pre-degree psychology. This expansion is providing rapidly-increasing opportunities for teachers of A-level, AS-level, and GCSE Psychology syllabuses in schools and FE colleges across England and Wales. Standard Grade and Highers in Scotland do not offer psychology, so it can only be taken at pre-degree level in the very small handful of centres which offer psychology amongst the A- and AS-level alternatives to Highers.

Information about the number of teachers involved in pre-degree psychology is not available from the examining boards and is almost impossible to calculate. In many FE centres such courses may be taught by University and HE teachers on a part-time basis rather than by full-time staff employed for the purpose. It is still not uncommon practice for the psychology syllabus to be taught by non-psychologists; that is, by those who do not have a qualification in psychology. The BPS has established its own Diploma in the Applied Psychology of Teaching specifically as a training for pre-degree psychology teachers, but the annual candidature is still extremely small and it may take many years before the teaching of pre-degree psychology is put on a proper professional footing.

One of the particular obstacles to this is that a teacher employed full-time to teach one or more of the psychology syllabuses in a school or FE college may not be employed exclusively as a specialist teacher in psychology and may be expected to teach other disciplines such as sociology or economics, for which other qualifications are appropriate.

THE GROWTH OF PRE-DEGREE TEACHING

The expansion of teaching opportunities can best be illustrated by the increase in centres and numbers of candidates. The total A-level candidature in the UK in 1990 was 8,907, which increased to 13,569 in 1992 and about 19,500 in 1994 (from provisional statistics). The number of centres offering A-level psychology was approximately 600 in 1993, by far the majority of FE colleges. Of the 49,000 candidates nationwide who sat A-level psychology between 1990–93, 81 per cent studied in FE or other colleges and only 19 per cent in schools. The Associated Examining Board (AEB) has about 90 per cent of the A-level market share, but other Examining Boards are now offering Psychology at A-level: the Joint Matriculation Board (JMB), and Oxford and Cambridge, which came into operation in 1994 and already has a candidature of about 1,500. The Northern Examination and Assessment Board (NEAB) started up a new modular A-level syllabus in September 1994 and will be making its first awards in 1996.

For AS-level psychology, the AEB has been the only examining board with a candidature of 1,728 in 1994, about 40 per cent of which was in schools. NEAB has just commenced an AS-level syllabus. Some centres offer AS-level as a second-string to A-level and as a cushion for those who are not sufficiently prepared for A-level.

GCSE in psychology is offered by four examining boards (Southern Examining Group (SEG), Midlands Examining Group (MEG), Northern Examining and Assessment Board (NEAB) and the Welsh Joint Examining Committee (WJEC)). The total 1992 candidature was 18,421; the 1994 totals are not yet published but are likely to be close to 25,000. The Southern Examining Group's total number of psychology candidates for 1994 is estimated at 7,219. Changes in Government code of practice brought about through the introduction of the National Curriculum are resulting in all the Boards having to rewrite their syllabuses for 1996.

There is also a small candidature for psychology associated with the International Baccalaureate. At the Higher Level, 31 schools were registered in 1994 with a total candidature of 310; at the Subsidiary Level 70 schools were registered with a candidature of 1,019.

Whilst giving these statistics to show the size of the 'industry' in pre-degree psychology, it is also worth indicating that for the AEB A-level syllabus, three-quarters of the candidates are female and one-quarter are male, showing roughly the same imbalance in preferences for psychology between the sexes as is reflected at degree level.

In addition to these 'conventional' pre-degree courses in psychology comes the huge recent expansion in NVQ and Access courses in which psychology is offered as an increasingly popular component. In some centres class sizes already run into the hundreds. This is inevitably going to make available a considerable pool of additional employment opportunities for psychology graduates, but it is impossible to determine at this stage what impact this will have on applications for degree courses. New developments are taking place very rapidly at this time.

Employment details

By far the majority of pre-degree teachers in psychology are employed in the public sector by Education Authorities, with the same contracts as those in other disciplines within the teaching profession. For some unknown reason, private schools and colleges are generally less likely to offer psychology as a pre-degree subject, but it is very difficult to obtain quantitative data in this area.

TEACHING RESPONSIBILITIES

Unlike university staff, teachers in schools, Sixth Form colleges and FE colleges are not free to select what they teach or to shape their own syllabuses. The Examining Board syllabuses dictate very much what the nature and balance of student learning experiences should be, in particular the balance between classroom learning and practical work (in the field or laboratory). Nevertheless, class size will have an influence on the style of teaching in terms of whole-class lectures, tutorials and small group work. The teacher is exhorted by the syllabuses to inculcate various skills in the students, and experimental approaches to teaching are on the whole encouraged. Teachers must provide opportunities for students to develop critical skills of analysis and interpretation, to relate psychological theories and methodologies to other disciplines, to develop skills appropriate to the implementation of psychological research, the consider psychological knowledge and ideas in the context of their own experiences and to make students aware of the ethical responsibilities of psychological researchers.

The AEB and JMB have three papers in their A-level syllabuses: one coursework paper involving the prior preparation and submission of four practical reports of work carried out in the laboratory or in the field. The two unseen papers (of three hours each) involve essays and one compulsory research methods/statistics question (both Boards). The Oxford and Cambridge A-level syllabus involves five papers: two based on coursework, one on research methods for problems sent out in advance, one on case studies and one on specialist choices.

Given the increasing trend towards professionalism, teachers of pre-degree psychology often register for higher degrees at their local universities if they have a first qualification in psychology. Their topics for research are usually based around their classroom experiences and around the opportunities which teaching young people afford. Typical research topics might focus on methods for making teaching and learning more effective, the impact of technology in the classroom, students' interaction with computers, study habits, and social interaction in the classroom. Teachers may also engage in research on the planning of the curriculum, on appropriate assessment criteria and assessments which facilitate learning or performance skills. It has to be added that not all teachers of psychology are in posts where there are opportunities or facilities to conduct research.

There are two organizations to which teachers of Psychology may belong for conferences, workshops, information and professional development purposes: the Association of Teachers of Psychology (ATP) which has a membership of about 800, mainly pre-degree level teachers, and the Society's Special Group for the Teaching of Psychology which has 400–500 members, a larger proportion of whom are degree-level teachers.

QUALIFICATIONS

Teachers in state schools must have a recognized teaching qualification. The Postgraduate Certificate of Education (PGCE) is a one-year course and is followed by work experience in school on a probationary basis. Training on a Bachelor of Education course is of four years' duration. Independent schools usually prefer teaching qualifications but these may not always be essential.

FE colleges also prefer a teaching qualification but in some cases it can be obtained via secondment on special training courses. As with independent schools, a qualification in psychology is not essential, although highly desirable. Non-psychologist teachers turning to psychology syllabuses are encouraged to take the BPS Diploma in Applied Psychology of Teaching, details of which can be obtained from the Society's office. Posts are typically advertised in the Education *Guardian* every Tuesday and in the *Times Educational Supplement*.

Since 1992 a new Licensed Teacher Scheme has been in operation, originally set up by the LEAs but now operated by the FE colleges using the scheme. This is a form of in-house, on-the-job training where a probationary teacher (with no certified teaching experience) is 'trained-up' by a mentor (one of the current specialist staff) and then approved by an external assessor.

SALARY AND PROSPECTS

Schools

The National Union of Teachers (NUT) issues information about teacher salaries on the pay spine applicable. The position on the pay spine depends on the number of spine points allocated to a teacher by the governing body on the following criteria:

1. *Qualifications*: 2 mandatory points for good honours graduates;
2. *Experience*: up to 7 mandatory points for good honours graduates (9 for other graduates);
3. *Responsibilities*: up to 5 points for additional duties and responsibilities (formerly rewarded by incentive allowances) which should be clearly defined in job descriptions.
4. *Special needs*: up to 2 points (one is mandatory) for teachers in special schools and teachers of statemented and visually/hearing-impaired pupils in mainstream schools;
5. *Recruitment and retention*: up to 2 points (3 in inner London) reviewed every two years;
6. *Excellence*: up to 3 points, reviewed annually.

Increments and reviews take place in September. Points for recruitment and retention and excellence may be withdrawn; points awarded for 1–4 mentioned previously are usually retained as long as the teacher remains in that post. London Area allowances operate from 1st April 1994 but the Inner London Supplement is no longer paid to classroom teachers appointed to posts after 1st September 1993, nor to heads and deputies after 1st September 1994. They may be placed on a spine point equal to or above their current salary.

Teachers taking up their first appointment have their spine points assessed and will be paid at the appropriate pay spine point. They start no lower than Point 2 (good honours graduates) or Point 0 (other graduates). Re-entrants also have their spine points assessed but they must be paid at a pay spine point which reflects the salary point at which they were last paid. Part-time and supply teachers engaged for a whole day or less than a day are paid the appropriate proportion of the pay spine salary which they would receive if employed full-time. They are entitled to an additional spine point in September of each year if they have worked for at least 26 weeks in the previous twelve months.

Pay spine for classroom teachers (salary w.e.f. 1.4.94) Spine-point 0 £11,571 to Spine-point 17 £31,323. (Increments rise from £693 (6 per cent) at the lowest spine point to £1,347 (4.5 per cent) at the highest spine point.)

Pay spine for heads and deputies (salary w.e.f. at 1.4.94) Spine-point 1 £23,055 to Spine-point 51 £52,152. (Increments rise from £375 (1.6 per cent) at the lowest spine point to £882 (1.7 per cent) at the highest spine point.

Pay ranges for headteachers and deputy heads vary according to the size of the school across six groupings. Teachers are expected to teach on a maximum of 190 days during the school year. These are supplemented by five Inservice Training days per year. Most teachers join the Teachers' Occupational Pension Scheme, strongly endorsed by the National Union of Teachers.

Further and Higher Education

The National Association of Teachers of Further and Higher Education (NATFHE) are, at the time of writing, in dispute with employers over new contracts. No increases have been made in 1994. The pay scales for 1993/94 which currently apply in the Further Education sector are:

Lecturers Point 1 : £11,331 to Point 14 : £20,538. (Increments change from £705 (6.2 per cent) at the lowest point to £708 (3.7 per cent) at the highest point.)

Senior Lecturer Point B : £19,830 (rising through 0–5) to Point 6 : £24,789. (Increments change from £708 (3.7 per cent) at the lowest point to £705 (2.9 per cent) at the highest point.)

Part-time hourly rates are £14.17 through 5 points to £22.60.

The management spine for FE extends from Point 0: £20,595 to Point 35: £47,325. (Increments change from £675 (3.3 per cent) at the lowest point to £801 (1.7 per cent) at the highest point.)

Higher Education salaries are paid on a different pay scale (University and College Lecturers). A new scale was introduced on 1.9.94. The 1994/95 scales are:

Lecturer Point 3: £12,756 to Point 15: £21,264. (Increments change from £714 (5.6 per cent) at the lowest point to £711 (3.5 per cent) at the highest point.)

Senior Lecturer Point 0 : £20,553 to Point 8 : £26,223

Principal Lecturer Point 0 : £24,804 to Point 9 : £31,188. (Increments change from £711 (3.5 per cent) at the lowest point to £708 (2.3 per cent) at the highest point.)

Part time hourly rates are from £14.17 through 3 points to £22.69.

The Head of Department minimum is £26,304.

Additional income can be earned from other sources, in particular: examining and moderating for the Examining Boards, private tutoring and writing articles or textbooks which pay fees or royalties.

1.5.2 TEACHING AND RESEARCH IN HIGHER EDUCATION

Anthony Gale

THE BACKGROUND TO TEACHING AND RESEARCH

In Great Britain there are now some 100 or more higher education institutions with university status. Eighty or more have psychology schools, departments, or groupings of psychologists who offer undergraduate qualifications in psychology. Contractual arrangements with staff can vary. In the following account we refer to both the 'old universities' and the 'new universities'. While some of the old universities have been in existence for hundreds of years, this group includes many established in the 1950s, which flourished during the post-Robbins expansion of the 1960s, and which were resourced to pursue both teaching and research. The new universities are of recent origin by title, but many have a long history; the largest were called polytechnics before they achieved university status in the 1990s. In the past, the polytechnics sustained research activity but were not funded in such an explicit way to support research. Both groups are currently in a state of active development and change.

The basic contract

Until recently all lectureship appointments in higher education within the older universities included a contractual obligation to *carry out research* and *perform administrative tasks*, as well as *teach*. These three areas of responsibility cannot be treated as independent; for example, teaching involves considerable administrative skill in course organization, preparation of learning materials, development of assessment methods and processing of examinations, as well as maintaining records of student progress. Research, particularly when the lecturer leads a research team, also demands considerable administrative skill in financial planning and control, preparation of applications for funding of research, negotiating with funding bodies and government departments, writing reports for non-specialist bodies and clients, and in team management. Again, teaching is unlikely to be fresh and convincing to students unless it is informed by the personal research of the teacher. Knowledge soon gets out of date and the good teacher has to keep in touch with current developments. Without research, the disciplines of psychology would cease to develop. In the former polytechnics which now constitute a large proportion of the new universities, policies relating to involvement in research by teaching staff can vary. Several of the new universities have distinguished psychological researchers on their staff. However, promotion and recognition have not been so dependent on research achievement as in the older institutions.

The trend towards differentiation

There is now a trend across higher education to shift the balance between teaching, research and administration. Many departments have developed schemes for estimating an individual's total workload and varying the three components in the light of the needs of the department, the individual's personal skills, and the stage of personal development of the individual. Some major departments have appointed administrative officers with a view to releasing academic staff to devote the majority of their time to teaching and research.

Local custom and practice

At present, however, there are no national arrangements for determining individual workloads, working hours, or expected levels of contribution. Rather, workloads tend to be a matter of agreement between the individual and the head of their department, bearing in mind the norms, custom and practice of the institution. Thus, newly appointed staff may be given less administrative work; staff with major research interests may be allowed to reduce their teaching commitment, and so on. Some institutions are appointing very junior teaching staff at the level of Teaching Assistant, Teaching Fellow or Research Demonstrator, allowing the individual to conduct research but requiring a major contribution to teaching. Others are making appointments to essentially teaching posts at the Lecturer level, but such appointments are rare.

Research-only careers

Few universities have appointed individuals to permanent contracts purely to conduct research and the most common pattern is the traditional requirement for teaching, research and administration. There are individuals working in universities who have largely research posts, but these are people appointed to research units and individuals who hope for a lifelong career in research. However, such posts (for example, at the Medical Research Council Applied Psychology Unit at Cambridge) are relatively few and far between.

The impact of government policy: the grading of departments

Because central government is the principal source of funding for higher education, custom and practice in institutions are influenced by government policy. Recently, all universities have been subject to peer review of their research achievements; this means that each department must identify those individuals who can provide objective evidence of being active researchers. The research funding provided by government is based on a formula which includes the research standing or grade of the department (currently 1 to 5) which is multiplied *(inter alia)* by the number of active researchers. Funding for teaching purposes is based on a separate formula.

The department you work in is important

A Grade 5 Department is a department of the highest research standing at international level and institutions will wish to protect that grading, not least because of its financial implications. Thus, in such a department, research will be highly regarded and distinguished researchers may be protected from other duties. In contrast, a Grade 2 department might be expected to generate its principal income from recruiting additional students thereby increasing the student:staff ratios, which in turn will increase the teaching load and reduce the time available for research. Government policy therefore has a direct impact on the working life of the lecturer. A parallel exercise is conducted to assess the quality of teaching departments. Initially, when the methodology for assessment was in its infancy, departments were graded *excellent, satisfactory,* or *unsatisfactory,* and not all departments were visited, some being given a *satisfactory* rating on the basis of a paper submission. Recently, the methodology has been improved and made more explicit. All departments are visited. Six core aspects are assessed; *curriculum design, content and organization; teaching, learning and assessment; student progression and achievement; student support and guidance; learning resources,* and *quality assurance and enhancement.* Four-point assessment scales are used to yield a profile together with a reasoned assessment report. A poor profile might lead to withdrawal of funding; a strong profile, well above threshold standards, will not be rewarded with additional funding, although this might change in the future. But since the results will be published, as are the research gradings, a department which warrants a very positive profile will enhance its reputation.

Collegiality   One of the most positive features of academic life is the fact that colleagues have been appointed to their posts for many years and develop together as a community of scholars. There is relatively little job mobility. There is much sharing of experience and many activities are carried out in collaboration. Many departments meet weekly to listen to presentations of individual research or to a presentation by a visiting researcher. Individual autonomy and the notion of academic freedom, whereby the individual pursues their own scholarly interests, is complemented by a sense of group membership. This can be beneficial for individual health and well-being, as research and teaching at this level can involve a great deal of personal challenge and even anxiety. Group coherence and a sense of identity with the discipline, the department and the institution, are a special privilege of working in a university. Of course, as in other organizations, enforced proximity to colleagues with whom one has less positive relationships can be stressful. But the balance in terms of group support and personal identity is beneficial and it is very rare for a job to be advertised which does not attract many candidates, although salary levels for university posts are not particularly competitive.

Higher participation rates in higher education

This is a time of major change in higher education. Given the desire of psychologists to ensure that all individuals have an opportunity to develop their skills, the expansion in student participation rates, which is a major plank in government policy, should be welcomed. However, as with all publicly funded activities, priorities have to be determined, and the funding bodies concerned have decided to implement a policy of differentiation between departments in different institutions. Typically, funding for research and teaching is provided according to known formulae which in turn means that management policy can be driven by financial need and the financial status of individual disciplines within institutions. The late 1980s and the 1990s have seen a real revolution in the running of universities in the United Kingdom.

Implications of public accountability

The notion of public accountability is associated with a policy of tying funding to achievements; thus there is now a great deal of regular data gathering, particularly relating to performance indicators. Government has also required institutions to implement regular appraisal procedures for staff; thus staff development and training policy are driven in part by a government desire to enhance the quality of university staff performance. Such developments and the rapid pace of innovation in management and financial control, make the higher institutional scene very changeable and unpredictable, particularly where resources for public funding are under pressure. Each university has to make a detailed annual return specifying very precisely how much it has cost to carry out specific activities; the preparation of this return is a major activity for each university and the data aggregated across the university sector as a whole forms part of the model for future funding. The external assessment of teaching quality has been referred to above. In addition, whole institutions are subject to quinquennial audits by the Higher Education Quality Council whose auditors visit institutions and publish a report on the operation of the institution's arrangements for quality assurance. There are few aspects of a university's procedures which are not subject to public scrutiny and such audits typically include course development; assessment; personal tutoring; residential accommodation; library, computing and welfare provision; staff development; student recruitment and careers guidance; and student evaluation of courses.

CATEGORIES OF STAFF

All posts in higher education are advertised in the press and in the appropriate scientific and professional publications. There are currently about 1,506 fulltime staff teaching psychology at undergraduate or postgraduate level. Applicants submit a full curriculum vitae and/or a formal application form. Appointment is by interview of shortlisted candidates; some departments will also require applicants to present a research seminar. Candidates are well advised to visit the department beforehand and to explore any resource issues which will affect their work, particularly if they need major facilities for their research. Young teaching staff are typically appointed at Lecturer A grade in the older universities and Lecturer in the new. Psychology graduates might also be appointed to research or teaching support posts such as Experimental Officers or Technicians, where the salary expectations are much lower. Lecturers are placed on a three year probationary period, during which time there will be formal monitoring of their progress. They are likely to have undergone further training following completion of their undergraduate degree in psychology and to have obtained a Masters or Doctoral qualification in a specialist area, funded by a Postgraduate Training Award (provided by the Research Councils) or as a Research Assistant on a research project, or as part of training in professional psychology (for example a Doctorate in Clinical Psychology). Satisfactory completion of probation and/or transition to Lecturer B grade will also involve a formal procedure. Evidence will be required of developing a programme of research, of achievement in teaching, and participation in the life of the department through taking on administrative tasks. Appointment to Senior Lecturer in the older universities is usually on a competitive basis and demands a high level of demonstrable achievement, with research achievement playing a major role. Such appointments usually come after at least 12 years in post. The term Senior Lecturer is used in the new universities to describe the career grade for the majority of staff. Individuals with exceptional research achievement can be appointed to a Readership or to a Personal Chair or Professorship; such appointments usually involve external referees who are asked to evaluate the personal achievements of the candidate. In the past the head of a department was usually a Professor (appointed to an established Chair) but quite often nowadays heads might be Senior Lecturers or even Lecturers. A Professor has many professional obligations, not least to *profess* the discipline within and outwith the institution. The inaugural lecture, presented in most institutions by a newly appointed Professor provides an opportunity to explain why their research is intrinsically interesting and constitutes a major contribution to knowledge.

Personal development

Most institutions have training officers who are responsible for organizing workshops and seminars focused on key aspects of personal development (such as teaching, enhancing research, management skills, counselling skills and so on). One instrument for personal development long in use in the older universities, and used more strategically in the new universities, is sabbatical leave. The intention is to ensure that the individual is relieved of normal duties and has a term or semester in which to develop their research, either at their parent institution, or at a specialist centre elsewhere or abroad. Leave entitlement is typically one term or semester every three years, although it is rarely treated as a right. Staff need to present a case to justify their absence, particularly since it will lead to additional work for colleagues who must take over their duties. At the end of leave a report might be required so that the individual can demonstrate they have used the time effectively.

Personal appraisal is a means of reviewing the individual's achievements across the board, setting targets, and identifying needs for training. The frequency of appraisal might depend on the seniority of the individual; probationers are likely to participate in appraisal on an annual basis.

TEACHING

The new teacher

We have all been on the receiving side of teaching. Students claim that the best teacher is enthusiastic, well-organized, and sensitive to the needs of students, treating them as individuals. It is rare for a newly appointed lecturer to satisfy all these requirements from the outset and most institutions recognize the need for training and personal development in teaching skills. Newly-appointed staff might well be given lower teaching loads initially and be encouraged to develop new courses and course materials with the help and guidance of a mentor or experienced member of staff, preferably someone familiar with the specialized field of the individual. Senior staff will sit in on teaching sessions and provide the probationer with constructive feedback on their teaching performance.

The teaching task

Teaching does not just consist of classroom or laboratory encounters with students. Most departments are required to have a *curriculum*, which stretches over the three or four years' duration of an undergraduate degree course, is planned in a developmental way, and within which are individual *syllabuses*. Departments plan their staffing complement to satisfy the needs of the curriculum and specialists will be appointed to develop and deliver particular syllabuses. At the end of their course students are awarded a grade or class of degree. In order to assess students' knowledge and competence there are assessment procedures, including traditional written examinations, open book examinations and coursework, consisting of essays, dissertations, practical and project work and other modes. The teacher has to design appropriate assessment methods and these have to be integrated into a general assessment scheme which is internally compatible and not so excessive that students cannot cope with the demands imposed on them. Because of their knowledge of psychometrics and assessment, psychologists should be particularly well-equipped to ensure that assessment is reliable, valid and free of bias. It takes a great deal of experience to select appropriate assessment procedures and teachers tend to deploy a variety of techniques over their career. Most teachers are not left to solve such problems alone; most departments have course development committees or departmental meetings at which such issues can be discussed. Programmes of staff development training will also include a variety of facets of the teaching process. While individual lecturers are appointed as specialists they will need to be flexible and could be required to teach in several areas of psychology not necessarily covered by their own research specialty.

Face to face teaching

Lecturing is analogous to acting: one has to capture the interest and hold the attention of the audience, one has to have a compelling script, and the show must go on however one feels. As the numbers of students increase the audience increases and the rules or script for the task change. The behaviour of the teacher in the lecture theatre will be different from their behaviour in the small tutorial or seminar setting, or in the practical laboratory, dealing with individuals or small groups. The new teacher has to learn that these various situations have their own rules or roles and social scripts. Because of increasing numbers of students, classes have become much larger and small group teaching is at a greater premium. One of the challenges for the 1990s is to maintain and enhance standards of teaching under circumstances which might make the student feel just one of a large crowd. At the same time most universities enable students to evaluate the quality and effectiveness of courses, thus providing valuable feedback to the lecturer.

Examining (see also Section 4.6)

Examining procedures are usually highly structured and formal, the aim being to deal with all candidates in a fair and equitable fashion. Where possible most institutions employ anonymous marking so that the identity of candidates is concealed. Most institutions have agreed standard procedures for combining and converting individual marks into a final degree class or grade. External examiners are appointed from other institutions: their key role is to ensure that academic standards are high and that students are treated fairly. Recently the role of external examiners has been expanded so that they are typically required to provide the institution with a general evaluation of the curriculum and the quality of teaching as well as commenting on the conduct of examinations and the assessment procedures. Their annual reports are generally public documents which can be used in the evaluation of the teaching achievements of the department. Thus the role of the external examiner in terms of public accountability has been enhanced.

External accreditation

Where universities offer courses which confer professional qualifications or which are precursors to professional training, such courses are typically accredited by external professional bodies. Undergraduate psychology degrees need to be recognized by The British Psychological Society, either for Graduate Membership (which enables a person to become a member of the Society), or more importantly for the Graduate Basis for Registration (which enables a person to proceed to professional training). The Society publishes clear guidelines for those who wish to have their undergraduate degrees so recognized and departments are usually able to submit existing documentation as part of the evidence to justify recognition. In the case of professional training, all postgraduate courses are subject to a thoroughgoing periodic review by the Society including a visit to the department by a team of experienced applied psychologists. The visiting team prepares a report which is then scrutinized by various committees within the Society which can set requirements and recommendations for full recognition of the course, including the provision by the institution of appropriate levels of resource.

Pastoral care

In most institutions, students have a *personal tutor*, the member of staff to know most about them and to whom they can turn for advice on courses, study habits, personal problems, and ultimately for a personal reference. Advice to students about course selection may not be easy to give, especially as course structures have been loosened in recent years. Many institutions have introduced modular courses, giving students a great deal of choice; in some settings, a student may be able to construct the title of their final degree by virtue of the particular combination of courses completed. But recognition of a psychology undergraduate degree by The British Psychological Society may require the student to follow particular courses within a modular structure; otherwise they will not have experienced the depth and breadth considered essential by the Society. Apart from advice on academic matters, students often need personal advice. Student concerns can include worries about feeling unable to work effectively, personal relationships, marital conflict or illness in the family, personal illness, or financial difficulties. Mature students and overseas students can have a special set of problems. While most institutions have specialized *counselling services*, lecturers are expected to sustain a pastoral role, without necessarily being trained or having an aptitude for it. When students are in particular difficulties, staff can consult with colleagues to ensure that the student receives the best possible advice. However, dealing with student problems can be stressful for the individual lecturer.

POSTGRADUATE COURSES

Most departments in the leading universities offer postgraduate instructional courses in specialized areas of psychology (such as social or developmental psychology, cognitive science, health psychology) which reflect the special interests of staff. There are also some conversion courses for students who have graduated in cognate but non-psychological disciplines. Many departments also run professional training courses in clinical, educational or occupational psychology (which are covered elsewhere in the *Handbook*).

Psychology taught to other professions

Psychology has become an essential element in the training of several professions. A psychology lecturer might well have to provide specialist teaching for medical students, paramedical students (such as nurses, radiologists, physiotherapists and occupational therapists) or students following courses in business studies, social work, or education. Such teaching typically has three aims: to introduce the student to fundamental theory and research in psychology (for example, in child development or ageing); to demonstrate how psychological knowledge may be used to enhance professional practice (for example, in interviewing patients or in group decision-making); and to encourage the budding practitioner to reflect on their own view of the world and their personal beliefs, which might in turn affect their interaction with others. In several institutions psychologists have been appointed to undertake this specialist teaching and may find themselves within a medical school, college of nursing or management school, rather than in a psychology department teaching honours psychology undergraduates.

RESEARCH

Research and self esteem

Academic life is centred upon research and scholarship, which are the founts of knowledge for teaching. Psychologist academics derive much of their self- esteem and sense of personal worth from their research and the reputation it gives them with their peers in the academic community. Thus national and international recognition are important and are reflected in publications in prestigious journals, publications of research monographs and key texts, major book series, membership of journal boards, the award of major research grants, honours such as medals and prizes, membership of distinguished bodies, and invitations to speak, as well as acting as a consultant and adviser to government bodies, research councils and scientific journals. Very distinguished researchers are likely to spend periods of work in the key world centres for their specialty as a visiting fellow or professor. Research in psychology typically involves empirical work, although some do focus on scholarship and theory, and many have made a name through the development of new methods, particularly in statistics. Over a research career an individual's focus may vary, both in terms of specialty and in the mode of research activity; many psychological scientists move between field and bench and theory development and experimentation.

Lonely scholar or collaborator? As in the arts and humanities psychologists can be individual scholars, publishing work under their sole authorship. However, as in the natural sciences, psychologists also work in teams and collaborative groups, particularly in the light of new sources of funding (such as the European Union) which tend to promote special initiatives involving inter-disciplinary and multi-centre research. While the research councils will still fund individual research projects, submitted by individual psychological scientists, money is also distributed for research in areas identified as calling for a special research effort (such as HIV infection, exploitation of new technology, inter-disciplinary studies of diet and pollution). On the other hand, the newly introduced procedures for determining research funding within institutions through excellence in particular areas, may pull the pendulum back towards individual research or research collaboration between colleagues within a more narrowly defined field.

Supervision of postgraduate research

Supervising research students is one of the most challenging jobs for an academic and can also be the most rewarding. Research students are likely to be very bright, highly motivated, independent in thought, and ambitious for their own future. Supervisors often develop lifelong friendships with their research students as well as longstanding research relationships. All universities have formal procedures for monitoring the progress of students and most have introduced formal training modules to broaden the education and training of research students and enhance their advanced research skills. The Biotechnology and Biological Sciences Research Council (BBSRC) and the Economic and Social Research Council (ESRC) are the main providers of research training awards for psychology Ph.Ds and there is considerable competition for them. Research students typically undertake demonstrating and other forms of teaching to supplement a rather meagre stipend. Within four years (and three if possible) the student submits a thesis which is examined by an external examiner who is an authority in the field, for the award of a Ph.D. (Note that this section could have been introduced under the *Teaching* heading, but supervision of research students is much closer to research than to teaching.)

ADMINISTRATION

Administration: a curse or a blessing?

While people often refer to administrative tasks, committees and business meetings in derogatory terms, there is no doubt that little could be achieved without them. Resources have to be allocated in a way which is seen to be fair and acceptable. Public accountability requires the open publication of performance data (such as publications, research grants, numbers of students graduating) and records have to be maintained for individual students. Examination procedures have to be formal and systematic. The recruitment of students at both undergraduate and postgraduate levels is a major task for any department. Individual departments have to respond effectively to government and institutional initiatives and requests for information and views.

The inspired amateur

Until recently, there was little formal training in management skills or administrative effectiveness for university staff and indeed that is largely still the rule. Unless the head of department has an understanding of such matters, individual lecturers can find themselves thrown in at the deep end, depending on folklore and convention, rather than formal theory. In contrast, individuals might be paired with others to carry out major tasks, such as undergraduate admissions. Although universities are responsible for major financial resources, central administrators in the older universities are rarely free to act independently of committees largely made up of academics. Within departments most of the major administrative tasks (including finance, library collections, monitoring of expenditure for research, examining, admissions, course development) are carried out by academics. Collegial government usually means full participation by peers in decision-making, lengthy meetings and full consideration of the pros and cons of every possible course of action. Of late, the wish of the government to include representatives of industry and commerce on university governing bodies has shifted the style of management to a more hierarchical model of decision-making. Such a style of management has indeed been more common in the newer universities where administrators have been relatively unfettered by the participation of academic staff. Without making any judgements about the merits of either approach, it can be asserted as fact that universities have for many years achieved their objectives in producing new graduates and in conducting research, improving productivity on a regular basis, with diminishing resources, yet without major strikes, student unrest, or damaging financial failures. Presumably, the style of government has something to do with the achievements of the organization.

Career development
There is a tendency for more senior academics to become involved in administration, including policy and university-wide decision-making. Typically heads of department and deans (heads of faculties or groups of departments) are drawn from among older staff. Senior staff also tend to become involved at a national level with committees and academically related bodies, such as the research councils or committees conducting assessments of research and teaching quality. However, there are a number of distinguished academics who throughout their working career manage to remain at the leading edge of their research field, without being drawn into too many major administrative tasks.

Equal opportunities issues

For many years the ratio of female to male undergraduates on psychology courses has been circa 4:1 and similar ratios apply at postgraduate professional training level. At the same time the ratio of female to male lecturing staff in the older universities has been the reverse and the number of senior female academics is very low. In the newer universities also the ratio of male to female staff is unbalanced but less so. Differences in seniority between the sexes may be due to a time lag, with males having been in the organization much longer, but the general position in universities is that there may be one female professor for every twenty males. It is hard to account for this other than by reference to systematic biases in the system. The situation in relation to members of ethnic minority groups and to individuals with disabilities is even worse. Some institutions have an effective equal opportunities policy, with training for staff in all aspects, from student recruitment to staff appointments. Given the requirement for research achievement in both initial appointment and subsequent promotion procedures, the fact that many women decide to take time out to rear children constitutes a *de facto* barrier to seniority. At the same time, as universities make progressively more part-time posts as a means of employing individuals at lower cost, female appointees are particularly vulnerable to a role as a second class citizen within a department.

Consultancy

Some of the most creative psychologists in the history of the discipline have moved regularly between field and bench, applying psychological know-how to practical problems and using practical problems to drive theory. One way of maintaining functional links between academic and applied psychology is to undertake consultancy in your own specialty, providing practical advice for government, commerce and industry. Some institutions require staff to hold consultancies, others allow a number of days per annum without special authority, although it would certainly be courteous to inform the institution of additional commitments taken on. Fees are negotiated and guidelines and advice about fees are given in trade union handbooks. It is also important to negotiate in advance about ownership of the work; commercially sensitive work could suffer from impediments to publication. Most institutions give advice about intellectual property. An individual also has to decide, when allocating precious time, whether it is more sensible to conduct research which will lead to publication and indirectly, to promotion, or to raise additional income doing work for which little other formal credit may be due.

CURRENT SALARY SCALES

The 1994–95 salary scales (incremental) in the older university sector range from £14,756 (Lecturer Grade A) to £33,077 (Senior Lecturer and Reader Discretionary Scale). The starting salary for Professors (who are not on a fixed scale) is likely to be in the range £30,533 and upwards.

In the new universities, the salary scale (incremental) ranges from £13,140 (Lecturer at Point 4) to £30,426 (Principal Lecturer). The starting salary of professors is not determined nationally and some of the new universities have expressed an interest in locally determined pay scales. At the time of writing, the new university scales looked set to increase by 2.5 per cent.

1.6 COUNSELLING PSYCHOLOGY

Mary Watts and Robert Bor

ORGANIZATION AND STRUCTURE

COUNSELLING psychology is that branch of applied psychology concerned with helping people make informed choices in their lives and to adjust to new and sometimes unwelcome circumstances. Counselling psychologists work directly with clients spanning the full human lifecycle. They have skills for therapeutic counselling with individuals, couples, families and groups. Consultation and liason with colleagues and other professionals forms an important part of their work. Counselling psychologists in the UK are trained to work both as independent practitioners as well as members of organizations and multidisciplinary teams.

A fundamental feature of counselling psychology is the relationship between the counselling psychologist and the client, with the client being seen as an equal partner within the therapeutic alliance. As a consequence, counselling psychologists are required to undergo personal psychological counselling in the course of their training and to arrange for ongoing professional development once they have qualified. A range of therapeutic approaches is taught in training and applied in practice, including the mainstream schools – psychodynamic, cognitive behavioural, systemic and client-centred.

Counselling psychologists are practitioners who are able to apply the results of systematic research, and insights gleaned from professional experience, to their understanding of the evolution, maintenance and resolution of human problems. They may also be involved in teaching, supervision of trainee psychologists, and research designed to broaden the knowledge-base of psychology in general, and counselling psychology in particular.

Counselling psychology has a long and distinguished history in some other overseas professional psychology associations (for example the American Psychological Association (APA)). By way of contrast, counselling psychology in the UK is among the youngest of the specialities in applied psychology.

Counselling psychology was first recognized by The British Psychological Society in 1982, when the Counselling Psychology Section was established. The rapid growth in membership, reflecting the escalating interest in counselling psychology both nationally and internationally, led to the Section becoming a Special Group in 1989, and a Division in 1994. The Division of Counselling Psychology (DCoP) now has approximately 1,200 members, of whom approximately 110 are accredited members (Chartered Counselling Psychologists). There are also general and affiliate members. The Division of Counselling Psychology is the second largest of the Society's six Divisions.

In order to qualify as a Chartered Counselling Psychologist, individuals must have completed The British Psychological Society's Diploma in Counselling Psychology, have been awarded a Statement of Equivalence in Counselling Psychology (which indicates that they have qualifications and experience deemed to be equivalent to the Society's Diploma in Counselling Psychology), or have graduated from an approved training course in counselling psychology.

Who employs counselling psychologists?

The number of psychologists with a primary qualification in counselling psychology has increased steadily since the introduction of the BPS Diploma in Counselling Psychology in 1993, and a diverse range of employment opportunities are available to these people. Counselling psychologists are employed in the Health Service, universities, schools, Social Services and in specialist counselling agencies (for example in drugs counselling, HIV counselling and career counselling settings), among others. Some work as independent practitioners.

An increasing number of counselling psychologists are employed in higher education institutions to teach psychology and counselling psychology, and to conduct research. Teaching activities include:

- advanced training for psychology graduate students on Counselling Psychology courses;
- introducing the theory and practice of counselling psychology to students on relevant courses (for example, social work, psychology);
- counselling skills for health care professionals (for example, doctors, nurses, physiotherapists);
- management and consultation skills to students and col-

leagues from a range of undergraduate and postgraduate courses;

- counselling skills for the police, firefighters and ambulance staff.

Counselling psychologists apply a range of research approaches and methodologies. There is probably a greater emphasis in counselling psychology on the qualitative and process aspects of research than has been conventional within psychological research.

To whom do counselling psychologists offer a service?

Since counselling psychology is a new and evolving profession, employers are still learning what knowledge and skills counselling psychologists can offer. Employment opportunities are therefore in a state of flux and new employment opportunities are emerging. Examples of some of the specialist services offered by counselling psychologists are given below. These services all reflect the utilization of a combination of counselling experience and formal research-based knowledge.

Counselling psychologists work to assist in the alleviation of psychological distress that may accompany life stage developments such as parenting, relationship breakdown, and sexual identity, as well as specific problems including infertility, difficulties in adjusting to retirement, and bereavement. Psychological counselling can help people to clarify the issues associated with their psychological distress, and with the assistance of the counselling psychologist, work towards their management or resolution, and in some cases, the prevention of problems.

A number of counselling psychologists work in hospital and school settings and have trained to work with children, young people and adolescents. Working alongside child and educational psychologists, clinical psychologists and child psychotherapists, they are able to assess and treat problems in the context of the child's family and school. Typically, they provide counselling for children who refuse to attend school, those with developmental problems, children whose behaviour brings them to the attention of the authorities (for example, truanting behaviour, shoplifting), and those experiencing relationship problems within the family and beyond, as well as children affected by physical illness. The issues and difficulties experienced by students in higher education are assisted by counselling psychologists through student counselling services, career evaluation, psychometric assessment and educational and career guidance.

An understanding of the dynamics involved in human relationships and family systems, are offered to those meeting difficulties in the family or within other significant relationships. Counselling psychologists are also trained to work with couples and to provide counselling for psychosexual problems where this is indicated. They work closely with family therapists and sexual and marital therapists. Counselling psychologists have skills in helping family members to adjust to divorce, separation, a reordered family, loss in the family, childlessness, childbirth and other changes in the structure of the family.

Problems confronting the elderly, including retirement, bereavement, chronic illness, and loss, are the province of counselling psychologists. The emphasis is on ameliorating the psychological effects of these problems, increased self empowerment and the creative use of the client's available resources, including his or her family and social support network.

Through their employment in the Health Service, GP practices, and specialist agencies, counselling psychologists work alongside clinical and health psychologists to assist those affected by acute and chronic illness, and disabling conditions. They have a role in helping people to prepare psychologically for medical investigations and treatment, and to adjust to new and sometimes unwelcome circumstances. They work with their colleagues in matters pertaining to health promotion and disease prevention, treatment noncompliance and disaster counselling. Counselling psychologists, through their research skills, are able to evaluate their work and contribute to health service auditing activities. They also work in a specialist medical counselling services, for example, for infertility, HIV, pregnancy termination, substance misuse, and staff support counselling.

Counselling psychologists in industrial and organizational settings typically work in close collaboration with organizational psychologists. Counselling in the workplace focuses on issues such as job loss, retirement, productivity, improving the organizational climate, reducing stress and fatigue, consultancy and employee assistance activity.

With whom do counselling psychologists work?

The diverse skills and work settings of a counselling psychologist mean that they work alongside a wide range of professionals both in organizations and in the community. For example a counselling psychologist working in a primary health care setting may receive referrals from a GP but also work very closely with a district nurse, or community psychiatric nurse. A counselling psychologist working in a school setting will develop close working relationships with the teaching staff, and a counselling psychologist working in a community or social setting is likely to have close contact with social workers and receive referrals from them.

Problems arising from relationships in communities, disability, ethnicity and gender may also be managed by counselling psychologists, in conjunction with other social support services.

RESPONSIBILITIES AND RIGHTS OF A COUNSELLING PSYCHOLOGIST

The responsibilities and rights of a counselling psychologist are described in detail within the Division's proposed *Guidelines for the Professional Practice of Counselling Psychology*. It is worth noting that in an early part of the guidelines, the humanistic value base of counselling psychology is affirmed. In order to recognize the diversity of the work undertaken by counselling psychologists, the guidelines focus on general principles and do not attempt to account for specific cases or instances.

The counselling psychologist has an obligation and responsibility to him or herself as well as to the client, society, and colleagues. These must be considered and met in order to protect the client, oneself, and other colleagues, and to ensure professional competence and ethical practice.

A primary responsibility of the counselling psychologist is to ensure that they recognize their personal strengths and limitations in training and ability. Personal competence is continually monitored and advanced through supervision, consultation, and continuing professional development. Counselling psychologists are expected to hold adequate professional indemnity and maintain personal safety (see *Appendix C: Professional Liability Insurance*).

Supervision

There is an ethical requirement for all practitioners to have regular supervision or consultative support from a suitably qualified professional. The supervisory contract must be clearly defined, confidential, and proportional to the volume of work and experience of the counselling psychologist. A counselling psychologist is expected to speak out against any breach of professional or ethical conduct, but care should be taken not to denigrate colleagues publicly.

Respect for the client's autonomy and confidentiality

An emphasis in the practice of counselling psychology is to devolve power to the client, and to seek ways of promoting the client's autonomy in matters pertaining to their life and relationships. There is recognition and respect for clients' values, however diverse these may be. It is the responsibility of practitioners to ensure they do not exploit their clients, especially in relation to financial, sexual, and emotional matters. Due regard should be given to the Society's paper *Sexual Harassment at Work and the Ethics of Dual Relationships*.

Where a counselling psychologist works with a young person or with someone who is emotionally or physically vulnerable, care should be taken to explain and clarify the goals and process of counselling with the client and with any person having legal responsibility for them.

The relationship a counselling psychologist has with a client is confidential and it is a requirement that case records be safely kept and made available to the client upon request. Information on computer must conform to the requirements of the Data Protection Act (see Section 2.2.2). The extent and nature of confidentiality should be explained from the start, particularly in relation to multi-disciplinary team work and ethical issues. Counselling psychologists, like other professionals, work within the remit of the law.

Responsibilities and obligations to society

The counselling psychologist has a responsibility to respect cultural diversity however it may present. As the practitioner's relationship with the public is based on confidence, an important role of the counselling psychologist is to promote a continuing regard for the status, knowledge, and understanding of psychology and counselling psychology. This is achieved via the maintenance of high standards of ethical counselling practice, and the advancement and appropriate dissemination of knowledge relating to the theory and practice of counselling psychology. Complaints pertaining to the practice of counselling psychologists are dealt with by the Investigatory Committee of The British Psychological Society (see Section 3.4).

REGISTRATION, QUALIFICATION AND FURTHER TRAINING

To become a Chartered Counselling Psychologist, individuals must first have gained The British Psychological Society's Graduate Basis for Registration (GBR), usually obtained on completion of a recognized first degree in Psychology, and subsequently complete either (a) the Society's Diploma in Counselling Psychology, (b) an accredited equivalent course, or (c) have been awarded a Statement of Equivalence to the Diploma by the Society.

Information on courses leading to GBR, and on routes to Chartered Status for counselling psychologists, can be obtained from the Society.

The BPS Diploma in Counselling Psychology

A Diploma Course in Counselling Psychology was set up by the Society in 1993. Students may either register directly with the Society to follow a course of study and supervised practice designed to meet the requirements of the Diploma, or with an institute of higher education which runs an accredited postgraduate course of study. The British Psychological Society supplies information on the routes to registration as a Chartered Counselling Psychologist, and on those institutions which provide approved training courses.

Duration of training

A minimum of three years' full-time study is required to complete the Society's training. The Diploma is divided into two parts, and candidates are required to successfully complete Part I or its equivalent (for example, a Society-accredited M.Sc. course deemed to meet all of the Part I requirements), before proceeding to Part II. In addition to meeting academic course requirements, students must also meet the practice requirements, which are approximately six hours per week of supervised practice for Part I of the examination, and twelve hours per week for Part II of the examination, if taken full-time.

Content of the Diploma

In order to complete Part I of the Diploma, students must successfully meet the supervised counselling experience requirements, as well as complete a course of study which integrates psychological knowledge with knowledge of counselling practice. Areas of study include, among many others, theories and models of the counselling relationship, assessment and intervention strategies, ethics, counselling skills, the historical development of counselling psychology, and research methodologies relevant to counselling psychology. Students participate in a programme of experiential workshop training and also in a personal development programme, which involves a minimum of 40 hours of personal psychological counselling.

In order to complete Part II of the Diploma, students must again meet the requirements relating to academic work, supervised counselling experience, and experiential workshop training.

By successful completion of Part II of the Diploma in Counselling Psychology, students are able to work as experienced and competent practitioners of counselling psychology. As in all professions, they are expected to undergo continuing professional development throughout their practice.

PAY, PROSPECTS AND CONDITIONS

Posts relevant to counselling psychologists are advertised in the BPS *Appointments Memorandum*, and also in national newspapers such as *The Guardian*. There is a wide range of work settings in which counselling psychologists are employed. At the time of writing, there is still lack of uniformity in pay and conditions for counselling psychologists, largely because counselling psychology is a new speciality, and employment, recruitment, and conditions of service have yet to be standardized. The Division of Counselling Psychology maintains the view that comparable applied psychologists should be entitled to equivalent pay and conditions. It is therefore expected that those for counselling psychologists will be similar to those of clinical psychologists. The pay for a clinical psychologist ranges from £15,651 after qualification to £46,934. Most counselling psychologists should therefore expect to earn a salary between these ranges, depending on age, experience and level of responsibility.

Many counselling psychologists work in independent practice. The independent practitioner will therefore set his or her own fees and negotiate contracts with potential clients.

It is important to closely monitor issues relating to equal opportunities and discriminatory practice in the employment of counselling psychologists, for instance relating to employment decisions which disadvantage a particular group according to ethnicity, disability, or gender.

Regulations governing the practice of counselling psychologists, counsellors, and psychotherapists, are currently being developed in Europe. Counselling psychologists who wish to work abroad should check these with the local psychological association within the country in which they wish to work.

THE FUTURE

Counselling psychology as an emerging speciality complements clinical psychology, health psychology, occupational psychology, counselling and psychotherapy. Prospective trainees will find that there is an increasingly wide choice of courses available to them in counselling psychology. It is a distinguishing feature of counselling psychology training that a range of psychotherapeutic approaches are taught, thereby increasing the choices available to trainees.

Practitioners of counselling psychology face a future that is both exciting and challenging. There will be opportunities to work collaboratively with a wide range of colleagues representing different professions and approaches, and in an almost unlimited number of settings.

Acknowledgements

Sections of this chapter are based on literature supplied to the authors by the Society's Leicester Office, written by members of the Special Group (now Division) in Counselling Psychology. Particular acknowledgement is given to Jennifer Elton-Wilson, Chair of the Division of Counselling Psychology, and Carol Shillito-Clark, Chair of the Sub-Group for Practitioner Members Affairs.

FURTHER READING

Directory of Chartered Psychologists 1994. Leicester: The British Psychological Society. This contains an outline of the services offered by counselling psychologists.
Chartered Counselling Psychologists. Leaflet available from The British Psychological Society.
Guidelines for the Professional Practice of Counselling Psychology (1995). Available from The British Psychological Society.
A Code of Conduct for Psychologists. Available from The British Psychological Society.
Regulations For The Diploma In Counselling Psychology. Available from The British Psychological Society.
Routes to Chartered Status For Counselling Psychologists. Available from The British Psychological Society.
Sexual Harassment at Work and the Ethics of Dual Relationships. Available from The British Psychological Society.

1.7 HEALTH PSYCHOLOGY

Marie Johnston and John Weinman

ORGANIZATION AND STRUCTURE

HEALTH psychology is a study of psychological and behavioural processes in health, illness and health care. The extent of the discipline is extremely wide and, to provide an illustrative overview, five broad content areas are identified for convenience. In each, we have given examples together with a general statement about intervention strategies.

1. *Health risk behaviours* – the nature, causes and health effects of such behaviours as smoking, substance-abuse, unsafe sexual behaviour, harmful dietary choice; the role of stress and dispositional factors in the aetiology and exacerbation of disease; psychological theories and interventions for primary prevention and health-related behaviour change in community and workplace settings.

2. *Health protective enhancing behaviours* – the uptake and maintenance of such behaviours as exercise, healthy dietary choice, teethbrushing, health checks/self-examination and attendance for preventive medical screening; psychological approaches to health promotion.

3. *Health-related cognitions* – cognitive processes which mediate and determine health and illness behaviours. These include general health beliefs/attitudes; attributions, control and self-efficacy beliefs; symptom perception; and illness representations in children and adults. There are a range of theoretical models and frameworks which can be used not only for explanation and prediction, but also for developing interventions (for example, to modify health beliefs, increase internal control or self-efficacy beliefs).

4. *Processes influencing health care delivery* – the nature and effects of communication between health care practitioners and patients; patient satisfaction and adherence to treatment and advice; the uptake and response to preventive health services such as screening; stressful

medical investigations and treatment; hospitalization; health-care staff attitudes; decision-making, work stress; quality assurance; measurement issues in audit and outcome evaluation; psychological interventions to improve communication, facilitate adherence, prepare for stressful medical procedures, and so on.

5. *Psychological aspects of illness* – the psychological impact of acute and chronic illness on individuals and their families and carers across the lifespan; pain behaviour and pain coping; social support; disability; quality of life; rehabilitation and health-related behaviour change; dying, death and bereavement. Psychological interventions to promote self-management, facilitate coping with pain or illness, to improve quality of life and to reduce disability and handicap.

In all these areas, a wide range of skills is used, including assessment, evaluation, communication, teaching and intervention. The work of a health psychologist is targeted at the problems of public health, the provision of health care and of the response to illness. The problems may be identified by health care agencies, including NHS trusts and Health Authorities, health professionals including GPs, nurses and rehabilitation therapists, and organizations and employers outside the health care system.

It is a new and rapidly evolving area of professional practice both in the UK and abroad (see Johnston, 1994), and therefore many of the organizational elements are in a transitional state. While some health psychologists have their roots in clinical psychology, others have their basic training in social psychology, psychophysiology or some other area or discipline.

Approximately 800 UK psychologists are members of the Special Group in Health Psychology of the BPS. Of these, 29 per cent are also members of the Clinical Division, 15 per cent of the Counselling Division, and 2 per cent of the Occupational Division.

Who employs health psychologists?

The main employers are health services (40 per cent) and universities (40 per cent). Within health services, psychologists are frequently employed in services to patients, usually in primary care, acute medical or physical rehabilitation services. More recently, they have also been employed directly by the management of NHS trusts to deal with general problems of quality assurance, preventive health care or intervention at an organizational level. In addition, purchasers of health care may employ health psychologists to assist in setting and evaluating targets for health care.

In universities and other institutes of higher education,

health psychologists are employed in psychology departments to teach and conduct research which frequently depends on specific expertise and practising skills. They are frequently involved in training health professionals; all UK medical schools employ psychologists to train doctors. They give training in both knowledge of psychological aspects of the work of the professional group, and the skills appropriate to their practice, for example communication skills. Thus their employment depends not only on their general teaching and research skills, but also on their specific knowledge and skills relevant to health, illness and health care. Health psychologists may also be employed by Departments of Public Health especially for their expertise relevant to preventive health care. A substantial number of health psychologists are employed on research contracts supported by research councils, NHS research schemes or charitable organizations.

Other possible but less common employers are Health Education Departments. A few health psychologists are in private practice, some offering a clinical service to individually referred clients. With the recent developments in the NHS, some psychologists currently holding contracts with NHS trusts may in the future operate privately and contract their services to NHS trusts.

With whom does the health psychologist work?

The location and work relationships will be determined by the specific kind of employment. Since it is a recently emerging professional group, health psychologists may work in isolation from other health psychologists, although there are now a number of departments with a cluster. Most health psychologists will work co-operatively with other health professionals and health managers on a day-to-day basis.

To whom does the health psychologist offer a service?

Health psychologists work on problems at individual, group, organizational or community levels. Some may be restricted to specific problems such as pain management, with referrals coming from relevant clinical agencies, or quality assurance in outpatient services. Others may have a more general brief with contracts being negotiated with management as specific issues arise, for example stress and uncertainty in staff associated with hospital closure. The client may be an individual with a clinical problem, a health centre, a hospital clinical directorate, the chief executive of a health authority, the director of a company, a health research funding body, a university or some other body.

REGISTRATION, QUALIFICATION AND FURTHER TRAINING

At present there are no specific restrictions on practice beyond those which apply to any psychologist. However this is probably only a transitional stage as courses develop and potential employers have the opportunity to employ more highly trained candidates.

Most UK psychology degrees contain a component of health psychology which gives an introduction to the subject. Courses may go under titles such as 'Stress and Coping', 'Psychophysiological Processes', 'Health and Behaviour'. In the UK, there are now at least five Master's courses (City, London, Middlesex, Stirling, and Surrey) in Health Psychology accepting students who already hold the Graduate Basis for Registration (see Section 3.2). [Some of the courses also train non-psychologists in health psychology.] These courses are of one year's duration full-time or two years part-time. They provide a knowledge base in the subject, plus skills in assessment, evaluation and research methods. In addition some give training in psychological interventions. Graduates of these courses have been employed in contract research, health services, private compannies, lectureships, and so on.

Other psychologists train in health psychology by completing a doctoral degree in a relevant area. A review (Psy-PAG, 1993) of current doctoral students in psychology (N = 185) found that 24 per cent (44) were conducting research in the area of health psychology; only one area of psychology, cognitive (42 per cent) was more common, and social psychology had similar percentages to health psychology. While many students were involved in more than one area, these data suggest that research is an important source of training. Such training gives more specialized training in a restricted area of the subject, and these graduates are typically employed in universities or other institutions to conduct further research and to teach health professionals.

The issue of training is under active consideration by the Special Group in Health Psychology. Throughout 1992 and 1993 there have been a series of publications in *Health Psychology Update*, the newsletter of the Special Group. The Training Subcommittee of the Special Group has produced a document (Rumsey *et al.*, 1994) which summarizes their current thinking as a basis for further discussion in developing guidelines for a core curriculum for training in health psychology. The key issues identified were:

- *Level of teaching:* it is assumed that Master's level training is essential, but is training also necessary at undergraduate and doctoral levels?
- *Eligibility for training:* should training be restricted to those holding the Graduate Basis for Registration?

- *Course content:* which elements constitute core theoretical knowledge and skills, and which should constitute specialist options?
- *Format of training:* what should the balance be between course work, skills training, research work, and supervised practice?

The *aims* of the proposed training programme are to enable trained health psychologists to:

- apply psychological approaches to disease prevention and to health care delivery;
- conduct and advise on research in these areas;
- to teach health psychology; and
- to supervise others engaged in such applications, research or teaching.

The proposed core curriculum makes a broad distinction between the academic knowledge base which needs to be acquired and health psychology practitioner skills which should be developed during postgraduate training. The suggested knowledge base is very broad and includes the following modules:

i) *Development of health psychology and main theoretical perspectives* – including an awareness of its relationship to other disciplines (for example, to medical sociology).

ii) *Background epidemiology of disease and biomedical knowledge* – basic understanding of demographic distribution and the main causes of morbidity/mortality, and main biomedical mechanisms.

iii) *Health-related behaviour and theories* – health-risk behaviours; health beliefs, perceptions of cause/control; social and individual representations; individual differences in illness behaviours, symptom perception, health and illness.

iv) *Stress, coping, health and illness* – coping; social support; chronic illness, disability, handicap; rehabilitation; outcome measurement.

v) *Treatment and the treatment context* – health-care professional–patient communication; stressful medical procedures; screening; hospitalization; satisfaction; placebo effects; decision-making by health-care professional and patients; psychological interventions.

The proposed *practitioner skills* are equally broad and these would need to be soundly based in the development of research skills in health psychology. Training would be acquired in various placement settings, often health care settings such as hospitals or health centres, but also in other community settings and worksites. The skills would include: research skills; teaching and training skills; consultancy/supervisory skills; problem formulation and intervention skills, with particular emphasis on stress-management, cognitive–behavioural approaches, provision of information and organizational approaches.

There are differing views as to the most appropriate balance of knowledge and skills in postgraduate health psychology training. One view is that training should be discipline-based with an emphasis on research skills, whereas others have proposed a more practitioner-based approach with an emphasis on intervention skills for the prevention and management of health problems.

The Special Group will use information from the experience of health psychology in other countries, especially USA and European countries, and from other Divisions within the BPS, especially Clinical and Counselling, to guide the development of its recommended training.

In Europe, training in health psychology is currently being addressed by a multinational task force of the European Federation of Professional Psychologists Associations (EFPPA) (see Section 5.2 on links with other countries). In the USA, the APA gives accreditation to courses in health psychology. It is thus unlikely that the current very flexible, but unregulated, situation in the UK will continue.

PAY, PROSPECTS AND CONDITIONS

Posts are not necessarily advertised as being for 'health psychologists'. Employers may request applications from psychologists with the relevant skills to work in the health area such as clinical or counselling psychologists, or from health professionals in general. Thus in addition to the BPS *Appointments Memorandum*, posts may be advertised in national newspapers such as *The Guardian* or *The Independent* in both university and health/social service sections. Posts are also advertised occasionally in the *Health Services Journal* and in local newspapers.

Pay and employment conditions vary with the employer and nature of the contract. Many contracts, especially at more junior grades, are for a limited term, often three years, supported by research grants from research councils, charities or health authorities, trusts, or boards. In addition to limited-term contracts, some contracts may be for part-time work. Health psychologists do not necessarily stay with the same type of employer; an individual may move from a university to a health authority and vice versa and there may also be joint appointments between universities and health service units or Trusts. It is thus important to take note of superannuation schemes and pension rights. When changing posts it may be possible to continue with an existing scheme even though it is not the usual one for the new employer. Health psychologists employed on more than one part-time contract simultaneously should be particularly attentive to issues of superannuation and pension rights. Similarly, those working freelance privately will need to address such issues as taxation, pension, and insurance and to integrate this with periods of work or simultaneous work as an employee.

In general, there is no simple career structure for health psychologists. There are other career structures such as university lecturer, career research worker, clinical psychologist, or occupational psychologist, which may be applicable for some individuals or at some stage in one's career. While most of these careers are described elsewhere, the career of research worker may be particularly relevant for health psychologists.

Research contracts are frequently paid on University Academic and Related Staff Scales, with Grade 1B scales (currently (1994) up to £17,183) for graduate researchers and Grade 1A scales (currently up to £21,786) for post-doctoral researchers. Higher scales (Grades 2 and 3) are available for career-level professional researchers and attract salaries of up to £28,756 for Grade 2, and up to £33,007 for Grade 3.

To some extent the diversity of employment and career structures reflects the immaturity of the profession, but it is likely to be a continuing feature as the problems addressed and the clients served will be from diverse organizational structures simply because 'health' is such a pervasive issue. Frequently, the career structure of an individual reflects the development of their individual talents and contributions to their client or employer.

Sixty-four per cent of the membership of the Special Group are women. There is no specific evidence of discriminatory practice in employment, but since there are no well-defined career structures and irregular employment patterns are common, it is possible that employers' decisions can serve to disadvantage women (or men in some cases), ethnic minorities, those at the extremes of the age distribution or where a disability is involved. Equal opportunities issues are an important current concern of the Special Group in Health Psychology.

Opportunities for working abroad are limited by the different stages of development of this area of work in each country. More commonly, psychologists from abroad have been funded to train in the UK and then returned to work in their own countries.

THE FUTURE

The future is uncertain but potentially exciting for health psychology. There are currently major developments in training and in the need for trained health psychologists.

Changing patterns of health care and health care delivery are leading to new opportunities and needs for the skills of health psychologists. The growing emphasis in health care on the prevention of disease (Marks, 1993) has led to a need for professional skills relevant to understanding and altering health-related cognitions and behaviours. The increased prevalence of chronic rather than acute disease has created a need for the understanding of emotional responses and problem-solving coping skills in addition to the existing biomedical knowledge. Changes in the structure of the health services in the 1990s has increased the need to evaluate the impact of these services on the users. This is apparent in the use of audit to assess whether targets are being met; these targets are frequently specified by descriptions of required behaviours by health care providers. Contracts between Health Authorities in the role of purchasers, with NHS Trusts in the role of providers, typically include some estimate of consumer satisfaction, and Trusts have similar endpoints in their Quality Assurance procedures. These innovations demand expertise in both measuring and improving behavioural and psychological processes. The best informed organizations will employ psychologists with the relevant expertise, but others will employ other professionals with a lay knowledge of these techniques.

It will be essential for psychology, and the Society in particular, to have structures that are compatible with the training and marketing of psychological skills to these emerging organizations and with the new demands for psychological skills. The development of Health Psychology from a Section to a Special Group is clearly progress in identifying a relevant knowledge and skill base. Relevant skills are also found in the Clinical and Counselling Divisions. However, one of the challenges for the Society will be the development of structures which facilitate the new skills and training relevant to these changing patterns of health and health care so that psychologists with appropriate knowledge, skills and professional status can be identified.

REFERENCES

JOHNSTON, M. (1994) Current trends in health psychology. *The Psychologist*, 7, 114–118.

MARKS, D. (1994) The role of psychology in *The Health of the Nation*. *The Psychologist*, 7, 119–121.

Psy-PAG (1993). *Survey of PhD students 1991/2*. Personal Communication, Julie Williams.

RUMSEY, N., McGUIRE, B., MARKS, D., WATTS, M., WEINMAN, J., WRIGHT, S. (1994). Teaching and training in health psychology. *The Psychologist*, 7, 129–131.

SECTION II
PROFESSIONAL ISSUES

Contributors:

Andrew Colman
Reader in Psychology, University of Leicester

Martin Herbert
*Professor of Clinical and Community Psychology, University of Exeter, and
Consultant Clinical Psychologist, Exeter Health Authority*

Bernard Kat
Psychology Services Manager, Community Health Care North Durham NHS Trust

Tony Black
*Head of Psychological Services, Broadmoor Hospital 1959–86, and Mental Health
Act Commissioner 1986–90*

John Sheppard
*Chartered Educational Psychologist and Past Chair of the Division of Educational
and Child Psychology*

Harry Rafferty
*Course Director, M.Sc. Developmental and Educational Psychology, Queen's
University, Belfast*

Tommy MacKay
*Principal Educational Psychologist, Dumbarton West Psychological Service;
Honorary Lecturer in Psychology, University of Strathclyde; and Chair of the
Scottish Branch of The British Psychological Society*

Paul T. Brown
Consulting Clinical and Occupational Psychologist, Jackson Brown and Co., London

Anne E. Abel Smith
*Associate Research Fellow, Centre for Research in Social Policy, Loughborough
University*

Eugene Burke
*Consultant Psychologist, London Fire Brigade, and Chair of the BPS Steering
Committee on Test Standards*

2.1 TESTIFYING IN COURT AS AN EXPERT WITNESS

Andrew M. Colman

Expert opinion has played a part in the legal process for centuries. At first, experts were invited to serve on juries, then in the late Middle Ages they began to testify as witnesses. During the eighteenth century, the testimony of experts in various fields became institutionalized in England (Cross and Tapper, 1990; Hodgkinson, 1990; Learned Hand, 1901).

The first psychologist to be called as an expert witness was probably the German Albert von Schrenck-Notzing, who testified in 1896 in the trial of a Munich man accused of murdering three women (Bartol and Bartol, 1987). His evidence focused on retroactive memory falsification – confusion among witnesses between what they saw and what they subsequently learned of an event. At about the same time in the United States, Hugo Münsterberg acted as a psychological consultant in two murder trials, and although his own evidence was not admitted in court, he became a forceful advocate of psychological testimony in particular, and forensic psychology in general. He was the first psychologist to collect empirical evidence specifically for use in legal cases, and his research into reaction times between rifle shots (Münsterberg, 1899) was still considered relevant more than half a century later in the controversy surrounding the number of assassins involved in the killing of President John F. Kennedy (Haward, 1979).

Münsterberg's (1908) pioneering (though controversial) book on psychological testimony, *On the Witness Stand: Essays on Psychology and Crime*, was followed by many others dealing exclusively or largely with this topic. Present-day psychological witnesses will find the following books, in differing ways, especially useful: Brodsky (1991), Gudjonsson (1992), Gudjonsson and Drinkwater (1987), Haward (1981), Lloyd-Bostock (1988), Loftus and Ketcham (1991), Shapiro (1984), and Weiner and Hess (1987).

PSYCHOLOGISTS WHO TESTIFY

Recent decades have seen a dramatic increase in the frequency with which psychologists have been called as expert witnesses in the United States, and to a lesser extent in Britain. A survey carried out by The British Psychological Society revealed that 92 per cent of psychologists who had testified in court or in front of a tribunal were either educational or clinical psychologists (Lloyd-Bostock, 1988, p. 137). Educational psychologists are often involved in the assessments of juvenile offenders and of children who are the subjects of custody disputes between divorcing parents, and are sometimes called as expert witnesses. A growing minority of clinical psychologists specialize in forensic psychology and spend a large part of their working time preparing evidence and testifying in court.

Other categories of psychologists who are called as expert witnesses from time to time include prison psychologists, who often contribute to assessments of offenders and occasionally give supporting evidence in court; occupational psychologists, who sometimes testify in cases involving employment discrimination or personal injury; and academic psychologists, a small number of whom testify on other specialized issues.

The law allows most witnesses to testify only about facts, but expert witnesses are uniquely permitted to give evidence of their opinions as well. Questions that have been put to expert psychological witnesses include the following (adapted from Haward, 1981): *Is the accused's confession likely to be genuine?; Did the plaintiff suffer brain damage, and if so what are its likely long-term effects?; Is the appellant a fit person to have custody of his child?; Is the memory of this witness likely to have been improved by hypnosis?; Is this person's mental condition such as to require her to be detained under the Mental Health Act for the protection of others?; Is the accused psychologically fit to stand trial?; What psychological evidence is available regarding the suggestibility of child witnesses when being interrogated by police officers?; Is this person's eyewitness identification of the accused likely to be trustworthy?; Does this person suffer from severe learning difficulties, and if so, how is this likely to affect his earning power?; What are the likely effects of long-term alcohol abuse on this person's memory?; Is the accused's behaviour likely to have been significantly influenced by social psychological effects during this incident of mob violence?*

PREPARATION

Testifying in court is a daunting ordeal for almost anyone, and few, if any, expert witnesses ever become comfortably habituated to it. The awe-inspiring architecture and furnishing of the courtroom, the bizarre dress conventions in some courts, and the solemn rituals governing courtroom proceedings are all calculated to impress on witnesses the gravity of the occasion. If all that is not impressive enough, then hostile and determined cross-examination is virtually guaranteed to disconcert even the most nonchalant expert witness – that, after all, is often one of its primary objectives.

The outcome of a case may depend crucially on expert testimony, and the expert knows that a great deal is at stake, otherwise the matter would not have ended up in court. The expert's own professional reputation is inevitably on the line, which increases the pressure still further. Nothing can be done to make the job easy or stress-free, but adequate preparation can go a long way towards reducing anxiety and facilitating the effective presentation of evidence. This involves judicious preparation of evidence and, equally importantly, mental preparation.

Preparing evidence and writing reports

The expert witness's first task is usually to prepare a written forensic psychological report based on information gathered from interviews and (if appropriate) from psychological tests. The report, to which is normally attached a brief curriculum vitae outlining the expert's formal qualifications and experience, is usually disclosed to lawyers representing the opposing party. Its preparation and organization can have a significant bearing on the outcome of a case. Practical advice on preparing reports can be found in Carson (1990, pp. 30–32), Gudjonsson (1992, pp. 304–305), Hodgkinson (1990, pp. 84–88), and Shapiro (1984, pp. 181–189).

Forensic psychological reports often need to deal with issues that do not arise in other types of psychological reports. Perhaps most importantly, expert witnesses often have to be alert to the possibility that clients are malingering, whereas in other circumstances psychologists can usually take the behaviour and symptoms presented by their clients at face value. Malingering is often a pivotal issue in criminal trials, because a person who was mentally disordered at the time of an alleged offence may for that reason alone be found not guilty, and one who is mentally disordered at the time of evaluation may even be declared unfit to stand trial. In civil litigation, a plaintiff who suffers from some psychological incapacity as a result of a head injury sustained in a road traffic accident, for example, may be entitled to substantial damages. In such cases, the likelihood of malingering should be evaluated in the light of all the available evidence, and the issue should be addressed directly in the report.

A report should be confined to answering the question(s) posed by the instructing solicitors. The individual who is the subject of the report should be interviewed and assessed with diligence and circumspection, using the most appropriate techniques and instruments. All available evidence, including tape-recorded police interviews where relevant, should be asked for and studied. A diligent expert witness will also review current literature in the relevant field before preparing a report. The report should be written in plain, jargon-free language, and should be balanced and scrupulously honest. Its conclusions should be concrete and explicit, citing wherever possible the facts on which they are based. Uncertainties, where they exist, should be incorporated with appropriate qualifiers, such as 'probably', 'I feel fairly certain', 'in most cases of this kind', and so on. It is a dangerous fallacy that only absolute, cut-and-dried conclusions are acceptable in court.

If the instructing solicitors are not satisfied with the conclusions of the report, they may simply ignore it and decline to call its author as a witness. They may then instruct another psychologist, in the hope of obtaining a more favourable report. Alternatively, they may ask the original psychologist to modify the report or to delete the unfavourable points. A psychologist who is asked to alter a report in a way that might mislead the court should, of course, refuse to do so (Gudjonsson, 1992), but reasonable suggestions designed to improve the clarity of the report should not be rejected out of hand.

It is a good idea to structure the report as a series of numbered points or paragraphs (Carson, 1990). This helps to systematize the material and makes it easier for everyone concerned to refer to specific parts of the report during the presentation of oral evidence and the judgment. A report that is presented clearly, comprehensively, succinctly, and above all persuasively, is often accepted by the lawyers on both sides of the case without the psychologist having to testify orally.

Mental preparation

Before testifying in court for the first time, a psychologist should, if possible, visit the court while it is in session in order to become familiar with its layout, rituals, and general ambience. The discomfort that most people feel in court tends to diminish quite rapidly as a function of the amount of time spent in it. It may be useful to know that the law allows experts, unlike lay witnesses, to sit in court and listen to the evidence of other witnesses in their own cases before testifying themselves (Hodgkinson, 1990, p. 107).

In the United Kingdom (with the exception of Scotland),

most minor criminal trials take place in magistrates' courts. The magistrates who hear a case are either three unpaid Justices of the Peace, selected from the community, or one legally trained stipendiary magistrate, and the lawyers who argue for the prosecution and the defence are solicitors. Serious criminal cases are heard in a crown court in front of a judge and (except in Northern Ireland) a jury of twelve members of the general public. In a crown court, the prosecution and defence lawyers are barristers rather than solicitors, and both they and the judge wear wigs and black gowns. In both types of court the proceedings are run by a clerk and a court usher who calls witnesses and carries messages and exhibits. Most civil (non-criminal) cases are heard in county courts presided over by circuit judges and recorders or, in difficult or specialized cases, in the High Court, both of which resemble crown courts.

Scotland has its own legal system and structure of courts. Although this is different from other parts of the United Kingdom, the same general principles apply when witnesses are cited to give evidence.

PRESENTING THE EVIDENCE

Expert witnesses are often anxious about how they should dress for court. It is advisable to avoid casual dress but, as far as possible, to wear familiar and comfortable clothes. Clothes that are likely to attract attention for any reason at all are inappropriate.

Taking the oath

The first thing that happens after a witness has been ushered into the witness box is the administration of the oath. The witness is asked to swear on the Bible or other appropriate holy book to tell the truth. The witness normally reads the oath off a card, and an atheist, agnostic, or heathen is allowed to affirm by reading a non-religious declaration, but it is worth considering whether this could convey an unfavourable impression to the magistrates, judge, or jury.

Carson (1990, pp. 11–12) has pointed out that the ritual of taking the oath provides witnesses with a golden opportunity to range their voices in order to establish the optimal volume and pitch for audibility and comfort across the unnaturally large spaces of a typical courtroom. Carson advises witnesses to take their time and to declaim the words of the oath with feeling: nothing but good can come from appearing to take them seriously, and magistrates, judges, and juries form their crucial first impressions of witnesses at this point. It is inadvisable to repeat the oath from memory, unless it has been very carefully memorized, because if even one word is wrong the witness will be corrected immediately and may consequently feel (and look) foolish.

After taking the oath, expert witnesses usually begin their evidence-in-chief by testifying about their qualifications and experience in order to establish the basis of their expertise. The lawyer leading the examination-in-chief usually draws attention to key points from the expert witness's curriculum vitae and simply asks the witness to confirm them. During this preliminary phase of the evidence, since no cognitive effort is required, a witness has a further opportunity to settle down.

Forms of address

An appropriate form of address should be used when speaking directly to the court. Witnesses should address magistrates as 'Your Worship(s)'; but if that expression sticks in the gullet, then 'Sir' and 'Madam' are generally acceptable, although neither is grammatical when addressing a full bench of three magistrates. Circuit judges, recorders in county courts, and crown court judges, apart from judges in the Central Criminal Court in London (the Old Bailey), should be addressed as 'Your Honour'. High Court judges, and by tradition, judges in the Old Bailey, although it is really only a crown court, are addressed as 'My Lord' or 'My Lady'. In tribunals, 'Chairman', 'Madam Chair', 'Sir', or 'Madam' are generally appropriate forms of address.

Witnesses are often advised to stand in the witness box facing the bench and to direct their answers directly to the magistrate(s) or the judge and jury, if there is one. This is a difficult and unnatural way of conducting a dialogue, because our natural impulse is to reply directly to the person who asks the questions. As long as the replies are loud and clear enough to be audible throughout the courtroom, replying directly to the lawyer who is asking the questions should do no harm, although replying to the court is more correct and preferable for various other reasons (Carson, 1990).

Expert witnesses may take whatever notes they wish into the witness box, but if they do, lawyers representing the opposing party are then entitled to ask to see them and to base questions and arguments on their contents. Formal psychological reports are usually taken into the witness box, because they have usually been disclosed already and because questions are likely to refer to them repeatedly.

Cross-examination

Testimony begins with the examination-in-chief, in which the psychologist often simply confirms and clarifies the evidence in the written report. This is followed by cross-examination, conducted by a lawyer representing the opposing party, which is designed to undermine the testimony. Brodsky (1991) and Carson (1990) have suggested numerous guidelines and maxims for handling difficult questions during cross-examination. The golden rule is to listen attentively and to answer carefully and objectively. Expert witnesses should keep the limits of their expertise clearly in mind, and if they do not know the answer to a question, they should not hesitate to say so. The most common faults of expert witnesses include waffling instead of confining themselves to answering the questions; being afraid of expressing opinions; exaggerating; answering questions defensively; speaking inaudibly; over-qualifying statements; using jargon; and appearing to be partisan rather than objective.

Expert witnesses should unhesitatingly concede valid points that appear to favour the opposing side, but they should be assertive enough to stand their ground and to avoid crumpling unnecessarily in the face of hectoring or intimidating cross-examination. They should never fall into the trap of becoming angry in response to sarcastic or bullying cross-examination (or cross-making-examination, as it might be called). Emotions aside, it is seldom, if ever, right to change a professional opinion as a result of cross-examination; expert opinion should be grounded in the relevant literature and data.

ETHICAL AND PROFESSIONAL ISSUES

Psychologists who are asked to testify as expert witnesses often face ethical and professional dilemmas (Colman, 1991; McLoskey, Egeth, and McKenna, 1986). If a defendant appears to be guilty of an especially despicable crime, the first dilemma may revolve around whether simply to refuse to testify for the defence. Although there is no compelling professional duty to testify – nothing comparable to the 'cab-rank rule' according to which barristers are obliged to accept briefs within their fields of practice as long as they are available – there are at least three powerful arguments in favour of testifying in these circumstances. The first rests on that precious element of the rule of law known as the *presumption of innocence*, according to which any defendant is rightly considered innocent until proven guilty. The second argument is that it is the job of the magistrate(s), judge, or jury, and not the expert witness, to decide questions of guilt or innocence. The third argument is that innocent people are often falsely accused, and those charged with the most heinous crimes – who face the heaviest sentences if convicted – should be defended at least as vigorously as anyone else.

After agreeing to testify, a dilemma often arises between presenting controversial psychological issues even-handedly or slanting them selectively in favour of the client's case. This dilemma arises from the incompatibility between the methods of truth-seeking of psychology and of the law (Colman, 1991; Loftus and Monahan, 1980). Psychologists are taught to seek the truth through the detached and dispassionate application of the scientific method. Lawyers, in contrast, seek the truth through adversarial court cases in which each party presents the arguments and evidence that support its own case and vigorously attacks those presented by the opposing side, and the magistrate, judge, or jury referees the debate and decides where the truth lies.

Expert psychological witnesses who are caught between these two incompatible approaches to truth-seeking should remain true to their own profession. Although they may be subjected to direct and indirect pressures from lawyers, they should adhere firmly to the *Code of Conduct, Ethical Principles and Guidelines* of The British Psychological Society (1993). They are duty bound to give fair and balanced testimony, especially on controversial issues. Although the client's lawyers hope and expect that the evidence will help their case, the expert's proper function is not to help the client to win the case but to help the court to reach the right decision. Prejudicial testimony undermines the reputation of both academic and professional psychology and the credibility of all future expert psychological witnesses.

REFERENCES

BARTOL, C. R. and BARTOL, A. M. (1987). History of forensic psychology. In I.B. Weiner and A. K. Hess (Eds), *Handbook of Forensic Psychology* (pp. 3–21). New York: Wiley.

BRITISH PSYCHOLOGICAL SOCIETY (1993). *Code of Conduct, Ethical Principles and Guidelines*. Leicester: The British Psychological Society.

BRODSKY, S. L. (1991). *Testifying in Court: Guidelines and Maxims for the Expert Witness*. Washington, DC: American Psychological Association.

CARSON, D. (1990). *Professionals and the Courts: A Handbook for Expert Witnesses*. Birmingham: Venture Press.

COLMAN, A. M. (1991). Crowd psychology in South African murder trials. *American Psychologist, 46*, 1071–1079.

CROSS, R. and TAPPER, C. (1990). *Cross on Evidence* (7th ed.). London: Butterworths.

GUDJONSSON, G. H. (1992). *The Psychology of Interrogations, Confessions and Testimony*. Chichester: Wiley.

GUDJONSSON, G. H. and DRINKWATER, J. (Eds). (1987). *Psychological Evidence in Court*. Leicester: The British Psychological Society.

HAWARD, L. R. C. (1979). The psychologist as expert witness. In D. P. Farrington, K. Hawkins, and S. M. A. Lloyd-Bostock (Eds), *Psychology, Law and Legal Processes* (pp. 45–53). London: Macmillan.

HAWARD, L. R. C. (1981). *Forensic Psychology*. London: Batsford.

HODGKINSON, T. (1990). *Expert Evidence: Law and Practice*. London: Sweet and Maxwell.

LEARNED HAND (1901). Historical and practical considerations regarding expert testimony. *Harvard Law Review*, 15, 40–58.

LLOYD-BOSTOCK, S. M. A. (1988). *Law in Practice: Applications of Psychology to Legal Decision Making and Legal Skills*. Leicester and London: BPS Books (The British Psychological Society) and Routledge.

LOFTUS, E. and KETCHAM, K. (1991). *Witness for the Defense: The Accused, the Eyewitness, and the Expert Who Puts Memory on Trial*. New York: St Martin's.

LOFTUS, E. and MONAHAN, J. (1980). Trial by data: Psychological research as legal evidence. *American Psychologist*, 35, 270–283.

McLOSKEY, M., EGETH, H., and McKENNA, J. (Eds). (1986). The ethics of expert testimony [Special issue]. *Law and Human Behavior*, 10 (1/2).

MÜNSTERBERG, H. (1899). *Beiträge zur experimentellen Psychologie*. Freiburg: Mohr.

MÜNSTERBERG, H. (1908). *On the Witness Stand: Essays on Psychology and Crime*. New York: McClure.

SHAPIRO, D. L. (1984). *Psychological Evaluation and Expert Testimony: A Practical Guide to Forensic Work*. New York: Van Nostrand Reinhold.

WEINER, I. B. and HESS A. K. (Eds). (1987). *Handbook of Forensic Psychology*. New York: Wiley.

TRAINING

The British Psychological Society has produced a 75-minute, four-module video training package entitled *Expert Testimony: Developing Witness Skills*, suitable for group or self-tuition. It is priced at £650 + VAT (BPS members £580 + VAT). Further information and copies available from the BPS office (Tel: 0116 254 9568).

The Behavioural Science and Law Network at the University of Southampton holds expert witness training courses, including one entitled 'Developing Witness Skills' run by

David Carson, around the country. Further details available from Jill Elliot (Tel: 01703 592376).

The Department of Psychology (Clinical Section) at the University of Leicester will be running courses on psychology and the courts and other forensic issues. The first course, *Psychology and the Courts: Preparing Legal Reports and Appearing as a Witness* will be run in June 1995. Further details from Viv Doughty, Course Administrator, Department of Psychology (Clinical Section), University of Leicester (Tel: 0116 252 2481).

Other departments or organizations may be running similar courses, but at the time of writing these were the only ones of which we were aware.

2.2 ACTS OF PARLIAMENT

2.2.1 THE CHILDREN ACT 1989

Martin Herbert

*I*T *should be noted that while the underlying principles of the Act are the same, there are minor differences in the Act's applications in N. Ireland. For example, the section numbers referred to here will not parallel those of the Children (N.I.) Order. Also, where references are made to local authorities, in N. Ireland the corresponding responsible body will be the Department of Health and Social Services. English High Court appeals will be at County Court level in N. Ireland. At the time of writing, the Children Act 1989 does not apply to Scotland (except for Section 10 which concerns registration of childminders). There will be legislation in the near future, and a Children (Scotland) Act is likely to overlap considerably with English legislation. However, there will be a number of areas of difference reflecting Scottish terminology and other legislative differences.*

BACKGROUND TO THE ACT

Child care law, on issues of child protection and preventive work, prior to the Children Act 1989 was complicated and sometimes contradictory. The framework it provided for professionals in this area (and indeed parents) was felt to be inadequate. It also failed to facilitate parents' involvement in the lives of children accommodated by local authorities. The Short Committee's concerns about these shortcomings led to the setting up of the DHSS Review of Child Care Law in 1984. Major changes in the law were recommended. Added to these initiatives were the devastating reports of three child death enquiries concerning Jasmine Beckford, Kimberley Carlile and Tyra Henry. A need for greater clarity of law and increased powers for social workers were priorities in drafting the new legislation.

The overriding aim of the ensuing Children Act was to

provide a clear and consistent code for the *whole* of child care law which was comprehensible to all who work in the field.

Impact of the Act

The Children Act reforms and brings together the public and private law relating to children, and will now apply in all three levels of court permitted to deal with family proceedings: the High Court, the County Court and the new Magistrates' Family Proceedings Court. What is its impact on the profession of psychology? Certainly there is a general, and more particular, requirement of clinical child psychologists and educational psychologists to familiarize themselves with the powers and duties defined by the Act. The far-reaching implications of the legislation for children and their parents demand a clear understanding of the various orders, so as to be in a position to advise clients (parents and children) of their rights and duties. In addition, the practitioner's work should be informed by an accurate knowledge of the law; that is to say by reality, rather than by wishful thinking about what can, and cannot, be done to help and protect children.

At a more particular level, clinical child psychologists (like child psychiatrists) and educational psychologists are likely to be called on to provide reports and (in certain circumstances) to appear in Court to give expert opinions on various matters arising from the legislation (see also Section 2.1 on acting as an expert witness). These requests may come (*interalia*) from the Courts, from Social Services and from Guardians *ad litem*. The need for rigorous, and developmentally-based assessments, is a key issue, as we shall see, in the Act. The training of psychologists in theory and methods of measurement, in traversing the minefield of making predictions, and in behavioural theory and child development, gives them an advantage shared by few, if any, other professions. In the author's experience, the emphasis by psychologists on objective evidence, systematic data collection and unemotive formulations, is highly valued by solicitors, barristers and judges. So, too, is their knowledge of the empirical literature (see, for example, Schaffer, 1990; Sutton, 1988). Likewise, the expertise of clinical and educational psychologists in psychological therapies – remedial and preventive – fits, neatly, the ethos of the Children Act with its emphasis on parent participation and keeping families together. What of the Act itself? It is now a cliché, but one worth repeating, that the Children Act, with its 12 parts, 108 sections and 15 schedules (generating numerous sets of rules and regulations) introduced radical changes in the legislative base of childcare work and resulted in the most comprehensive changes in local authority casework for several decades.

MAIN MESSAGES OF THE ACT

The main messages of the Children Act can be summarized as follows:

1. The child's welfare is paramount

A 'welfare checklist' is included to facilitate consistency across different levels of courts across the country. (See Masson, 1990, for an excellent commentary and annotations on the Act.) A crucial principle of the Act is that the welfare of the child should come before and above any other consideration in deciding whether to make an order. It is a matter of policy that the court should not make an order unless it considers that to do so would be better for the child than making no order at all [s. 1(5)]. This has important implications for practitioners, in that, at the very outset, one must consider whether the court is likely to make any order at all.

The Act states that the court shall have regard in particular to the child's welfare as defined in the following welfare checklist [s. 1(3)]:

a) The ascertainable wishes and feelings of the child concerned (considered in the light of the child's age and understanding).
b) The child's physical, emotional and educational needs.
c) The likely effect on the child of any change in circumstances.
d) The child's age, sex, background and any characteristics that the court considers relevant.
e) Any harm the child has suffered, or is at risk of suffering.
f) How capable each of the child's parents, and any other person in relation to whom the court considers the question to be relevant, is of meeting the child's needs.
g) The range of powers available to the court under this Act in the proceedings in question.

2. Children should be brought up in their own families

The Act highlights this point by creating a duty to provide adequate services to help the family maintain the child at home. Local authorities have a duty to promote the upbringing of *children in need* by their families. 'Children in need' becomes a technical term which covers *children who need services to secure a reasonable standard of health and development*. It includes children who are disabled.

3. Parents are responsible

The new concept of parental responsibility shifts the emphasis from parents' rights over a child, to their duties and responsibilities towards him or her. Parental responsibility is defined in [s. 3(1)].

4. There is a continuing role for parents and the wider family
Parental responsibility cannot be taken away (except by adoption) and is, therefore, shared with everyone else who acquires it (for example, the local authority). When parental responsibility is shared with the Social Services Department (SSD) they have the power to decide how much the parents may exercise their parental responsibility, but may only do so if it is necessary to safeguard or promote the child's welfare. The SSD *must* allow parents reasonable contact with children who are the subject of a care order, and try to promote such contact, unless this will put the child's welfare at risk.

5. Child protection is crucial but open to challenge
The Act addresses the difficult task of protecting children from harm, families from unwarranted intervention and the right of families to challenge decisions.
The child protection orders include:

- a child assessment order [s. 43];
- an emergency protection order [s. 44];
- removal and accommodation of children by police in cases of emergency [s. 46];
- recovery of abducted children etc. [s. 50].

Care and supervision are the two main public law orders:

- a care order places the child into the care of a local authority [s. 31];
- a supervision order puts a child under the supervision of an SSD or a probation officer [s. 35].

The grounds for obtaining care or supervision orders are new. Section 31(2) provides that a court may only make a care order or supervision order if it is satisfied (a) that the child concerned is suffering, or is likely to suffer, significant harm; and (b) that harm, or likelihood of harm, is attributable to (i) that care given to the child, or likely to be given to him/her if the order were not made, not being what it would be reasonable to expect a parent to give to him/her; or (ii) the child's being beyond parental control.
The SSD will have to produce a plan for the future of each child in its care, and the progress of each child will be subject to periodic review to ensure that the child is being provided with the right kind of care. 'Looked after' (by the local authority) is the generic term to describe a child's situation when in the care of (on a care order), or provided with accommodation by, the local authority. Because *protection* of children, quite rightly, is such a major preoccupation of the law, the issue of the *welfare balance* can create a considerable intellectual, emotional and moral tension for the professional. Because social and health workers are

enjoined to give priority to the protection of children while, at the same time, having to bear in mind that children are generally best looked after within the family, both parents playing a full part (indeed, even when the child is removed from the family), these sometimes contradictory requirements make for difficult judgements, decisions and recommendations. The Act seeks to protect children both from the harm which can arise from failure or abuse within the family, and from the harm which can be caused by unwarranted intervention in family life.

The courts are given wide powers to intervene to protect children at risk of harm within the family. If an assessment of the child is needed to decide whether significant harm is likely and it is clear that there is not an emergency calling for an emergency protection order, the Act allows an application for an order or an assessment which can last up to seven days.

6. The child's voice should be heard; the child should be informed about what is happening

The first item on the 'welfare checklist' considers the ascertainable wishes and feelings of the child. When a court determines any question with respect to the upbringing of a child, it has regard, in particular, to the ascertainable wishes and feelings of the child concerned (considered in the light of his/her age and understanding). Thus there is a greater emphasis than in earlier legislation on consulting children and finding out their views. The courts, according to Masson (1990), should not merely suggest that a child is too young to be consulted nor should they rely on what a parent says the child wants. Guardians *ad litem* in care proceedings attempt to discover the views of children as young as three years old.

So how does one find out what the child wants? As with all persons, the major methods used are observation, questioning and giving a sympathetic hearing. Interviewing, because of the opportunity it gives to 'ask them', 'question them', and, by no means least, 'listen to them', becomes a prime instrument of assessment, investigation, intervention and evaluation. Verbal report, based upon clinical conversations, may be a fairly good predictor of real-life behaviour, but it can also be very misleading and therefore unreliable.

These issues of assessment, including communicating with children and their reliability as witnesses, are dealt with by the author elsewhere (Herbert 1991a; 1993).

Public law orders:

- Investigation and assessment [Sections 43 and 47]: the local authority's responsibilities in investigating cases where a child may be harmed, are clarified.

- Emergency protection orders [Sections 44 and 45]: 'place of safety orders' are replaced with more restrictive 'emergency protection orders'.
- Supervision orders [Sections 31, 35 and Schedule 3].
- Care orders [Sections 31–34]: there used to be 20 or so routes into care. Now there is only one – the one defined in the Act.

Health professionals may be called upon to give an expert opinion in either private or public law cases.

Psychologists with a training in psychometrics, developmental counselling and various forms of therapy, are in a good position to design, supervise or implement assessments and interventions to help parents or caregivers to be more responsive, effective, self-reliant and confident in the care and management of their children and in their relationships.

The local authority, when providing services (for example, day care or accommodation), and when cancelling registration under Part X, must give due consideration to the 'child's religious persuasion, racial origin, cultural and linguistic background'. (Part X is that section of the Children Act dealing with childminding and day care (for example, nurseries), for young children; issues such as registration, requirements, protection and inspection are covered.) A specific duty is required so that arrangements are made to ensure that issues of race, religious persuasion and cultural background are taken into account when recruiting foster parents.

7. Standards of child care are monitored
There are greater powers to monitor child minders, residential homes and other providers of child care, and their standards. The new court system enshrines several new principles, including:

No delay – courts must draw up a timetable for the disposal of an application without delay. They should give priority to children's cases.

No order – no order will be made 'unless it is considered better for the child than making no order at all'.

The 'Domestic Court' is renamed the 'Family Proceedings Court' and is able to handle most cases. Care cases will usually start in that court, but the rules contain a power to transfer cases to specified County Courts of the High Court.

Most public law cases will thus be heard by magistrates drawn from new Family Panels and will be specially trained to deal with cases under the Children Act. If cases are particularly complex or urgent, they will be heard by judges who have been specially trained, and who sit in courts designated as care centres or family hearing centres. The procedure in the courts will be made to feel less threatening and more informal, especially for children.

Appeals in care cases will be heard in the High Court. Care proceedings are brought within the civil legal aid scheme.

REFERENCES AND FURTHER READING

BLACK, D. and WOLKIND, S. (1991). *Child Psychiatry and the Law*, 2nd edn. London: Gaskell (for the Royal College of Psychiatrists).

HERBERT, M. (1991a). *Child Care and the Family. A Resource Pack*. Windsor: National Foundation for Educational Research – Nelson.

HERBERT, M. (1991b). *Clinical Child Psychology: Social Learning, Development and Behaviour*. Chichester: Wiley.

HERBERT, M. (1993). *Working with Children and the Children Act*. Leicester: BPS Books (The British Psychological Society).

H.M.S.O. (1989). *An Introduction to the Children Act 1989: A New Framework for the Care and Upbringing of Children*. London: Her Majesty's Stationery Office.

H.M.S.O. (1990). *The Care of Children: Principle and Practice in Regulations and Guidance*. London: Her Majesty's Stationery Office.

H.M.S.O. (1991). *Patterns and Outcomes in Child Placement – Messages from Current Research and Their Implications*. London: Her Majesty's Stationery Office.

MACDONALD, S. (1990). *All Equal Under the Act*. London: Race Equality Unit, N.I.S.W.

MASSON, J. (1990). *The Children Act 1989: Text and Commentary*. London: Sweet and Maxwell.

SCHAFFER, H. R. (1990). *Making Decisions About Children: Psychological Questions and Answers*. Oxford: Basil Blackwell.

SUTTON, C. (1988). *A Handbook of Research for the Helping Professions*. London: Routledge and Kegan Paul.

2.2.2   THE DATA PROTECTION ACT AND OTHER ACTS CONCERNING RECORDS

Bernard Kat

Mr Smith sees a psychologist at the request of someone, perhaps his employer or doctor. The psychologist asks Mr Smith to com-

plete a number of questionnaires and also takes notes of their conversation. Mr Smith knows that the results of the question- naires and the notes of the discussion will form the basis of a report from the psychologist to the person who asked him to see the psychologist. Mr Smith also knows that important decisions affect- ing his future will be influenced by the content of the report. Should he ask for a copy? Will he be offered one? Suppose the psychologist has misunderstood him; can he have the report cor- rected? Suppose he disagrees with the psychologist's conclusions; can he have them changed?

Mr Smith's predicament is shared by almost everyone at some time in their lives. Almost any contact with almost any service, whether statutory or non-statutory, pro- fessional or commercial, gives rise to a written or compu- terized record containing information such as the client's name, address, gender, date of birth, the reason for the contact, and so on. Such records have many purposes. They provide an *aide-mémoire* for the person who dealt with us; they enable the organization providing the ser- vice to monitor its activities; they may be passed on to other organizations which 'mailshot' unsolicited adver- tisements for products in which we might be interested. But what control do we have over that information? What are our rights to stop it from being misunderstood or mis- used?

The rights we do have are those given to us by legislation which was designed to answer those questions. These rights derive from several Acts of Parliament, not just one, and they are rooted in European legislation as well as British laws. Several different Acts have been required because the problems of access to records and confidentia- lity are complex and have been approached from a number of different angles.

BACKGROUND TO THE ACT

So far as the United Kingdom is concerned, the story begins in 1970 when the Government of the day appointed the Younger Committee to consider whether legislation was needed for the protection of individuals and organizations against intrusions into privacy. The microprocessor and personal computers were only a gleam in designers' eyes at the time, and there were probably only 6,000 computer systems in the country, all of them based on 'mainframe' computers which required whole rooms, even buildings to themselves. Nonetheless, the Younger Committee set out some general guidelines for information users which have been incorporated into all subsequent legislation.

In 1975, a White Paper on Computers and Privacy identified computer operations as a particular threat to privacy. This is because through the use of computers:

- extensive record systems which would not be feasible without the power of computers can be created and maintained;
- data can be accessed easily and quickly via networks;
- data can be transferred very easily from one system to another without the knowledge of the people to whom the data refer;
- several databases can be used simultaneously, permitting the user to select and combine data about individuals, thereby discovering information about them which had not been recorded in its own right;
- all of these activities can be undertaken using data stored and transmitted in such a way that ordinary people are unable to understand what is being done or check the data for accuracy or intrusiveness.

In 1978 the Government set up a further committee, the Lindop Committee, to advise on the legislation required. That Committee's work finally led to the Data Protection Act, 1984.

Council of Europe Convention

This 'potted history' of one of the main sources of personal rights in relation to information would not be complete without reference to events in Europe. Business depends on the free flow of information, both between companies in the same country and across national and international boundaries. But that information often refers to individuals whose privacy ought to be safeguarded. In 1981, the Council of Europe created a convention, called the *Convention for the Protection of Individuals with regard to the Automatic Processing of Personal Data*, the aims of which were:

- to codify the rights and freedoms of individuals in relation to the computerized processing of information which refers to them;

- to regulate flows of data across borders in such a way that countries which ratified the Convention could refuse to send data to countries which did not observe the same standards of data protection.

The Data Protection Act has two main purposes:

1. to meet public and professional concern over threats to privacy arising from the use of computers, their ability to analyse and process large amounts of information about individuals, to give wide access to the data and to merge data held for different purposes;

2. to enable the United Kingdom to ratify the Council of Europe Convention and so minimize the risk to UK international trade that would arise if we did not ratify it and other countries would therefore not share data with us.

Thus the Data Protection Act is primarily about information held on computers, or in a form which would allow a computer to process it. This could include text that could be read by a suitable input device such as a scanner, and might soon extend to handwriting as the technology to read it directly into the computer becomes available. It is a wide-ranging Act which makes only a few references to specific areas such as health care.

Access to records

In the middle 1980s, as the Data Protection Act came into force, another aspect of public concern was making itself felt. It appeared that a significant number of people wanted to be able to find out what was in their medical records, or in the records held about them by their university or about their child by their child's school. Many of these are not, or were not at the time, held on computers; they were so-called 'manual' records, that is, hand-typed or hand-written. The Data Protection Act had created new legal rights of access to information for individuals and new legal obligations on those who hold data. Why couldn't the same rights and obligations that apply to computerized records also apply to 'manual' records? As a consequence, a sequence of Acts was passed by Parliament, of which the Access to Health Records Act, 1990 is a particular example.

IMPLEMENTATION AND ADMINISTRATION OF THE ACT

The Data Protection Act created the office of Data Protection Registrar and set up a register of computer users, data users and computer bureaux. The Registrar reports direct to Parliament and has the responsibilities of implementing and administering the Act.

The Act requires computer users to comply with three main obligations. Firstly, to register the use of personal data. The definition of 'personal data' is important. 'Personal data means data consisting of information which relates to a living individual who can be identified from that information (or from that and other information in the possession of the data user), including any expression of opinion about the individual, but not any indication of the intentions of the data user in respect of that individual.' Registration involves a description of the data, the purposes for which they are held, from whom they will be obtained and to whom they will be disclosed.

Secondly, to operate in accordance with the Data Protection Principles. (The Data Protection principles are reproduced in the *Appendix* to this section.) If a data user fails to observe this requirement, the Data Protection Registrar can intervene and can even stop the offending data user from operating at all. The Data Protection Principles, which originated in the Younger Report but have since been incorporated into European legislation, seem quite bland and abstract at first sight. Nonetheless, when used as criteria against which to test the appropriateness of a course of action, they often turn out to be both clear and powerful.

Thirdly, there is an obligation on computer users to give any individual access to the personal data which is being held about him or her.

On the other hand, the Act gives the individual three main rights. Firstly, to inspect the register. In other words, the register is a public document which lists everyone who holds personal data. It is available (through public libraries) to anyone who wants to read it and therefore everyone has the opportunity to exercise the other two rights.

Secondly, to be told (by the data user) whether a particular data user is holding data which refers to them as an individual and what those data are, and to be supplied with a copy of the data in a form which is intelligible. The person to whom the data refers is known as the 'data subject' and this right is known as the right of 'subject access'.

Thirdly, to be compensated for damage or distress caused by the loss, inaccuracy or unauthorized disclosure of personal data, and in some circumstances to have that inaccurate data rectified or erased.

HOW DOES THE ACT RELATE TO THE PROFESSIONAL PRACTICE OF PSYCHOLOGY?

Many psychologists are employees and usually it is their employer who is the registered data user. This undoubtedly raises questions about who controls the data created by a psychologist's work. Mr Smith, whose predicament was outlined at the beginning of this section, would have to exercise his rights in relation to his psychologist's records about him via the psychologist's employer, rather than directly. It is not always clear how this reality can be kept consistent with the basic assumption of the Society's Code of Conduct; that the primary responsibility for a psychologist's records lies with the psychologist. (See also Section 2.3 on Confidentiality and Access.)

Subject Access Modification Order 1987

The Act explicitly permits the Secretary of State to modify the subject's right of access to data about their physical or mental health. The Subject Access Modification Order 1987 permits data users to withhold or modify such information where disclosure would be likely to cause serious harm to the physical or mental health of the data subject. The arrangements within the National Health Service for decision-making about whether to withhold information from a patient, or modify it on the grounds of potential for harm, are quite elaborate. For further information, see Department of Health circulars HC(87)26 and HC(89)29. (The 1987 Order is of interest for another reason: it is almost the only piece of legislation which refers specifically to 'clinical psychologists'. They are listed in the schedule which defines 'health psychologists'.)

Disclosure of information

Personal data covered by the Act can only be disclosed to the organizations and people who have been registered as the potential recipients of such disclosures. Thus the requirements of professional confidentiality are accommodated within the Act but they are not required by it. The breaking of confidentiality in exceptional circumstances (paragraph 4.3 of the Society's *Code of Conduct*), that is disclosure of information to third parties without the subject's consent, is permitted by section 28 of the Act. However, the prior consultation with an experienced and disinterested colleague which is required by the Code may only come within a strict interpretation of the Act if the consultation does not identify the data subject, or the colleague in question is covered by the same registration, or has been registered as a recipient of disclosures.

At the time of writing, the management of data pertaining to patients is the subject of a great deal of debate and some concern. Since the 1989 reforms of the NHS, many health services have been provided on the basis of contracts between a purchaser of services (a Health Authority or a fund-holding General Practitioner) and the provider of the services (usually an NHS Trust). In order to verify activity and justify payments, providers have to make available a considerable amount of data about patients to purchasers. No less a person than the Data Protection Registrar has expressed concern about some aspects of current practice. In the middle of 1994, the British Medical Association (BMA) published a draft Parliamentary Bill on behalf of twelve organizations representing health professions, including The British Psychological Society. The Bill codifies the principles which the health services should observe regarding disclosures of personal health information without the consent of the person to whom it relates; in other words, it is a Bill about the maintenance and breaking of confidentiality. Towards the end of 1994, the Department of Health sought comments on draft guidance to the NHS on confidentiality, some aspects of which were considered very contentious by the health professions.

The outcomes of all this activity may well have implications for psychologists working in health and social care. Issues arising out of multi-profession and particularly multi-agency clinical teams have also been a matter of concern. Under the circumstances it is premature to offer any advice, except to seek patients' and clients' explicit consent to proposed disclosures of information to third parties, and to test any new proposals against the Data Protection Principles. In particular, principle 2 emphasizes the importance of clarity about the purposes for which data are held and principles 3, 4 and 6 build on that fundamental point.

The Access to Health Records Act gives individuals the right of access, subject to certain exemptions, to health information about themselves which has been recorded since November 1st 1991 other than on a computer. Basically, it extends the principles and procedures of subject access to cover all health records. The procedures to be followed in the NHS are virtually identical to the procedures for subject access under the Data Protection Act.

Two other Acts preceded the Access to Health Records Act, all with similar principles: the Access to Personal Files Act, 1987, and the Access to Medical Records Act, 1988.

The general principles promoted by these Acts are:

• no right of access to records made before a certain date;

• a balance between the rights of the data subject to access information pertaining to themselves and the rights of others to privacy;

• likely harm to the data subject or others as the criterion for limiting access;

• specified situations where the interests of the community can take priority over the data subject's right to privacy;

• in other situations, an obligation to gain the client's or data subject's permission before disclosure about them.

The Access to Health Records Act has another significance. There are only very limited grounds for refusing a patient access to notes about themselves. For all practical purposes, it should be assumed that any notes that are made and any questionnaires or tests that are administered would be available to the patient if the patient asked to see them.

Professional practice must take this into account so that neither we nor Mr Smith are in a predicament any longer.

Appendix: The Data Protection Principles Concerning Personal Data Held by Data Users

1. The information to be contained in personal data shall be processed fairly and lawfully.

2. Personal data shall be held only for one or more specified purposes.

3. Personal data held for any purpose or purposes shall not be used or disclosed in any manner incompatible with that purpose or those purposes.

4. Personal data held for any purpose or purposes shall be adequate, relevant and not excessive in relation to that purpose or those purposes.

5. Personal data shall be accurate and, where necessary, kept up to date.

6. Personal data held for any purpose shall not be kept for longer than is necessary for that purpose or those purposes.

7. An individual shall be entitled:
   (a) at reasonable intervals and without undue delay and expense:
      (i) to be informed by any data user whether he holds personal data of which that individual is the subject;
      (ii) to have access to any such data held by a data user; and
   (b) where appropriate, to have such data corrected or erased.

Personal data held by data users or in respect of which services are provided by persons carrying on computer bureaux

8. Appropriate security measures shall be taken against unauthorized access to, or alteration, disclosure or destruction of personal data and against accidental loss or destruction of personal data.

BIBLIOGRAPHY

BRITISH PSYCHOLOGICAL SOCIETY (1993). *Code of Conduct, Ethical Principles and Guidelines*. Leicester: The British Psychological Society.

COWLEY, R. (1994). *Access to Medical Records and Reports*. Oxford and New York: Radcliffe Medical Press.

2.2.3   THE MENTAL HEALTH ACT

Tony Black

The Mental Health Act 1983 is the current legislation providing for the rights of 'mentally disordered' people (as defined in the Act) to receive or refuse treatment for their disorder; for the general public to be protected from possible damage or injury resulting from the behavior of mentally disordered people; and for members of the professions involved to carry out their duties in this context.

BACKGROUND TO THE ACT

The previous Act, the Mental Health Act of 1959, was the first amending legislation following the 1939–45 war, and introduced sweeping changes to pre-war thinking and procedures. The Royal Commission of 1954–57 (the Percy Commission) was the influence on this and, of course, its recommendations must be set in the context of the National Health Service Acts which had been introduced in 1946–47. The 1959 Act was reckoned to have been a major piece of liberalizing legislation, and it certainly radically changed the definitions and procedures that had gone before. For instance, certification by magistrates was abolished and compulsory admission into care became a medical matter. Previously, those who could afford it had signed their insane relatives into private care, but 'paupers' had needed a magistrate to decide whether they should be admitted to an asylum or to the workhouse. The magistrate therefore acted less in defence of the liberty of the subject and more in the public's interest, ensuring that those with the best chance of recovery received treatment.

With the 1959 Act, and following the creation of the NHS, 'mental hospitals' no longer only constituted a form of social and moral intervention by society for its own protection and the care of the insane. 'Mental patients' were to be treated like 'physical' patients and were to be able to enter or leave hospital, and accept or reject treatment, of their own free will. Thus much of the 1959 Act contained safeguards to protect the civil liberties of patients – how they were to be detained and have their detention renewed, if that was necessary, and how they could appeal against their detention to a Mental Health Review Tribunal (MHRT). At the same time, the immediate post-war period had seen sweeping advances in the development and efficacy of new medical treatments for mental disorder, where the range of radical new drugs was expected to replace leucotomy and insulin coma and electro-convulsive therapies. The war had also brought psychological concepts and measurements into the picture and, with the development of social work, occupational and other therapies, and of a more distinct professional philosophy and independence in the nursing profession, the clinical team was created.

The influence of psychology

From the standpoint of the profession of psychology, the legislative changes of the crucial 1959 Mental Health Act and its 'tidying-up' successor, the present 1983 Act, represent something of a 'two steps forward and one back' situation, or perhaps more accurately 'two steps sideways'. For all its faults, the pre-war situation was better suited to the introduction of psychological principles of both explanation and 'treatment' (behaviour change) than the 1959 and 1983 Acts have been. In the context of a philosophy of institutional containment where a stress-free life in the country and bland occupational pursuits were concerned, it should have been but a short step to the introduction of individually-programmed change, using psychological approaches. The 'attendants' of those institutions, prior to the arrival of modern psychiatry and largely managing themselves before the 1959 Act created the 'Responsible Medical Officer' (RMO), operated in the main a system of benign support, sympathy and encouragement (or their converse, as circumstances seemed to them to require) which might well have lent itself to translation into more systematic cognitive–behavioural programmes. Later on, when required to operate within the more explicitly medical framework of the 1959 and 1983 Acts, this *modus operandi* faded out and the development of patients' coping skills as a primary treatment objective, instead of just a useful adjunct, only re-emerged with the arrival of psychologists very much later. Unfortunately, clinical psychology was only just arriving as a significant profession at the time of the framing of the 1959 Act, deriving its rationale from work done during the war on both assessments in the armed services and the study and treatment of wartime neuroses and head injuries. There were then only some 300 clinical psychologists countrywide. The profession was not, therefore, in a position numerically or developmentally to influence legislation in the direction it might favour today, and which was vigorously represented by the Society at the time of the Amendment Bill of 1982 which led up to the present 1983 Act. Despite its vigour, this Society initiative did little to change or even to supplement what had by then become a well-entrenched medical model of 'mental disorder'.

Influence of the civil rights philosophy

This confinement to a medical model was partly due to Parliament's natural reluctance to widen the authority for the detainment and 'control' of people's lives; it had already allowed more of this to pass from lawyers to doctors than it was really comfortable with. At the same time Parliament was dealing with a similarly vigorous lobby from the various civil rights organizations (led by MIND) which were concerned to correct those parts of the 1959 Act considered to be too discriminating in favour of the powers of doctors to detain people, and too little orientated to the rights of people to challenge their hospitalization or the imposition of treatment against their will. However, civil rights cut both ways: on one hand there are the rights of people deprived of their freedom by being detained in hospital; and on the other hand the rights of the public and the families of mentally disordered people to be protected from the demands and possible dangers posed by some sufferers of mental disorders. Freedoms, rights and responsibilities, therefore, are largely what the 1983 revision of the 'mould-breaking' 1959 Act is all about. It revises and reformulates definitions to many of the procedures, including the detention of someone in hospital involuntarily and for the professional opinions which should be involved in this; the imposition of treatment against people's wishes or when they are not capable of deciding for themselves; and the second opinion consultation process which applies to some treatments at any time and to others when patients refuse or are incapable of making a decision for themselves.

The medication boom, the 'open door' and community care

During this period between the 1959 and 1983 Acts other crucial changes were taking place which influenced the revision of legislation. As well as the philosophy of greater personal freedom and the reaction against shutting people away in Victorian institutions, there were advances in medication. Although not the panaceas or 'cure-alls' originally hoped for, they did enable many mentally ill patients to be helped more quickly towards recovery and the incidence of chronicity to be reduced. In this the later arrival of 'depot medication' was crucial, involving periodic injections effective over a period of weeks. 'Mental hospitals' knocked down their peripheral walls, opened their doors and were redesignated 'district psychiatric hospitals'. From this it was but a short step to outmoding them altogether, creating instead psychiatric units in general hospitals and dealing with increasingly more people through out-patient facilities and day centres. More psychiatric patients were then enabled to live at home, or in hostels under supervision, rather than having to be admitted to hospital; their progress was monitored and support given periodically by visits from community psychiatric nurses.

The remaining hard-core and the 'enactment' of psychopathic disorder

Unfortunately there remained a small group of psychiatric patients whose delusions prompted them to behave with often sudden and unexpected violence. Only the closed wards of the old 'mental hospitals' provided the necessary safety for them and for the rest of the community. (This excludes patients with dementia.) The 1959 Act had also broken new ground in introducing 'psychopathic disorder' (but not in the equivalent Scottish legislation) as an additional category of mental disorder to those of 'mental illness', 'mental subnormality' and 'severe mental subnormality' (in the 1983 Act the last two were changed to 'mental impairment' and 'severe mental impairment'). By definition, 'psychopathic disorder' features 'abnormally aggressive or seriously irresponsible conduct' so that secure institutional containment was frequently required for this new category of disorder – just when locked wards were being unlocked or abolished, and staff accustomed to dealing with aggressive outbursts were becoming a scarce resource. Another group requiring long-term care were those patients who had suffered brain damage.

SPECIAL HOSPITALS AND REGIONAL SECURE UNITS

The result of these two phenomena (aggressive and violent patients and the new category of psychopathic disorder) was a considerable increase in admissions of both categories to Special Hospitals. These had originally been 'Criminal Lunatic Asylums', becoming Board of Control 'Institutions' following the creation of the NHS, and then Special Hospitals (directly administered by the then Ministry of Health) as a result of the 1959 Act. With three such hospitals for England and Wales and one for Scotland, they were able to transfer patients to and from the district psychiatric hospitals as a result of that Act. They also quickly became overcrowded as a result of both the transfer innovation and the transformation of the former mental hospitals into the more open, district, psychiatric facilities described earlier. This problem was addressed by a succession of select parliamentary and other committees, one of which, the Committee on Mentally Abnormal Offenders (the Butler Committee 1975), introduced the concept of Regional Secure Units.

Creation of the Mental Health Act Commission

The result of all these events and changes of philosophy and outlook was for the current Mental Health Act (1983) to show a general 'tightening up' of definitions and procedures, resulting in more explicit safeguards for the protection of both individual patients and public safety. In creating the Mental Health Act Commission, the 1983 Act restored a provision that had existed in earlier legislation. The 'Board of Control', which had replaced the 'Commissioners in Lunacy' in 1930, disappeared with the 1959 Act, leaving no independent body with a statutory duty to monitor the rights of detained patients and their standards of care. Following the reports of several inquiries into alleged incidents and 'scandals' at mental illness and disability hospitals, there had been a widely felt need to restore this watchdog function. Other changes towards greater public and patient safeguards are illustrated in *Appendix 1*, which lists the principal differences between the 1959 and 1983 Acts.

SIGNIFICANCE OF THE ACT FOR PSYCHOLOGISTS

As mentioned, post-war legislation has gone in the direction of defining the problems and needs of the 'mentally disordered' (a Mental Health Act-defined term) in terms of medical concepts, thus bringing them in line with the patients of other hospitals. Consequently, there has been a tendency for concepts of behaviour change, drawing upon cognitive-learning models, to be seen as ancillary issues instead of, as they often are, fundamental to the patient's problems. Thus the medical concept of rehabilitation, in which skills lost through illness are regained, would be diametrically opposed to the concepts underlying much psychological treatment where new behaviours, replacing the former unwanted ones, must be acquired and practised in progressively more realistic environments, in order to compete with and successfully replace them. This particularly affects those patients 'sectioned' under the Mental

Health Act, and especially those under Part III (concerned in criminal proceedings) who may be thought 'unsafe' to move out of a secure environment until 'cured'. However, they cannot be said to be 'cured' until a period of 'treatment' can be carried out in the 'natural' environment where the 'problem' originated – for example, a compulsive gambler, phobic or sexual offender cannot confidently be said to have completed 'treatment' until alternative behaviours successfully survive in real life gambling, phobic or opposite sex situations.

Psychologists have no statutory duties or obligations under the current legislation. Doctors have numerous statutory duties, of course, including dealing with documentation for patients' admission, treatment (and its renewal) and discharge. Social workers are statutorily involved at various stages, notably on admission and in arrangements with local authority social services for statutory aftercare of certain 'sectioned' patients. Managers have statutory documentation to complete, especially on admission or if a patient appeals to them (for example, for discharge). It should be noted that in Northern Ireland the doctor initially recommending admission is external to the psychiatric unit and is preferably the patient's GP, while in England and Wales the psychiatrist is involved in the recommendation.

However, there are situations where it would be important for a psychologist to be available and possibly negligent for them not to be, as in the admission or discharge of a 'sectioned' patient where the problem is clearly psychological or involves a psychological component (and almost certainly with a patient in the 'psychopathic disorder' category where treatability is now the issue). Similarly, when an MHRT appeal is involved, a psychologist might expect to have to provide a report or at least respond to the relevance of any psychological report already on file.

An obligation for psychologists exists under the statutory requirement for a 'Second Opinion Approved Doctor' (SOAD) to be called in when a patient refuses treatment which the 'Responsible Medical Officer' (RMO) feels must be given. The SOAD must consult with two other professionals involved in the patient's treatment, one a nurse and the other neither a doctor nor a nurse. This second professional is often a social worker, especially if they were involved in the original admission, or also commonly an occupational therapist. Psychologists are rarely involved, either through unavailability (thin on the ground and likely to be elsewhere in the district) or simply through not knowing the patient. This can cause difficulty for the SOAD who statutorily has to consult (although they may do so by phone). Likewise, another professional is statutorily required to be available but, of course, is not specified and may not be a psychologist. In the case of a patient who has undergone treatment with or been reported upon by a psychologist, or where an important psychological problem arises (for example, the SOAD may ask if there is a feasible psychological alternative to ECT, or the patient may be classified as 'psychopathically disordered'), there is a forceful argument that a psychologist should be available as the second professional and it is an interesting legal point whether he or she might be held to be negligent if not available in such circumstances.

Occasions where consent *and* a second opinion are required are rare, involving almost invariably psychosurgery or a hormonal implant. Nevertheless, in such circumstances it will often be the case that an alternative treatment may be psychological and, as hormonal implants are usually for some sexual disorder, it will be appropriate for a psychological opinion to be available. Again, this is not a statutory requirement, but failure to be involved, provided a referral or request had been made, would raise questions of lack of professionalism, if not negligence, within the requirements of a chartered profession.

CONCLUSIONS

Any legislation must reflect the needs of a society at a particular time. The current Mental Health Act of 1983 cannot be understood without a consideration of the legislation preceding it and of the social circumstances and pressures which have prevailed in the interim. Professional applications of psychology have arrived late on the scene, relative to the history of medicine and of the law itself. Nevertheless, first the strides in psychology which the 1939–45 war greatly accelerated, and now the influence of computerization, both on the understanding of systems and in the processing of information from those systems, will no doubt bring substantial further changes to the social climate which will, in turn, influence future legislation. It will be for future revisions of the mental health legislation to incorporate and reflect psychological concepts, and for the profession to ensure that it does.

Appendix I: Some important changes in the 1983 Act by comparison with the 1959 Act

(a) DEFINITIONS
- Mental 'subnormality' became 'impairment' which included a 'conduct' element.
- Psychopathic disorder's age limits were removed, but the requirement was added that only the treatable were admitted to hospital. Sexual deviancy, and drug and alcohol dependence on their own were excluded. (In Northern Ireland legislation, psychopathic disorder is excluded whether treatable or not.)

(b) ADMISSION TO HOSPITAL
- Application and consultation conditions strengthened.
- Admission 'for assessment' introduced.
- Renewals, reviews, checks and appeals strengthened.
- Nearest relative definition clarified and extended to include cohabitee.
- 'Treatability' introduced (see (a)).
- Holding powers introduced for nurses.
- Remands to hospital and interim hospital orders introduced for offenders.
- Further facilitation of transfer of prisoners.

(c) CONSENT TO TREATMENT
- Codified with regard to those treatments requiring consent AND a second opinion (mainly psychosurgery), and those requiring consent OR a second opinion (ECT; medication).
- Exclusions specified for first 3 months (not ECT) and urgent treatment (i.e. to save life; prevent violence, serious deterioration or suffering).
- Second opinion procedure specified, including consultation with other staff who are clinically involved in patient's treatment.

(d) APPEALS TO MENTAL HEALTH REVIEW TRIBUNALS (MHRTS)
- In general, opportunities for appeal increased.
- Powers introduced to delay discharge following successful appeal (to allow appropriate planning to be undertaken).
- Automatic reviews for long-stay patients who fail to appeal on their own behalf.
- Legal Aid introduced.
- 'Restricted' patients brought within MHRT powers when tribunal chaired by a judge (previously authority restricted to the Home Secretary)

(e) MENTAL HEALTH ACT COMMISSION INTRODUCED
- Watchdog body with powers to visit and report on detained patients (visiting psychiatric hospitals annually, special hospitals more frequently).
- Responsibilities: to appoint and review 'second opinion' doctors; to check on statutory documentation, complaints, appeals, seclusion and policies (for example, aftercare requirements), to draw up and keep under review a Code of Practice.

Appendix II: The main provisions of the Mental Health Act 1983.

(The parts and sections referred to will of course differ in N. Ireland legislation.)

SECTION	DESCRIPTION	COMMENT (e.g. duration or implications)
Part 1 (Application of the Act)		
1	*Definitions*	Mental Disorder, Mental Impairment, Severe Mental Impairment and Psychopathic Disorder defined, but not Mental Illness
Part II (Compulsory admission to Hospital and Guardianship)		
4	*Emergency Admission*	72 hours, convertible but not renewable (48 hours in Northern Ireland)
5	*Emergency detention of patient already in hospital*	
5(2)	*...by doctor*	72 hours, not renewable (48 hours in Northern Ireland)
5(4)	*...by nurse*	6 hours, not renewable
2	*Admission for Assessment*	28 days, convertible but not renewable (14 days in Northern Ireland)
3	*Admission for Treatment*	6 months, renewable for 6 months then at 12 monthly intervals, indefinitely
7	*Application for Guardianship*	Powers and circumstances defined, for LASS or person accepted by them
17	*Leave of absence from hospital*	During which 'detained' conditions continue to apply; often used as 'trial discharge'
20	*Duration of authority*	Procedures for renewal of sections, etc.
Part III (Patients concerned in criminal proceedings or under sentence)		
35	*Remand for Assessment ('Reports')*	28 days, renewable by court twice, up to 12 weeks in all
36	*Remand for Treatment*	28 days, renewable by court twice, up to 12 weeks in all
38	*Interim Hospital Order*	Up to 12 weeks, renewable in 28 day steps up to 6 months total
37*	*Court Order for Hospital Admission or Guardianship*	6 months, renewable for 6 months, then at 12 monthly intervals indefinitely
41	*Power of higher court to restrict discharge*	Applied with s.37 for specified or indefinite time
47*	*Transfer to hospital of sentenced prisoner*	6 months, renewable as for s.37
48	*Transfer to hospital of other (e.g. remanded) prisoners*	Not specified, but ends with trial
49	*Restriction on discharge*	Can be applied to s.47 and some s.48s as s.41 may be applied to s.37 above

Part IV (Consent to Treatment)

57	Treatment requiring consent AND a second opinion	Effectively surgical and hormonal treatments
58	Treatment requiring consent OR a second opinion	Effectively ECT at any time and medicines after 3 months
59	Plans of treatment	Applying to treatments under sections 57 or 58
60	Withdrawal of consent	When sections 57 or 58 will be required
61	Review of treatment	Reports variously required, e.g. when renewing s.3, 37 and 47 orders
62	Urgent treatment	Conditions over-ruling lack of consent, i.e. to save life; prevent deterioration; alleviate suffering; or prevent violence or danger to self or others

Part V (Mental Health Review Tribunals)

66	s.2	Entitled to appeal within 14 days
	s.3, 37, 47, 48	Entitled to appeal within first 6 months, second 6 months then annually BUT......(see s.70 following)
68	Various duties of managers	Including referral to MHRT of patient after 3 years who has not appealed on own behalf

*Note that before these sections can be applied for psychopathic disorder or mental impairment, it must be established that the condition is treatable (likely to be alleviated or deterioration prevented).

70	s.41 and 49	Restrictions rule out appeal at the end of the first 6 months

Part VI (Removal and Return of Patients within United Kingdom)

Part VII (Management of Property and Affairs of Patients)

Part VIII (Miscellaneous Functions of Local Authority and Secretary of State)

114	Appointment of Approved Social Workers	Requirements of LASS to appoint 'approved' social workers (i.e. appropriately trained and qualified)
115	Powers of Entry and Inspection	By 'approved' social workers, with an 'authenticated' document if required
117	Aftercare for patients discharged under sections 3, 37, 47, or 48	Planning and liaison between health and local authority required
118	Code of Practice	Required from Secretary of State, in effect from the Mental Health Act Commission. Unacceptability of first two drafts led to delay; Parliament accepted third draft, Nov. 1989

| 120 | *Protection of Detained Patients* | Sets out requirements for patients to be visited, interviewed, and their complaints investigated |
| 121 | *Mental Health Act Commission* | constitution and functions |

Part IX (Offences), i.e. in the operation of the Act

Part X (Miscellaneous and Supplementary)

131	*Informal admission of patients*	
132⎱ 133⎰	*Duties of managers*	
134	*Correspondence of patients and duties of MHAC in respect of mail*	When special hospital patients' mail may be withheld, and to whom they may correspond without inspection.
135	*Warrant to search for and remove patients*	Powers of police accompanied by approved social worker and doctor to enter premises.
136	*Mentally disordered persons found in public places*	Powers of police to take a person to a place of safety for examination
139	*Protection for acts done in pursuance of this Act*	Provides protection for staff, e.g. to restrain patients 'in good faith' without necessarily incurring risk of prosecution

2.2.4 THE EDUCATION ACT 1993

John Sheppard

The Education Act 1993 was one item in a spate of legislation which was introduced by the Conservative Government in the late 1980s and early 1990s, and designed to completely overhaul the education system in England and Wales. The bill was proudly proclaimed to be the longest ever education bill, and by the time it gained the Royal Assent it was considerably longer, having 308 sections. The Act generally came into force on 1 September 1994.

BACKGROUND TO THE ACT

The so-called Butler Act, the Education Act 1944, set the framework for education over the next half century. A basic principle of the Act was that children should be educated according to their age, aptitude and ability. Section 33(2) specially provided for the 'less handicapped', to be catered for in ordinary schools, and during its debate a senior Government minister declared a desire to see 'as many children as possible retained in the normal stream of school life'. Nevertheless, one outcome was the rapid growth of special education in separate schools. Educational psychologists gradually became involved as a matter of routine in the assessment of children's suitability for special education or, until implementation of the Education (Handicapped Children) Act 1970, placement outside the school system. The replacement of HP forms (handicapped pupil) by SE forms (special education) in 1975 firmly positioned the educational psychologist in the process of selection for special education. By this time there was a growing realization that special education need not mean placement in a special school, and that the nature of the child's needs and the resources required to meet those needs had to be defined more closely as part of this process. At the same time there was a backlash against the segregationist trend, with section 10 of the 1976 Act (never implemented) placing the emphasis very firmly on integration of pupils with special needs. The Education Act 1981 resulted from the Warnock Report, albeit with some of the Committee's recommendations watered down, and introduced a further evolutionary stage in the paperwork, the now familiar collection of advice leading to a statement of special educational needs. The primary rationale was now one of defining needs and resourcing, rather than one of determining placement with some justification appended; the spirit of the Act was integration into mainstream as the first option; and psychologists were an integral, and for the first time a statutory, part of the process.

It is only necessary here to consider Part 3 (sections 156 – 191) and schedules 9 and 10 of the Act which together formed the new legislative base for special education, assessment of needs, determination of resources required, and provision. The Act itself is supplemented by various sets of Regulations, Departmental circulars, and a Code of Practice, and will gradually acquire its own case law. With minor but important exceptions, Part 3 of the 1993 Act is effectively a rewrite of the 1981 Act.

Definition of special educational needs

For the purposes of the Education Act 1993, a child (up to age 19) has special educational needs if that child has a learning difficulty which necessitates special educational provision (section 156). This rather circular definition is operationally meaningless, so an assessment procedure is required (section 167) wherein the education authority consults parents and seeks 'medical, psychological and educational advice and such other advice as may be prescribed' (schedule 9(2)). This involvement in the assessment process represents only a small part of the wide contribution made by educational psychologists not only to the special needs field but also to education more generally, but remains their only *statutory* function.

Under this Act an education authority has to make a statement of special education needs if this is necessary (section 168). The test of necessity, rather than of reasonableness as under the 1981 Act, was seen by the Department for Education as a way to cut down on the number of statements issued and maintained.

Special educational provision

The Act imposes a qualified duty to secure education of children with special educational needs in ordinary schools (section 160). The qualifications, however, may prove fatal to the duty – compatibility with the child receiving suitable provision; other children receiving an efficient education; and the efficient use of resources.

The education authority must keep under review its arrangements for special educational provision (section 159), in conjunction, where applicable, with the Funding Agency for Schools.

Special educational provision can be made otherwise than in school (section 163) or outside England and Wales (section 164). The latter provision is thought to have been introduced particularly to enable access to the Peto Institute in Budapest.

Parents' rights Parents can request assessment (section 173); or re-assessment (section 172); request that assessment not take place (section 168); appeal against a decision not to make a statement (section 169); or appeal against the contents of a statement (section 170). Appeals are heard by a new body established under section 177 of this Act, the Special Educational Needs (SEN) Tribunal. Under the 1981 Act, parents could appeal in some instances to an LEA panel with only advisory powers, and in other cases to the Secretary of State who could criticize the LEA, apply some moral influence and only ultimately wield legal powers under the 1944 Act. Parental power through appeal was thus significantly increased by the 1993 Act.

A parent is enabled to state a preference for a school (schedule 10(3)) and the LEA must have good reasons to deny provision at this school. This is in line with other recent legislation relating to school placements generally.

Code of Practice

The Secretary of State must issue and occasionally revise a *Code of Practice* (section 157). This new provision appeared at first glance frightening in its bureaucracy, but soon appeared a useful way of tightening up proper procedures which had been neglected under the previous Act. In particular, the Code issued to come into force in September 1994 specifies time limits to formal assessment, and specifies stages of assessment, individual programming, monitoring and reviewing with parents which are clearly the responsibility of the school before ever formal assessment is begun. The responsibility of the LEA to ensure that this happens largely falls in practice on the educational psychologist, who is in a good position to advise the school in adjusting its procedures and to help make them work properly.

The SEN Tribunal

The SEN Tribunal must include at any sitting one lawyer and two other members, one of whom has experience of education administration and one who has knowledge of special educational needs. Since educational psychologists meet both criteria, it is not surprising that more than a quarter of Tribunal lay members are psychologists. It can be expected that at most hearings before the Tribunal the LEA will call its educational psychologist as a witness, and in many cases the parent may also choose to call a psychologist. The rules of the Tribunal emphasize informality and the interests of the child. This seems more in keeping with the spirit of the Children Act 1989 than with education legislation, which hitherto had been in the adversarial/pro-prietorial tradition of parental rights versus LEA and State rights.

The future

At the time of writing, the Education Act 1993, the various associated Regulations and Circulars, and the Code of Practice are all newly operational, or even in some respects not yet so. It remains to be seen how they work in practice, but the first signs are hopeful that they will enhance parental influence and children's rights, while clarifying and tightening school and LEA practice. Psychologists are retained as part of the statutory process, and potentially have considerable influence at all points of the special education system and, indeed, the education system more generally. The pressures created by the Act and its *Code of Practice*, however, may lessen the scope for psychologists to operate effectively throughout the system, tending instead to limit them to the narrowly defined statutory duties.

SPECIAL EDUCATIONAL NEEDS LEGISLATION IN NORTHERN IRELAND
Harry Rafferty

The pattern of SEN legislation in Northern Ireland has developed along broadly similar lines to that in England and Wales. Having said this, it is important to realize that some differences do exist. Firstly, there are some procedural and technical differences in the way legislation is formed and implemented in Northern Ireland. Though these differences are not unimportant legally, they need not concern us here.

Secondly, and more relevant to the present purpose, there is a time-lag between the enactment of legislation in Britain and the subsequent implementation of functionally similar legislation in Northern Ireland. Thus the requirements of the Education Act 1993 and the associated *Code of Practice* have already been felt in Britain, while the corresponding legislation for Northern Ireland is still some way off. This delay potentially has some advantages for Northern Ireland because it allows time for the impact of the Education Act 1993 to be assessed and subsequent lessons to be learned.

In broad terms, therefore, the present legislative situation regarding SENs in Northern Ireland is not unlike that pertaining to Britain before the implementation of the Education Act 1993.

Some of the differences which do occur arise from the

fact that Northern Ireland has its own framework of local government which is quite unlike that existing in England and Wales. A pertinent example of this is that Northern Ireland has a layer of Education and Library Boards (instead of Local Education Authorities) between central government and schools. These Boards are not just LEAs under a different name, but are quite different from them in structure, function, composition and accountability.

Other differences are due to the fact that Northern Ireland has its own legislation (The Education and Libraries (N. Ireland) Order 1986), which is quite separate from the corresponding English and Welsh legislation (both the Education Act 1981 and the Education Act 1993). For example, an Education and Library Board in Northern Ireland is only required to provide an assessment of SENs when it is *'of the opinion'* that a child has, or probably has, special educational needs requiring special educational provision to be made. Likewise a Board is only required to make a statement on a child if it is *'of the opinion'* that it should determine the special educational provision to be made for the child.

This contrasts with the situation in England and Wales, where an LEA had to make a statement under the Education Act 1981 if it were *reasonable* to make special educational provision, and has to make a statement under the Education Act 1993 if it is *necessary* to make special educational provision. Clearly the necessity test of the 1993 Education Act is less stringent than the reasonableness test of the 1981 Education Act. Though both appear at first sight less strict than the *opinion* test set down in the 1986 Northern Ireland Order, it may be that an Appeals Tribunal would decide whether or not an opinion formed by an Education and Library Board was indeed *reasonably* based. In this case, there would in effect be no practical difference between the *reasonableness* test and the *opinion* test.

In conclusion, therefore, SEN legislation in Northern Ireland is broadly similar to that which existed in England and Wales immediately before the 1993 Education Act. Some of the differences which do exist may be more apparent than real, though this has been a matter of some legal debate. The definitive and precise meaning of Northern Ireland legislation is entirely a matter for the courts to decide.

An equivalent of the 1993 Education Act is expected in Northern Ireland within the next two years.

REFERENCES

DEPARTMENT OF EDUCATION AND SCIENCE CIRCULAR 2/75 / Welsh Office circular 21/75. *The Discovery of*

Children Requiring Special Education and the Assessment of their Needs. London: HMSO.

DEPARTMENT OF EDUCATION AND SCIENCE (1978). *Special Educational Needs: Report of the Committee of Enquiry into the Education of Handicapped Children and Young People (The Warnock Report)*. London: HMSO.

DEPARTMENT FOR EDUCATION (1994). *Code of Practice on the Identification and Assessment of Special Educational Needs 1994*. London: HMSO.

Education Act 1944. London: HMSO.

Education (Handicapped Children) Act 1970. London: HMSO.

Education Act 1981. London: HMSO.

Education Act 1993. London: HMSO.

2.2.5 SCOTTISH EDUCATIONAL LEGISLATION

Tommy Mackay

Educational legislation in Scotland shares a common foundation with similar legislation in the rest of the UK. It is based on the same philosophy of making adequate and efficient provision of school education (including special education) and further education, taking account of age, ability and aptitude. The provisions made for children and young persons with special educational needs are extensive, and include a commitment to educating such pupils along with their peers in mainstream schools wherever possible. The legislative context is mediated through Acts of Parliament, regulations, government circulars and official reports.

Beyond this common foundation, however, the position in Scotland is different from the rest of the UK in many important respects. It is governed by separate Scottish education acts which do not always correspond in timing or in purpose with acts applying to England and Wales. For example, there is no equivalent (either existing or intended) to the Education Act 1993, with its *Code of Practice* and Special Educational Needs (SEN) Tribunals. Even where there are similar provisions, the terminology used is often different, and this reflects a different legal system and structure of courts. The statutory duties of educational psychologists are very different indeed.

This section will outline first, the general background to Scottish educational legislation; second, the relevant provisions of the Education (Scotland) Act 1980; third, the statutory functions of the educational psychology services; and fourth, the legislation governing access to educational psychologists' records

GENERAL BACKGROUND

Free, compulsory education for children of school age in Scotland was introduced by the Education (Scotland) Act 1872. This act required that 'efficient and available provision' should be accessible to every child, and children with special educational needs were not excluded from its scope. It was clear, however, that additional resources for children with special needs were required in order to fulfil the provisions of the act, and, as a consequence, a further series of acts in the late nineteenth and early twentieth centuries established wide ranging provision for this purpose. For the most part this took the form of a segregated special school system.

The Education (Scotland) Act 1946 greatly extended the legislative arrangements for children with special needs. It placed a duty on education authorities to ascertain which children who had reached the age of five required special education, and to meet requests from parents to examine children from the age of two for this purpose, unless the request was deemed unreasonable. Although the statutory examination of such children was still a medical concern, the same act made it lawful for education authorities to provide a child guidance service, the functions of which would include involvement in the special education process.

The 1946 Act also required the Secretary of State for Scotland to make regulations 'defining the several categories of pupils requiring special educational treatment'. The preparations for this exercise were remitted to the Advisory Council on Education in Scotland, which produced seven comprehensive and forward-looking reports between 1950 and 1952. On the basis of these, the Secretary defined nine categories of handicap in the Special Educational Treatment (Scotland) Regulations 1954. These categories were similar but not identical to the categories used in England and Wales, and they formed the legislative basis of Scottish special education for the next 30 years. These were pupils who were deaf, partially deaf, blind, partially sighted, mentally handicapped, epileptic, suffering from speech defects, maladjusted or physically handicapped. At the same time the Secretary issued a strong commitment to integration of children with special needs into mainstream schools, although in practice most pupils with more pronounced needs continued to be segregated.

Between 1960 and 1967 the Scottish Education Department appointed a number of working parties to review various areas of special educational needs. The subsequent reports formed the background to a revision of special educational legislation in the Education (Scotland) Act 1969. The minimum age at which a child could be ascertained as requiring special education was abolished, and recognition was given to the fact that provision for special needs is a continuing process. A structure for reviews and appeals was therefore established.

The 1969 Act had major implications for educational psychologists. First, the decision to ascertain a child was no longer to be only a medical one. In every case there also had to be a psychological examination. In addition, the power given to education authorities in 1946 to provide a child guidance service became a statutory duty. Mainly as a result of this legislation, the number of educational psychologists in Scotland doubled within ten years.

At the beginning of the 1970s there was still a group of children who were deemed to be unsuitable for education or training either by ordinary or by special methods of education, and who were therefore placed outside the school system. It was not until the passing of the Mentally Handicapped Children (Scotland) Act 1974 that these children became the responsibility of the education department.

The move from a *deficit model* to a *needs model* of special education in Scotland in the 1970s followed a very similar pattern to changing approaches in the rest of the UK. The scope of the Warnock Committee extended to Scotland as well as England and Wales and prepared the way for the special educational needs legislation of the early 1980s.

THE EDUCATION (SCOTLAND) ACT 1980

The 'principal act' governing Scottish education both for ordinary children and for those with special educational needs is the Education (Scotland) Act 1980. This was an act of consolidation which drew together the various changes which had affected legislation since the previous act of consolidation in 1962. The principal act must be interpreted as including all of the amendments which have been enacted between 1980 and the present time. The main amendments affecting special education and psychologists are laid down in two subsequent acts. These are the Education (Scotland) Act 1981 and the Disabled Persons (Services, Consultation and Representation) Act 1986.

The Education (Scotland) Act 1981

Two main areas were tackled by the 1981 Act. First, parents were given greater choice in selecting the school they wished their children to attend. This was in fulfilment of a major strand in government policy, and covered both ordinary and special education. Second, statutory categories of handicap were abolished, and terms relating to handicap and disability were replaced with the expression 'special educational needs'. At the same time extensive legislative machinery was put in place for assessment, documentation, review and appeals. In parallel with developments in England and Wales, special education now occupied a very prominent position in the statutes. This is reflected in the space devoted to it in the various education acts – three pages in 1946, 15 in 1969, 20 in 1981.

The main change made in 1981 was a conceptual one. The old concept of 'special education' affected a very small percentage of pupils with marked disabilities, most of whom would be likely to attend special schools. The new concept of 'special educational needs' represented the Warnock view of the 15 per cent or so of children whose learning difficulties indicated the need for special consideration within the ordinary schools. Nevertheless, virtually all of the Act was still devoted to the small group of 'children and young persons with certain special educational needs'. These were described as pupils who 'have pronounced, specific or complex special educational needs which are such as require continuing review'. For each such child or young person the education authority must open a 'Record of Needs', the Scottish equivalent of the Statement in England and Wales.

Regulations governing Records of Needs

The regulations governing Records are closely similar to those which relate to Statements. Medical and psychological assessments are carried out, and are supplemented by educational and other available reports. The views of the parent are requested in writing both at the time of the assessment and at the stage when a draft Record has been prepared. Parents may appeal against a decision to Record or not to Record, against the terms of the Record and against the school nominated. For this purpose there is an appeal structure involving a local appeals committee or the Secretary of State as appropriate. There is also a requirement placed on the authority to review the Record at appropriate intervals. Throughout the process the parent may be represented by a 'named person' who is specified in the Record.

In keeping with the spirit of the Warnock Report and the legislation and circulars following from it, the proportion of children attending segregated special schools in Scotland has shown a steady decline. It is important to note, however, that this process of increased integration in mainstream schools is not a result either of Warnock or of the legislation. Rather, the act and the various reports were the outcome of a process which had already been established. The move towards increased mainstreaming had been taking place throughout the 1970s (MacKay, 1994a).

Educational legislation in Scotland has probably shown greater divergence from England and Wales since the 1980s than at any other period. In the area of special educational needs there is no parallel to most of the provisions of the Education Act 1993 and none is envisaged. A draft circular on *Children and Young Persons with Special Educational Needs* was issued by the Scottish Office Education Department for consultation in 1994. This is being revised for publication later in 1995, and is supported by a manual of good practice. While the Circular occupies a similar official position to the *Code of Practice* in England and Wales, it does not relate to it closely in terms of content. Perhaps a significant factor underlying the difference and the lack of pressure for Special Educational Needs Tribunals is the very low number of appeals made in Scottish education authorities. Several authorities will have had no appeals at all during the years since the 1981 Act came into force.

The Record of Needs procedures represent only a small part of the statutory duties of the educational psychologist, but they tend to demand an increasing proportion of the psychologist's time. It is generally the psychological service which is responsible for co-ordinating the whole process from the initiation of the statutory assessments to the preparation of the draft Record. While this gives the psychologist a central and influential role it has wider implications for the general work in which services are engaged.

STATUTORY FUNCTIONS OF EDUCATIONAL PSYCHOLOGY SERVICES

The statutory development of psychological services in Scotland has been fundamentally different from other parts of the UK (MacKay, 1995). Probably the single most important legislative statement that can be made about educational psychology in Scotland is that it is *not* a school psychological service. Nor are its statutory duties tied exclusively – or even principally – to the arrangements for children with Records of Needs. The separate development of a child guidance service and a school psychological service in England and Wales was not a pattern adopted in Scotland. The Scottish legislation made provision instead for a statutory child guidance service with a wide range of functions. The child guidance clinics were funded by the education authority and directed by psychologists, with appropriate access to social work and medical services. It was also from the child guidance clinic that the service to school and to special education was provided.

It is this pattern which has continued to provide the basis for the work of the psychologist in Scotland, where services are available to the population of children and young persons aged 0–19 years. The functions are specified in section 4 of the Education (Scotland) Act 1980 as amended by the Education (Scotland) Act 1981 and the Disabled Persons (Services, Consultation and Representation) Act 1986. The precise form of words is as follows.

It shall be the duty of every education authority to provide for their area a regional or island authority psychological service in clinics or elsewhere, and the functions of that service shall include –

    (a) the study of children with special educational needs;

    (b) the giving of advice to parents and teachers as to appropriate methods of education for such children;

    (c) in suitable cases, provision for the special educational needs of such children in clinics;

    (d) the giving of advice to a local authority within the meaning of the Social Work (Scotland) Act 1968 regarding the assessment of the needs of any child for the purposes of any of the provisions of that or any other enactment.

The 1981 Act introduced the term 'special educational needs' to replace previous terminology used to describe the children in question. The 1986 Act replaced the term 'child guidance service' with the term 'regional or island authority psychological service'. Otherwise the statement remained essentially the same as in 1969 when the service became mandatory.

Scottish Children's Hearings

The duties outlined in paragraph (d) relate to the Scottish Children's Hearings. Since 1969 children who have committed offences or who require compulsory measures of care have been referred to the Reporter to the Children's Panel as an alternative to the court system. A panel of people from the local community consider each case and recommend an appropriate response. If the grounds of referral are not accepted by the child the option of trial in the sheriff court is still available. The educational psychologist has a statutory function to give advice on any cases referred by the Reporter, and acts as part of a team with other professionals.

Interpretation of 'special educational needs'

It is important to note that the term 'children with special educational needs' is to be interpreted as having the meaning assigned to it in the Scottish statutes, as supported by official circulars, statutory instruments and government reports. It is not to be understood as relating narrowly to pupils requiring a Record of Needs or to school education.

It was a modernizing of the old term 'handicapped, backward and difficult children' and continues to describe the same group as in earlier legislation. This is the group of children who show the full range of problems of learning, behaviour or development. All of this group have access to psychological services, whether referred through the schools or by their parents or other professionals. The educational psychologist in Scotland therefore covers by statute an extensive range both of educational and of clinical functions, and provides a service both to the school and to the community.

ACCESS TO EDUCATIONAL PSYCHOLOGISTS' RECORDS

The Access to Personal Files Act 1987 was part of the fulfilment of the government's commitment to providing access for individuals to information held about them by various authorities. It extended only to local authorities and to social services, but not to education. Nevertheless, it was a significant step in a wider programme, and it was soon followed by a number of regulations providing access to information held by other departments.

In Scotland, access to education records was provided by the Secretary of State on the basis of powers conferred under section 2 of the Education (Scotland) Act 1980. After a process of consultation The School Pupil Records (Scotland) Regulations 1990 were issued. This is the statutory instrument which governs access to manual records held by regional authority educational psychologists, and it is supported by Scottish Office Education Department Circular No. 7, 1991.

Regulations governing access to files

Files held by psychologists contain a great deal of highly sensitive information, and in this respect they are quite different from records held by most other education department personnel. It is therefore of crucial importance that psychologists understand the precise nature and extent of the regulations (MacKay, 1994b). The information to which the regulations give access is 'personal information in any record held by the authority for the purpose of the discharge of their functions under section 1 of the Education (Scotland) Act 1980 in relation to school education'. While some of these functions in relation to school education are supported by the psychological service, it has been noted that the duties of the service are considerably wider than this and are separately detailed in section 4 of the act.

This leads to a very important distinction for psychologists. The only records held by them to which access must be provided are records of an *educational* nature. All other personal information held in their files continues to be protected. This distinction is made clear in Circular No. 7. This means that when a formal request for access is made there requires to be a 'prepared file' which contains only such information as relates to school education.

Although as a matter of good practice psychologists adopt an open approach with children and their parents, and provide informal access to information whenever it is appropriate to do so, the protection given to their files is of considerable importance. This is because the person to whom access may be granted is the parent and not the child. While in the majority of cases the interests and well-being of the child are represented by the parent, there is a significant minority of cases in which this is not so, and indeed where the parent may be acting against the child's interests. By providing for access only to educational information and not to the wider range of more sensitive personal information held by psychologists, the law affords considerable protection to the child.

Persons who may have access to educational records
The arrangements for access to the educational records are set out in detail in the regulations. The person who may have access is the parent of a pupil under 18, but also the pupil if aged 16 or over. Under that age the pupil may also have access with the consent of the parent. The definition of the term 'parent' is very broad for the purpose of the regulations. It includes not only the actual parent or legal guardian but also any person with custody of the child or liable to maintain the child. It also includes a parent without custody and even a parent with no legal access to the child. Even within the limited range of information to which the psychologist must give access there are several important exemptions. There is no access to records made prior to October 1990 or to information which might identify a third party. Records held solely for the employee's 'own use' are not accessible. This would cover information held only for research purposes, but is not intended to exclude case notes, whether recorded in the child's file or kept in any other place. Information likely to cause serious physical or mental harm to the child or any other person is also exempt, but the interpretation of this exemption is strict and 'serious harm' does not equate with personal distress. There are also special provisions relating to access to reports which have been received from the Reporter to the Children's Panel or from a health professional.

Access to information must be provided within a given timescale, and information already recorded may not be modified during that period. There is a mechanism for erasure or amendment of inaccurate information and for appeal.

Summary

Education in Scotland is governed by a separate system of legislation, mediated through Acts of Parliament, statutory instruments, official circulars and government reports. While sharing a common foundation with the rest of the UK, the position in Scotland differs in several important respects. As well as different terminology and a separate legal system there are different arrangements for children with special educational needs, wider statutory functions for the educational psychologist and distinctive regulations governing access to psychologists' records.

REFERENCES

DEPARTMENT OF EDUCATION AND SCIENCE (1978). *Special Educational Needs: Report of the Committee of Enquiry into the Education of Handicapped Children and Young People (The Warnock Report)*.

MacKAY, T. (1994a). The trend of Scottish special educational statistics. *Scottish Educational Review, 26, (1),* 27–33.

MacKAY, T. (1994b) The confidentiality of psychologists' files. *Educational Psychology in Scotland, 1,* 10–15.

MacKAY, T. (1995). The statutory foundations of Scottish educational psychology services. *Educational Psychology in Scotland, (in press)*.

Scottish Office Education Department Circular No. 7, 1991.

Scottish Office Education Department Draft Circular, *Children and Young Persons with Special Educational Needs, 1994*.

The Education (Scotland) Act 1946.

The Special Educational Treatment (Scotland) Regulations 1954.

The Education (Scotland) Act 1969.

The Education (Mentally Handicapped Children) (Scotland) Act 1974.

The Education (Scotland) Act 1980.

The Education (Scotland) Act 1981.

The Disabled Persons (Services, Consultation and Representation) Act 1986.

The Access to Personal Information Act 1987.

The School Pupil Records (Scotland) Regulations 1990.

2.3 CONFIDENTIALITY AND ACCESS

Tommy MacKay

The work of psychologists who provide services to the public is based on a confidential relationship between professional and client. This chapter covers the following aspects: the importance of this area to professional practice; confidentiality and the law; professional codes of conduct; legal access to psychologists' records; children and young persons; and pointers to good practice. Further information on specific aspects of the legal background will be found in Section 2.2.2 on the Data Protection Act, which also covers the question of access to health records, and in Section 2.2.5 on Scottish educational legislation

IMPORTANCE FOR PROFESSIONAL PRACTICE

The issue of confidentiality is of crucial importance and involves two fundamental principles. First, clients expect that the information they give to a professional psychologist will be treated in confidence and that all reasonable steps will be taken not to divulge it to a third party. Second, clients expect that information held about them by psychologists will be generally accessible to them. Underlying these principles is a more general foundation governing psychological practice. While it is accepted that psychologists may have several different clients with competing interests, it is upheld that the interests and well-being of the individual child, young person or adult with whom they are concerned is of the highest importance at all times. This foundation informs all practice relating to confidentiality and access as well as all other fields of activity.

Both professional and administrative issues arise in this field. Confidentiality is a professional issue which concerns the relationship between psychologists and their clients. Access is to a large extent an administrative matter concerning the arrangements whereby clients may inspect files and other records which are held on them. It is the interface between these two areas, and the legal context governing them, which is of central significance for psychologists. Often the answers to dilemmas which may arise are not absolute but involve judgement and discretion, and lead to potential conflict between professional integrity, contractual duties of employment and legal obligations.

This may be illustrated by considering the following questions.

Can the psychologist's claim to a confidential relationship be legally upheld?;
What is the position of a psychologist who is privy to information regarding a crime?;
What happens if there is a conflict between a professional code of conduct and a request for access to files?;
How do psychologists who work with children and young persons safeguard the rights of their clients to privacy in the face of parental demands for access to information?;
Do officials of employing authorities have access to records held by psychologists?;
How is confidentiality to be handled within organizations and departments, since access may have to be available to clerical staff and colleagues?

Recent changes in practice and in the law

While these issues have always been of importance to professional psychologists, the whole issue of confidentiality and access has for several reasons become much more central in recent years. First, for psychologists working for local authorities there have been changes in practice. An example of this is seen in the official procedures to be followed in the area of child protection. These procedures at local authority level have the force of law and may place an obligation on psychologists to disclose information to which they are privy. Second, there have been changes in the law. The most important have been the Access to Personal Files Act 1987 and the Access to Health Records Act 1990. These and other enactments led to statutory regulations specifying how people could have access to records held about them in some of the main public departments in which psychologists are employed – health, education and social services.

Third, in 1989 the United Nations General Assembly passed the Convention on the Rights of the Child, and in 1991 it was ratified by the UK Government. While this did not give the Convention the force of law in this country, it did imply a commitment on the part of the government to amend existing legislation to accommodate its provisions. Several articles in the Convention are relevant to confidentiality and access for psychologists who work with children. Article 3 states that in all actions concerning children, whether undertaken by public or private social welfare institutions, courts of law, administrative authorities or legislative bodies, the best interests of the child shall be a primary consideration. Article 12 asserts that children shall have the right to express their views freely in all matters affecting them and that these views shall be given due weight in accordance with age and maturity. Article 13 gives freedom to seek, receive and impart information and ideas of all kinds. Article 16 gives protection against arbitrary or unlawful interference with privacy. Article 18 recognizes that parents have the primary responsibility for the upbringing and development of the child and that the best interests of the child must be their basic concern. Article 28 requires the state to make educational and vocational information and guidance available and accessible to all children.

Fourth, there is the question of increased public accountability. Psychologists and others who offer services to the public, whether through government bodies or in private practice, have become more accountable for their actions than ever before. Related to this is the fact that society has become more litigious, and professionals are therefore increasingly likely to have requests for access to their records within the context of litigation.

CONFIDENTIALITY AND THE LAW

There is no such thing as an absolute obligation of confidentiality, neither for a psychologist nor for any other person. It may be generally stated however that the law will support confidentiality and will act against breaches of it. The law will also take account of the context in which a claim of confidentiality occurs. Thus, it is understood that there is an undertaking of confidentiality implicit in the relationship between doctor and patient or solicitor and client. Similar obligations relating to confidentiality would be likely to be recognized in the relationship between psychologists and their clients.

Implications for psychologists

This has two important implications for psychologists. First, they would be regarded to have a general duty not to disclose confidential information relating to their clients. Second, while no citizen is exempt from a duty to disclose information required by a court of law, the obligations of confidentiality between psychologists and their clients are likely to be given reasonable consideration.

The duty to disclose information provided to a psychologist in confidence may be clarified by two questions: 'Is there any information which a psychologist is obliged to disclose simply by virtue of being the recipient of it?', and, 'What information may a psychologist be required to disclose in court?'. Apart from one or two prescribed situations, such as terrorist offences and road traffic offences, there is no general duty for members of the public to report any information involving criminal conduct. It is a different matter if a psychologist is cited to appear in court as a witness or to give a precognition on oath. In such cases questions must be answered truthfully on the basis of all information held, but as previously indicated, claims of professional confidentiality will not be disregarded if this can be avoided, and in practice conflicts between professional and legal obligations do not arise frequently.

PROFESSIONAL CODES OF CONDUCT

It is generally accepted in society that professional persons work within an implicit or explicit ethical code which governs their practice and which is based on pursuing and upholding the best interests of their clients at all times. This includes an understanding that relationships between professionals and their clients operate within a confidential framework. The Society's *Code of Conduct, Ethical Principles and Guidelines* (see Section 3.4) sets out minimum standards for conduct with which psychologists are expected to comply. The guiding principle in relation to confidentiality is that 'psychologists must take all reasonable steps to preserve the confidentiality of information acquired through their professional practice and to protect the privacy of individuals or organizations about whom information is collected or held'.

These requirements are developed in detail in section 4 of the *Code*. Psychologists are not at liberty to divulge information without consent, must make it clear to clients if information is likely to be shared within a team and must recognize that the interests or safety of the client or others may override confidentiality. In addition, their records must be adequate, securely safeguarded, kept no longer than necessary and have information entered discreetly where control over access is limited. The revision of the *Code* in 1993 accommodated the term 'agreed working practices' as a basis on which confidentiality may require to be broken. This is designed to cover contractual obligations set out in local authority guidelines.

The *Code* represents an important interpretative framework against which the conduct of professional psychologists may be judged whether they are members of The British Psychological Society or not, since they make explicit the implicit standards which society may reasonably expect of those engaged in the professional practice of psychology. The *Code* is also important in providing added protection to psychologists as well as to the public, and in strengthening the position of psychology within the context of local authority practice.

LEGAL ACCESS TO PSYCHOLOGISTS' FILES

During the 1980s the government made a commitment to providing individuals with access to information held about them by local authorities and other bodies. This led to a range of legislation and regulations including the Access to Personal Files Act 1987 and the Access to Health Records Act 1990. The arrangements vary for England and Wales, Scotland and Northern Ireland, and for health, education, social services and other agencies. Non-manual records continue to be governed by the provisions of the Data Protection Act 1984.

Regulations governing access

The regulations stipulate detailed provisions for access by clients to their records. They identify who may be afforded access, which records are accessible, the timescale within which access must be provided, whether the applicant may have copies and the arrangements for appeal and for correction or erasure of inaccurate information. They also cover important exemptions. In general these include records prepared before a certain date, information which would identify a third party and information which would be likely to result in serious harm to the client or another party. The application of exemptions is intended to be strict, and does not serve as a catch-all for information a professional might have anxieties about disclosing. It is essential that psychologists should be familiar with the regulations which apply to their own situation. This may have important implications for many aspects of record-keeping and discussions with clients. For example, while the *Code of Conduct* requires that psychologists' records must be adequate, it also requires that a discreet approach must be taken to the type of information which is entered if control over access is limited. It may also be necessary before files are prepared to advise clients on the arrangements for access to their records.

The psychologist must also know the procedures which will be followed if a formal request for access to information is made. This may vary from one department to another and many important issues could arise. For example, will the psychologist be consulted regarding the specific information which is to be made available? If not, who will take responsibility for this, and how will the records be prepared? How will a decision be reached on any exemptions? Will access be provided in the presence of the psychologist so that questions can be answered, or will the information simply be made available by administrative staff? Some departments will already have a clearly defined policy for access to records, and this may include arrangements which go beyond the demands of any legal regulations. Others will have no fixed procedures and will respond on an individual basis when requests are made. It is therefore most important that psychologists should have knowledge both of the legal requirements which apply to them and of the procedures adopted within their own department or organization. Formal access requests tend to be few, but when they occur they may have many implications and may also arise within a context of litigation.

Children and young persons

Familiarity with the appropriate regulations is particularly crucial for psychologists who deal with children and young persons. Legislation extending the rights of individuals to have access to information held about them has in general been welcomed by psychologists, and good professional practice has encouraged a very open approach when dealing with children and their parents. However, these legal developments have generally taken place within a context of parental rights but have not given separate consideration to an approach based on the rights of the child. In most cases the rights and interests of parents correspond with those of their children, and therefore any strengthening of the rights of parents would be expected likewise to support the interests and well-being of children and young persons. Nevertheless it is recognized that the rights of children and parents are not indivisible and indeed at times may be in direct conflict. This is particularly the case in the population referred to psychological services, where problems of family conflict, child abuse or other difficulties relating to child–parent relationships may be prominent.

This again highlights the need for psychologists who work with children and young people to study carefully the specific regulations governing access to their files, and to recognize that what applies to one part of the United Kingdom or to one public body may not apply to another. The young person's enquiry, 'Can I speak to you in confidence?', can best be answered when the psychologist is familiar not only with the demands of professional integrity but also with the regulations which control access to records. Again, there are many implications for file-keeping practices and for the initial discussions the psychologist may wish to have with the young person or parents when a referral is taken on.

An approach to confidentiality and access based as far as possible on children's rights is compatible with all current developments. In keeping with the principles outlined in the UN Convention, the trend of recent legislation in such areas as child care and legal capacity to consent to treatment has been to strengthen the recognition of children's rights. This is relevant to the rights of the child in making a self-referral to a psychologist. There is nothing in law to limit a child's right to take this course of action without parental consent, account being taken of age and maturity. A primary consideration in such cases is the best interests of the child. The particular access regulations applicable to the psychologist may determine the extent to which the child may expect that the fact and the details of the referral can remain confidential in the event of a parental request for access.

GOOD PRACTICE

The promotion of the best interests of clients in the areas of confidentiality and access will be fostered not through formal legal arrangements but by a commitment to good practice. Difficulties will seldom arise in a context which is marked by clear written policies, communication of these to clients and a general confidence on the part of clients that information held about them will not be divulged to other parties but will be accessible to themselves. For this reason it is helpful to aim for complete openness, and to provide access to information informally as far as possible. It is often useful to discuss confidentiality and access with clients from the start, to let them know the arrangements for seeing records held on them and of any circumstances in which information could be available to any other party. This should include the practice followed when reports are to be sent to other professionals, as well as any arrangements for sharing information with colleagues who work in the same service or department. From this point of view it is helpful to consider confidentiality as residing in organizations rather than in individual professionals so that the legitimate requirements of professional support, administration and management can be met, but with any necessary safeguards. At times it may be necessary for access to records to be provided to departmental administrators, but for this there should be an agreed set of procedures.

Record-keeping often represents a fine balance between entering information discreetly and yet ensuring that it is sufficiently relevant and detailed to meet the needs of the case. Careful consideration should always be given to any statement which is of dubious validity or which a client might find undermining. At the same time a psychologist's file will inevitably on occasions contain information and interpretation which a client may not like. There are circumstances in which unpalatable information must be recorded, and there is also a place for a psychologist to enter something as being a professional opinion.

Good practice on confidentiality and access within a psychological service or department will be marked by agreed policy statements, defined procedures, adequate staff training, clear communications, efficient support structures and regular review.

2.4   PRIVATE PRACTICE

Paul T. Brown and Anne E. Abel Smith

There is, to the best of our knowledge, no systematic research in the UK as to why a psychologist might go into private practice. In conversation the reasons usually advanced include a wish to be free of the imposition of organizational constraints; the hope of financial returns that are greater than in employment; a wish to deliver services at a standard higher than is possible within the public sector; and having the freedom to work with a variety of colleagues on a co-equal and expert basis. In any event, engaging in private practice is for applied psychologists still a consciously chosen process rather than one of slipping unquestioningly into the long-accepted habits of a profession, as could easily be the case within law and accountancy.

DEFINITION OF PRIVATE PRACTICE

What defines private practice is that the individual psychologist is in a direct, fee-for-service relationship with a client (individual or organizational) or patient as an alternative to being employed on a full- or part-time salaried basis; and is in consequence taxed as a self-employed person on full or part earnings.

An individual may earn all of his or her income through fee receiving; or may be in full employment and additionally engage in some private work; or may have structured a professional life around part-time salaried employment combined with independent earnings. In the absence of firm data, it is our impression that many psychologists in full-time salaried employment (especially within the NHS, university teaching departments, and in educational psychology) engage in varying amounts of private, fee-receiving work; that a much smaller number engage in a mix of part-time employment and private practice; and that there are very few full-time private practitioners.

The Association of Chartered Clinical Psychologists in Private Practice The Association of Chartered Clinical Psychologists in Private Practice (ACCPPP), which has been in existence for some ten years, is the only grouping of psychologists especially devoted to the aims of private practitioners. It has a core of around 80 members, with up to 40 others who drift in and out of membership. Half the core group combine a little private practice with full-time NHS employment, while the remainder have varying commitments to a larger proportion of private practice.

SALARIED EMPLOYMENT AND PRIVATE PRACTICE

It is an essential requirement of conducting private practice whilst being in full-time salaried employment within the public sector that proper contractual relationships are established with the employer regarding this mode of practice, and especially so if publicly-funded facilities such as consulting rooms, test materials and equipment are used in the pursuit of private fee-earning.

We cannot think of any other chartered profession where the boundaries between salaried employment and simultaneous independent fee earning are as fluid as they are among psychologists. This is perhaps a consequence of the relatively unsophisticated or uninformed approach that most psychologists appear to have about independent fee earning. The embryonic development of private practice in the UK appears to be not unlike that noted by Reid and Lord (1990) in Australia. A survey of 300 members of the Australian Psychological Society showed that there was no strong private practice sector and that a very high proportion of the small number of private practitioners were part-timers.

The situation is complicated by the fact that a growing number of psychologists, especially in the occupational field, may appear to be in private practice but are in fact organized through a formal private (limited company) structure. We have excluded these from our definition of private practice by virtue of the fact that they are employed, even though the company through which they are employed may be in a fee-receiving relationship, with its clients. Where individuals are in a formal partnership, however, and are rated for taxation purposes on the basis of Schedule D earnings, then they are included in our consideration. It is our impression that formal partnerships are very rare among professional psychologists, and we know of no formal partnership having more than three principals. The commonest form of private practice – whether it is full- or part-time – is of a single practitioner who might employ one or more assistants with psychological qualifications or other support staff (technical/secretarial).

THE DEVELOPMENT OF PRIVATE PRACTICE IN THE UK

Our impression is that private practice in psychology is at a very immature stage of development at present, with a small number of entrepreneurial individuals well-established in private practice in metropolitan London but without there being any mechanisms for their experience to feed back into general professional awareness. For some comparison with the USA, where the traditions of private practice are very much more established, see Kralj (1992). She discusses the experiences of several full-time consulting psychologists in the States who have been able to maintain successful practices in spite of the recession, and she offers a seven-point checklist based on their comments; no comparable guidance is available in this country.

Outside London there is an almost complete dearth of full-time private practice. This position perhaps derives in part from the fact that most applied psychologists train within large, publicly-funded bodies (the NHS, the Prison Service, and Education) where there have been well-defined career structures and, until recent time, an antipathy towards private practice; and, in part, from the traditions of psychology as an academic rather than applied subject. However, with the spirit of free enterprise and contracting out of services appearing in all the applied areas, it may be that we are on the brink of substantial change in the way that psychologists pursue their professional lives – a situation predicated by Brown and Loftus (1988). Ford (1992) has tracked the growth in occupational psychology consultancies in the UK, and describes a very substantial growth over the past ten years, though starting from a very small base.

SETTING UP

The formal processes of setting up in private practice are not dissimilar to those in any other profession or, indeed, the start-up of any small business. These can be addressed through any of the excellent publications which are now available free of charge from the high street banks (for example, the National Westminster Bank, 1992; Barclays Bank, 1992).

Zager (1990) explored the factors involved in beginning an independent psychology practice in a metropolitan area in the US. In the UK, professional training for psychologists (other than occupational) does not generally include a training in the rudiments of managing a private practice (though training in business might include a great deal of psychology). Most psychologists in the UK who engage in private practice appear to stumble into the issues involved rather than approach them in a systematic or disciplined manner. Indeed we doubt whether any UK psychologists in fields other than occupational psychology begin their training with the primary intention of becoming a private practitioner. These last remarks do not apply, however, to those psychologists who intend to take a later specialist training in psychoanalysis or psychotherapy, where private practice has a long and well-established tradition. We have, however, excluded the practice of psychotherapy and psychoanalysis from our consideration here, as anyone with formal training of this kind and consequent membership of the relevant training body will have access to referral networks and a body of experience about setting up in private practice which are particular to their specialty.

The development of counselling psychology as an independent professional discipline within the Society will, we expect, lead to there being an increasing number of psychologists who are in some form of private practice as the demand for private counselling services grows.

We have observed that many psychologists who engage in private practice start doing so on an *ad hoc* basis, responding opportunistically to circumstances that present themselves. This is especially true in the clinical and counselling fields, where a medical colleague seeking private referral resources might intentionally or accidentally encourage a clinical or counselling psychologist into a fee relationship with a private patient or client. The growth of compensation litigation is also creating opportunities for clinical and counselling psychologists to take private instructions. In a recent (1993) civil litigation case in the High Court, six chartered psychologists were involved in the hearing. All of them (three on each side) had distinct contributions to make for either the plaintiff or the defence. Of these six, four were in full-time private practice and two were in full-time employment but able to act as expert witnesses on a fee-receiving basis (see Section 2.1 on testifying as an expert witness). Whether the fee-receiving was by formal contractual arrangement with the Health Service's employing authority in each case or by common consent as established professional custom is not known. Paralleling a growth in the use of psychologists in compensation litigation, there is also a growing demand for child and educational psychologists to act as expert witnesses on residence issues under the Children Act 1989 (Spencer and Flin, 1990; Bridge and Bridge, 1990). Thorburn (1990) has challenged the dichotomy between the local education sector and private practice as being simplistic when considering the future of educational psychology services.

BUSINESS ISSUES

As in any business start up, there are seven key issues in establishing a private practice:

1. What is the product?
2. How will business be found and acquired?
3. How will customers (organizations/clients/patients) be serviced?
4. How will the business be financed?
5. What are the criteria for failure?
6. How will it be managed?
7. What will the rewards be?

We shall address each of these issues in turn. In doing so, and in the absence of any established and agreed professional practices in the UK, we make a caveat that these are the authors' own views, based, for the first author, on over 30 years' experience in clinical and occupational psychology, 20 of that in private practice; and for the second on ten years' independent research contracting.

The product

It is axiomatic in fee-receiving (market-based) relationships that customers will only buy what they want and are under no necessary obligation to take what is offered. Given that the UK population is perhaps one which is neither very aware of psychological services and the benefits which might accrue from them, nor sophisticated in seeking them out, this places a special onus upon practitioners to clarify to themselves, and to their potential customers, what exactly are the 'products' that they might offer.

Defining the product

As colleagues in other professions (such as medicine, teaching, the law, management and so on) might be sources of referral, they too require private psychologists to define their services through the discipline of attempting product definitions. Under the pressures of contracting-out of services, these are increasingly issues for the institutional providers and users of psychological services too. Beach and Goebel (1988) surveyed 375 psychologists in private practice in Illinois, examining demographic characteristics, patient contacts and fees in an attempt to develop a model description of a psychologist and to consider the implications for professional licensing.

Different approaches can be seen to create different, if competing, products which have a similar theoretical base. In our experience, psychologists other than occupational are not yet very skilled at defining and presenting ('packaging') their products for their potential customers. It is almost certainly true to say that many possible users of psychologists do not even distinguish between different branches of psychology, let alone differentiate specific products. Indeed, many quite sophisticated individuals and related professionals remain chronically unclear about the differences between psychologists, psychiatrists, psychotherapists and psychoanalysts, and this is a confusion in the general mind which is of disadvantage to occupational and other applied psychologists too. It is highly likely that a general inadequacy of product definition contributes to this lack of clarity. As previously noted, psychologists in the private sector are working in a very immature and poorly-developed market; yet they may well be doing less than they could to help the market grow by failing to address issues such as product definition within normal business conventions.

Product definition is most advanced within occupational psychology, where practitioners typically have to sell their services to a demanding and value-driven commercial market in carving out their own particular niches.

How will business be found and acquired?

Psychologists are trained within academic and reactive environments rather than commercial and proactive settings. In the absence of any traditions or support within the profession for private practice, those contemplating leaving the public employment sector should be aware that they will almost certainly enter the mysteries of the experience alone, unprepared and unprotected.

Nowhere are the mysteries more arcane than in the processes by which business will be found and acquired – marketing and selling. Wiggins (1989) discusses the development and maintenance of a psychological practice in the US, and outlines a strategy to cope with competition and meet marketing objectives.

Advertising Throughout this century there has been, in the UK, a general ethical embargo upon the marketing of professional services, and especially upon advertising. This standard of professionally accepted behaviour, which became in itself one of the distinguishing characteristics of belonging to a profession, has been overturned by the changing practices within law, accountancy and medicine where restrictions towards advertising amongst members were relaxed most radically in 1987 (law), 1987 (accountancy) and 1990 (medicine) respectively.

The *Code of Conduct, Ethical Principles and Guidelines* of The British Psychological Society (1993) should form the basis of any approach to the marketing and selling of psychological services to the general public or to third parties. Marketing and selling within the commercial environment is not specifically distinguished from an approach to the general public, so it can be taken that similar rules apply. However, 'advertising' is especially the behaviour to which the *Code* addresses itself. In this context it has a rather wider connotation – the offering of services for fee or reward – than would be the case in the commercial world, where advertising forms only one part of any marketing or sales strategy.

Third party referral

For the individual practitioner, perhaps the most effective form of marketing is still what is called 'third party referral': that is to say, a recommendation from a previous client or trusted source. Whether the new client who is recommended or referred is a commercial firm or an individual, this kind of introduction typically results in the highest conversion rate from introduction to sale; that is, from a potential into a paying client.

In professional and especially clinical circles it is generally regarded with opprobrium to offer fees for this kind of introduction, though the Society's *Code* makes no specific reference to this matter. In the commercial world, however, a 'finder's fee' may often and quite properly be negotiated for the introduction of commercial work. In the absence of specific guidelines, the distinction which needs to be kept in mind is that if an individual were referred for personal help, anything that smacked of an exchange of money for such an introduction or referral would generally be thought highly improper. However, if a commercial organization is the user of the psychologist's services, then a finder's fee to the source of introduction might not be inappropriate. If, though, the introduction of the commercial organization were to result in an individual of that organization being referred for personal help largely outside the area of his or her company responsibilities, then again a finder's fee would be quite inappropriate even if the organization were the source of the psychologist's fees.

It is important to clarify at the beginning of any relationship who is responsible for the payment of fees: will it be the individual, a commercial organization, the referring practitioner, or an insurance body? In the case of health insurers, psychologists are advised to seek the specific approval of the insurer for the particular consultations proposed before entering into an agreement with the patient or client.

Advertising materials

Many psychologists develop their own brochure describing themselves and their services, or at the very least have a card which introduces them by name, professional qualification, status and perhaps specialism. The glossier the brochure, and the higher the design content, the more it is likely to cost. Most brochures require the skills of a graphic designer, though it is doubtful whether the services of a copywriter for the text should be employed as, if the practitioner has condensed his or her thinking to a position where a copywriter can be briefed succinctly, the need for a copywriter has been superseded. A well-developed brochure, letterheads, bill or invoice forms, and cards, might cost up to £10,000.

Titles

The Society has given particular thought to the question of individuals attributing to themselves the title 'consultant' without such a title having been accorded by an outside (and preferably public) body (see the *Code of Conduct*). It prefers the designation 'consulting', and indicates very clearly that even that word is not one to be used lightly or by psychologists of limited experience. We support this view ourselves, though it cannot but be noted that the word 'consultant' is now used very widely in all parts of the commercial world and often indicates the over-inflated status of a junior person in the financial services sector!

The Society's concerns here fit very well with the general principles of marketing and product definition. For these reasons alone they deserve thoughtful review by psychologists both considering, and established in, private practice.

It is the authors' experience that it takes at least two years to establish a full-time private practice, and this has been confirmed anecdotally by others.

The service

Under this heading come all those aspects which directly bear upon contact with the client. These range from the initial encounter on the telephone to the ambience of one's office; from the nature of the first greeting to whether or not coffee or tea is offered; from the comfort of seating arrangements to the discussion about how and when payment is to be made; and, fundamentally, the quality of the professional encounter that the client experiences and the sense of comfort and efficiency with which professional skills are made available.

In the service industries it is generally considered that every act that passes between the provider and recipient of the service has significance for the recipient's satisfaction. It is therefore incumbent upon the provider to examine in fine detail every aspect of the service offered; whether it fits into an overall sense of meeting the main objectives of whatever the encounter is intended to achieve; and whether there is congruence between all the various components. No amount of subdued lighting will compensate for poor and inefficient paperwork in providing, say, a report as part of the main professional endeavour, while an unwelcoming reception and thoughtless inattention to a client's comfort will set a tone which makes effective professional relationships harder to establish.

It is a considerable advantage of the private sector that, given due deference to costs, the practitioner can create whatever style and ambience best suits what he or she wishes to offer to clients. In a competitive world these are not unimportant considerations.

Choosing where to work
The selection of where to work is a key part of the service. It may be convenient to start a private practice from home. This defrays initial costs, may have some tax advantages (though long term may incur capital gains tax disadvantages), and eliminates the wasted time of travelling. However, it should be fundamental to practice of any kind from home that there are properly-designated waiting, consulting and toilet facilities, and that domestic matters do not impinge in any way at all upon contact with clients. A home is the most personal statement of oneself to which a stranger can be readily admitted. The competing requirements for a home to be a home as well as an office may be too difficult to reconcile. If a separate business line has not been installed, all members of a family who answer the telephone will need specific instruction in the form of answering for the purposes of the practice so that, as already indicated, clients feel in an effective encounter from the start. Matters of third-party liability insurance and security also need to be addressed with insurers, and the interests of mortgagors should also be properly addressed. Practising from home also requires that special attention be paid to the development of working colleague relationships, lest colleagues feel more like visitors than working partners.

Perhaps the most effective method of working from home is to use space away from the main house – a converted garage or barn. This unhappily conflicts for most people with the fact that the majority of private practice occurs in metropolitan areas where external spare space of this kind is rare, or the opportunity costs of using it are high, or practice is conducted from a residential flat. There are practitioners, however, who have successfully created additional buildings to their homes and practise very effectively from them.

Finance

On the assumption that it takes two years to establish a private practice, it is prudent to ensure that financial resources are available both to meet cash needs during that time and, should the practice fail, to know what the exit route is. Borrowings in which the equity in a house is given as security against future earnings may be especially unwise.

The only sensible way to approach the matter of finance is through a detailed cash-flow forecast. High street bank guides will give a clear understanding of what is required. Most small business start-ups are underfunded. They founder not so much through lack of potential business but through lack of cash to finance the enterprise whilst business grows. Some banks (Coutts & Co. being a particular example) have traditionally serviced the long-term financial requirements of private professional practice and such a bank should be sought out.

It is also crucial to ensure that proper arrangements are made for retaining earnings in respect of tax and national insurance payments due; VAT – compulsory if earnings are over the VAT threshold (voluntary otherwise), in which case all services supplied are subject to VAT charges; self-employed pensions; and professional indemnity as well as other third party insurance matters (see *Appendix C* on Professional Liability Insurance). The Society has an excellent scheme in the last area, organized through brokers, covering professional indemnity (malpractice, errors and omissions); libel and slander; public liability; product liability; and disciplinary hearings.

It is also important to establish your criteria for failure; that is, to decide on a point or signs which will indicate to you that setting up in private practice has been unsuccessful. This should not be when bankruptcy is looming, but at a point where it will still be possible to salvage something from the exercise.

Management

Staffing

Psychologists in private practice find themselves having to take on and fulfil a myriad of roles, unlike their colleagues in public sector employment who enjoy an administrative and support structure which permits them to give full concentration to the psychological task. In the private sector decisions about permanent staffing to provide technical or secretarial back-up can be delayed until the practice is established. In this event, routine tasks inevitably fall to the practitioner who also has to act as sales, marketing, financial and general manager as well as being the main provider of the professional services involved.

It should not be forgotten that businesses are driven by the graduate disciplines of sales, marketing and financial management, which are functions just as specialized as that of applied psychology. A psychologist in private practice is clearly ill-advised if he or she fails to acquire either professional back-up in these areas or the appropriate level of skill.

WHAT WILL THE REWARDS BE?

Setting fees

The setting of fees requires a sensitive appreciation of what the particular market will bear and what the practitioner considers the services supplied are worth, both these being linked to the practitioner's own practice overheads and financial ambitions. The Society does not attempt to stipulate the fees which should be charged for psychological services.

A minimum hourly charge of £30.00 would create, for a 48-week year, an annual gross income of £57,600. It is however highly unlikely that eight hours a day, five days a week, over 48 weeks of the year would be continuously filled with billable time. A figure of 50 per cent of this annual total would be a reasonable basis on which to consider a sole practitioner's private practice well-established, though it clearly leaves no real margin for overheads. It can be calculated that incremental additions of £5.00 per hour in charge-out rates make interesting differences to annual income.

There are in fact enormously different fee levels existing throughout the country. Charges of up to £150.00 per clinical hour have been recorded in London, though this at present would be considered the top of the profession's expectations and £70–£100 might be more usual. Court work for a senior expert might be costed at between £1,000 and £1,500 per day's attendance at court, with hourly fees pro rata for the preparation of an expert witness report. These levels of clinical fee parallel those in the occupational field, where a senior individual might be charged out to a commercial client at up to £1,800 per consulting day, though down to £300 per day for a newly-qualified person.

On an annual income basis, therefore, a psychologist in private practice at the peak of professional earnings might establish an income of somewhere between £100,000 and £150,000, whilst across private practice as a whole the viable range may go to a low of £25,000. Informal soundings suggest that, in well-established private practice, there is a median gross earning level somewhere in the range £40,000–£60,000, exclusive of overhead-related earnings. This level of remuneration is not substantially different from that of the senior end of the public sector when pension and other benefits are taken into account.

Non-financial benefits

There are of course non-financial benefits to be considered, not the least of which is the freedom of professional action which private practice confers. Nevertheless, the market place can be as much a tyrant as the rapid changes in public policy which affect professional practice in health and education settings. In public or private settings, however, the duties of the psychologist to engage in proper professional practices are equal.

Appendix: Checklist of matters for consideration in starting a private practice of consultancy in applied psychology

1. PRODUCT AND PROFESSIONAL MATTERS

1.1 Professional base
- range of skills on offer and (mix of) specializations
- levels at which skills are offered (principal, assistant, technician)
- training of new professionals/junior staff
- professional equipment
- new product/service development

1.2 Form of organization
- sole trader
- associate relationships with others in private practice
- formal partnership
- private limited company

2. MARKETING AND SALES

2.1 Sources of work/markets
- referrals
- direct mail
- networking
- indirect advertising
- media advertising
- professional directories (e.g. *The Directory of Chartered Psychologists*)
- niche v. generalist offerings
- assessment of market opportunities

2.2 SWOT (*strengths, weaknesses, opportunities* and *threats* analysis

2.3 Sales-related matters
- forms of contract
- fee rates/payment schedules/discounts
- marketing and advertising materials

2.4 House style
- furniture, lighting, ambience
- stationery
- communications/report style
- toilet accommodation
- refreshment supply

3. BUSINESS PLANNING, CONTROL AND FINANCIAL

3.1 Planning and management
- formal business plan
- partnership/employee terms and conditions
- hourly, daily, product charge-out rates
- keeping and communicating client records
- access to relevant other professional services, especially accounting and legal

3.2 Financial management
- keeping business records
- billing, credit and debt collection procedures
- cash flows
- profit and loss accounts
- annual accounts
- sources of funds
- taxation matters
- banking relationships
- indemnity and third party insurances

3.3 Logistical matters
- premises – full or part-time; purchase or rent; home-based or business/professional; sessional
- access to premises by car and public transport
- statutory provisions for premises and employment

REFERENCES

The Association of Chartered Clinical Psychologists in Private Practice (ACCPPP), Box 2EB, London W1A 2EB. Tel: 0171 323 2370.

Barclays Bank PLC (Sept. 1992). *Services for Business: Thinking of starting a business?; Setting Up and Running Your Business; Managing your Business.*

BEACH, D. A. and GOEBEL, J. R. (1988). Psychologists in Private Practice: A Survey of Illinois Practitioners. *Journal of Training and Practice in Professional Psychology*, 2, 6–24.

BRIDGE, J. and BRIDGE, S. (1990). *Blackstone's Guide to the Children's Act*. London: Blackstone Press.

BRITISH PSYCHOLOGICAL SOCIETY (1993). *Code of Conduct, Ethical Principles and Guidelines*. Leicester: The British Psychological Society.

BROWN, P. T. and LOFTUS, M. (1988). Clinical Psychology in Crisis. *The Psychologist*, 393–396.

FORD, R. (1992). *Occupational Psychology in the UK*. (Available from Psychology Consulting Services Ltd (PCS), 235 Old Marylebone Road, London NW1 5QT.

KRALJ, Mary M. (1992). Seven ways to build a practice during a recession. Centennial issue: Learning from our history. *Consulting Psychology Journal: Practice and Research, 44,* 28–29.

NATIONAL WESTMINSTER BANK, PLC. (1992). *The Business Start-up Guide.* London: National Westminster Bank.

REID, J. M. and LORD, Margaret M. (1990). Survey of Members of the Australian Psychological Society who Derive All or Part of Their Income from Private Practice. *Australian Psychologist, 25,* 77–102.

SPENCER, J. R. and FLIN, R. (1990). *The Evidence of Children: the Law and Psychology.* London: Blackstone Press.

THORBURN, L. N. (1990). LEA v. Private Practice: a false dichotomy. *Educational Psychology in Practice, 6,* 19–25.

WIGGINS, J.G. (1989). Maintaining a competitive edge in your practice. American Psychological Association 95th Annual Convention (1987, New York). *Psychotherapy in Private Practice, 7,* 67–73.

ZAGER, K. (1990): Starting a new old-fashioned practice. *Psychotherapy in Private Practice, 8,* 21–26.

2.5   PSYCHOMETRICS

Eugene F. Burke

The past 10 years have seen a substantial growth in the use of psychometric instruments in the UK. Why? Well, as any textbook will tell you, in comparison with other common methods such as the one-to-one interview or observational assessment, psychometric tests and questionnaires offer a cheaper and more consistent approach to defining individual strengths and weaknesses. But what qualifies a test or questionnaire as psychometric? This section will try to answer this question through describing some basic steps in psychometric analysis and looking at some of the issues involved in the use of psychometric instruments. Finally, the efforts of The British Psychological Society's (BPS) Standing Committee on Test Standards to ensure informed practice in the UK will be briefly described.

WHAT ARE PSYCHOMETRICS?

Comparisons of one person to another are a natural and necessary part of everyday life. Psychometric instruments serve to make such comparisons explicit by providing numerical scores that indicate how much of a particular quality an individual possesses. The purpose of what Suen refers to as the *psychometric process* is to devise a scoring system that is meaningful, reliable and valid, and to define a *psychological scale* along which individuals can be compared. The psychometric process may begin from a number of starting points, such as psychological theory and published research, or such procedures as job or content analysis that are used to identify the knowledge, skills or attitudes required for success in an occupation or in a programme of instruction.

Evaluation of instruments

Once a prototype of a new instrument has been produced, the next obvious step is to administer it and collect data to evaluate its psychometric properties. Psychometric theory provides mathematical and statistical formulae for such analysis. Though closely allied to statistical theory, a key distinction is the nature of what is being analysed which, in psychometrics, tends to be covert and in the form of latent rather than manifest variables (for example, psychopathy versus height). Given the psychometric model to be used in analysing an instrument, the collection of data requires consideration of appropriate sampling strategies, target populations, and procedures for administration that safeguard the integrity of the data obtained.

Psychometric analyses focus on two types of relationships; those concerned with the internal functioning of the instrument, and those concerned with relationships to variables external to the instrument. Both types of analysis are concerned with the extent to which a measure is subject to error. With respect to internal characteristics, the focus of analysis is to determine whether the content of the instrument is uniform (*Are there any poor items/scales that detract from the precision of the instrument?*); whether it measures more than one thing (*Was it meant to?*); and whether it is consistent in the distinctions it makes between people (*Will the same classification/ranking of individuals be obtained if the instrument is administered to them again?*). With respect to external characteristics, the focus of analysis is on whether the instrument leads to accurate diagnosis and predictions of behaviour, and the extent to which a score incorrectly classes someone as acceptable (*false positive*) or unacceptable (*false negative*) against some external criterion of behavior.

Reliability

A key concept in psychometrics is *reliability* – the accuracy with which the score observed for an individual reflects his or her true score. A basic tenet of psychometrics is that scores observed for individuals can be broken down into two components: a true component arising from the endeavour to answer a question correctly or truthfully and an error component arising from the design or administration of a test or questionnaire. The more an instrument is subject to irrelevant content or factors associated with poor administration, then the more unreliable or error-prone the score obtained from that instrument or administration. Different reliability indices reflect different facets of the instrument. An *internal consistency coefficient* indicates whether the questions or rating scales making up the instrument are consistent in their contribution to an overall score. A *retest or stability coefficient* indicates whether the same ranking or classification of individuals will be obtained if the instrument is administered more than once to the same people. An *alternate forms coefficient* indicates whether two versions of an instrument give similar rankings or classifications. These indices of reliability are not interchangeable since they address different concerns, and information from all three perspectives should be sought when reviewing a test or questionnaire.

Validity

Once an instrument has been refined through the analysis of its internal properties, the next step is to examine its relationships with other variables. This leads us into the most complex aspect of psychometrics, *validity*, which has been described in some texts as *'whether the instrument measures what it purports to measure'*. This suggests that validation is an all-or-nothing process leading to a yes or no conclusion. Rather, validation is an accumulation of data obtained from a variety of sources, locations and times. Such data might be obtained through a *content validation* in which experts evaluate whether an instrument is an adequate representation of some domain of interest. This might be obtained for a *factorial validity study* which examines the relationships between different instruments, the direction of these relationships mapping out what is being measured. Such data might be obtained for a *predictive* or *criterion validation* that examines how well a score predicts criteria such as job performance or educational achievement. Evidence from studies contributes to a better understanding of the instrument's *construct validity*, where a construct might be mathematics ability, anxiety, or leadership potential. With a catalogue of data on an instrument, one can obtain a better idea of the nature of the construct(s) evident through it. Indeed, it is really these constructs rather than a particular test or questionnaire that is being validated. This knowledge then defines the valid uses to which an instrument may be put (see Messick, 1989).

To sum up, what qualifies a test or questionnaire as psychometric are mathematical and statistical models through which an instrument is analysed, and through which empirically based statements about its qualities and its usefulness can be made. One of the features often claimed for psychometric instruments is that they are *objective*, as if this is some quality they obtain in their own right. What one should look for in evaluating a psychometric instrument is objective evidence of that instrument's strengths and weaknesses.

APPLICATIONS OF PSYCHOMETRIC INSTRUMENTS

Psychometric methods provide a general framework for the analysis of individual differences and are frequently used to evaluate assessments other than tests or questionnaires, such as those based on observation. Papers describing the use of these methods will be found throughout journals in the areas of occupational, cognitive, social, educational and clinical psychology, as well as in journals specifically dedicated to psychometric research. This chapter will limit itself to a brief review of three types of psychological measure and focus on issues associated with their history and current use. This will provide the reader with a flavour of current research and practice that can be pursued through the references provided at the end of this chapter.

Ability tests

The distinction between ability and aptitude tests is one that can lead to some confusion and is really more one of usage than of intrinsic psychometric properties. Ability tests have been characterized by Cronbach as *maximum performance measures* containing questions to which there is only one correct answer. Such measures represent a scale of how quickly or correctly someone can perform the task represented by a test. The term 'aptitude' has a more general referent in defining a variable as a predictor of a particular outcome such as training or job performance, and ability tests are widely used for this purpose.

At present, ability tests are generally held as the most consistent and predictive of personnel selection procedures, though this marks a shift from previous opinion. The work of Ghiselli had indicated that predictions were generally moderate and varied by type of job, leading to the conclusion of *situational specificity* in the predictions from ability tests. Ghiselli's analytical methods were somewhat crude, and the 1970s saw the development of more sophisticated methods of analysing data across independent studies. Hunter and Schmidt developed a *validity generalization* model that focuses on both the average prediction across studies and on variation from study to study in the predictions that they report. Their model also takes into account the conditions of data collection in each study, and their analyses have indicated that predictions from ability tests are high and consistent. Indeed, they have concluded that general ability is a dependable predictor across all job types.

Various validity generalization models were produced in the 1980s, though all yield equivalent results and Hunter and Schmidt's model is the most widely used. Their model has been subject to a detailed debate and more recent meta-analyses have shown promising predictions from other types of selection procedures (notably the structured interview, though such interviews show properties akin to those of a test). Nevertheless, the predictions achieved by tests are still widely held as the standard against which other selection methods are compared.

Two considerations weigh in favour of using tests in personnel selection. First, they provide a referent to psychological theory and a systematic understanding of what factors contribute to successful job performance, and what manipulations of those factors affect levels of success. The other practical consideration is that of cost benefit. The 1970s and 1980s saw substantial work on the development of *utility models* for estimating the return that can be expected from investing in a selection procedure, and these models show that substantial returns can be expected from only a few hours of testing (Cascio provides a very readable description of utility with several worked examples).

One factor that weighs against tests is the score differences found between males and females and between ethnic groups. Results to date indicate that these differences can be substantial and generally favour white, male applicants (although scores for Asian groups often match and even exceed those of white majority members). If psychometric tests are valid predictors of job success but disadvantage minority members, then two questions need to be answered.

1. *What do the differences in test scores represent?* The relative contribution of genetics and environmental factors to the development of abilities has a long history of heated debate. Today, group differences in scores tend to be interpreted from an environmental or *nurture* perspective. This could be seen somewhat cynically as bowing to social acceptability, but it is a view that is supported by a wealth of cross-cultural, longitudinal and learning research which shows differences in problem solving strategies between cultures, that intellectual development within cultures is influenced by social and economic factors, and that performance on both tests and criterion measures can be significantly improved through training. One of the issues researched in detail in the 1970s and early 1980s was the extent to which tests were biased against females and members of ethnic minorities. Bias in the psychometric sense of the word refers to whether an instrument functions differently for different groups. Examples are whether members of different groups with identical ability levels perform differently on a specific test item; whether a test or questionnaire is equally reliable for different groups; and whether a test or questionnaire is equally predictive of outcomes for members of different groups. Studies of test bias have shown that well-constructed tests measure ability equally well irrespective of group membership, and as such, the differences in test scores are not due to psychometric or measurement bias. It should be noted that

it is not common practice for test constructors to deliberately write biased tests, and that differences in ability test scores seem to be picking up true differences related to non-psychometric factors, reflecting social issues that psychometric tests are not designed to resolve.

2. *What can be done to reduce the degree of disadvantage?* Various strategies have been proposed to minimize group differences. One suggestion has been the use of separate group norms and selection within groups, but this has been criticized for encouraging selection by quota and not by pure merit. Such a procedure would be strongly supported if score differences occurred in the absence of between group differences on performance criteria, but evidence suggests that score differences often reflect differences in job performance. This leaves us with the recommendation that fair practices be applied to selection, training and appraisal, and that organizations should seek to provide documentation of why a selection procedure, test or otherwise, is being used. Action that is gaining popularity in the UK is that of providing practice materials to reduce anxiety about the testing procedure and improve understanding of what it entails.

Evidence that a test is unbiased does not mean that its use is fair. These are distinct and separate issues since it is possible to use an unbiased test unfairly. The reader is directed to Arvey and Faley (1988) and to articles by Schmitt, Pearn, and Williams in Smith and Robertson (1989) for details of issues and actions in fair use of tests in personnel selection.

Intelligence and educational attainment

Another common confusion in labels is that between aptitude and attainment tests. Both terms can refer to measures of ability and the distinction again depends on the purpose for which the test is used. Aptitude tests are used to predict training or job success (future behaviour). As the word attainment suggests, they measure the level an individual has reached (present behaviour). This distinction blurs when one considers that attainment tests are used to diagnose and predict an individual's likely achievement at some future time. The distinction between intelligence and attainment measures is also one that can lead to misunderstanding. In fact, the development of both types of tests is closely associated, as a brief history will serve to show.

Concern over identifying the need for remedial education led Binet to develop the *Binet-Simon Scales*. Published in 1904, these scales were derived from problems based on observations of children. Each problem was graded in terms of the proportion of normal children at different ages answering it correctly, giving a simple index of an individual's mental level. Terman translated and adapted the scale for use in the US, resulting in the *Stanford-Binet Intelligence Scales* and the introduction of the term *intelligence quotient*. Wechsler later extended the scope of individually administered measures to intelligence scales that differ in content and by the psychological process measured.

Parallel to research on intelligence scales, work by Terman and colleagues at Stanford University and by Burt at the University of London developed and incorporated measures of scholastic achievement in psychometric research. The lines of research pursued in the two countries led to different models of intelligence based on analyses of relationships between such measures. The British psychologist Spearman conducted a review of published studies which led to his suggestion that scholastic performance was primarily determined by a single factor of *general intelligence* or *g*. The American psychologist Thurstone subsequently posited that intelligence could be described by *primary mental abilities* covering verbal, numerical, spatial, memory, perceptual and general reasoning abilities. Thurstone suggested that profiling by these abilities would be more useful in interpreting educational problems than the IQ.

Burt's research began to pave the way towards a middle ground between these two models. He proposed a hierarchical organization of ability from a comprehensive general factor down to more specific factors in terms of content. This hierarchical arrangement was further pursued by Vernon to develop a model that is currently receiving renewed attention. In his model, *g* is subdivided into two major groups of *v:ed* (verbal-numerical-educational attainment) and *k:m* (practical-mechanical-spatial-physical). While *g* provides a useful prediction, Vernon felt that practical assessment for educational and vocational guidance should encompass the specific elements of the two major groups (which respectively conform to what are sometimes perceived as attainment and aptitude). Humphreys, Lubinski and Yao (1993) have recently presented results of a longitudinal study suggesting that science and engineering may be losing talent by undue weight on *v:ed*. They call for a greater balance in research and practice between the two intellectual cultures of *v:ed* and *k:m*, reflecting growing concern over the need to tie assessment to specific educational goals.

Another difference between the two countries is the conditions that contributed to a testing culture in the US. Prior to such tests as those produced at Stanford, supervisory bodies overseeing standards for college entry were already actively involved in examination programmes. Several of these bodies were merged in the 1940s to form the Educational Testing Service, influential in producing attainment tests and developing psychometric methods. Another factor was research in the 1920s and 1930s which showed low consistency in the marking of essay questions by teachers, and that the newer objective item format yielded better predictions of educational criteria (the factor of validity mentioned earlier). Yet another factor was the invention of automatic scoring machines in the 1930s. Today, entry to American colleges and universities is strongly influenced by scores on such tests as the *Scholastic Aptitude Test (SAT)* and the *Graduate Records Exam (GRE)*. Such tests may be supplemented by measures of knowledge in specific subjects such as the *Medical College Admissions Test*. More specific content tests are also widely used in the US, in particular *criterion-referenced* tests that indicate whether a person has mastered a particular body of knowledge.

Thus, attainment measures vary quite widely in their scope. Anastasi has characterized measures of educational attainment as lying along a continuum from narrowly defined tests of knowledge to broad measures of general ability. She notes that as one moves to the broader end of the continuum, the more attainment tests begin to resemble intelligence tests.

Application of models of learning

An important recent influence on educational and psychometric research has been the application of models of learning from cognitive psychology. One testing programme that is generating a wealth of data combining cognitive and psychometric theories is the United States Air Force's *Learning Abilities Measurement Programme (LAMP)*. Kyllonen and Christal (1990) report a strong relationship between reasoning ability and working memory – the capacity of an individual to hold and manipulate information in the mind. The measures of working memory were based on Baddeley's work and comprise simple tasks in contrast to, say, questions measuring comprehension of text or carrying out a series of arithmetic calculations. This substantial relationship can be explained by the synthesis of two lines of research. Ackerman has shown that the earlier stages of skill acquisition are heavily dependent on general intelligence. Research also shows that working memory load is highest in the early stages of skill acquisition as the individual develops a mental model of the task (consider learning to drive a car and the initial difficulty of remembering where all the pedals, sticks and gears are or *were supposed to be*). Mislevy (1989) has expressed the hope that contributions from cognitive theory will lead to more dynamic psychometric models of individual differences in learning.

Personality

In my experience in occupational testing, psychometrics is often seen as synonymous with personality measurement. This is not surprising since personality measures are widely used in occupational, educational and clinical assessment. They vary widely in theoretical orientation, content and administration, and range from individually administered projective measures such as the *Rorschach Ink Blots Test* in which ambiguous items are used to elicit perceptions and emotions, to group-administered questionnaires and rating scales which describe personality according to several dimensions, as in the *California Personality Inventory* and the *Minnesota Multiphasic Personality Inventory*.

Cronbach characterizes personality measures as an example of *typical performance* measures. In contrast to maximum performance measures, there are no right or wrong answers but an inclination to respond to people and situations in certain ways. The most common format for such measures is the self-report questionnaire in which people state how they are likely to act in social situations, what their likes or dislikes are, or which words or phrases best describe them. The first such questionnaire is attributed to Woodworth who developed a *Personal Data Sheet* to simulate a psychiatric interview and provide a standardized means of screening candidates for military service. It gave only a single score for the frequency of neurotic symptoms, but, coupled with the work of Allport in compiling a dictionary of trait names, it set a format that encouraged the construction of instruments describing a multitude of personality dimensions.

Self-report measures

Self-report measures suffer from a number of difficulties, the most serious of which is the pervasive problem of *response bias*; whether the pattern of responses recorded by an instrument reflects an individual's true character or a distorted image constructed for public consumption. Such bias stems from the natural desire of individuals to control the image that others have of them. This presents difficulties in basing judgements on self-report profiles in situations conducive to projecting a good self-image, such as applying for a job or promotion. Most personality questionnaires contain hidden indices to detect *faking good, social desirability* or *motivational distortion*, though such indices should not be over-interpreted as demonstrating deliberate deception. One attempt at controlling such bias has been the development of *ipsative* or *forced-choice* question formats. In contrast to *normative* questionnaires in which different dimensions are measured through questions which are answered independently of one another, the ipsative approach requires the subject to choose between dimensions within each question. So, the normative approach would tot up the scores for a series of questions keyed to particular dimensions, say sociability or culture, whereas the ipsative approach would tot up how many times sociability was selected in preference to culture or vice versa. While the forced-choice method has been shown to reduce response bias, it does not remove it entirely, and there are technical difficulties in the psychometric analysis of ipsative scales which do not occur with normative methods.

While they may be problematic, questionnaires have been the basis of many theories of personality. Two such theories are those of Cattell and Eysenck. Their models describe personality according to *traits*, persistent qualities that are common across individuals and which explain consistent patterns in social behaviour. Trait approaches have been criticized for omitting the influence of situational characteristics on behaviour (the situational specificity hypothesis again), leading to the development of *state* theories and measures which focus on feelings and moods that vary according to time and circumstance. Another criticism is that many questionnaires ignore the specific characteristics of an individual and only permit comparisons between individuals on broad dimensions. Such measures are referred to as normative or *nomothetic*, and the latter criticism has lead to *idiographic* measures (sometimes confused with ipsative methods) that focus on the balance of personality dimensions within a specific individual. Recent research has moved to a synthesis of different perspectives and the analysis of personality using theories drawn from social psychology. This encourages a perspective that combines both the intentions of an individual (the idiographic level) with traits that explain consistencies in behaviour across individuals (the nomothetic level) to generate a functional, goal directed explanation of personality. Krahe (1992) describes how both the nomothetic and idiographic approaches to personality measurement have been combined in recent research to explore patterns in people's perceptions of self, life and well-being.

Despite their critics, traits retain a useful organizing role in personality research. A taxonomy that has grown in popularity is that of the *Big Five Factors* of *extraversion, agreeableness (friendliness), conscientiousness, emotional stability,* and *openness to experience.* Though authors have differed in the interpretation of their results, many studies have repeatedly found five factors to account for the responses to personality questionnaires. These general factors do not explain personality but do provide a more reliable basis for its measurement and a more cohesive structure for its investigation (see the papers by Bentall (1993), Costa and McCrae (1993), Deary and Mathews (1993), and Kline (1993b) for a recent debate on the status of trait theory).

The need to work at different levels of personality description is an obvious requirement for the diagnosis of psychological illness, maladjustment, and psychological and neurological trauma. Both quantitative measures such as questionnaires and observational protocols are commonly used in conjunction with more qualitative information in diagnosis. The use of psychometric instruments is also generally complex as personality scales, intelligence and ability tests are frequently combined in educational and clinical diagnosis. The effective synthesis of quantitative and qualitative information relies heavily on the skill and experience of the individual diagnostician, serving to emphasize the importance of training and competence in the use of psychometric instruments.

QUALIFICATIONS AND GOOD PRACTICE

To encourage good practice, the BPS Steering Committee on Test Standards (SCTS) has for a number of years issued and updated guidelines for psychological testing. With the increase in test use witnessed in the 1980s, the SCTS devised and instigated a framework for the certification of competence in test use. So far, these efforts have resulted in the *Standards of Competence in Occupational Testing* dealing with ability and aptitude tests (Level A) and personality measures (Level B). These standards contain recommendations for the knowledge and hands-on experience that is expected for competent use and interpretation of tests used in selecting and assessing employees. An individual is not required to be a psychologist to acquire the *Certificate of Competence in Level A*, but it is required that the individual's competence be assessed and affirmed by a Chartered Psychologist from a register of verified assessors. Work is currently in hand to develop similar competence standards for the use of tests in educational and clinical assessment.

The list of competencies and guidelines on testing can be obtained from the BPS's office in Leicester, as can information on the recently published BPS Open Learning Programme for Level A. The Institute of Personnel Development (IPD) provides information on those offering Level A training, and the BPS has published reviews of aptitude tests (1992) and personality measures (1995) available in the UK.

This chapter can be followed up through the references which follow. For a general introduction to both technical concepts and types of instruments, the second of Anastasi's books listed is an excellent starting point. The books by Cronbach, Kline, Rust and Golombick, and Suen provide more technical information at varying levels of detail and difficulty. The other references provide detail on specific topics in research and the use of psychometric methods and psychological measures.

REFERENCES

ACKERMAN, P. L. (1988). Determinants of individual differences during skill acquisition: Cognitive abilities and information processing perspectives. *Journal of Experimental Psychology: General*, 117, 288–318.

ALLPORT, G. W. and ODBERT, H. S. (1936). Trait-names, a psycholexical study. *Psychological Monographs, 47*.

ANASTASI, A. (Ed.) (1965). *Individual Differences.* London: John Wiley and Sons.

ANASTASI, A. (1982). *Psychological Testing*, 5th edn. London: Collier Macmillan Publishers.

ANDERSON, J. R. (1983). *The Architecture of Cognition.* Cambridge, MA: MIT Press.

ARVEY, R. D. and FALEY, R. H. (1988). *Fairness in selecting employees*, 2nd. edn. New York: Addison-Wesley.

BADDELEY, A. D. (1986). *Working Memory.* Oxford: Clarendon Press.

BARTRAM *et al.* (1992). *Review of Psychometric Tests for Assessment in Vocational Training.* Leicester: BPS Books and The Training Agency.

BARTRAM, D. B. and LINDLEY, P. (1994). *Psychological Testing: The BPS 'Level A' Open Learning Programme.* Leicester: BPS Books.

BARTRAM *et al.* (1995). *Review of Personality Assessment Instruments (Level B) for Use in Occupational Settings.* Leicester: BPS Books.

BENTALL, R. P. (1993). Personality traits may be alive, they may even be well, but are they really useful? *The Psychologist, 6*, 307.

CASCIO, W. F. (1988). *Costing Human Resources: The financial impact of behavior in organisations*, 2nd. edn. Boston: PWS-Kent.

COSTA, P. T. and McCRAE, R. R. (1993). Bullish on personality psychology. *The Psychologist, 6*, 302–303.

CRONBACH, L. J. (1990). *Essentials of Psychological Testing* 5th. edn. New York: Harper Collins.

DEARY, I. J. and MATHEWS, G. (1993). Personality traits are alive and well. *The Psychologist, 6*, 299–311.

DIGMAN, J. M. (1990). Personality structure: Emergence of the five factor model. *Annual Review of Psychology, 41*, 417–440.

GHISELLI, E. E. (1966). *The Validity of Occupational Aptitude Tests.* New York: Wiley.

HALL, C. S., and LINDZEY, G. (1970). *Theories of Personality*, 2nd. edn. London: John Wiley and Sons.

HARTIGAN, J. A., and WIGDOR, A. K. (1989). *Fairness in Employment Testing: Validity generalization, minority issues and the General Aptitude Test Battery.* Washington DC: National Academy Press.

HUMPHREYS, L. G., LUBINSKI, D. and YAO, G. (1993). Utility of predicting group membership and the role of spatial visualization in becoming an engineer, physical scientist, or artist. *Journal of Applied Psychology, 78*, 250–261.

HUNTER, J. E. and HUNTER, R. F. (1984). Validity and

utility of alternative predictors of job performance. *Journal of Applied Psychology*, *96*, 72–98.

KLINE, P. (1990). *Intelligence: the psychometric view*. London: Routledge.

KLINE, P. (1993a). *Personality: The psychometric view*. London: Routledge.

KLINE, P. (1993b). Comments on 'Personality traits are alive and well'. *The Psychologist*, *6*, 304.

KRAHE, B. (1992). *Personality and Social Psychology: Towards a synthesis*. London: Sage Publications.

KYLLONEN, P. C. and CHRISTAL, R. E. (1990). Reasoning ability is (little more than) working-memory capacity?! *Intelligence*, *14*, 389–433.

MEEHL, P. E. (1957). When shall we use our heads instead of the formula? *Journal of Counselling Psychology*, *4*, 268–273.

MESSICK, S. (1989). Validity. In R. Linn (Ed.) *Educational measurement*, 3rd. edn. New York: Macmillan.

MISLEVY, R. J. (1989). *Foundations of a New Test Theory*. ETS Research Report RR-89-52-ONR. Princeton: Educational Testing Service.

ROID, G. H. (1985). Computer-based test interpretation: The potential of quantitative methods of test interpretation. *Computers in Human Behavior*, *1*, 207–219.

RUST, J. and GOLOMBICK, S. (1989). *Modern Psychometrics: The science of psychological assessment*. London: Routledge.

SMITH, M. and ROBERTSON, I. T. (1989). *Advances in Selection and Assessment*. London: John Wiley and Sons.

STAGNER, R. (1958). The gullibility of personnel managers. *Personnel Psychology*, *11*, 347–352.

SUEN, H. K. (1990). *Principles of Test Theories*. New Jersey: Lawrence Erlbaum Associates.

VERNON, P. E. and PARRY, J. B. (1949). *Personnel Selection in the British Forces*. London: University of London Press.

VERNON, P. E. (1961). *The Structure of Human Ability*. London: Methuen.

BPS PUBLICATIONS ON PSYCHOMETRICS

General Information Pack: Level A	Free
General Information Pack: Level B	Free
Guidance for Assessors: Level A	£15.00
Guidance for Assessors: Level B	In preparation
Review of Psychometric Tests for Assessment in Vocational Training (1990; updated 1992)	£125.00 (£100.00 BPS members)
Psychological Testing: the BPS Level A Open Learning Programme (1994)	£165.00 (£150.00 BPS members)
Review of Personality Instruments (Level B) for Use in Occupational Settings (1995)	£150.00 (£125.00 BPS members)

Prices are valid for 1995, but are subject to annual review. Please enquire about current availability and postage costs. *Enquiries to:* The British Psychological Society, St Andrews House, 48 Princess Road East, Leicester LE1 7DR, UK. Tel: 0116 254 9568 Fax: 0116 247 0787.

SECTION III
THE BRITISH PSYCHOLOGICAL SOCIETY

Contributors:

Helen Clark
Administrator, Psychological Affairs, The British Psychological Society

Graeme Geldart
Assistant Executive Secretary, and Clerk to the Investigatory Committee and the Disciplinary Board, The British Psychological Society

Jonathan Calder
Sub-editor, Subsystem Periodicals, The British Psychological Society

3.1 AIMS AND ORGANIZATION OF THE SOCIETY

Helen Clark

The British Psychological Society is the learned society and professional body for psychology in the UK. It was founded in 1901, and incorporated by Royal Charter in 1965. The Society has several objectives, which include 'to promote the advancement and diffusion of a knowledge of psychology pure and applied' (The Charter) and to maintain high standards of professional conduct and training. Since 1987 the Society has been authorized to maintain a Register of Chartered Psychologists (see p. 166), and the title Chartered Psychologist has become protected by law.

The Society carries out these objectives through its various committees and sub-systems. Answerable to the Membership in general meeting, the Council is the body within the Society which has ultimate responsibility for Society policy and activity. It carries out its responsibilities through a number of Standing Committees, and through the three main Boards of the Society. The diagram on p. 157 shows the main committees of the Society.

The Society has a democratic structure. Some of the officers serving on Council, and the Boards, have been elected at the Annual General Meeting. Others are chosen by sub-systems of the Society to represent their interests. The President is elected at the Annual General Meeting for a term of one year. The Honorary General Secretary is also elected at the AGM for a term of one year, but will usually stand for re-election on two further occasions. The President, President Elect, Vice President (who is the immediate past President) and Honorary General Secretary serve on Council, the Finance and General Purposes Standing Committee (F&GPSC), and all three Boards. Other elected officers of the Society are the Honorary Treasurer and Deputy President.

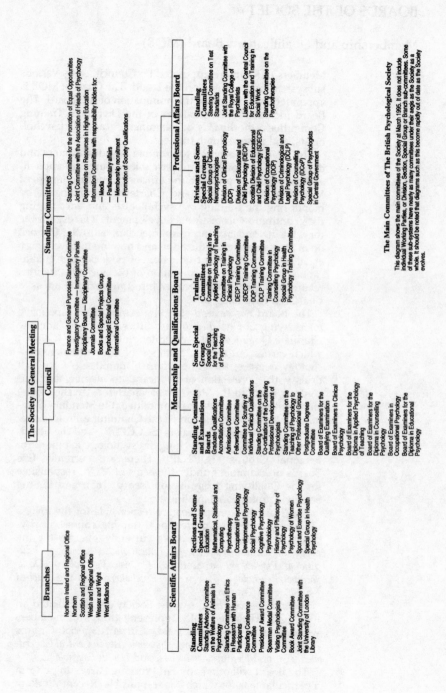

The Society in General Meeting

Branches

- Northern Ireland and Regional Office
- Northern
- Scottish and Regional Office
- Welsh and Regional Office
- Wessex and Wight
- West Midlands

Council

Standing Committees

- Finance and General Purposes Standing Committee
- Investigatory Committee — Investigatory Panels
- Disciplinary Board — Disciplinary Committee
- Journals Committee
- Books and Special Projects Group
- Psychologist Editorial Committee
- International Committee

Standing Committees

- Standing Committee for the Promotion of Equal Opportunities
- Joint Committee with the Association of Heads of Psychology Departments on Resources in Higher Education
- Information Committee with responsibility holders for:
  - Media
  - Parliamentary affairs
  - Membership recruitment
  - Promotion of Society Qualifications

Scientific Affairs Board

Standing Committees

- Standing Advisory Committee on the Welfare of Animals in Psychology
- Standing Committee on Ethics in Research with Human Participants
- Standing Conference Committee
- Presidents' Award Committee
- Spearman Medal Committee
- Visiting Psychologists Committee
- Book Award Committee
- Joint Standing Committee with the University of London Library

Sections and Some Special Groups

- Education
- Mathematical, Statistical and Computing
- Psychotherapy
- Occupational Psychology
- Developmental Psychology
- Social Psychology
- Cognitive Psychology
- Psychobiology
- History and Philosophy of Psychology
- Psychology of Women
- Sport and Exercise Psychology
- Special Group in Health Psychology

Membership and Qualifications Board

Standing Committee and Examination Boards

- Graduate Qualifications
- Accreditation Committee
- Admissions Committee
- Fellowships Committee
- Committee for Scrutiny of Individual Clinical Qualifications
- Standing Committee on the Co-ordination of the Continuing Professional Development of Psychologists
- Standing Committee on the Teaching of Psychology to Other Professional Groups
- Postgraduate Degrees Committee
- Board of Examiners for the Qualifying Examination
- Board of Examiners in Clinical Psychology
- Board of Examiners for the Diploma in Applied Psychology of Teaching
- Board of Examiners for the Diploma in Counselling Psychology
- Board of Examiners in Occupational Psychology
- Board of Examiners for the Diploma in Educational Psychology

Some Special Groups

- Special Group for the Teaching of Psychology

Training Committees

- Committee on Training in Applied Psychology of Teaching
- Committee on Training in Clinical Psychology
- DECP Training Committee
- SDECP Training Committee
- DOP Training Committee
- DCLP Training Committee
- Training Committee in Counselling Psychology
- Special Group in Health Psychology Training Committee

Professional Affairs Board

Divisions and Some Special Groups

- Special Group of Clinical Neuropsychologists
- Division of Clinical Psychology (DCP)
- Division of Educational and Child Psychology (DECP)
- Scottish Division of Educational and Child Psychology (SDECP)
- Division of Occupational Psychology (DOP)
- Division of Criminological and Legal Psychology (DCLP)
- Division of Counselling Psychology (DCoP)
- Special Group of Psychologists in Central Government

Standing Committees

- Steering Committee on Test Standards
- Joint Standing Committee with the Royal College of Psychiatrists
- Liaison with the Central Council for Education and Training in Social Work
- Standing Committee on the Psychotherapies

The Main Committees of The British Psychological Society

This diagram shows the main committees of the Society at March 1995. It does not include individual Working Parties, or Division, Section, Special Group or Branch sub-committees. Some of these sub-committees are very nearly as many committees under their aegis as the Society as a whole. It should be noted that diagrams such as this become rapidly out of date as the Society evolves.

BOARDS OF THE SOCIETY

Membership and Qualifications Board (MQB)

Members of MQB are appointed by Council, or by various subsystems represented on the Board. The Chair of MQB is appointed by Council on the nomination of the Board. The Board includes representatives of the Divisional Training Committees, the Boards of Examiners, academic psychologists, and postgraduate trainees.

The Board is concerned to promote the advancement and diffusion of a knowledge of psychology pure and applied, and especially to promote the efficiency and usefulness of Members of the Society and Chartered Psychologists by monitoring the training of psychologists and encouraging their continuing professional development. It is responsible for advising and making recommendations to the Council on matters relating to education and training in psychology at all levels, on the introduction of new Society qualifications, and on the interpretation of the Society's Statutes relating to grades of membership and registration as a Chartered Psychologist.

The Board has several standing committees responsible for carrying out its day-to-day duties. These include the Graduate Qualifications Accreditation Committee (GQAC) which carries out the accreditation of undergraduate psychology degrees, the Admissions Committee (AC) which deals with the election of applicants to membership and controls entry to the Register of Chartered Psychologists, along with the Fellowships Committee, the Standing Committee on the Coordination of the Continuing Professional Development of Psychologists (SCCCPDP), and the Standing Committee on the Teaching of Psychology to other Professional Groups (TOPTOP). There are currently five Boards of Examiners under the aegis of MQB, responsible for the Qualifying Examination (see p. 165), and for the Society's professional qualifications.

The Training Committees are responsible for the review of Society-accredited professional training courses in psychology. Training Committees currently operate for the areas of *Clinical Psychology, Educational Psychology, Educational Psychology in Scotland, Forensic Psychology, Occupational Psychology, Counselling Psychology*, and the *Applied Psychology of Teaching*.

Several Special Groups of the Society are represented on the MQB. These typically represent groups of members working in a particular field. Current Special Groups include *Teachers of Psychology, Psychologists in Central Government, Clinical Neuropsychologists*, and *Health Psychologists*.

The Board will often appoint Working Parties to perform a particular task for which it is responsible. Recent Working

Party reports have included a briefing paper on sexual harassment at work and the ethics of dual relationships. The Working Parties spend time looking in detail at a particular problem, and make recommendations to the Board about possible solutions or actions. The Board will discuss these proposals, and amend them accordingly. The document may then go to Council for ratification before the policy is implemented.

Scientific Affairs Board (SAB)

Two key functions of the Society are to act as a professional body for psychologists in the UK, and to be a learned scientific Society. These functions are reflected in the existence of two complementary Boards – the Scientific Affairs Board (SAB) and the Professional Affairs Board (PAB). The two Boards communicate through Council and through cross-representatives.

The Scientific Affairs Board oversees the learned scientific functions and as such is made up of representatives of the various Sections of the Society, along with the President, the President Elect, the Honorary General Secretary, Chair of the Animal Welfare Committee, the Honorary Librarian, Honorary Conference Secretary and co-optees to the Board. It is concerned to promote the advancement and diffusion of a knowledge of psychology pure and applied, and especially to encourage new developments in psychological science and its applications.

The Scientific Affairs Board is parent to several Standing Committees which are responsible for providing guidance on such matters as the standards for psychological research and teaching involving animals, and ethics in research with human participants. Other Standing Committees of the Scientific Affairs Board are responsible for selecting the recipients of the various awards given by the Society, such as the Presidents' Award, the Book Award, and the Spearman Medal.

Recent Working Parties considered issues such as Management Education and Research and the Dissemination of Information on Research Funding. Recent Working Party reports have included the *Report on Recovered Memories*.

Professional Affairs Board (PAB)

The Professional Affairs Board deals with the concerns of the professional applied psychologists of the Society. It is concerned to promote the efficiency and usefulness of psychologists in their professional work, the advancement and continuing development of high standards of professional education and knowledge in psychology, and standards of professional conduct for psychologists especially in relation to developments in psychological practice.

Board membership includes, amongst others, representatives from the six Division committees, representatives of the Special Groups in Clinical Neuropsychology, and Psychologists in Central Government, Chairs of various Standing Committees, representatives elected at the AGM, and the President Elect, the President, and the Honorary General Secretary.

Standing Committees of the Professional Affairs Board include the Steering Committee on Test Standards, the Joint Standing Committee with the Royal College of Psychiatrists, the Standing Committee on the Psychotherapies, and the Liaison Committee with CCETSW (Central Council for Education and Training in Social Work).

Current Working Parties of the Professional Affairs Board include the Working Party on Applying Psychology with Offenders, and the Joint Working Party with The Royal College of Psychiatrists on Psychological Therapies for Adults in the NHS. Recent Working Party reports have covered District Psychology Services for Offending and Anti-Social Behaviour, Graphology in Personnel Selection, Psychological Wellbeing for Users of Dementia Services. The Board is responsible for approving numerous responses each year which the Society makes to Government green and white papers, relating to issues of social concern affecting the lives of the client populations served by professional psychologists in the United Kingdom.

HOW THE SOCIETY IS STRUCTURED

Branches

Each Branch represents a geographic region, and any Society member living in that area is automatically a member of the Branch. Branches of the Society hold regular meetings, courses, seminars and conferences and publish newsletters.

Divisions

Divisions exist where there are clear professional groupings, with specialist qualifications required for membership. Full membership of a Division will usually be available only to those psychologists who have undertaken an approved course of training in the relevant area of psychology. The Society currently has Divisions in the following areas:

Division of Clinical Psychology (DCP)

Division of Counselling Psychology (DCoP)
Division of Criminological and Legal Psychology (DCLP)
Division of Educational and Child Psychology (DECP)
Scottish Division of Educational and Child Psychology (SDECP)
Division of Occupational Psychology (DOP)

Special Groups

Special Groups exist to represent groups of members who are working in particular areas. The entrance criteria are not based on possession of a formal qualification, and members will not necessarily have undergone a Society-approved course of training. Special Groups currently exist in the following areas:

The Special Group in Clinical Neuropsychology
The Special Group for Psychologists in Central Government
The Special Group in Health Psychology
The Special Group for the Teaching of Psychology
The Special Group of Psychologists and Social Services

Sections

The Society has several Sections which represent various academic fields within the discipline of psychology. Sections are scientific interest groups and exist for members to exchange ideas and knowledge. For a small fee, members may join any Section of the Society which interests them. The following Sections currently exist:

Cognitive Psychology
Developmental Psychology
Education
History and Philosophy of Psychology
Mathematical, Statistical and Computing
Occupational Psychology
Psychobiology
Psychotherapy
Psychology of Women
Social Psychology
Sport and Exercise Psychology

3.2 SOCIETY MEMBERSHIP

Helen Clark

At the end of 1994, the Society had a total of 18,448 Members in various grades. In addition there were 3,994 Contributors (Affiliate, Foreign Affiliates, and Student Subscribers), making a total of 22,442.

Student Subscribers

This is a financially subsidized grade of Society membership open to students of psychology who are registered on a United Kingdom course at an institution recognized by the Society. Students from the Open University will be required to send evidence with their application forms of enrolment on, completion of, or exemption from, courses DS 261, DS 262 or DSE 202 (Introduction to Psychology).

No one can remain as a Student Subscriber after completing their course and/or becoming eligible for Graduate Membership of the Society. The grade of Student Subscriber is not normally open to students who are studying on courses outside the United Kingdom. Student Subscribers are entitled to attend Scientific Meetings and Branch Meetings, although they may take no part in the government of the Society or its subsystems. Further information and application forms are available from the Society.

Graduate Members

In order to become a Graduate Member an applicant normally must have a Society-accredited degree in psychology, at either undergraduate or postgraduate level, or a pass in the Society's Qualifying Examination (see p. 165). Graduate membership may also be awarded on the basis of a Ph.D. in psychology, or by a 'points route' where various aspects of a person's experience may be taken into account. Details of the various routes to membership are outlined in the booklet *Criteria for Membership* which is available from the Society's office on request.

The Graduate Basis for Registration (GBR)

Since the introduction of the Register of Chartered Psychologists in 1987, the GBR has become a prerequisite for postgraduate training in psychology. All those who are entered to the Register must hold the GBR, along with any necessary postgraduate training which may be required.

In order to be eligible for the GBR an individual must either have passed the Society's Qualifying Examination or hold a qualification in psychology which has been accredited by the Society as conferring the GBR. Usually this will be an approved Honours degree in psychology, although it may be an approved postgraduate conversion course. Information about conversion courses, and about studying psychology at undergraduate level, is available from the Society's office.

It is important to understand that the GBR is not the same as Graduate Membership. Those who do not hold the GBR will not be able to pursue postgraduate training in psychology leading to registration as a Chartered Psychologist.

In order to establish eligibility for the GBR, it is necessary to apply to join the Society as a Graduate Member. Eligibility for the GBR will be assessed at the same time. If you have undertaken a Society-approved course, your tutor or course organizer should be able to tell you if you are eligible for the GBR.

Affiliates

This grade of Society membership is for those people who are interested in psychology but do not have the qualifications necessary for Graduate Membership. The grade of Affiliate was created to allow those working in fields related to psychology to have an association with the Society allowing them the benefits of Society membership, although they take no part in the government of the Society. There is no limit to the length of time for which a person may continue to be an Affiliate, although anyone eligible to be a Graduate Member may not become an Affiliate. Applications for the grade of Affiliate cannot normally be accepted from people who are resident overseas (but see section on Foreign Affiliates).

Fellows and Associate Fellows

The letters 'AFBPsS' after a psychologist's name indicate that the person is an Associate Fellow of The British

Psychological Society. Associate Fellowship is open to Graduate Members who, since becoming eligible for Graduate Membership, have either met the requirements to become a Chartered Psychologist (see p. 166) and completed an aggregate of a further two years' study or practice of psychology, or have been 'engaged in the application, discovery, development, or dissemination of psychological knowledge or practice' (Statute 5) for an aggregate of at least seven years.

The letters 'FBPsS' indicate a Fellow of the Society. Fellowships are awarded in recognition of higher psychological qualifications and achievements. Honorary Fellows are recommended by Council for election by a General Meeting. They will be persons of distinction who have contributed to the advancement of psychology.

CANDIDATES FOR MEMBERSHIP FROM OVERSEAS

The Society has no facilities to accredit degree courses in other countries. Therefore applications for membership from psychologists educated overseas are considered on their individual merits by the Admissions Committee.

The Admissions Committee will examine an applicant's qualifications to determine if the requirements of the Society's Statutes are met. The qualification must have been gained at an institution which is a recognized university (the Society has several guidebooks to indicate this) and be at least equivalent to a UK Honours degree in standard. Different countries do not all use the same words to indicate the standard of a qualification, and the Society is guided by British Council publications when judging whether or not Honours standard has been reached. The content of an Honours standard degree is then considered; if studies of psychology comprise at least half of the degree content, then that applicant will usually be elected to Graduate Membership. If these studies of psychology also cover the breadth of the Qualifying Examination, then the Graduate Basis for Registration will usually be granted.

The only way for an overseas-educated psychology graduate to establish eligibility for the Graduate Basis for Registration is to submit an application for membership or sit the Qualifying Examination. As the GBR is a prerequisite for any Society-accredited postgraduate training in psychology, applicants to these training courses are advised to establish their position with the Society in good time, remembering that applications may take some time to process. The Admissions Committee will not consider an application until referees have replied and all relevant information is available, and as the Committee itself meets only once every two months, delays are inevitable. Admissions tutors for accredited training courses should also be aware of these special arrangements for overseas applicants.

Foreign Affiliates

If a candidate for membership of the Society is resident in a country which has a national association affiliated directly, or indirectly, to the International Union of Psychological Sciences (IUPsyS) or to the European Federation of Professional Psychologists' Associations (EFPPA) (see also Section 5.2 on overseas psychological associations), the Society expects the candidate to belong to that association.

Applicants for Foreign Affiliateship from countries in which there is no national association affiliated to the IUPsyS or the EFPPA will be offered Foreign Affiliateship provided they would qualify for Graduate Membership of the Society.

Foreign Affiliates who subsequently take up residence in the United Kingdom are required to transfer to a different grade of Society membership within a year of ceasing to be resident overseas. Most applicants for Foreign Affiliateship also have the choice of becoming Graduate Members of the Society should they wish to apply for this grade of Society membership instead. Further information and application forms are available from the Society's office.

THE QUALIFYING EXAMINATION

For graduate applicants who do not meet the requirements for the Graduate Basis for Registration, the Society conducts a Qualifying Examination to enable those applicants to attain GBR status.

The Qualifying Examination is conducted annually and assesses the applicant's knowledge and understanding to the breadth and depth required for GBR. The examination comprises five three-hour papers, one each in the areas of *Biological Foundations and Cognitive Processes; Individual Differences, Social and Developmental Psychology; Research Design and Quantitative Methods in Psychology;* a *General Paper;* an *Advanced Option Paper* (covering Educational Psychology, Clinical Psychology, Occupational Psychology, Psychobiology, Cognitive Psychology, Social Psychology, and Developmental Psychology). There is also an assessment of a *Practical Component* through the submission of a practical work portfolio.

All components of the Qualifying Examination must be passed before GBR can be awarded.

3.3 CHARTERED PSYCHOLOGISTS

Helen Clark

Currently in the UK, and unlike certain other countries, there is no statutory control over the use of the title 'psychologist'. As psychological services have expanded over the last decade, concern has built up that there are people practising as psychologists who have no suitable training or qualifications.

In response to such concerns, in 1987 the Society sought and obtained authority under its Royal Charter to set up the Register of Chartered Psychologists. The title 'Chartered Psychologist' became protected in law. This affords some protection to the public, as by consulting or employing only Chartered Psychologists they can be assured that the person has undergone a full training, has had their qualifications properly scrutinized, and is answerable to an independent body for their professional conduct (see Code of Conduct p. 173).

To be eligible for registration an individual must have achieved the GBR (Graduate Membership alone is not sufficient) followed by a Society-accredited postgraduate training in the relevant area of psychology. This will take a minimum of three years to achieve, and details of the requirements of this training are available in the leaflet *Criteria for Registration as a Chartered Psychologist*.

Registration will often be in one of the areas of professional applied psychology for which the Society has a Division, or on the basis of a Ph.D. by research in psychology.

Conditional Registration

Conditional Registration will be granted where an applicant is following a training route which will render them eligible for full registration within three years. Psychology graduates who are undertaking such training are advised to apply for Conditional Registration, so that they may be assured that the training they are undertaking is appropriate. Being Conditionally Registered will also assure clients that the psychologist is undertaking an approved course of training and is under the supervision of a Chartered Psychologist.

Titles

All those who are entered on the Register of Chartered Psychologists are able to use the title Chartered Psychologist. If a Chartered Psychologist is, or has been, a Full Member of a Division, they are also entitled to use a specialist term. This is an adjectival title; for example, 'Chartered Clinical Psychologist' for those who are or have been members of the Division of Clinical Psychology. The title 'Chartered Psychologist', and the various approved specialist terms between the words 'Chartered' and 'Psychologist' are protected by law, and may not be used by anyone who is not currently Registered.

Clinical psychologists

Clinical psychologists must undertake a Society-accredited clinical psychology training course. On successful completion of such a qualification the psychologist will be eligible for registration. If they should also join the Division of Clinical Psychology, they will become eligible to use the adjectival title 'Chartered Clinical Psychologist'.

Educational psychologists

In order to train as an educational psychologist in England, Wales or Northern Ireland, a psychology graduate must have the GBR, a teaching qualification, and normally at least two years post-qualification teaching experience with children and young people up to the age of 19 years. They may then enter an educational psychology training course. These courses usually last for one year, and lead to an MEd or MSc in Educational Psychology. The psychologist must then work as an educational psychologist under the supervision of a Chartered Psychologist for a period of one year before becoming eligible to register. Where the training course lasts for longer than twelve months, the required period of supervised practice will be reduced pro rata. Those who are then elected to Full Membership of the Division of Educational and Child Psychology on the basis of their educational psychology qualifications will become eligible to use the adjectival title 'Chartered Educational Psychologist'.

Since 1990, to register as an educational psychologist in Scotland has required the GBR and completion of an accredited educational psychology training course at a Scottish university. All of these courses are of two years' duration, and must be followed by one year's supervised practice in a post with a Regional Council Psychological Service which has been approved by the Society as an accredited training service. Teacher training and experience are not required for entry to an educational psychology training course in Scotland. The educational psychology course includes an orientation to education for educational psychologists. Those who consider training in Scotland should remember that LEAs south of the border will usually only employ educational psychologists who have teaching experience.

Occupational psychologists

Postgraduate training as an occupational psychologist will take a minimum of three years to complete. This must include successful completion of either a Society-accredited training course in occupational psychology, or the Society's Postgraduate Certificate in Occupational Psychology, along with supervised practice in several areas of occupational psychology. (Further details on the requirements of this supervised practice are available from the Society.) Following this three year training period, psychologists should apply to become Full Members of the Division of Occupational Psychology. If accepted, they will then become eligible to be Chartered Occupational Psychologists. Those whose experience is not considered broad enough to become members of the Division may still be eligible to become Chartered Psychologists, although they will *not* be entitled to call themselves 'Chartered *Occupational* Psychologists'.

Forensic psychologists

The largest group of forensic psychologists is prison psychologists, employed by the Home Office. These psychologists will undertake a three to five year in-service training, which may include secondment to a Society-accredited training course in forensic psychology. Other forensic psychologists, for example those who work in special hospitals and regional secure units, will usually be qualified clinical psychologists. Some forensic psychologists will have undertaken a Ph.D. by research in an area of forensic psychology, or may have trained in another area of applied psychology before specializing in a criminological or legal setting. Those Chartered Psychologists who become Full Members of the Division of Criminological and Legal Psychology become entitled to use the specialist title 'Chartered Forensic Psychologist'.

Counselling psychologists

Since 1992 it has been possible to register as a Chartered Psychologist on the basis of training and experience in the field of counselling psychology. Psychology graduates with the GBR wishing to qualify as a Chartered Counselling Psychologist should undertake the Society's Diploma in

Counselling Psychology, or a Society-accredited training course. The first accredited counselling psychology training courses became available in 1995. Some training courses have been designed to fulfil all requirements of the Society's Diploma in Counselling Psychology, whilst others aim to meet the requirements of Part I only (graduates of these courses would then need to undertake Part II of the Diploma as independent candidates). It is important to check these arrangements with the course organizer before accepting a place on the course.

Those people who have been practising as counselling psychologists may be eligible to register as Chartered Counselling Psychologists under transitional arrangements, by applying for a Statement of Equivalence in Counselling Psychology. **However, all such 'grandparent' applications should be submitted by February 1997.**

Academic or research psychologists

Where an individual is eligible for the GBR, and in addition holds a Ph.D. or D.Phil. by research in an area of psychology, they will usually be eligible for registration as a Chartered Psychologist. This is on the grounds that the Ph.D. has demonstrated that they have sufficient expertise as a research psychologist to warrant registration. Occasionally applications for registration are received from research psychologists who do not hold a PhD. In line with the general principles, these psychologists may be considered eligible for registration if they are able to demonstrate that they have worked as a research psychologist for a period of at least five years under the supervision of a Chartered Psychologist, and they have a publication record which the Admissions Committee deems to be at least equivalent to a Ph.D.

Teachers of psychology

Since the introduction of the Diploma in the Applied Psychology of Teaching in 1991, teachers of psychology who do not qualify for registration via another route (for example, the research route mentioned in the preceding paragraph) may pass this Diploma in order to become eligible for registration.

Other psychology graduates

The majority of applications for registration are received from psychologists trained in one of the areas mentioned. However, occasionally the Admissions Committee is asked to consider applications from psychology graduates working in areas of professional psychology that fall outside the areas already mentioned. For example, they may be employed by industrial firms, in market research, or as psychologists in the police force. Where psychologists apply for registration with work experience and *ad hoc* training in areas not covered by the Society's usual accreditation procedures there can be difficulties in granting registration. Such applications are considered on their own merits by the Admissions Committee. Where an applicant does not qualify for registration via one of the routes already outlined, they will be required to prove to the Admissions Committee that they have undertaken an adequate training in psychology, supervised by a Chartered Psychologist, which renders them capable of the professional practice of psychology without supervision. This postgraduate training will have been of at least five years' duration, and will usually involve specialization in one area of practice. In principle the Council wishes to see recognition of psychology graduates who develop innovative professional applications of psychology. However, the Society must bear in mind at all times that the function of the Register is to protect the public, and therefore more information and evidence than is usual may be required when considering applications in these other fields. In some cases it may be that in the judgement of the Society these psychology graduates have not undertaken an adequate postgraduate training, or are not practising as psychologists, and in these cases registration will not be available.

Candidates for Registration with Qualifications from Overseas

The Society does not automatically approve any qualification gained outside the UK. However, applications for registration from psychologists trained overseas are considered by the Admissions Committee on their own merits. Candidates are asked to complete an additional application form providing detailed information about their training and postqualification experience. In general, the Committee will determine if the applicant has met the requirements of the GBR and the postgraduate requirements for registration in the relevant area of applied psychology. This will usually mean that the applicant has met the entry requirements for one of the Society's Divisions. If successful, the applicant will be able to use the adjectival title of whichever Division's entry requirements they have met. Applicants who have not obtained their psychology qualifications in the English language will usually be required to pass the Cambridge Local Examinations Syndicate Certificate of Proficiency in English at Grade A.

Owing to the large numbers of overseas-trained clinical psychologists wishing to register as Chartered Psychologists, a special scrutiny process has been set up to meet the particular needs of clinical psychologists. Candidates must submit an application for a Statement of Equivalence in Clinical Psychology to the Committee for Scrutiny of Individual Clinical Qualifications. Where an individual's training and experience are considered to be equivalent to the training required by a UK clinical psychologist (at both undergraduate and postgraduate level) a Statement of Equivalence will be granted. The Committee will take into consideration the length of time that a person has been qualified. Where a Statement of Equivalence cannot be awarded straightaway, a statement of training needs will usually be issued to the candidate, who may then work as a clinical psychologist under supervision within the NHS whilst undertaking any further training required. The award of a Statement of Equivalence in Clinical Psychology indicates eligibility both to join the Division of Clinical Psychology and to register as a Chartered Psychologist.

Applying for registration

Application forms and further information about applying for Graduate Membership or registration as a Chartered Psychologist are available from the Society's office on request. Applicants should bear in mind that the Admissions Committee meets six times a year, and therefore it may take some months to process applications, especially where it is necessary to collect reports from referees who may be resident abroad. For this reason applicants are urged to submit applications as early as possible. Applicants from overseas are advised that they should seek to establish their position with the Society as soon as they consider relocating to the United Kingdom.

Further information about how to train as a Chartered Psychologist and on the Register of Chartered Psychologists is available from the Society's office.

SOCIETY EXAMINATIONS AND ASSESSMENT

Candidates holding GBR and wishing to attain chartered status, but who are not on a Society-accredited postgraduate course route, may enrol for examination and assessment through one of the specialized individual candidate routes.

Boards of Examiners for Clinical Psychology, Counselling Psychology, Occupational Psychology, Educational Psychology, and the Applied Psychology of Teaching assess applicants who are *en route* to chartered status as independent candidates.

Candidates must enrol in the relevant area of expertise and have a plan of training, co-ordination and supervision of their training, approved by the appropriate Board of Examiners. The assessment processes undertaken by each Board differ slightly and the processes and syllabus for each are laid down in the relevant Regulations.

The Society does not conduct 'taught' courses, and these examination processes are designed only as an assessment process. Upon fulfilling the requirements of the examination and assessment process, candidates are awarded: for Clinical Psychology, a Doctorate/Masters/or Diploma; for Counselling Psychology, Educational Psychology and the Applied Psychology of Teaching, a Diploma; and for Occupational Psychology, a Postgraduate Certificate.

The successful completion of the Society Diploma/ Masters/Doctorate assessments gives the candidate the requisite qualifications for admission to chartered status through that specialized route. The Postgraduate Certificate in Occupational Psychology is awarded only for the knowledge base in that specialized area and successful candidates must also complete an approved supervised training before being entitled to chartered status.

3.4 CODE OF CONDUCT, ETHICS, INVESTIGATORY AND DISCIPLINARY PROCEDURES

Graeme Geldart

THE CODE OF CONDUCT

Under the terms of its Royal Charter, the Society is required to maintain a code of conduct. A Code of Conduct has been adopted with provision for an Investigatory Committee and Disciplinary Board to consider complaints of professional misconduct brought against members of the Society. The Statutes appended to the Charter state that a 'Disciplinary Committee shall be guided by the Code of Conduct, but that mention or lack of mention in the Code of Conduct of a particular act or omission shall not be taken as conclusive on any question of professional conduct'. Nevertheless, the Code sets out certain minimum standards for conduct with which psychologists are required to comply.

The Code is supplemented by several other guidelines and statements on matters of ethics and conduct produced by the Society and its sub-systems, which set out standards of good practice at which psychologists should aim. These additional statements give detailed guidance on matters such as advertising and descriptions, research with human or animal participants, use of non-sexist language, sexual harassment and dual relationships, and equal opportunities. Other guidelines deal with specific fields of professional practice, or concern the special provisions of law and practice on such matters as confidentiality and the disclosure of information (see also Section 2.2.2 on the Data Protection Act and Section 2.3 on Confidentiality and Access). Failure to observe the provisions of these additional statements and guidelines may lead to disciplinary action being taken under the Code of Conduct.

The Code of Conduct is framed under five broad headings:

General Conduct
Competence
Obtaining Consent
Confidentiality
Personal Conduct

If a member is charged with professional misconduct the charge(s) will be related to one or more of the Sections contained under those headings in the Code.

INVESTIGATORY AND DISCIPLINARY PROCEDURES

The Royal Charter requires the appointment of a Disciplinary Board from which a Disciplinary Committee shall be appointed as necessary. The composition of the Disciplinary Board from which a Disciplinary Committee is drawn is of at least three past Presidents of the Society and a greater number of non-psychologist members drawn from nominations requested by Council from other professional bodies for suitable senior members from within their ranks; for example, The Institute of Chartered Accountants, The Law Society, The Royal College of Nursing. A Disciplinary Committee of three will be appointed from the membership of the Disciplinary Board to hear allegations of professional misconduct and that Committee's composition must be two non-psychologist members and one past President. The reason for the Disciplinary Board and Disciplinary Committee comprising a majority of non-psychologist members is to ensure that the profession is not seen to be judged by its own membership on allegations of misconduct. Decisions of a Disciplinary Committee are binding upon the Council of the Society.

The Investigatory Committee

Before any matters are brought before a Disciplinary Committee, a procedure of receipt of complaints, and investigation and recommendation with regard to complaints, is stipulated in the Statutes. Council is required to appoint an Investigatory Committee consisting normally of four Fellows or Associate Fellows of the Society, at least two of whom shall be officers of the Society (President, President-Elect, Honorary Treasurer, Honorary General Secretary, Vice (immediate past) President, and Deputy President), and one of those officers shall be appointed as Chair. Members of the Investigatory Committee cannot sit concurrently on the Disciplinary Board.

Most complaints originate with an accusation of pro-

The British Psychological Society
Investigatory and Disciplinary Procedures

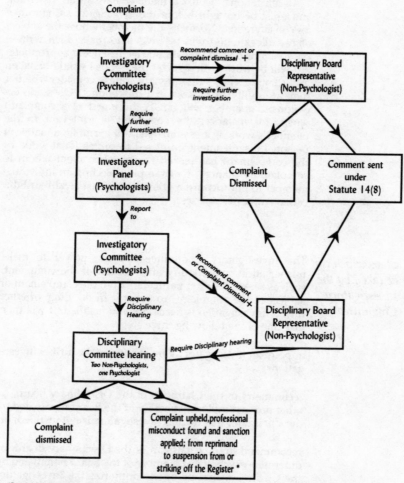

*Remedial measures may be required such as retraining under supervision. Alternatively medical or psychological treatment may be required where there are extenuating circumstances involving the psychologist.

+ `Recommend Comment' refers to BPS Statute 14(8). This Statute authorizes the Investigatory Committee to comment and advise on the professional conduct of the subject of the complaint, even when it has been decided by the Disciplinary Board Representative that referral of the complaint to a Disciplinary Committee hearing is not justified because any breach of the Society's Code of Conduct is only minor. (By analogy, the Society can in such circumstances, issue the equivalent of a `caution' from a police officer.)

fessional misconduct raised by a member of the public or by a professional colleague. The Investigatory Committee itself also has a duty to the public to initiate the investigatory process if it becomes aware of allegations of a member's professional misconduct not reported directly, for example, through media coverage.

All allegations against a member have to be in writing and must be brought before the Investigatory Committee for consideration. Normally the member who is the subject of the allegation(s) will be invited to make such written observations on the allegation(s) as they deem appropriate, but will be warned that such observations would be taken into account at any subsequent hearing to consider whether they are guilty of professional misconduct. On some occasions, a member will not be informed of a complaint when, for instance, the complaint is irrelevant to the member's work as a psychologist, for example, a matter of personal disagreement unrelated to professional work; or the complainant has picked the member about whom to complain by chance – for example, selecting an individual member to put forward a grievance against Health or Education Authority policies.

Steps which can be taken by the Investigatory Committee The Investigatory Committee has the power to make further additional enquiry after receipt of the complaint, such as seeking further particulars from the complainant or subject of the complaint, to assist it in deciding whether further investigation is necessary and justified. It will then take one of the following three steps:

appoint an Investigatory Panel to undertake further investigations;

recommend to the Chairman of the Disciplinary Board, or other non-psychologist member of the Board nominated by the Chairman, that further investigation is not justified; or

recommend to the Chairman of the Disciplinary Board, or other non-psychologist member of the Board nominated by the Chairman, that he or she authorize the Investigatory Committee to write to the subject of the complaint and, when reporting that the matter will not be referred to a Disciplinary Committee, may advise in relation to the Code of Conduct (under Statute 14(8)).

In the latter two cases, the Disciplinary Board representative shall either accept the recommendation, or reject it and require the Investigatory Committee to appoint an Investigatory Panel to undertake further investigation.

The Investigatory Panel

If the subject of the complaint is not prepared to accept the Investigatory Committee's advice given under Section 14(8), he or she could request the appointment of an Investigatory Panel to undertake further investigation. An Investigatory Panel consists of two to five Fellows or Associate Fellows or members of Council, and has the power to call for further information as it considers necessary to its investigation. It is the duty of every member to provide information requested by an Investigatory Panel. The Panel's task is to seek to establish the facts, and in so doing must be satisfied that the subject of the complaint has been given the opportunity of making written representations to it. It has the discretion to give the subject an opportunity of being heard before it or requesting a personal interview. There is no right on the part of the subject to require such an interview.

Possible recommendations of the Investigatory Committee

At this stage of the enquiry the subject has not been charged with professional misconduct, but has been notified of allegations and requested to give his or her account of the matter. At the conclusion of its investigations and enquiries the Panel makes a written report to the Investigatory Committee and may make recommendations, but the responsibility lies with the Investigatory Committee to decide to recommend to the Chairman of the Disciplinary Board or other non-psychologist member of the Board nominated by the Chairman that:

no further action should be taken;

the Investigatory Committee be authorized to write to the subject and when reporting that the matter will not be referred to a Disciplinary committee, advise in relation to the Code of Conduct; or

the matter be referred for formal consideration by a Disciplinary Committee.

If the Disciplinary Board representative accepts a recommendation that no further action be taken, the complainant and subject will be advised and the matter will be closed. No record of the matter appears on the personal membership file of the subject. If the Disciplinary Board representative agrees that advice on the Code of Conduct should be given to the subject without referral to a Disciplinary Committee, this will be done formally by the Investigatory Committee. If the subject is not prepared to accept the advice, he or she may request the appointment of a Disciplinary Committee to consider the matter.

The Disciplinary Committee

In the event that a Disciplinary Committee is appointed, it will be composed of three members of the Disciplinary Board, two lay non-psychologist members and one psychologist who is a past President of the Society. One of the non-psychologist members of the Disciplinary Committee will be appointed as Chair. The Disciplinary Committee may be advised by a lawyer and by up to two Fellows of the Society with special expertise relating to the issues in the matter before the Committee. The advisors do not share in the judgment of the Committee. The Disciplinary Committee may appoint legal counsel to act on the enquiry, and the subject may either present his or her own case or be represented by legal counsel or by another person of their choice, for example, trade union official or friend. The subject will be given a full and fair opportunity of being heard, of calling witnesses, and cross-examining any other witnesses testifying before the Committee. Written evidence may be presented. It may not be necessary for the complainant to appear before the Disciplinary Committee to give formal evidence, and this will be dependent upon the circumstances of the case. It is the Society, not the complainant, who brings the charges of professional misconduct before the Disciplinary Committee, and the complainant's role is as a witness relating to those charges.

Actions which can be taken by the Disciplinary Committee

The Disciplinary Committee must then decide whether the member is guilty of misconduct. If it does find the member guilty, it may take one or more of the following actions;

reprimand or severely reprimand the member;

require the member to give an undertaking to refrain from continuing or repeating the offending conduct;

suspend the member from the Society or the Register or both for a period not greater than two years;

expel the member from the Society, or remove them from the Register, or both.

Appeals and re-instatement

There is no appeal from a decision of the Disciplinary Committee other than by way of judicial review through the High Court. Council of the Society is also bound by decisions of a Disciplinary Committee.

A member who is expelled or removed from the Register of Chartered Psychologists may apply for re-instatement, but no sooner than two years from the disciplinary hearing or one year from a previous application for re-instatement.

No re-instatement may be made without the agreement of the Disciplinary Board or its Chairman. The Disciplinary Committee has the authority to publish the names of those disciplined. This publicity will usually be in the Society publication, *The Psychologist*, but may be on a wider scale if the Disciplinary Committee directed, or journalists follow up the publicity in *The Psychologist*. Employers of a member who had been disciplined would normally be notified of the decision.

Clerks to the Committee and Board

The Statutes provide for members of the Society's office staff to serve as Clerks to the Investigatory Committee and Disciplinary Board. The role of the Clerk is to advise the Committees on procedure, arrange hearings, and communicate with the subject of the complaint. The Clerks are neutral in the proceedings and take no part in the decisions of the Committees. The Clerks provide advice when required by a subject as to their rights under the Charter and Statutes and with regard to the investigatory and disciplinary process.

Up until the conclusion of the disciplinary process, proceedings are confidential and the Disciplinary Committee meets *in camera* to protect the interests of the complainants who may often wish to make allegations about matters of great personal sensitivity such as those which arise in therapy.

Note: The title of *Chairman* has been used with regard to the Chairman of the Disciplinary Board as it is the required and stipulated terminology to be used in the Royal Charter by direction of the Privy Council.

3.5   PUBLICATIONS OF THE SOCIETY

Jonathan Calder

THE PSYCHOLOGIST

THE Psychologist is the official monthly bulletin of The British Psychological Society. It publishes official statements on behalf of the Society and provides a forum for discussion and controversy among members of the Society. It is sent free to all members of the Society (except Affiliate members) as part of their subscription. Affiliate members may subscribe at a reduced rate, and subscriptions and single copies are also available to non-members. An educational discount is also available. Enquiries about subscriptions should be made to The British Psychological Society office in Leicester.

Submitting articles

The Psychologist has pioneered in the development of articles designed to communicate the kind of information normally found in academic journals to psychologists with a wide range of academic and professional interests, and wishes to encourage contributions from psychologists in all areas, both academic and applied. Articles should be written for an intelligent, educated but non-specialist audience; shared knowledge of theory should not be assumed and references should be kept to a reasonable minimum. Papers may provide a broad overview of a particular area of issue, review the literature or include original research, discuss theory, or debate applied issues, practical and professional problems.

All articles accepted for publication may be subject to editing. Authors will be asked to provide brief summary sentences which may be used as the basis of the introduction: this serves as an invitation to the reader to read the article, and replaces the standard academic abstract.

Authors will be sent the final version for consultation before publication. Articles may be illustrated, and should be of a maximum of 3000 words, typed on A4 paper, double-spaced, with complete references. Sexist and racist language should be avoided. All articles published, with the exception of invited articles, are subject to anonymous review, so authors' names and affiliations should not appear on the typescript but on a separate page. Five clear copies should be submitted to the Leicester office. If the article is accepted for publication, authors will be asked to supply the text on an IBM-compatible 3.5" disk if at all possible. (Please do not send the first submission on disk.) Submission of an article to *The Psychologist* implies that it has not been published elsewhere and that it is not currently being considered for publication elsewhere.

Anyone who wishes to discuss an idea for an article, or who would like advice on the suitability of a piece that has already been written, should contact the Society's office in Leicester, who will then put them in touch with the appropriate Associate Editor.

Copyright

Copyright for all published material is held by The British Psychological Society, unless specifically stated otherwise. Authors, illustrators and photographers may use their own material elsewhere after publication without permission, but the Society asks that the following note be included in any such future uses: 'First published in *The Psychologist*, The Bulletin of the British Psychological Society, vol. no. and date'. Permission is required and a reasonable fee charged for commercial use of articles by a third party.

Brief reports on published research (200–400 words) and on conferences of interest to a wider audience (200–500 words) are welcome, and should be sent to the Society's office within a month of the event. *The Psychologist* also welcomes humorous or satirical articles and cartoons with relevance to psychology; three typewritten copies of such pieces should be sent to the Society's office.

Book reviews

Book reviews are commissioned by the publication's Book Review Consultants. Anyone interested in reviewing books in a particular field (rather than a particular volume) should write to 'The Associate Editor (Books)' via the Society office.

Correspondence

The Psychologist carries a substantial correspondence section every month. Letters, marked clearly 'Letter for publication in *The Psychologist*' should be sent by e-mail (bps1@le.ac.uk) or addressed to The Editor, *The Psychologist*, The British Psychological Society, St Andrews House, 48 Princess Road East, Leicester LE1 7DR, UK. News of events, decisions, discoveries, people or any items which would be of interest to psychologists should also be sent to the Society's office.

Advertising   *The Psychologist* carries a substantial amount of advertising as well as notices of the Society's and its subsystems' own events. Potential advertisers should note, however, that *The Psychologist* does not carry any job advertisements. All such advertisements are carried in the Society's *Appointment Memorandum*. Advertising rates for both these publications may be obtained from the Society's office.

SOCIETY JOURNALS

The journals of The British Psychological Society are international in their contributors, editorial consultants and readership. Papers are invited from authors worldwide. All papers are peer reviewed and blind reviewing is encouraged (see also Section 4.1.2 on editing a journal).

Submitting articles

Publication is speeded by care in preparation. Papers should be typed in double spacing and on one side of the paper only. Four copies should be sent to the Editor of the relevant Journal c/o Journals Office, 13A Church Lane, London N2 8DX. (Tel. (+44) 0181 444 1040; Fax (+44) 0181 365 3413). The Journals Office also deals with all general editorial enquiries. Section 4.1.1 deals with the preparation of journal articles.

Subscriptions   Members of The British Psychological Society may subscribe to Society journals at special reduced rates, and should direct all enquiries and orders to the Society's office in Leicester. The office will also be pleased to provide further details of any Society journal, although subscription orders (except for *Selection & Development Review*) should be sent to Turpin Distribution Services Ltd, The Distribution Centre, Blackhorse Road, Letchworth, Hertfordshire, UK (Tel. (+44) 01462 672555; Fax (+44) 01462 480947). Any requests for back numbers should be sent to Leicester.

British Journal of Educational Psychology

The editorial board invites psychological research that makes a significant contribution to the understanding and practice of education. Empirical and theoretical studies, action research, case studies and psychometric and statistical methods are all welcome to the board, which aims to give access to research to a broad readership including researchers and educational practitioners.

Selection & Development Review (SDR)

Formerly known as *Guidance & Assessment Review*, this *Review* has changed its name to reflect more accurately an increasing focus on selection and development issues for professional people whose job it is to assess other people. Topics covered in recent issues have included new product teams, recruitment advertising design, use of selection methods in the UK, OPQ norms and scales, assessing and selecting employers as suppliers, practice testing and executive intelligence.

Selection & Development Review is sent free to those on the *Register of Competence in Occupational Testing* and is available at a special price to members of the Society's Section and Division of Occupational Psychology.

British Journal of Medical Psychology

This international journal with a traditional orientation towards psychodynamic issues aims to bring together the medical and psychological disciplines, and this is reflected in the composition of the editorial team. The Editor particularly welcomes collaborative studies between psychologists and psychiatrists. Original theoretical and research contributions are invited from the fields of psychodynamic and interpersonal psychology, particularly as they have a bearing upon vulnerability to, adjustment to and recovery from both medical and psychological disorders.

British Journal of Mathematical and Statistical Psychology

This journal is a major international outlet for papers on all aspects of quantitative psychology, including mathematical psychology, statistics, psychometrics, decision-making, psychophysics and relevant areas of mathematics, computing and computer software. The editor is actively seeking reviews of the literature, expository articles or short notes on useful techniques and routines in these areas.

British Journal of Psychology

The Editorial Board is prepared to consider for publication any of the following:

reports of empirical studies likely to further our understanding of psychology;
critical reviews of the literature;
theoretical contributions.

Readership is worldwide and includes academic and research workers in experimental, cognitive and general psychology.

Journal of Occupational and Organizational Psychology

This international journal of industrial and organizational psychology publishes conceptual and empirical papers which aim to increase understanding of people at work. Its domain is broad, covering industrial, organizational, engineering, vocational and personnel psychology, as well as behavioural aspects of industrial relations, ergonomics, human factors and industrial sociology. The editor particularly welcomes papers taking innovative or interdisciplinary approaches with a psychological emphasis.

British Journal of Clinical Psychology

The editor and editorial board wish to reflect the broad role of clinical and health psychologists and include descriptive studies as well as studies of the aetiology, assessment and amelioration of disorders of all kinds, in all settings and amongst all age groups. Empirical investigations from any theoretical perspective of the relation of intrapersonal and interpersonal processes to disorder are welcome, as are studies of the delivery of health care in hospital or community settings.

British Journal of Health Psychology

The special section on health psychology contained within the *British Journal of Clinical Psychology* has attracted so many high quality submissions that it will be launched as an independent journal in 1996. During 1996 the *British Journal of Health Psychology* will be sent out with the *BJCP*, but will be available separately from 1997.

British Journal of Social Psychology

The editorial team encourages submissions addressing a variety of issues, and employing a variety of methods, both quantitative and qualitative, and welcomes theoretical, review and methodological papers in addition to empirical papers of theoretical significance.

British Journal of Developmental Psychology

The Editor invites submissions relating to all aspects of development from infancy to old age, including: development during infancy, childhood and adolescence; abnormal development – the problems of disabilities, learning difficulties and childhood autism; educational implications of child development; parent–child interaction; social and moral development; and effects of ageing. Full length empirical, conceptual and review papers as well as brief reports of work in progress are encouraged.

Legal and Criminological Psychology

This new journal will be launched in February 1996. The editors invite theoretical, empirical and review studies in the field as broadly defined. Topics of interest include new legislation, legal decision-making, court processes, victimology, theories of delinquency, public attitudes, mental health and the law, policing and crime detection.

SUBSYSTEM PERIODICALS

The various subsystems of The British Psychological Society produce a wide range of publications, varying from informal newsletters to journals. Whatever their style, all these publications are intended primarily for the members of the particular subsystem, who receive them free of charge as part of their subscription. While contributors to subsystem publications will generally be members of the relevant subsystem, some editors are happy to consider contributions from other sources. Editors can be contacted via the Society's office.

The Society's library, held at the University of London, maintains a full collection of all subsystem publications. If a particular issue or a photocopy of a single article is required, it is sometimes possible to supply it from the stock held at the Society's office in Leicester. These holdings are not complete, however, and neither are they open to inspection by members of the general public.

Subsystem periodicals are carrying an increasing amount of advertising. As with *The Psychologist*, however, it should be noted that no job advertisements can be accepted. All such advertisements are carried in the *Appointments Memorandum*, which is sent out to all members of the Society with *The Psychologist*.

There follows a list of those subsystem periodicals for which subscriptions are currently available to non-members of The British Psychological Society.

Counselling Psychology Review

Counselling Psychology Review is published by the Division of Counselling Psychology. The Editorial Board invites contributions on any aspect of counselling psychology. Papers concerned with professional issues, the training of counselling psychologists and the application and practice of counselling psychology are particularly welcome. The Editorial Board would also like to encourage the submission of letters and news of forthcoming events.

Health Psychology Update

Health Psychology Update is published by the Special Group in Health Psychology and appears four times a year. Its intended readership is those who are concerned with the application of psychological models to the study of behaviour relevant to health, illness and health care. In addition to papers of significance to health, illness and healthcare, *Health Psychology Update* has regular special issues and topic reviews, research forum and book review sections, bibliographies, conference reports, correspondence and news from the Special Group.

Clinical Psychology Forum

Clinical Psychology Forum is published monthly by the Division of Clinical Psychology. In addition to papers of significance to health and social services, *Clinical Psychology Forum* has regular special issues, book reviews, conference reports, correspondence and news from the Division of Clinical Psychology.

Psychology of Women Section Newsletter

This newsletter is published twice a year by the Society's Psychology of Women Section and provides up-to-date information and comment on new developments in the psychology of women and related areas.

News from EFPPA

News from EFPPA is produced four times a year by The British Psychological Society for the European Federation of

Professional Psychologists' Associations (see Section 5.2. on links with other countries). All members of EFPPA receive copies as part of their membership entitlement. Issues to date have included papers on equal pay, reading standards, European psychotherapy and child sexual abuse, and reports on psychological training in Finland, the Netherlands, Spain and Hungary. Other regular features include profiles of member associations, conference reports and a diary of European events.

Psychology Teaching Review

Psychology Teaching Review has been established to encourage research on teaching and learning in psychology, to serve as a vehicle for the sharing of good practice and to improve the standard of psychology teaching at all levels. The editorial board welcomes articles on any aspect of psychology teaching.

Educational and Child Psychology

The *Papers* of the Division of Educational and Child psychology are published quarterly. Each paper consists of a number of articles with a common theme; recent themes have included core competencies, motivation and children's rights.

Division of Educational and Child Psychology Newsletter

This newsletter appears every two months and offers thorough coverage of Division and Society business of interest to educational and child psychologists. Other regular features include *In and Out of Parliament; Training Matters; Europe; The World; Research in Brief;* and *Book Reviews.*

Issues in Criminological and Legal Psychology

The *Occasional Papers* of the Division of Criminological and Legal Psychology are not published to a regular schedule, and it is anticipated that fewer will be published once the Society's new journal in this field has begun to appear. Recent issues have contained a selection of the papers presented at the Division's annual conferences.

Education Section Review

The *Education Section Review* is published twice a year with the main aim of publishing short papers, reports and information about current ideas and issues in educational psychology.

Forensic Update

The newsletter of the Division of Criminological and Legal Psychology appears four times a year. It contains articles, conference reports and book reviews covering the whole range of the Division's work.

THE DIRECTORY OF CHARTERED PSYCHOLOGISTS

The *Directory of Chartered Psychologists* is a 'yellow pages' of services offered by psychologists in the UK. The *Directory* contains a detailed guide to the various services provided by psychologists and a comprehensive index which helps potential clients to find the services they require. The entries submitted by 1,350 (figure for 1995) individual psychologists give details of their specialisms and their own comments on their special interests. The *Directory* also includes advertisements by local and national organizations. The *Directory* can be found in major references libraries and may also be purchased.

The main categories in the index are:

- Clinical psychology
- Clinical neuropsychology
- Counselling psychology
- Educational psychology
- Forensic psychology
- Occupational psychology
- Psychological services in social services settings
- Services by teachers of psychology
- Other psychological services

Within these main categories there are detailed descriptions of where psychologists are competent to work. For clinical psychology, clinical neuropsychology and counselling psychology there are, in all, 28 specialist subdivision descriptions. In the educational area 16, in forensic six, in social services 12, and in teachers of psychology five.

These descriptions are then indexed by geographical area, and the individual entries also detail specialist services and areas of interest, together with information on such things as contact details, foreign languages spoken and hours of work.

All Chartered Psychologists who hold a practising certificate are eligible for an individual entry in the *Directory*, and will be contacted by the Society whenever a new edition is to be produced.

THE REGISTER OF CHARTERED PSYCHOLOGISTS

The Society also publishes a *Register of Chartered Psychologists*, which is sent to all major reference libraries. This is an alphabetical list of the names and addresses of all Chartered Psychologists, including details of their academic and professional qualifications and of any specialist term they are entitled to use (for example, Chartered *Clinical* Psychologist, Chartered *Educational* Psychologist).

BPS BOOKS

BPS Books is the books and special projects publishing division of The British Psychological Society, and is based in the Leicester office. The main aim of the publishing programme is to disseminate good psychology as widely as possible, and this includes making the insights gained from psychological research available to non-psychologists as well as to psychologists. Many of the titles in the list are therefore books and textbooks for specialists in disciplines other than psychology (doctors, nurses, social workers, teachers, management), as well as self-help paperbacks, schools materials and books for the general reader. BPS Books also produces psychology careers and reference materials, including the *Compendium of Postgraduate Studies in Psychology in the UK and Ireland*. Recently the publishing programme has expanded into the area of distance learning, with the publication of *Psychological Testing: the BPS Level A Open Learning Programme*.

Members of the Society receive a discount on books published by BPS Books, upon quotation of their membership number. As there are now over 100 titles in print, the list has been split into subject catalogues – *Education; Careers; Personal and Professional Development; Health and Social Care;* and *Psychometrics* – and these are available from the Leicester office. A direct sales scheme to schools of the *Open Learning Units in Cognitive Processes, Research Design and Statistics*, and *Developmental Psychology* is also operated, and again details and sample material are available from the Leicester office. Books published by BPS Books are displayed at most of the Society's conferences, and at student psychology conferences run by other organizations.

To all intents and purposes, BPS Books operates in the same way as any other small commercial publisher. All titles are promoted and sold through the usual channels –

direct mail, display advertising, reviews, exhibitions, inserts in journals and through visits by reps to bookshops both in the UK and overseas. Titles accepted for publication are, therefore, judged to be commercially viable in the normal way.

Proposals for books relevant to the field of psychology are welcomed from both established and first-time authors, and a leaflet on *Writing the Outline Proposal for a Book* is available from the Leicester office (see also Section 4.1 on publishing). All proposals received will be considered by the editorial board, the Books and Special Projects Group, which meets every 6 weeks. The board is made up of psychologists from all areas of professional practice. Editing, marketing and promotion, and the sale of foreign rights are co-ordinated by the Leicester office, and BPS Books has a strong track record on negotiating translation rights.

SECTION IV
CONTINUING PROFESSIONAL DEVELOPMENT

Contributors:

Michele Benjamin
Journals Manager, The British Psychological Society

Susan Pacitti
Editor, BPS Books, The British Psychological Society

Anthony Gale
Director of Research and Development, Department of Psychology, University of Portsmouth

Joyce Collins
Publications Manager, BPS Books, The British Psychological Society

Paul Jackson
Senior Lecturer in Psychology, and Associate of the Institute of Work Psychology, University of Sheffield

Tom Carruthers
Occupational Psychologist, Carruthers Associates

Stephen White
Director of Information, The British Psychological Society

Bruce Napier
Head of Psychology Services (Mental Health), Gwynedd Community Health Trust

Neil Brooks
Director, Case Management Services, Edinburgh

Glenys Parry
Director, Sheffield Consulting and Clinical Psychologists, and Senior Psychological Officer, Department of Health

Ann Colley
Head of Department of Psychology, University of Leicester

4.1 PUBLISHING: JOURNALS AND BOOKS

4.1.1 HOW TO PREPARE A JOURNAL ARTICLE

Michele Benjamin

*O*UR *advice is: begin at the end. Write down your conclusions as clearly, precisely and economically as you can, and relate them to the hypothesis you have been examining . . . A scientific paper should not be the history of an inquiry but its outcome.*

Thus speak O'Connor and Woodford (1978) in their classic *Writing Scientific Papers in English.* 'Your writing should interest, inform and persuade your reader. Psychological writing should not be dull or stuffy', advises Robert Sternberg (1993) in his lively *Psychologist's Companion.* Both these titles are useful guides on how to organize the written presentation of research results.

DECIDING ON A JOURNAL

Once you know what you want to say, how you want to say it and have considered optimum methods of data presentation (see, for example, Leach's useful Chapter 7 in Sternberg, 1993), decide which journal is appropriate for your submission. Choose your target carefully: most peer-reviewed journals receive far more papers than they accept and expect a statement to the effect that your submission is not under consideration elsewhere. Thus, making an inappropriate choice is likely to waste a great deal of time.

Recent issues of potential target journals are a good guide to what has previously been found acceptable in terms of subject matter and style. A statement of the journal's editorial aims and objectives plus some guidelines on length of paper and details of presentation are usually included with each journal issue (most often on the inside journal cover or as the first or last page of the issue). Sources of more detailed guidelines may also be listed, for example, the APA *Publications Manual* or the *BPS Style Guide*.

STYLE OF PRESENTATION

Different journals follow different conventions and varying levels of take-up of new technology impose different media and coding requirements, but the journal itself is still the most authoritative source of what is expected. Certain journals will not even consider a paper for publication if it is not prepared in line with their style guide, so an initial inquiry to the journal's editorial office may save a great deal of later revision. In spite of the variety of styles, a few general statements about presentation can be made.

- Submission on disk should be accompanied by hard copy and this copy should usually be presented in the same way as conventionally prepared copy. In these days of sophisticated word processing, it is tempting to present a paper using all the best DTP wiles, with three-dimensional graphics and closely-spaced text resembling typesetting. Please resist this temptation. The reason for double-spaced typescripts is to allow easy annotation and DTP presentation completely defeats this objective.

- Type clearly, double-spaced, on one side of the paper only leaving a good left-hand margin.

- Number the pages consecutively.

- Make the hierarchy of headings quite clear either by consistent typographic treatment (for example, main headings centred capitals, second-level headings side, underlined, or an alternative designated in the style guide) or by numbering (for example, 1, 1.1, 2, 2.1).

- Literature referred to in the text should be listed in consistent detail in the reference list at the end of the paper. The exact details depend on the style adopted but the usual requirement is for all surnames plus initials of authors, year of publication, chapter and book title/ article and journal title, first and last page numbers, location and name of book publisher.

- Accompanying illustrations should be carefully prepared in black ink on plain white paper (without graph or grid background). If submitting originals, protect them but do not use damaging paperclips. Type captions on a separate sheet and identify figures by consecutive numbers outside the image area. Check with Leach (1993) on when and how to deal with tabular and graphical data.

Covering letters

The guidelines should indicate how many copies of the submission should be sent. Make sure you also keep a copy for your own records. Always send a covering letter addressed to the specific journal you want to target: journal editors change, editorial office addresses may change and many publishers' editorial offices deal with more than one journal. (The Society's comparatively modest Journals Office publishes eight journals (ten from 1996) and receives nearly a thousand unsolicited submissions a year.) Making your intentions clear does help at the receiving end.

When to contact the office

Finally, remember that envelopes get torn and misdirected and paper can go astray. If you have not received an acknowledgement or some other sign of life from the editorial office after three or four weeks, check that you have indeed made contact. Once that is ensured you have done what you can to facilitate consideration of your paper; the rest is up to the journal's editorial team.

REFERENCES

O'CONNOR, M. and WOODFORD, P. (1978) *Writing Scientific Papers in English.* London: Pitman Medical.

Publication Manual of the American Psychological Association 4th edn. (1994). Washington, DC: American Psychological Association.

STERNBERG, R. (1993). *The Psychologist's Companion: A Guide to Scientific Writing for Students and Researchers*, 3rd edn. Cambridge: Cambridge University Press.

Style Guide: Information and Advice to Authors (1989) Leicester: The British Psychological Society.

FURTHER READING

Journals in Psychology: A resource listing for authors (1993). American Psychological Association, c/o Eurospan, 3 Henrietta Street, Covent Garden, London WC2E 8LU, UK.

4.1.2 EDITING A JOURNAL

Michele Benjamin

The role and duties of a journal editor depend on the type of journal concerned and the organizational environment within which it operates. Some journals are owned and published by learned societies, some are owned by societies and published commercially, still others are wholly owned by a commercial publisher who may have special purchasing arrangements with members of certain societies. Agreements between societies and commercial publishers are usually subject to contractual arrangements and expert advice should be sought before entering into any such arrangement.

WHAT CONSTITUTES A JOURNAL?

Defining what constitutes a journal is also not straightforward. In terms of *content* there are periodicals of record which publish abstracts and papers previously presented at meetings; others carry news, reviews and events listings; some carry only original work which may be empirical, conceptual or theoretical; others encourage literature reviews and current awareness updates; and some combine one or more of these categories. In terms of *market*, some are directed only at members, others address purely professional concerns, some are parochial, others are international in appeal. In organizational terms, some may be edited by a staff (in-house) editor, others by an external paid or honorary editor; some may be peer reviewed, others vetted by and sometimes written by the editor alone; copy may be unsolicited or commissioned; produced in-house or by outside contractors. The number of possible permutations is enormous and all of them may legitimately be called 'journals' as long as they appear periodically. Within this wealth of possibilities, any definition of a 'journal' or a 'newsletter' draws arbitrary boundaries.

BPS Journals

For organizational purposes, the Society has defined a journal as a periodical publishing peer-reviewed original research of interest to the international community of psychologists. Each journal has an honorary editor elected by and from the membership for a period not exceeding six years. Editors meet together as the Journals Committee, a standing committee of Council. The Journals Committee discusses, formulates and makes recommendations to Council on publishing policy and to the Finance and General Purposes Standing Committee (F&GPSC) on budgets and finance. Thus, although the possible role of an editor can be as varied as the possible types of journal, the role described hereafter is that of an editor of one of the Society's learned journals as has been defined.

EDITORS

Editors are seen as captains of the Society's scientific flagships. They are entirely responsible for the content of their journal and this involves judgements about the suitability and acceptability of papers published, the balance of content and the development of editorial aims and objectives. Since the subject matter of a journal tends to be too broad for the detailed expertise of any individual, editors usually find it useful and necessary to appoint a team of associates to help in the decision-making process and to keep in touch with the various specialist subfields covered by the journal. The exact nature and number of the editorial team varies from journal to journal and is one of the early decisions facing a new editor. In general terms, the broader the area covered by the journal, the larger the number of associates required but other qualitative and quantitative factors influence the decision. The names of the team, once published in the journal masthead statement, should give a clear indication of the areas in which the journal hopes to attract submissions. Defining the editorial aims and objectives of the journal and making them clear to potential authors and readers is an important part of the editorial role.

SELECTING PAPERS FOR PUBLICATION

The mechanism used to select papers for publication in Society journals is that of *peer review*: submissions are read by at least two experts in the field and the editor or associate makes a publishing decision based on their reports. Peer review is not without its critics and cannot be held to be entirely objective. However, to date it is seen as the best available method of selecting those papers which are worth publishing from the deluge submitted to journals. It can be argued that selection is unnecessary and unreasonable and that a universal database would be preferable but, under the current structure of journal publishing, any individual publisher still works within resource constraints that make selection a necessity. The Journals Committee issues a summary of journal operations, published annually in *The Psychologist*, which reveals that journals publish only a fraction of the papers submitted (the median rejection rate was 68 per cent in the 1993 summary).

Peer review

The principle of peer review is that the editor or associate editor solicits reports from two or more experts in the field. A list of referees is built up from various sources including the editor's and associate editors' networks of colleagues and co-workers, authors, referees used previously by the editorial teams, self-selected volunteers and authors cited in the references of the paper concerned. The detailed guidelines for referees depends on the journal and editorial policy but referees are typically asked to comment on the submission in terms of:

- clarity of expression;
- economy of exposition;
- methodological adequacy;
- theoretical importance; and
- contribution to knowledge.

Specialist questions about professional and methodological issues may be added as appropriate. Referee names are not usually revealed to the author, although referees are given the option of signing their reports if they wish. Society practice is to send referee reports to authors and also to send each referee the comments from the other referee(s). Thus the refereeing process is intended to be instructional for all those involved.

Few papers are accepted immediately. Revision is requested in line with referees' comments and, depending on the degree of revision demanded – which may be anything from checking minor infelicities of phrasing to reworking the experimental design and collecting more data – the author will have to decide whether to revise and resubmit, try a different journal or accept the work as flawed.

Referees may return conflicting reports on the submission in which case the editor may seek the advice of further referees or exercise a casting vote.

Papers submitted to Society journals are reviewed blind; that is, authors' names are removed from the title page of the article. The intention is that the refereeing process is not influenced by authors' established reputations or that of their affiliated institution; that is, a fresh new researcher is treated the same as an *éminence grise*. Authors are asked to take note of this in the guidelines, but those who identify figures by author name, give fulsome thanks to colleagues at the same place of work or make more citations of their own previous work than anyone else's in the reference list leave abundant clues to authorship scattered round the paper.

FINANCIAL AND HUMAN RESOURCE CONSTRAINTS

Running a journal involves juggling with a number of different factors. Since the majority of papers are unsolicited, the flow of copy into the Journals Office is beyond editorial control, although one aim of marketing is to raise the journal profile within the community of possible authors. Considerations of accuracy, appropriateness, substantive contribution to the subject and interest to the readership are paramount but these operate within the financial and human resource constraints of the budget. Budgets are agreed between the Journals Committee and F&GPSC and specify, amongst other things, the number of pages the journal can publish in the year. Once decided, the budget needs to be defended from the often conflicting pressure of numbers of acceptable papers and desirability of a limited and relatively short publication lag. The Society's Journals Office works closely with editors in trying to maintain the balance between these factors while also meeting strict print, production and distribution schedules designed to optimize the service provided to readers and libraries.

Marketing

Within the Society, the Journals Office is also responsible for administering the peer-review process and for marketing, and editors are encouraged to visit and maintain regular contact with office personnel. Editors are also encouraged to take an active interest in marketing. From their position at the centre of the active research community, they have opportunities to encourage potential authors and readers of the journal, and their words carry far more credibility than even the smoothest publicity material. They are also in touch with new research developments affecting the direction of existing journals and sometimes leading to the establishment of new titles.

THE FUTURE

Encouraging and selecting the best possible material may be the foremost concern of the editor but the role imposes other difficult demands. In the modern world, journals are used as a measure of research productivity; staff selection and promotion may depend on the citation impact factor of articles published in the Society's journals and editorial decisions have wider implications than the mere fact of publication. Ethical considerations such as subject treatment and client confidentiality need to be taken into account and editors need to be aware of social and political sensitivities in the use, for instance, of non-sexist or non-racist language. The pressure to publish which generates multiple papers each containing the minimum necessary contribution to knowledge (so-called 'salami' publishing), multiple submission, plagiarism, duplicate publication and libel are all matters of concern, and the journal editor may need to refer sensitive material to 'experts' beyond the normal referees. More research workers are producing more papers, demanding larger and more journal issues than ever before, and yet library funding is being continually cut back. Technological developments are leading to computerized library networks, lower journal subscriptions and a call for on-demand document delivery in place of the conventional journal package. The whole system of scientific information is in a state of upheaval, and journal editors and publishers are in key positions to contribute to discussion and future developments.

4.1.3 FINDING A BOOK PUBLISHER

Susan Pacitti

The most important part of finding a publisher is targeting your manuscript appropriately. Looking along the appropriate subject shelves in your local bookshop or library will give you an idea of who publishes what. There is no point in approaching a purely academic publisher if you want to write a trade title (i.e. one with wide bookshop sales potential), and vice-versa. It is also worth asking around your published colleagues, and you can gain useful insights from their experiences of working with different publishers. Also think about books which you thought were well-produced, and who published those. Once you have come up with a list of possible publishers, their catalogues will give you an idea of whether your book might fit into their publishing programme (see also Section 5.3 on publishers of psychology books and journals). Other useful information to be found in publishers' catalogues will be the list of their overseas representation, which will give you an idea of how widely your book might be marketed by that particular publisher. There are several reference books available (see *Further Reading* section) which list publishers and their interests, and often list the managing or acquisition editor's name. As with job applications, it is always useful to be able to write to a named individual. If you do not have a named individual to write to, address your proposal to the editor in your subject area, e.g. 'Psychology Editor'.

SUBMITTING A PROPOSAL

Once you have drawn up a list of suitable publishers you should draft your proposal (see p. 211). Publishers will often ask to see a sample chapter, especially if you are a new author, so it is wise to have thought through the book thoroughly, for example, writing a contents page, thinking about the market and whether there are any competitors in this area, approaching a co-author or contributors if appropriate. After all, this is your book, and although the publisher will provide you with editorial help for structure and other issues, they will not expect to write the book for you. While you can submit your book proposal to more than one publisher at a time, unlike journal submissions, it is best to let publishers know you are doing so. Particularly if you are writing in a specialist area, the publisher may want to send the manuscript out for an expert opinion, and this will cost them money. Phoning first to sound out an idea with the commissioning editor is also a good idea, as they will be able to give you an idea of whether or not your proposal is suitable for their list.

If the publisher is seriously interested in your proposal, they may well wish to send it out to specialist referees, depending on the subject matter, and it may also go to an editorial board meeting. This can mean that it is quite some time before you hear whether or not your book has been accepted for publication.

Rejection letters

Publishers receive many unsolicited proposals, so don't be discouraged if you receive a rejection letter. It does not mean that your book is unpublishable. The subject may not have been right for that particular publisher's list, it may be too similar to another title they publish, or perhaps their list is full for the next year. Usually you will receive some indication in the rejection letter, with perhaps some useful suggestions as to who else you might approach.

Style

Every publisher will have their own house-style; this will cover such things as whether they prefer 'ise' or 'ize' spellings, and their style of references. A copy of the publisher's style guide can be obtained from them, or will in any case be sent out with the contract for the book once accepted.

A word of warning. Very, very few manuscripts require little editing, and although you will have done a lot of work on the manuscript before submitting it, it is very likely that it will come back to you covered in the editor's red pen. This might be disheartening, but the editor is as anxious as you are that this should be the best book in the field, and is only trying to help you to achieve that end. In fact, you may end up speaking to your editor more often than to members of your family during the course of the writing of the book!

There is no doubt that finding a publisher you enjoy working with and whom you can trust is a vital part of the process. Thus it is worth carrying out some market research and asking around for opinions and suggestions.

FURTHER READING

An Author's Guide to Publishing. Michael Legat. London: Robert Hale.

Blackwell Guide for Authors (1991). Oxford: Blackwell.

Getting Your Book Published, Christine S. Smedley et al. London: Sage. (Vol. 10 in the *Survival Skills for Scholars* Series).

International Literary Market Place (annual). New Jersey, R.R. Bowker and Co.

Literary Market Place: The Directory of American Book Publishing (annual). New Jersey: R.R. Bowker and Co.

The Oxford Dictionary for Writers and Editors (1981). Oxford: Oxford University Press.

Publishing Agreements, 4th edn. (1993). Charles Clark. London: Butterworth.

UK Publishers Directory. Edited by Ellen Rocco. London: Gale Research International.

Understanding Publishers' Contracts. Michael Legat. London: Robert Hale.

Writers' and Artists' Yearbook (annual). London: A&C Black.

The Writer's Handbook (annual). Basingstoke: Macmillan/ PEN.

4.1.4   BOOK AND SERIES EDITING

Anthony Gale

An apologia   I have edited or co-edited about two dozen books with different publishers. They include highly specialist texts, readings for undergraduates, books which were part of a series, and user-friendly texts for the general public. On occasion, a colleague has thought up an outline proposal and asked me to collaborate; sometimes the inspiration has been mine alone. Some projects have been initiated by publishers, who have approached me to act as editor.

Reflection on the process of editing brings about a mix of feelings from sheer cold sweat to brief glimpses of joy. I have learned to write tactful letters, to facilitate, to act tough, to make repeated and unproductive phonecalls and to wheedle. Getting a group of people to work together effectively is never easy. As a delinquent writer myself, addicted to accepting invitations to contribute to edited works, I have sympathy both for authors and for editors. This article is a very personal view of book and series editing.

THE PRODUCT RANGE

Academic publishers often produce multiple-author books on specialist topics, edited by an established authority in the field. These can be high level handbooks with state of the art accounts of an area of research, scholarship or professional application, published as free-standing single titles, or as a series of volumes, covering different aspects of the specialism, with one general editor and a series of volume editors. Lower level texts, aimed at a student population, may also appear in this format, again either in single volumes with several authors, or, more typically, a series of single author specialist texts, under the general editorship of an individual or of an editorial board.

There are also series designed for a popular audience – for the intelligent layperson or particular target groups, such as parents, carers of the elderly or potential consumers of psychological services. More popular books or 'trade' titles have an increased likelihood of being taken into stock in bookshops.

WHAT DO PUBLISHERS WANT?

Most psychology publishers prefer single author books, aimed at a student population, which are likely to become established standard or recommended texts. Publishers have very precise knowledge of the costs of production, distribution and other outgoings, and work from financially sound spreadsheets. They also know how many sales of an individual book are needed, not only to recoup the original costs and make a modest profit, but to enter a zone of maximum profit, where additional print-runs can be produced at a marginal cost. They also have a pretty shrewd idea of which existing books and authors are selling well, how their competitors are operating, and whom to approach within the psychological community for good advice. There is a considerable amount of professional know-how among the population of publishers serving the psychological community.

Obviously, publishers are looking for winners. Advanced texts, which by definition are specialist, are unlikely to attract a large audience. At best, they may be seen as so authoritative that they attract the attention of people responsible for purchasing stock for academic libraries. There may be only a few hundred people across the world who would use them in their daily work or refer to them on a regular basis for research or advanced teaching. This is likely to be true of particularly advanced texts. Since specialized volumes on, for example, observational methodology, or ambulatory psychophysiology can be rather weighty and might include costly illustrative material, their price is likely to be set very high, a factor which in turn, will limit sales and would certainly put them out of the reach of undergraduates, students following postgraduate instructional courses, or postgraduate researchers.

In contrast, a text on human development or on abnormal psychology, likely to be recommended for basic courses as part of an honours psychology degree, or for psychology courses taught to professional groups such as nurses or teachers, will be designed from the outset to capture a substantial market and ensure regular annual repeat orders from bookshops. Large annual sales will enable the book to be a regular and predictable source of income, perhaps cross-subsidizing more adventurous publishing ventures. Setting the price is important; high sales can make even a relatively low priced book cost effective and profitable.

It is important to recognize that publishing is a business. At the same time, however, many publishers have a strong sense of responsibility to produce monographs and other texts which help to advance the discipline. They know that the academic community will either respect or criticize their contribution. In recent years, this role of helping to advance the discipline has been satisfied in part by the production of specialist journals, which again have potential for library sales (see Section 4.1.2). Clearly, it would be beneficial to make financial gain from the production of good quality work.

The full impact of electronic publishing and the prospect of the electronic campus have yet to be assessed. Enthusiasts suggest that within ten years students will do much of their work from their home base, linked by computer to worldwide, multi-media information sources. Academics are already enjoying the benefits of a handful of electronic journals; they can submit articles which are refereed quickly, and can keep in touch with developments in their field in a way which may make the paper book or periodical seem redundant. Publishers are faced with both challenge and opportunity. Electronic publishing has other implications for academic editing, but much of the content of this article will still be relevant.

DECIDING WHETHER OR NOT TO EDIT

The potential volume or series editor should bear these points in mind when preparing a publishing proposal or when being invited to edit. Discussing a proposal with a publisher is likely to be a tough experience, not unlike raising a loan from a banker. Essentially one is offering a business plan in terms of potential audience, relevance to particular research developments, practitioner or curriculum demands, timeliness, and existing competition. The editor does not need to know about or discuss the financial aspects beyond having a sensible awareness of the financial costs of their proposal, for example, the cost of full colour illustrations or gold embossed lettering on the spine. But economics will be an important factor in the mind of the publisher and in part will be an essential element of the brief given to up to half a dozen independent reviewers asked to judge the worth of the proposal. It follows that reading the views of reviewers, normally anonymous, and receiving a letter of rejection from the publisher, can be quite a demoralizing experience. Hard questions are asked, and direct answers are expected. Enthusiasm and commitment need to be complemented by harsh reality.

The career and reputation of the editor should also be born in mind. A book which is known by the editor's name and which is well respected in the appropriate academic community will enrich the individual's reputation. However, the full effort required to produce a good quality volume, or to ensure that a full series is of appropriate standard is considerable. Individuals should therefore ask themselves whether the production of six good quality papers in high quality scientific or professional journals is of more value in terms of standing and career. The present funding of higher education institutions is specifically geared to achievement in scholarship and research; in psychology, the mode of publication most respected at present is the journal article. Again, issues of practical concern have an impact on decisions to publish.

Conference proceedings

Academics can be quite disheartened when a publisher informs them that the proceedings of a recent conference are unlikely to be accepted, even in camera ready format. Published conference proceedings are notorious for their unevenness of content and purpose, and are unlikely to attract support unless the editor is willing to ask authors to edit and rewrite their contributions and to invite additional contributors as well as applying a veto to some of the original list. Some publishers might be willing to agree in advance to a conference publication and even to support some of the conference costs, but, unless the authors are particularly distinguished and well-known, or the focus of the conference is a matter of burning concern, a commitment in advance of the event is unlikely.

HOW TO BEGIN

A series or single title proposal needs to be worked on for some time before it is ready to be shown to others. It should include a number of essential elements (see also the *Appendix* to this chapter).

- A *background introduction* will explain the purpose of the volume or volumes, the proposed content, and the significance or timeliness of the material.

- The editor should then provide a brief *curriculum vitae* which demonstrates personal expertise, standing and competence in the field in question, together with *a list of articles and books already published*.

- There will then follow a series of headings, including: *names of authors, target audiences* and *likely sales, appropriate curriculum demands or professional need*, an *analysis of the quality of competing texts, proposed number of volumes or chapters, proposed length,* and *expected date/s of publication*. The more information provided the better, although a proposal would not normally exceed three pages of single space type.

- A good quality proposal will include a *synopsis of content* and/or *chapter headings*, together with a *proposed layout, common format*, or *thematic structure*.

Preparation of a proposal demands more than effective creative writing. First, it is better to get potential editors, authors or contributors on board before submitting the proposal. Publishers will wish to see an authoritative list of authors and in the case of a high level text, they will need to be among the best people in the world, reflecting key potential markets and North America in particular. A proposal for an edited book which includes a set of top class experts and which covers countries associated with high achievement in psychology is likely to have good appeal and ensure sales outwith the UK. One should not include an individual's name without approaching them first. Indeed such people might be likely referees for the proposal and could regard either their inclusion without notification or their apparent absence, as discourteous and a sign of the proposer's lack of integrity!

Analysis of existing competing texts and their impact should demonstrate the authority and understanding of the editor. Knowing the competition in intimate detail is a measure of one's own general knowledge and competence in the field.

Understanding of page allocations, likely overall length and proposals for appropriate formats or themes is part of the professionalism of book editing and will again command the publisher's interest. However, such proposals need to be justified in a convincing way. Edited volumes are best confined within 250 or 300 pages, while handbooks tend to be longer. Texts designed for students must also work within reasonable operational limits. A schedule for obtaining draft manuscripts from authors, editing and preparing for delivery to the publishers should reflect practical reality. Authors typically take between six months and two years to produce text in draft even when they are authorities in the field and have information at their finger tips. The higher their standing (and therefore attractiveness as a potential contributor) the more commitments they are likely to have.

There is a chicken and egg problem here. Many publishers act as facilitators, both seeking the views of potential authors on proposals and seeking to encourage them to publish. They might be willing to engage in discussion at a preliminary stage, before you have secured promises of co-operation from others. It is possible that when you start writing to potential contributors, you may already have been given some initial undertaking on the publisher's part to proceed. But no publisher will commit themselves to a contract without having a full sense of what will be delivered to them. Indeed, if you already have a commitment from distinguished authorities that will demonstrate that you have their confidence and collegial support and will be able to coax them into producing their contributions on time and in good order, this will stand you in good stead.

Some major series are agreed as a package from the outset. Others develop over time, taking several years to emerge in full. If the first volumes in the series have received positive reviews, the publisher will be more receptive to proposals for further volumes and, given the reputation which the series has acquired, more willing to take risks with previously untested authors, who may need more encouragement and support. The ability of the series editor to coax good quality work from colleagues is likely to affect the publisher's approach to any subsequent proposals.

An editor proposing a series also becomes a sort of commissioning editor. For example, meetings with individual volume editors or authors are essential, to ensure that there is a full understanding of the scope and limits of their volume, and to gain a full sense of confidence in their capacity to produce what has been agreed, and on time.

The contract

Individual contracts will need to be prepared for all contributors. These are formal legal documents which set out the obligations of both the publisher and the author, including the agreed royalty terms. Royalties are typically related to net sales. Publishers usually offer differential royalty rates for different levels of sales and for overseas sales or translation rights. A series editor will receive a variety of payments, which might include an advance to cover essential costs, a payment on delivery of manuscript, a payment on publication, and a percentage related to subsequent sales. A substantial advance is rare for edited volumes or series but not unusual for single-author volumes. An editor might well gain from the prestige and reputation of the volume or series, but should not expect to enjoy a significant financial benefit. Royalties are likely to be modest, although academic writing and editing is recognized as qualifying for tax relief under Schedule D and costs incurred in the home can be offset against gains. Thus, to summarize, the financial benefit is in terms of royalties together with the opportunity to offset allowances for domestic costs such as heating, lighting and telephone.

Before signing a contract an editor is well advised to consult knowledgeable others, including their trades union or professional association handbook. However, royalty rates do not differ significantly among publishers. More important is a clear agreement from the outset about the likely cost of individual volumes and the sort of marketing activities and associated budget to which the publisher is committed. Such matters can be discussed informally, but then become hidden by the mists of time which can lead to misunderstandings and resentment. Having everything written down and ageed can help to avoid this. After all, it can be at least two years between initial contract and subsequent publication.

A good publisher will keep an eye on the venture as it evolves and will wish to receive regular progress reports on the development of individual projects, including any problems or delays which arise.

COMMUNICATING WITH YOUR EDITORS AND AUTHORS

It is important to set up a communication network to ensure you can actually get hold of your authors. Among academics e-mail communication is common and particularly useful if you need to communicate with authors who are overseas. An efficient editor will write to all contributors, ensuring that they have the names, addresses, fax or e-mail numbers of all colleagues within the writing team. He or she will make absolutely clear all the formal requirements of the project including maximum length, section headings, fonts and disk formats, layout for the bibliography, location of page numbers, authors' names, authors' affiliations and so on. For layout, it is sensible to produce a sample page, so that there can be no ambiguity about the requirements. The page editing of bibliographies and references is very time consuming and demanding; therefore, if they are all in the same format and have the same required layout, weeks of unnecessary work can be avoided. Most publishers provide their own author's guide, which sets out their requirements for layout and style.

Such precise specification of important details is essential at the outset, For example, if chapters of an edited volume are to be 8,000 words in length and to include a maximum of 50 references only, this must be spelt out clearly. It is very hard to cut down a contribution which is twice the contracted length or which does not conform to the agreed format. Bear in mind the fact that manuscripts typically come in late and near to the date for delivery, so that major changes are hard and painful to implement and can lead to unpleasant international and uncollegial exchanges. Author failure to abide by agreed guidelines is a major source of anxiety and stress for editors.

It is very important to communicate with authors during the period in which the work is being prepared. It is likely that authors will treat the delivery date as something happening well in the future and so assign the project low or delayed priority. Personal contact and encouragement are essential. There must be very few edited books or series where the participants have delivered their work on time. Those who are efficient and live up to expectations can be very aggrieved if publication of their work is delayed through the apparent indolence or incompetence of the editor or other authors. Thus the impact of late delivery by even a handful of contributors can be extensive and disruptive of otherwise good personal relationships.

RECEIVING THE MANUSCRIPT

Manuscripts need to go to the publisher in a well-organized and legible condition. Usually three copies will be required together with the preliminary pages (prelims) and subject and author indexes. Authors will have been asked to provide four copies (one being retained by the editor), clearly typed and in accordance with instructions. Some publishers now ask for a hard copy together with disks. You should ensure that you have read through all disks provided by authors, that the disks are in the required format, and that you send the publisher the final agreed version and not an earlier draft. You will need to include formal copyright permissions where authors have used previously published figures or illustrations; it is usually the responsibility of the individual author to obtain such permissions in advance of including the work in question.

Indexing usually takes place at the proofreading stage; however, it is helpful to ask authors to prepare either on disk or on cards, index information which can subsequently be incorporated into an overall index. In most edited volumes, bibliographies appear immediately after each contribution; however, some publishers and editors prefer to gather all references at the end of the volume.

With an edited volume consisting of, say, twelve contributions, the following outcomes are likely. Three authors will produce superbly professional chapters before or on time and virtually exactly conforming to the requirements which you specified a year or so earlier. Six of the chapters will be competent, moderately late, and requiring a reasonable amount of editing and revision. The remaining three will cause headaches. Among the usual sources of difficulty are: late delivery, overlengthy manuscripts, dense and unclear writing, failure to follow agreed thematic structure or required format, defective bibliography with missing or inconsistent listings, and worst of all, failure to include important and substantial content.

One problem which can occur with distinguished people is that they farm out their chapter to a young colleague, or submit their work under two names, when in fact the junior person has been the sole author. The junior colleague might be quite inexperienced and the original author unwilling to do necessary re-writing before sending the manuscript to you. Distinguished people can even let you down by failing to produce anything. You then have to secure a competent and respected replacement in a hurry.

When the full manuscript is complete its preliminary pages will include the list of contents, a list of authors and their affiliations, the foreword, and in a series, a brief statement by the series editor. Where there are several volumes in the series, each volume will list the remaining titles and their editors and their date of publication. A publication which is part of a set might also include the list of contents of all volumes within each volume.

THE PROOFS

Most publishers will wish to send the manuscript out to specialist independent readers prior to page editing and printing. This will certainly happen if the final manuscript deviates in a substantial way from the specification set out in the contract. But if the manuscript is in good order and consistent with the original agreements, it will go to the publisher's production department. Typically the individual responsible for production will then make contact with you and inform you of the schedule for production. They will wish to be sure that you will be available to do your work on the proofs when they arrive and that the authors will also be available. During page editing you may be contacted by the production person to check on any queries or ambiguities.

Proofs of individual contributions will be sent directly to authors together with any instructions (for example, for the preparation of index material) which you have agreed with the production manager. There will be a short turnaround period and the authors will return their corrected proofs to you. You will need to set aside at least a week for proofreading. IIt can take at least a half-day to check through the proofs of one chapter and incorporate the changes which the author has indicated on their copy. Again, the more you can do to anticipate problems, the easier the task. You are unlikely to pick up all typographical errors at one reading and are well advised to read everything carefully at least twice. Authors will have been informed that major changes at this stage are costly; some publishers may require them to contribute to the cost of *substantial* changes. When authors fail to send their amended proofs you will need to carry out the work yourself. However, it is essential for an editor to proofread all the material with great care, even when authors have been required to proofread their own contributions.

Series editors will also receive copies of all proofs of the volumes in the series; the extent to which they become involved in detailed proofreading at this stage will depend upon their own confidence in the individual volume editor or author. The publishers will also have arranged for an in-house or freelance proofreader to check the proofs; so, between you, you should catch all errors or changes.

CONCLUSION

While preparation of a sole author text has its difficulties, the positive delights of editing can be exaggerated. Essentially, editing is not just a scholarly task but a challenge to person management, relentless persistence and diplomacy. It you are not super-efficient and resilient or in contrast callous and insensitive to the reactions of others, you should think twice before engaging in a major editing project. It is very much like hiring a builder to work at your home. You think you have agreed about what is to be done. You think that everyone understands how long the job will take. But you rarely receive what you expect and time proves to be elastic. Where builders typically manage to double the price of the work before it is finished, fellow authors manage to double your expected effort and time allocation for the task. Just as builders can leave you in the lurch, so authors can find that personal circumstances, change of job, or pressure from demands of higher priority, can induce a cavalier attitude and indifference to the feelings of the editor.

However, it is a considerable pleasure to receive the first copy of the work, to show it to colleagues and close friends, and to place it on your shelf or refer to it in reading lists and lectures. Seeing the book or series displayed on the publisher's stand at a conference is also a source of positive reinforcement. Publishers can become friends as well as business associates. Reviews of the work can be positive and rewarding, convincing you of your personal worth and, if all has gone well there will be no sudden rush of anxiety when opening a book and discovering an error which should have been seen before it was too late.

To return to the start of this contribution. Practicalities are an essential element in editing a series. The preparation of a proposal and its translation into a final product is something of an assault course. Any colleague considering a venture of this sort should appreciate that like everything involving other human beings, publishing is a complex and dynamic experience, involving both positive and negative affect. It is difficult to believe that anyone who has edited a volume or series has not experienced personal growth through successfully coping with adversity.

Appendix: Writing the outline proposal for a book

Joyce Collins

In making a publishing proposal the author must consider the reasons for writing the book and also for buying and reading it. A proposal should consist of three parts:

(a) an accurate and DETAILED DESCRIPTION of the book as envisaged by the author, including contents, format and style;

(b) details of the author's QUALIFICATIONS and eminent suitability for writing the book (in the form of an up-to-date c.v.), accompanied in most cases by sample writing;

(c) a description of the main READERSHIP and the MARKET for the book.

The following check-lists may help authors in writing a proposal. Do not worry if you cannot answer all of these questions.

Description of the book
Proposed date of submission
Provisional title

Detailed contents, giving chapter headings and main sub-headings, and chapter summaries if possible

Approximate price and length of the book (an average-sized paperback contains c.400 words per printed page)

Level of writing: e.g. research monograph / essential text-book / supplementary reading / general interest / self-help / reference

Level of detail of references

Bibliography

Illustrations

Index

Author's qualifications
Previous publications

Experience of the area

Experience of writing for this kind of audience at this level

For edited books, please include details of possible contributors

Readership
Main readership group(s): please specify in detail and, if possible, give numbers

The book's market
Reasons for writing the book: e.g. Is there a gap in the market?

What other similar books are there? Are they in or out of print?

What makes this book different or unique?

What are the book's main geographic markets? UK only? UK and old Commonwealth? The English-speaking world?

Are potential sales mainly through general bookshops / academic bookshops / direct mail to specialist groups?

4.2   CONFERENCES AND WORKSHOPS

4.2.1   GUIDELINES ON ORGANIZING A CONFERENCE

Paul Jackson

*T*HE *following notes should be used as guidelines only and are no substitute for enlisting professional help either from an agency or from your own professional body.*

Organizing a conference is one of those experiences where the contingencies are upside down: if things go well, no one will notice all the work that you did to make it look effortless; if things go badly, you will be very visible. All the same, taking on the task will be rewarding.

Two key pieces of advice are:

Plan in advance. Planning is more fundamental than anything else, and the best way to do this is to work backwards from the date of the event. Most of the following points need to be addressed before the conference itself: **there is no substitute for forward planning;**

Know your audience. Will their conference fees be paid out of their own salary or are their employers paying? Are the delegates academics who cannot escape lecturing commitments during term time? You need to know the answers to these, and many more questions, in order to provide for their needs.

BUDGET

When deciding on your budget please seek advice about VAT, either from your local tax office or, if applicable, from your professional body. **If your professional body is VAT registered you need to charge your delegates VAT.** In addition don't forget to get adequate public liability insurance for your event and add the cost to your budget.

Keynote speakers

You may want some invited speakers, perhaps to give a keynote address or a commentary on the conference as a whole (you will need to decide whether to pay them or not). Invited speakers should be well known to the potential audience and be able communicators. You may find that good speakers are booked years in advance and come rather expensive (take this into account when you are planning your budget). However, invited speakers can be a big draw for delegates and if they accept your invitation early enough you can put their name on the call for submissions to help attract good quality submissions.

CALL FOR SUBMISSIONS

The call for submissions (in *The Psychologist* or other appropriate publication) is probably your first announcement that the conference is taking place. You should include details such as dates, venue, invited speakers and the form you require the submission in, e.g. symposia, papers, workshops, posters and video presentations. Also give details of where submissions should be sent and the date by which they should arrive. You may also want to advise where guidelines for submissions can be obtained (see following).

Review procedure

For presenters, giving a paper may be the only reason that they are able to obtain funding to attend a conference. However, this does not absolve you of the responsibility to ensure that they have something to say and know how to say it in such a way that they can be understood. It is therefore a good idea to produce guidelines asking for standard information to allow intelligent decisions to be made about the content of the programme. For empirical papers, you may want to ask potential speakers to indicate the context and aims of their study; the nature of the methodology (e.g. sample, procedure, etc.); an indication of the statistical analysis; the results obtained and their implications. For theoretical and review papers you may want to ask for an indication of the problems addressed by the paper; the empirical/historical context; the range of evidence/theories considered and the conclusion drawn.

Decisions that need to be made on the review process are:

- who will review;
- whether to have blind reviewing (this avoids the embarrassment of rejecting peers' work); and
- whether to provide information about why papers were rejected.

In general:

- beware of papers describing the design of a really exciting project (make them come back when they have results – designs are never as exciting as results);
- beware of an abstract that goes into a lot of detail on what was done and then says nothing about what was found (the chances are that the author hasn't analysed the results yet, so there may be nothing worth saying in the end);
- remember that famous names may not be good presenters (although on the other hand you may get delegates coming along to see the famous names in the flesh).

As a conference organizer, you also need to decide whether to reject or accept symposia as a whole or whether you are prepared to accept certain parts only.

Organizing the chairing of sessions

The overriding responsibility of a Chair is to see that speakers keep to time; your event will run far smoother with people to chair the sessions. Guidelines for chairing sessions are a good idea to make sure everybody is working towards the same goal.

PROVISIONAL PROGRAMME

The programme that you send to potential delegates is a good opportunity to sell the event. Try to get your presenters to give their papers titles that are informative, accurate and interesting.

A small event will probably offer no parallel sessions, while a larger event will offer choice. If you have parallel sessions then you must try to:

- arrange the programme so that related papers appear in the same session;
- ensure that papers which appear in parallel are not aimed at the same audience (many people will want to be at both);
- make sure the delegates are spread between sessions –

you don't want all your delegates crowded into one room
with no one listening to the poor souls presenting in the
other rooms;
- gauge the size of potential audiences so that you can
  make the best use of rooms of different sizes. Also know
  what audiovisual requirements your speakers have, so
  that the appropriate equipment can be set up, or the
  appropriate room used.

If you print a final programme which contains major differences from the provisional programme (e.g. changes of
speakers or *especially* of time slots), you must make delegates aware of these changes **before** the conference. This
will prevent delegates turning up to find a speaker other
than the one they expected or at the time (now changed)
that was given in the provisional programme. It is important to remember that some delegates may have chosen to
attend on a particular day because of a specific paper being
given.

Themes

Organizing a symposium with related papers around a
common theme can be very valuable. However, these need
special care in deciding how many slots they should
occupy, how to arrange questions and discussions, and co-
ordination of material across papers. In timetabling a symposium, be aware that some people will only want to hear
part of it, so there needs to be some synchrony between the
duration of papers in a symposium and individual papers
in other sessions. This will allow people to move in and out
of presentations of interest.

Attention spans are short, therefore sessions need to be
varied and interesting with a mixture of workshops, videos
and poster presentations as well as straightforward talks.
Bear in mind the 'graveyard slots' – after lunch and the last
session of the day. No one should be expected to concentrate for very long without the opportunity to move
around. Therefore, your timetable needs to allow for
people to move between papers if they wish; refreshments,
cloakrooms etc. should be located so that people can use
the facilities conveniently (and without getting wet!).

TIMING

Timing of a meeting is clearly important and there is a
strong case for knowing your audience. Major BPS conferences tend to take place during academic vacations, avoid-
ing the height of the summer holidays in July and August.
If you expect delegates from among staff or students then

follow this lead. For some groups weekends are your only choice because delegates will not be able to justify time off work to attend. London may be a better choice as a venue during the week, although often hotels aimed at the business market will offer good rates at the weekend in order to fill their rooms. The opposite may apply somewhere like the Lake District where such a venue may be better on a weekend but the rates may be cheaper in the week when the hotel is not full of holiday makers. Travelling by rail may be difficult on a Sunday and expensive on a Friday. With press coverage in mind, you may not get good coverage on a Sunday (see Section 4.3 on the media).

VENUES

There are a number of ways to find a venue – word of mouth, working through *The Conference Green Book* or by using a venue-finding agency.

Booking and choosing the venue

Many venues need to be booked well in advance, so you need to decide very early where you want your event to take place. Where you stage your event may have a big impact on its success. In general people will not make awkward journeys unless they expect major benefits, so try to choose a location which is accessible with relative ease from most places by road and rail (remember that accessibility for car drivers includes easy, and cheap parking). Sometimes London is a good location, not because it is necessarily close to where delegates live, but because train journeys to London are often of better quality and cheaper than those to other locations. Despite the fact that delegates will only see a taxi, a meeting room and their sleeping accommodation, a picturesque location can be a draw.

Type of venue

What type of venue you choose will depend on many factors, such as number of delegates, number of parallel sessions, your budget and whether you have an exhibition as part of the conference. There is a wealth of venues to choose from – academic venues, hotels, conference centres and many pubs and church halls who like to describe their floor space as conference facilities. So do be warned, what is advertised as a conference venue may not be suitable for your requirements. For example, ceilings need to be high enough for slides, rooms should preferably have the entrance away from the speaker so any movement in the room during a talk will not disturb them. A mixture of room sizes is important for papers which may attract different-sized audiences. Before you make a final decision about a venue, visit it and see for yourself, especially if facilities are not all on a single site (several hotels may work together to offer the number of bedrooms you need; in this case, you need to know about parking at each of them and the hazards of travelling between them).

Other facilities

You may also want to check wheelchair access and crèche facilities. Having a crèche for delegates who wish to bring children may be a service you need to provide, but be well aware that the amount of work involved is probably greater than for any other special provision. Local authority regulations surrounding crèches are very exacting (ask the conference manager of the venue for details) in relation to facilities such as washrooms and play space, location (not on a higher floor from the conference delegates – you don't want parents to run towards a fire in order to rescue their children) and staffing (properly qualified people and low child:staff ratio).

Catering

This aspect of a conference can be very difficult to get right because it is so hard to please everybody. There is often a reluctance to pay a lot for meals and the aim is to provide catering that the delegates perceive as value for money. Don't forget to cater for vegetarians and other special diets – have a section on the registration form for delegates to indicate any dietary requirements.

AT THE CONFERENCE

Information to delegates

As an organizer, you need to be at the venue well in advance, preferably the day before if your meeting lasts more than one day. You will need to make sure that you know who is coming, that you have all the material they will want when they arrive – name badge, conference programme with any last minute changes, list of delegates so that they know who to look out for. Delegates will also ask you whether their friends have arrived yet, so make sure you have some means of recording each arrival.

Stewards

Students are often willing to act as stewards at a large event in exchange for subsidized attendance. They can help with directing delegates, signposting the venue, giving out conference packs and many other jobs which aid the smooth running of the conference.

Steward/Staff briefing

Do not be the only one who knows what is going on – there is bound to be a crisis seconds after you have been called to the phone. Recruit people to staff the registration desk, and make sure they know what they are doing.

Signposting

Of course you need to tell people where things are, and you are probably the worst person to decide where they should be, because you know your way round the venue by now. Get someone new to the venue to help with this – they will point out where the tricky parts of the route are. Make the signs big, so people can read them, but not too big. Although your delegates are intelligent, mature adult professionals, they will still get lost, so be prepared to find people in odd corners.

Hand-holding

If all goes well, your speakers will arrive relaxed and in plenty of time to look over their room and find everything that they need is in the right place. Rather more likely though ... someone will have slides but won't have told you; someone else will have forgotten to prepare OHP slides and won't have brought any blank acetates; yet another speaker will want the layout of the room changed and the extension lead won't reach the equipment.

Make friends with the venue support staff (they are paid to save your life), plan ahead for the unexpected, and offer a spare room for speakers to practise in, to preview slides or just to relax quietly in.

THE WIDER AUDIENCE

Many people who cannot attend the conference will still want to know what went on. The publication of proceedings is expensive and a lot of work, but might be worth considering if you can get a sponsor, if your presenters give a written text in time, and if the theme is precise enough to make the proceedings a likely seller. You should take press coverage seriously too; unless your meeting is private and by invitation only, the public at large have the right to hear what your presenters have to say. You can play your part in helping to sell psychology to the serious press (see Section 4.3 on the media). Increasingly, the press are treating psychology more seriously as psychologists treat journalists more seriously.

The following appendices give the schedule and requirements list for a past BPS Annual Conference. They will give some idea of the attention to detail that a conference entails.

REFERENCES

Conference Green Book: The Special Interest Guide to Conference Venues in the British Isles.
Conference Blue Book: The Technical Guide to Conference Venues in the British Isles.
Both volumes published by M-G Information Services Limited, Riverbank House, Angel Lane, Tonbridge, Kent TN9 1SE, U.K. Tel: 01732 362666.

Appendix 1: Example of a conference schedule
The British Psychological Society Annual Conference, 9–12 April 1992

Tuesday 7.4.92	*Delivery of conference packs by TNT.* Please store securely until Thursday.
Wednesday 8.4.92 10.30–18.30	*Scientific Affairs Board Meeting* (Regency Room). Room to be set boardroom style for 30. Water jug and glasses.
11.30	Coffee and biscuits for 30.
13.00	Sandwiches, fruit, cake, orange juice and coffee to be served for 30.
15.30	Tea and biscuits
Wednesday 8.4.92	BT to install phones in Foyer and Vita Dome.
Thursday 9.4.92 08.00	*Get-In Conference* Access required for get-in. This is a no smoking conference. 5 Rooms to be set theatre style. Please supply in each room water jug and glasses. Portable PA system to be available.

Grand Hall
To be set theatre style for 500 – using ground floor only.
To be equipped with:
OHP
35mm slide projector
Screen for front slide projection
Stage Set
Top table for 6 with one microphone, positioned stage right.
One standing lectern with microphone, positioned stage left.
Theatre
To be set theatre style for 400 using ground floor only.
To be equipped with:
OHP
35mm slide projector and screen.
Stage Set
Top table for 6 with one microphone positioned stage right.
One standing lectern with microphone positioned stage left.
Music Room
To be set theatre style for 100. Top table for 6. 35mm slide projector, screen and OHP to be installed.

13.00–14.00	*Sandwich Lunch* (Ocean Room) Charge to account. £2.85 per head including VAT. Numbers 120. Bar on a cash basis. Delegates will have tickets. BPS to collect.
14.00–15.30	*Conference Sessions* (Grand Hall, Theatre, Music Room, Regency 1 & 2)
15.30–16.00	*Tea*, coffee (and decaffeinated), fruit juice and biscuits for 350. (Ocean Room) Charge to account.
16.00–18.00	*Conference sessions* (Grand Hall, Theatre, Music Room, Regency 1 & 2)
17.00–18.00	*Psychobiology Section Meeting* (Promenade Lounge) Boardroom style for 12. No catering required.
17.00–1800	*Special Group of Teachers AGM* (Promenade Lounge) Boardroom style for 20. No catering required.
18.00–19.00	*Civic Reception*
19.30–21.30	*Public Lecture (Grand Hall)*

Friday 10.4.92

08.15	*Access* required to all rooms.
09.00–10.30	5 *Conference Sessions* (Grand Hall, Theatre, Music Room, Regency 1 & 2)
10.30–11.00	*Coffee* and (decaffeinated), tea, fruit juice and biscuits for 350. (Ocean Room) Charge to account.
11.00–13.00	*Conference Sessions* (Grand Hall, Theatre, Music Room, Regency 1 & 2)
13.00–14.00	*Sandwich Lunch* (Ocean Room) Charge to account. £2.85 per head including VAT.

	Numbers 150. Bar on a cash basis. Delegates will have tickets. BPS to collect.
13.00–14.00	*Sport Psychology Section Meeting* (Promenade Lounge) Informal layout for 10. Sandwiches and coffee required for 10.
13.00–14.00	*Psychology of Women Section Meeting* (The Fish Bowl) Boardroom style for 10. Vegetarian sandwiches, tea and coffee for 10.
13.00–16.00	*Cognitive Psychology Section Meeting* (Promenade Lounge) Boardroom style for 14. Sandwiches and coffee for 14 at 13.00.
14.00–16.30	*Occupational Psychology Section Meeting* (Promenade Lounge) Boardroom style for 10. Tea and biscuits for 10 at 15.00.
14.00–15.30	*Conference Sessions* (Grand Hall, Theatre, Music Room, Regency 1 & 2)
15.30–16.00	*Tea*, coffee (and decaffeinated), fruit juice and biscuits for 350. (Ocean Room) Charge to account
16.00–18.00	*Conference Sessions* (Grand Hall, Theatre, Music Room, Regency 1 & 2)
18.15–19.00	*AGM* – (Theatre)
19.00–20.00	*Division of Clinical Psychology AGM/Open Meeting* – (Music Room)

Saturday 11.4.92

08.15	*Access* required to all rooms.
09.00–10.30	*5 Conference Sessions* (Grand Hall, Theatre, Music Room, Regency 1 & 2)
10.30–11.00	*Coffee* and (decaffeinated), tea, fruit juice and biscuits for 350. (Ocean Room) Charge to account.
11.00–13.00	*Conference Sessions* (Grand Hall, Theatre, Music Room, Regency 1 & 2)
12.00–14.00	*Food, Health and Nutrition Working Party* (Promenade Lounge) Boardroom style for 5. Sandwiches, coffee and biscuits for 5 at 12.00.
13.00–14.00	*Sandwich Lunch* (Ocean Room) Charge to account. £2.85 per head including VAT. Numbers 150. Bar on a cash basis. Delegates will have tickets. BPS to collect.
14.00–15.30	*Conference Sessions* (Grand Hall, Theatre, Music Room, Regency 1 & 2)
14.00–16.00	*Social Psychology Section Meeting* (Promenade Lounge) Boardroom for 12. Tea, coffee and biscuits for 12 at 15.00.
15.30–16.00	*Tea*, coffee (and decaffeinated), fruit juice, and biscuits for 350. (Ocean Room) Charge to account.
16.00–18.00	*Conference Sessions* (Grand Hall, Theatre, Music Room, Regency 1 & 2)

18.00–19.00	*Open Meeting* (Theatre)

Sunday 12.4.92

08.15	*Access* required to all rooms.
09.00–10.30	*5 Conference Sessions* (Grand Hall, Theatre, Music Room, Regency 1 & 2)
10.30–11.00	*Coffee* and (decaffeinated) tea, fruit juice and biscuits for 350. (Ocean Room) Charge to account.
11.00–13.00	*Conference Sessions*
13.00–14.00	*Sandwich Lunch* (Ocean Room) Charge to account. £2.85 per head including VAT. Numbers 100. Bar on cash basis. Delegates will have tickets. BPS to collect.
14.00	END OF EVENT

Appendix II: Example of equipment requirements

Regency 1
To be set theatre style for 150. Top table for 6. 35mm slide projector, screen and OHP to be installed.

Regency 2
To be set theatre style for 70. Top table for 6. 35mm slide projector, screen and OHP to be installed.

Registration Get-In (Foyer)
6 Tables
6 Chairs
Telephone (BT)

Press Office (Vita Dome)
8 Tables
15 Chairs
4 Phones – 5 Phone lines (BT)
Flipchart
Photocopier – to be supplied.
Coffee machine (including decaffeinated)
Selection of soft drinks (coke, orange juice, mineral water) required for 35. Replenish as necessary. Sandwiches and fruit for 35 required daily (Thursday–Sunday inclusive). Serve at 12.00.

Quiet Room for Press Interviews (Vita Dome Meeting Room)
2 Tables
4 Chairs

Exhibition (Ocean Room)
44 5FT × 2FT Tables
40 Chairs
Electricity supply
Exhibition plan attached
Exhibition will run throughout the conference.

Poster Displays (Ocean Room)
6 Poster Boards

Meeting area (Promenade Lounge)
2 areas to be set boardroom style for 20–25 people.

Slide Preview Room (Press Office)
1 Table
2 Chairs
Slide projector, screen and carousels

Cloakroom
Charge to delegates

4.2.2   PRACTICAL ASPECTS OF PRESENTING A CONFERENCE PAPER

Tom Carruthers

WE believe that the following will be useful to you. However, before you consider this section, remember that you already have within you a resource of your own experience. This is your memories of lectures which you have attended and papers which you have heard.

The questions below are intended to help you organize your memories of such times so that you can develop and extend your *own* guidelines.

Think of a lecture or paper which you enjoyed and appreciated.	*Think of a lecture or paper which you found abysmal.*
What was helpful in:	What was unhelpful in:
arrangement of the subject matter?	arrangement of the subject matter?
the language used?	the language used?
the style and attitude of the speaker?	the style and attitude of the speaker?
the visual aids used?	the visual aids used?
the lay-out of the room?	the lay-out of the room?

* * *

Conferences happen in order to promote communication between colleagues and practitioners. This communication can be the informal, often extremely valuable, exchanges over a drink or a meal. It is also the organized part of the conference – the papers, the seminars, the workshops. Our interest is in the latter.

Participants benefit if a presentation is a good one. What

follows is intended to help you if you have the prospect of presenting a paper in the near future. To that end, this section is written as a direct address to 'you', the prospective presenter, from 'us', your prospective audience and participants.

Our basic theme is the idea of effective communication – the process whereby you, the speaker, shape a complex message so that it suits the situation and the resources and limitations of us, your hearers and receivers. Our needs, our resources and our limitations are the conditions within which you, the speaker, have to operate.

YOUR AIMS AND YOUR AUDIENCE

To start you need to focus your attention on the basis of your preparation:

- What is your direct aim in presenting the paper? That is, what change do you want to bring about in us, your audience?

- Who are we, your audience? What is our background of knowledge? What can you take for granted? (Would you present the same paper to a gathering of fellow specialists in your field as you would to a general audience of psychologists?)

- What are our interests? Do we want to hear about results, about a new theory, or about methods and techniques?

From your answers will come the shape and the emphasis of your paper.

Arrangement of Subject Matter

You know your subject very well. You have been working with it and on it for some time. We, your audience, have not. Respect our intelligent ignorance. Help us to join you in your knowledge by starting from where we are. Set your topic in relation to some general model in your field with which we are likely, being psychologists, to have some knowledge and understanding, and indicate the relationship of your topic to that. Then take us into your special field. Remember, you are our guide. We depend on you. If we were reading your account we could backtrack, taking time to review and reflect. *Hearing* your paper, we have to keep up with you as our guide, so suit your path and your pace to our capacities.

Tell us what we need to know. Avoid confusing us by telling us everything you know. Recall the old guidelines:

- tell them what you are going to say;
- say it;
- tell them (briefly) what you have said.

The Language Used

A conference contributor sometimes presents a paper by reading to an audience a journal article which is in preparation. The reader benefits: the audience suffers.

The language of a paper written for a journal is not spoken language. It differs from spoken language (that is, language comprehensible when spoken) in the length and construction of sentences, in vocabulary, and in a lack of repetition/redundancy. For a given number of words, it carries more meaning than spoken: it is a more densely packed language.

The printed format also allows the reader random access (for example, starting at the back by scanning the references), the possibility of re-reading, of cross-checking, of actively searching back, forward and through, in order to get the full meaning from a text. He or she can even take time to consult a dictionary. A writer can rely on this active exploring by the reader, and can, in consequence, produce densely packed material.

Hearing a paper at a conference, none of these possibilities are open to us. We are in your hands; we follow the sequence of words as you utter them. Repetition happens only if you make it happen. We depend on your choice of language, on your suiting it to us so that we grasp your meaning as you utter the words, for we cannot readily ask you for a replay. (Although the request, 'Would you say that again, please?' is sometimes heard.) Speak to us as interested friends.

Above all, remember **KISS** – Keep It Short and Simple.

STYLE AND ATTITUDES

All this puts a great burden on you – planning your presentation so that it suits us, we who will be members of an audience you may never have met. Keeping in mind the following points can help.

- Please, in your preparation, do not depend only on yourself. Enlist colleagues as try-out audiences.

- In your actual presentation, you are not alone. You have us, your audience. Work with us. Consult us. Do we want more time to consult a visual? Is a point clear or would we like it clarified

- Monitor us as you talk. Watch for the slight nod of comprehension or agreement, or for the frown of puzzlement. Use that to guide your pace. Pause in a way that shows that you are ready to take questions seeking elaboration of a point. We recognize that this feels risky. It is. But almost all of us will appreciate your attention to us. We are with you. We want you to succeed and we will do all we can to help.

- Limit your paper to two thirds of the time allowed. That gives us time for questions and comments, and protects you if the chairman has to shorten the time allowed. Remember **KISS**.

- A presentation is a theatrical performance. No actor would go on without rehearsal. No more should you. So:
  - write the paper, for an audience, in good time;
  - rehearse it and listen to the feedback which is offered to you;
  - prune it;
  - rehearse it again;
  - on the day, as any actor does, work us, your audience, and work with us.

VISUAL AIDS

Here a change of tone – from generally supportive to fairly prescriptive.

Try something: using a broad-tipped marker pen write a series of capital letters on a piece of paper, varying them in height from one to six inches. Note, below each letter, its height. Then see how well you can read them from a distance of 20 feet. That distance is the same as if you were 10 or 12 rows from a flip chart or screen in a meeting room. What size can you read comfortably?

The size of the letters of the words which you put up for us to read must be large enough for those of us who are furthest from the screen (or other display device) to be able to read them. Check the room size, and plan accordingly. Thus:

- for a maximum distance of 10 feet (small group work) – 2 inch letters.

- for a room with 10 rows of seats – 6 inch letters.

- for a room with 20 to 30 rows – 10 inch letters.

In a large lecture theatre a screen will usually be about 10 feet from top to bottom, so you could plan on about a maximum of eight lines of text on the slide which is to be projected.

Flip Charts

These are on A1 size paper (2 feet 9 inches by 2 feet). A pad contains about 25 sheets.

You could prepare a sequence of sheets in advance and reveal them in turn to accompany your presentation. The advantage of this is that, as you finish the presentation of material on one sheet, it can be detached and blu-tacked to a side wall. This allows you to build up a continuous visual summary of the material you have presented.

The limitation is that what you write is what the audience gets. With two inch letters and space in between lines, you can have some 12 lines of headings, phrases or statements on one sheet at a maximum viewing distance of 12 or, at most, 15 feet.

The great advantage is that you are independent; no problems of power supply, of cable length, of bulb life and of projector technology. These do affect you if you choose slides.

Slides

There are two kinds.

- *Overhead Projector (OHP) slides*
  These are transparent acetate slides 10 inches by 10 inches or A4 in size. You can use water soluble ink pens or permanent coloured ink pens of different thicknesses. The water soluble ones allow for easier corrections.

  It is better not to type material for a slide. Typewriter sized type has to be enlarged by four to six times before it is printed on a slide if it is to be legible, and the letters are inevitably thin. Bolder letters are needed. Word processors usually have heavy enough fonts of type to produce material which can be suitably enlarged. *A straight (unenlarged) copy of typed material on an A4 acetate is illegible when projected for an audience. Avoid the temptation.*

  If possible, have a graphic artist prepare your material. Ask at your organization's audio-visual support services.

- *2 inch by 2 inch (2" × 2") slides*
  These dimensions refer to the size of the slide frame which will go into the projector. Usually such a frame takes a slide made by a camera using 35mm film. You provide the original – headings, diagrams, photos; and the professional service does the rest. Again, some PC programmes can produce photo ready copy.

Content of a slide

Three kinds of information can usefully be presented on slides.

- A set or a list of topic headings. You talk about each one, perhaps revealing each heading as you wish to draw attention to it.

- Information on results. A summary can show an overall trend or pattern. (If you wish the audience to have details, use hand-out sheets. One A4 can hold a lot of detail and we can take it away with us. Tell us that sheets will be available but hold onto them until the end, or put them on seats beforehand. Either will do, so long as we are not distracted from your presentation by the actual distribution.)

- Diagrams, flow charts and graphics generally. Actual photos of equipment or events can be accommodated on 2" × 2" format.

One suggestion is to put as much information on a slide as you would have on a T shirt. Again, **KISS**.

In general

By presenting a strong visual image you are likely to make a point forcefully.

- When presenting words, keep the number of words to a minimum. Use bullet points where possible. (See Box A for examples of the use of bullet points.)

- Sometimes an OHP slide or a flipchart can be used to outline your presentation and to act as a prompt for you, saving you the need to consult notes.

- Display any sheet or slide long enough for us to take in the material on it.

Box A
Information Guidelines on Text

- Use a maximum of title and 36 words per visual aid.

- Use a maximum of 6 lines for a big audience.

- Use bullet points where possible.

- Ensure that the words can be **easily** read from the back of the room.

- Where possible, present information graphically or in diagram.

A bit more than 36 words – but it does highlight the points.

NERVES

Yes, it is normal to be nervous. You are putting yourself in an exposed position and you are submitting yourself and your work to scrutiny. Consult the various resources available on relaxation techniques. Tense and untense your muscles, deliberately slump, breath deeply and steadily, out as well as in. It all does help. So does thorough preparation and rehearsal. If it is any comfort, Sir Isaiah Berlin (Oxford philosopher, noted as a lecturer) said, 'I have never enjoyed giving a lecture in my life. I have always been extremely nervous, before, during and after.' (*Observer*, 14 Oct., 1990)

IN CONCLUSION

Perhaps Berlin can also provide us with our conclusion. At the age of 81 he was still drawing them in.

The thing about being a scholar is that you combine two incompatible things – one is the quiet scholar in the library (or lab) undisturbed by any specious factor such as popularity. The other is Ham Actor. Some people are afraid of being Ham Actor, so they suppress it and become dull.

(ibid.)

While we would not suggest that your success might depend on your becoming a ham actor, we hope that we have encouraged you to add a certain smokey tang to your presentation.

4.3 DEALING WITH THE MEDIA

Stephen White

MANY psychologists, especially those in the public sector, will have employers who have developed a PR/Press/External Relations channel. These employers will probably have developed guidelines for employees' interaction with the media. Some will say you can't; some will want your output vetted by a manager or by your 'Press Office'; some will say that you can't comment on employer policy – the variations are endless. So, the first point to make is: if you are employed in an organization where you think there may be a 'press policy', then find out what it is – pleading ignorance after the event is never a good defence.

FREE TO TALK

If we assume that you do have some freedom of action, what can usefully be said to help in that interaction?

A good first step in any relationship is to find out as much as possible about your potential partner. This goes for working with the media just as much as it goes for working with your colleagues or ensuring domestic bliss and harmony. Find out how the media work; what constraints they have; what resources they have; and what general policies they pursue. For most psychologists the great majority of their media interactions will be with the locals, both print and broadcast.

The local media

Firstly, the local media thrive on local stories. Secondly, they are always desperate for quality stories and serious stories, and whatever you are doing, be it service delivery, research, service development, training, or conference attending is likely to make a story in their terms.

The local media, whether it's print or broadcast, run on very limited staff resources. Although there might be a local government or health services correspondent, there will not be a science specialist or a psychology expert. Therefore, you'll have to start at first principles and simplify (but not trivialize) your work so that it can be disseminated to the local audience.

More often than not you will interact with a 'news reporter'. Whilst these people are not subject specialists, they *are* trained to elicit your story (in the fastest possible time) and then to write it or put it on tape to the desired length.

The news story

The news story can be visualized as an inverted triangle, with the widest part at the top. The top contains the most important information – the news – and the rest tails away with the least important material at the end. This is done so that if the space available is cut, then the story (or tape) can simply be cut from the bottom (end) paragraph until the requisite number of words are left.

So the first couple of sentences of any story are the most important. If you read the news pages and just read the first paragraphs you'll see that they conform to a pattern. This is called the five 'W's' – **What?; Who?; When?; Where?; Why?** 'What?' is the news, what has happened, what someone has said or proposed. 'Who?' is exactly what it says – who has said it, or has been found guilty, or has found a development on the road to a cancer cure. 'When?' is usually today; news always happens today or yesterday, but never last week. 'Where?' is the geographical location – 'in Toytown', or even 'in the District Psychology Department of Toytown Education Authority'. 'Why?' is a very simple, usually single phrase, explanation of what. This is how news stories are written, so be prepared for questions which get this information and especially be prepared to present the 'What?' of the story – the news – very clearly.

Of course the local media also run other types of items, such as features, editorials, letters, phone-ins, documentaries. Space here limits any further notes at this stage, but a useful book to read, which goes into all these aspects (and many more) is *Hitting the Headlines: A practical guide to the media* (White *et al.*, 1993).

HOW TO GET THE MEDIA INTERESTED

As was said earlier, virtually anything you do could easily be a story as far as the media are concerned. The crucial element is ensuring it becomes a story is to tell the media.

So, what is the best way of doing that? Writing and sending a media release.

The Media Release

The media release (see the example on p. 240) is the most efficient way of making an initial contact with journalists, because they expect and are happy to receive releases, because a single release can be sent to numerous different outlets, and because a release forces you to distil your story into one side of A4 paper (good discipline for psychologists.

There are four keys to producing a good media release.

Design

The design of the piece of A4 paper is just as important as what it says. Starting from the top, the first thing to have is an indication of where it comes from. Your usual letter headed paper is often enough, but you must add the words 'Media Release' or the journalist may mistake it for a 'Letter to the Editor' or some other form of communication. Next should be a date line, and this is the date you send the release out. Next down the page is an embargo – a date and time before which the media cannot use your story. This device allows you to send out your news well in advance of the event and gives the journalists time to check, come back to you for more information or simply to put it in their diary so that on the day they are ready. Next is a heading (try not to write Guardianesque headlines; few of us are clever enough to get away with it). This should be no more than four, five or six words simply stating what the story is about. Don't use technical language; make your heading as audience friendly as possible.

Next is the text. This should be double-spaced with a wide left hand margin, and no longer than one side of A4.

After the text should come a heading, 'For further information', after which should come names plus telephone numbers (work and home) of people who know enough about the content of the release to be able to answer journalists' questions. If this item is missing and the journalists don't have a contact, your chances of getting your story covered are severely diminished.

Timing

Your release has to arrive with the media in time for them to be able to react and write or broadcast the story. All parts of the media have different deadlines, both during the week and during the day. Giving a hard and fast rule is not possible, but if for instance you are organizing a local conference then give the media five to ten days' notice so that it can go in the office diary and resources can be allocated.

Distribution   Your story should be of interest to all types of media, so the building of a local media distribution list is an essential ingredient of getting coverage. This list should contain all the local press, daily and weekly as well as the free sheets; the local radio, both BBC and independent; the local TV, again BBC and ITV; the local press agencies, as well as any local freelance journalists and magazines. In the great majority of instances sending your release to the news desk will do, but it is much better if you can send it to a named reporter. If you don't know a name, phone and ask.

Composition   This refers back to your text. The object of the exercise (in print media terms) is to write your release so that it can be printed exactly as it is written. This means you have to study and ape the news journalism style. Remember the five 'Ws' and make sure that the first sentence is the news, the story.

Other points to note when you are news writing are:

- use the active voice – 'The research committee meets next week' *not* 'A meeting will be held by the research committee next week';
- don't use negatives – 'The experiments failed' rather than 'The experiments were not successful';
- only have one idea in your sentence;
- use a preponderance of simple and compound sentences;
- avoid jargon and technical language like the plague (see Table A for words to avoid and their alternatives);
- use first names and titles; and
- be honest and check your facts.

BEING INTERVIEWED – HINTS AND TIPS

The interview by a professional from the media can be a nerve-racking experience but it needn't be. Indeed, if handled correctly it should at best be enjoyable and at worst painless. There are some simple hints, tips and rules which should make your performance better and therefore make the media happy that they've got a good piece of tape or print.

The basic guidelines are:

- know the basis of the interview
- know the questions
- know your subject

Beyond the three guidelines there is one further fundamental; whenever you are talking to a journalist *you are being interviewed* (unless it is specifically stated to the contrary). Journalists generally don't talk to research scientists for

Table A 'Banned' words and their alternatives
'Don't use big words where shorter ones will do.'

TRY TO AVOID:	USE INSTEAD:
accordingly	so
apparent	clear, plain
commence	start, begin
consult	talk to, see, meet
discontinue, terminate	stop, end
dwelling, residence,	home
economical	cheap
endeavour, attempt	try
erroneous	wrong, false
facilitate	help
in consequence of	because
in excess of	more than
initiate	start
necessitate	need, require
obtain, receive	get
regulation	rule
state	say
statutory	legal, by law
supplementary	extra, more
utilize	use

their health, they talk to them (you) because they want a story.

Although the general hints are the same for all parts of the media, there are some minor differences. For ease of explanation I will deal with TV, radio and newspapers/magazines separately.

Television

TV interviews come in three types – the live studio interview, the filmed studio interview, and the location (usually your place of work) interview.

What to do beforehand

First, find out the purpose of the interview; in other words, why you are there. This may sound obvious, but there are many examples of interviewees being completely thrown by questions because they hadn't checked on the ground rules. So, find out the purpose and find out at least the first question that you will be asked (more if possible, but the first will give you a chance to prepare a brief and direct response). It also gives you an opportunity to negotiate the first question if you think it is inappropriate or unhelpful.

Some TV (and radio) journalists or interviewers won't tell you the exact wording of the first question. They say, and with some justification, that if they do then your answer will be rehearsed and lack spontaneity. When you meet this situation, insist they at least tell you the gist of the first question.

Other things
you should find
out about

Will the interview be

- Live or recorded; if it's recorded will the tape be edited? If it is to be edited, this gives you the chance to stop the interview, apologize and ask to do your answer again.

- How are you going to be introduced? This saves you being called something totally inappropriate. It also saves them getting your name, title and place of work wrong.

- How long is the interview to last – three, six or ten questions? This will give you a good guide as to whether you must be succinct or whether you can be slightly more leisurely.

- Are you to be interviewed alone or is there another guest? If there is someone else, get a good breakdown of their position so that you know whether the interview is going to be mutually supportive or confrontational.

If you are going to a studio get there at least an hour in advance. This will give you the chance to calm down, have a coffee (only one and *no alcohol*), check with the producer or interviewer on questions, and gives you the chance to become familiar with the studio – a rather daunting place of lights, cameras, microphones, monitors and lots of people.

During the
interview

If you have followed the pre-interview rules, then the event itself should be painless. However, a few tips may help your performance.

- Many novice interviewees attempt to pack their answers with a welter of information – *don't*. Try to work out, in advance, the three or four most important points you wish to get across and say them in the simplest way you can. It doesn't matter whether you directly answer the question; the object of the exercise is to get your points over.

- Your language is vital. Your audience will not understand jargon and technical terms, so find simple alternatives or explanations (see Table A for a list of words to avoid and their alternatives).

- Although your audience could be several millions, the best interviews are those where the interviewer and interviewee are in conversation. So don't declaim, patronize, or lecture and don't look straight at the camera – your eye contact should be with the interviewer. (The only time when you have to look at the camera is when you are being interviewed in a remote studio, with your interviewer perhaps hundreds of miles away.)

- Try to dress quietly. Busy cloth patterns are accentuated by TV and your audience may remember your checked shirt, striped tie or floral blouse rather than what you said.

- Tinted spectacles on screen make you look like the mafia.

- Don't take notes into the studio – you will be forever looking down or sideways to check if you have made all your points. If you've only got three points to make you should be able to remember them.

- Try not to jump about, or wave your arms; even a relatively small movement can mean you disappear out of shot.

- Finally, if you have a speech impediment or just freeze at the prospect of cameras and lights, get a colleague to do the interview.

Radio

What has been said about television interviews goes for radio too, except that the pressure of being seen is removed. So your clothing doesn't matter, and neither do your gesticulations, but also remember that where a gesture can be worth a thousand words on TV you can't use a gesture on radio. You can also take some simple notes into a studio with you. In fact, for the phone-in, a pad and pen is essential. (First write down callers' names and then the pertinent point(s) of their question.)

Radio interviews can also be done down a phone-line. If possible avoid this path, as the sound quality is never perfect; always try to get to the studio, or get the reporter to come to you and tape the interview face-to-face.

The Press

General news reporters on the national, regional or local press, and magazine feature writers are unlikely to know anything about science or your particular research, but they are skilled at asking pertinent questions and extracting information. Specialist science or medicine correspondents will at least have a rough knowledge of the field but the watchwords are 'don't assume knowledge'.

The printed press virtually always has 'an angle' – an editorial point they wish to make. So, when approached, always ask what the angle is and if you don't like it, either attempt a re-negotiation or simply say 'no thanks'.

Print journalists tend to collect their stories and comments over the phone, and it is very easy to be more forthcoming than intended down a phone line.

Two tips may help:

• pretend that your professional colleagues are in the room with you;

• don't answer the questions on the spot. Ask the journalist to give you all the questions, then put the phone down and call back in 10/15/30 minutes. If you use this technique you *must* phone back. This technique also gives you the chance to sort your thoughts, work out the most important points, and write down a few direct quotes. Of course there will always be subsidiary questions and points of clarification but if you have done your homework these shouldn't prove either difficult or embarrassing.

Off the record

'Off the record' is a means for you to provide information to a journalist without being quoted. There may be occasion for the use of this device, and you can be 95 per cent sure that a journalist will not break this convention. If a journalist does, then you will never speak to them again, and as journalists live by their sources this is a serious repercussion.

Remember always to say 'this is off the record' before you say something. There is nothing more frustrating to a journalist than to have taken copious notes and then be told 'by the way, that's off the record'.

Other points to note

• Always remember that when a journalist comes to you they want a story and you are the source (or one of them) they have chosen. This means you are in control – you have the power position. But don't abuse that power; there may be occasions in the future when you want journalists to do something for you.

• Don't forget that if you don't provide the information needed, the journalist will go elsewhere – probably to someone less qualified.

• If you really are being asked questions outside your area of competence, refer the journalist to someone you know and trust who can answer the questions.

Remember, being interviewed by a journalist from either TV, radio or the press should not be a harrowing experience as long as you have followed the rules:

• *know the basis of the interview*

- *know the questions*

- *know your subject*

This is only the barest outline of a media guide. For a fuller guide read *Hitting the Headlines* (published by BPS Books, 1993). Another point to note is that the Society regularly runs Media Training day courses. Details are available from the Director of Information at the Society's address.

FURTHER READING

Taylor, R. and White, S. (1991). *Written Evidence for the Outside World*. Leicester: The British Psychological Society. White, S., Evans, P., Mihill, C. and Tysoe, M. (1993). *Hitting the Headlines: A practical guide to the media*. Leicester: BPS Books (The British Psychological Society).

Appendix: Example of a media release

Telephone: 0116 254 9568
Fax: 0116 247 0787
E-mail: bps1@le.ac.uk
Compuserve: 100020,73

St Andrews House
48 Princess Road East
LEICESTER
LE1 7DR

Masthead

The British Psychological Society

Incorporated by Royal Charter – Registered Charity No. 229642

MEDIA RELEASE

Dateline   Date: Monday 6 April 1992

Embargo   Embargo: 14.00 hrs Saturday 11 April 1992

Heading   PROBLEMS IN ASSESSING AND TREATING
SPECIAL HOSPITAL PATIENTS

Text   How do you decide if someone who has committed a violent
crime should be sent for treatment or sent to prison? This is
one of the difficult questions raised in a symposium presented
by members of Broadmoor Hospital's Psychology Department
at The British Psychological Society's Annual Conference in
the Spa Complex, Scarborough, today, Saturday 11 April 1992.

The symposium convened by Carol Sellars, a Chartered Clinical Psychologist, discusses the question of 'treatability' in
those diagnosed as 'psychopaths', under the Mental Health
Act (1983). This Act changed the law so that in order for an
offender to be admitted to a Special Hospital like Broadmoor,
psychiatrists and psychologists have to say that he or she will
be treatable. Carol Sellars argues that this is almost impossible
to do, given our present state of knowledge, and actually stops
some people getting the care they need.

Other papers in the symposium include one by Dr Mary Hall,
who looks at the evidence for brain damage in some of Broadmoor's patients and tries to relate this to offending.

Dr Derek Perkins talks about the problems of assessing and
treating sex offenders, while Lona Roberts explains the role of
the Mental Health Act Tribunals in deciding when and how
Special Hospital patients should be released.

For Further   FOR FURTHER INFORMATION CONTACT: Sue Cavill,
Information   Press Officer, Tel. 0116 254 9568 (work), 0116 200 0000 (home)
Stephen White, Director of Information, Tel. 0116 254 9568
(work) 0116 200 0000 (home).
ON WEDNESDAY 8 APRIL ONLY CONTACT Sue Cavill or
Stephen White at the Cornelian Suite, Hotel St Nicholas, Scar-
borough. Tel. 01723 364101.
DURING THE CONFERENCE telephone 01723 377616 or
377618. Fax 01723 377667.

4.4 CONDUCTING MEETINGS AND TELECONFERENCES

Bruce Napier

MAKING MEETINGS WORK

MEETINGS are a part of professional life, but all too often they fulfil the cynical definition of a committee as 'a body that keeps minutes and wastes hours'. This section sets out to help you make good use of the meetings that you attend, and to develop a reputation for running effective and worthwhile meetings yourself.

The Principles

One of the insights that I had whilst working for the Society is that the Laws of Thermodynamics apply to the organization of meetings. In particular, the entropy of the system shows a tendency to increase, or at best to remain constant, unless energy is used to achieve a local reduction. This means that things will disorganize themselves unless active steps are taken to keep them in order.

Let me give some brief examples of what I mean. When arranging a meeting, obviously it is important to book a venue in good time, where the notice required is related to the size of the meeting, and whether it is local, regional or national in nature. However, unless the meeting is a small local one arranged quickly, it is a good idea to phone the venue at the stage of despatching the agendas to people, just to check that your booking hasn't got lost because your letter of confirmation went astray.

Similarly, for a meeting which is one of a series, good organization says that the minutes should be despatched as soon as possible, so that people are reminded of what was agreed in good time before the next meeting. However, **do not expect people to bring that copy of the minutes to the next meeting**. Some will, but most won't. Send them another copy with the agenda of the next meeting, and have spare copies of everything at the meeting.

It will be apparent from this that I am writing as though you are the secretary or other person responsible for the meeting. Naturally, often this will not be the case, but:

(a) if you see things from the secretary or convener's point of view, much that happens in meetings will make more sense;

(b) if you know what is supposed to happen, you may be able to influence the future organization of the meeting; and

(c) this in turn means that you will very likely be asked to arrange more and more such events.

If this last bit fills you with horror, remember that those who set the agenda and write the minutes have a direct influence on outcomes, and you can always decline such requests if you don't fancy the job.

There are two other principles to be set out before getting down to the nitty gritty of organization. Firstly, don't lose sight of the aims and objectives of the meeting, either whilst organizing it or taking part in it. By *aims*, I mean the broad statement of what the meeting is about and what it is trying to achieve – the 'Mission Statement'. By *objectives* I mean the operationally defined goals of this particular session – for example, 'By the end of this meeting, everyone will know who is to write the operational policy, what its main headings are to be, and by what date the first draft is to be complete.'

Keeping sight of this principle is your safeguard against the operation of those natural laws recorded by Parkinson, Murphy, Sod *et al*. They can't be circumvented completely, but their effects are much mitigated if everyone knows what they are doing in the same room at the same time.

The other essential is to understand the different roles of the Chair and Secretary. As I've said, most of this chapter is aimed at the Secretary, but it is vital that the Chair and Secretary agree on the aims and objectives and that the Chair chairs and the Secretary organizes and records. Anything else is a recipe for chaos.

The Agenda

The agenda is the list of items to be considered at a particular meeting. Formal agendas also include other useful information like where and when it is to be held, and what arrangements have been made to preserve the lives of the participants whilst it is going on (coffee, tea, lunch and so forth). Very formal agendas for AGMs and the like will probably be defined in Statutes or Rules.

Before setting out the conventional format, some general points are worth making. Firstly, make sure that all involved know the deadline for the despatch of the agenda, and the latest date by which items need to be with the Secretary for inclusion. Secondly, take an active decision about the style of the thing. Is it to be a list of headings, or will there be a clue as to what the headings really mean? A really useful agenda makes the objectives explicit, but this can lead to protests that the secretary is dictating to the committee.

It is the Chair's job to try to ensure that the agenda and its expressed or implied objectives are adhered to, and that all items on the agenda get a fair share of the available time.

The format

The following is a fairly standard format for an agenda, although some items may be unfamiliar.

Heading: the name of the committee, and details of where and when the meeting will be held;

Apologies for absence;

Minutes of the last meeting for approval as a true record;

Matters arising from the minutes (major items should have their own slot on the agenda);

Business from the Chair (an opportunity for the Chair to bring forward urgent new business which needs more attention than it is likely to get under Any Other Business);

Main items for discussion (ideally, each should be supported by a document, thus allowing people to consider the issues in advance of the meeting);

Any Other Business (the Chair should only allow brief discussion on such items; everyone is tired, there hasn't been advance warning of the issue and the probability of poor decision-making is very high);

Date and time of next meeting (for a series of meetings, it is better to arrange all the dates in advance, so that this slot is for confirmation rather than a bad-tempered end of meeting discussion about whose non-availability is important and whose isn't).

The Meeting

Much of what I have to say about the conduct of the meeting is covered either in the previous section as 'The Agenda', or in the following section as 'The Minutes'. However, it seems appropriate to say a few words about the physical arrangements. Just as when organizing a teaching or training session, it is important to try to ensure that learning is not impeded by discomfort or anxiety on the part of the participants, so it is with meetings. It should barely need saying, but the venue should be clean and comfortable, adequately heated and ventilated. Any deficiencies should be rectified, or else an explanation given to those present as to why nothing can be done.

When arranging refreshments, take into account the preferences of the participants as to caffeine, meat and other dietary requirements. The Chair should be clear as to what the arrangements are, and, if necessary, consult the participants about the timing of breaks.

The Minutes

'The minutes should record, not what people said, nor even what people think that they said, but what they would have said had they thought.' This philosophy, expounded to me by the then Chair of the Division of Clinical Psychology may seem just a little extreme to some, but it contains a kernel of truth. Discussion in committees does not proceed with the measured order of a Court of Law, but in fits and starts, in circles and oblique lines and, most definitely, in ellipses.

The competence of the Chair makes a difference of course, but a good Chair senses when to let things have their head for a while, so that the steam can run off from feelings and sensible discussion can resume. The Secretary thus must decide for each meeting how much of the discussion to include in the minutes, and what to leave out, and the decision must depend on the aims and objectives of the meeting and who else will read the minutes.

I think that it is worth saying here that circulating the minutes is the very poorest way of briefing others on the issues discussed. They will inevitably fail to give the flavour of the debate unless, Hansard-like, they are ludicrously detailed, almost verbatim. Any meeting must address as part of its objectives how to communicate with the rest of the world (see also Sections 4.2.1 and 4.3).

The minutes, then, must address the needs of the meeting itself for a record of decisions and who is to put them into effect. This means that, very often, briefer is better, although they may need to record enough of the debate to enable the Chair to forestall one of a committee's most pernicious and destructive habits, namely re-debating everything all over again under the pretext of matters arising.

The most important thing is to try to ensure that the minutes record the outcomes and who is responsible for moving things on in a way that fits with the objectives. The purpose of the meeting is *not* to generate minutes, but to achieve its objectives.

Washing-up

After the meeting is over, thought should be given to the best way to follow through to ensure that decisions are put into effect. Although getting the minutes out in good time is important, with frequent meetings there may not be much time between receiving the minutes of the last meeting and the agenda for the next. The moral is clear; don't wait for the minutes before doing what you agreed to do.

The Secretary may find it helpful to send a brief letter or memo to those who undertook tasks before working on the minutes. He or she should in any event be clear as to who is to do what by when, and should make sure that they are clear too. How individual participants organize themselves to do their bit is a matter of preferred time management style. Personally I use a combination of notes in my diary for small tasks to do shortly after the meeting, and a task list drawn up during the meeting and transferred to my main task list for the big jobs. The Secretary should not be afraid to remind people of their undertakings with regard to deadlines. Every committee seems to acquire one or two members whose enthusiasm outstrips their available time or other resources, and if tasks remain undone for more than one or two meetings, the Chair may need to undertake some tactful negotiations. At all costs he or she should avoid humiliating the participant concerned in the meeting: willing horses are too scarce to be shot out of hand for lack of speed.

THE ALTERNATIVES

This brings us to the alternatives to holding a meeting. For some jobs, a one person committee is the answer. Sometimes, the required policy or task needs the skills or knowledge of more than one. An answer to consider then is to select those who in combination have the skills, give them a deadline and let them get on with it. Often, one will draft and the other comment on the draft, perhaps by post.

Bulletin boards

The high tech solution for team drafting is to use an electronic bulletin board such as PSYCHE which is operated by the Division of Clinical Psychology. If you can use a word processor and a telephone, you can use a bulletin board, often by using the same approach if you are uneasy with IT. For many people, learning to use a word processor means acquiring a set of procedures which meet their needs, and the same is true for the bulletin board.

Teleconferences

For things which need discussion as well as drafting, a teleconference may be the cheapest and quickest solution.

In a teleconference, several people, perhaps from all over the country, are connected together on their phones. It costs the price of the individual calls to the teleconference centre, plus an additional fee billed to the organizer. BT has a special bureau called Conference Call which can set them up. They prefer 24 hours' notice, but can do it quicker in an emergency. Mercury Communications offer an Audio Conferencing facility which has a ten minute connection guarantee following a completed reservation.

Running a teleconference needs much the same skills as chairing a conventional meeting, but with the following provisos.

The Chair must be firm about people taking it in turns to speak, and should take care to ask for input from each participant. In particular, he or she should work systematically round the conference when a decision has to be made.

It is impossible to discuss things in a teleconference without precirculated material. This means that they are not good for brainstorming type meetings, but excellent for considering decisions for which there are clear criteria, such as membership applications.

For reasons which are not wholly clear to me, teleconferences do much more business in a given period of time than do face-to-face meetings. There is less inclination to chat, and a tendency to proceed with the items with despatch, possibly because of the need for firm chairing. They are also more tiring; one and a half hours is a sensible maximum, and two the very limit. In that time, though, you can expect to complete an agenda that would otherwise take half a day at least.

If you require further information on teleconferences, a leaflet entitled 'Advice to Those Participating in a Teleconference' can be obtained from the Society's office.

CONCLUSION

A systematic approach to meetings is needed to reduce the boredom and avoid wasting precious time. By paying attention to clarifying aims and objectives, and by clarifying the roles of Chair and Secretary, meetings can be made to work effectively. Being a valued participant in meetings can be an essential element in your career strategy.

4.5   DOING RESEARCH

4.5.1   WRITING A GRANT APPLICATION

Neil Brooks

OBTAINING research grants has never been easy. With the continuing heavy decline in the Government funding for biomedical research, the situation concerning Government monies (the British Medical Research Council, DoH, etc.) has become ever more difficult. Nevertheless, although the picture is gloomy for Government funded research, this is not the case for Charitable research. Indeed, a compilation of British Charities Funding Neuroscience Research identified 24 Charities disbursing amounts from £300 to £20,000, and some Charities (e.g. the Wellcome Trust) are major rivals to Government sources of research funding.

Whatever the amount and range of sources of research money available, the fundamental exercise is one of competition. Inevitably, any researcher seeking limited funds is competing with others equally keen to obtain those same funds. While it is rare that one can identify a direct competitor – 'direct' in the sense that they are seeking similar money for an identical project, there are often a number of projects in a similar area, and a deciding factor will then be quite simply the quality of the research application. The better the application the more likely it is to get funded.

Although the 'bottom line' is one of quality of research application, any experienced obtainer of research monies will admit that the process of research application is at least partly a gamble, with an element of luck. The prudent applicant is the one who reduces the odds in his/her favour, and this can be achieved by a variety of means. This chapter is essentially about ways of reducing those odds. There are some very simple strategies that are worth describing at the outset, and then the chapter will discuss a series of more detailed procedures to assist in an application.

Whatever the source of research money, an application

involves a series of discrete processes. Firstly, the Officers of the funding body will check that the grant application matches the formal requirements and funding policies of that body (length of application, total amount of money requested, duration of grant, etc.). Secondly, the application will usually go to referees who will concern themselves with the quality of the science, the adequacy of the case made for the amount of money requested, and the practicalities of the application (is it possible to complete the research in the time proposed, etc.). The referees will then report back to the awarding body with the recommendation for funding or not. Some bodies add an extra stage at which requests for clarification made by referees can be fed back to applicants for their comments prior to a final decision about funding. Finally, some bodies in the event of an unsuccessful application will give feedback of varying degrees of length and detail.

Any research application must address a range of issues. For the major grant awarding bodies (in the UK, the Medical Research Council, Department of Health, Scottish Home & Health Department, Mental Health Foundation, Wellcome Trust, etc.), these may be addressed by means of the detailed application form with its clear guidelines for submitting the proposal. The guidelines are crucial, and the applicant who fails to conform to them will quite simply not get past the first round. The exact information sought by the different fund awarding bodies varies, but a number of headings appear so consistently on the application forms that they are worth using to structure much of the rest of the chapter. Even if the applicant is applying to a body that does not have clearly specified application procedures, the headings about to be described are worth using in order to impose maximum structure and clarity on the application.

THE RESEARCH APPLICATION – HOW TO FILL IT IN

Introduction

Obviously the purpose of an application is to obtain research funding, but bearing in mind that the applicant is competing with others for limited resources, it is worth considering the different justifications which need to be made. Any applicant must justify tackling a particular problem, in a particular department, using a particular method, with a particular group of patients/subjects in a particular amount of time. Applicants will have to indicate why they themselves and those whom they hire are so crucial to the project, and must justify why the research will cost the amount of money which is being requested.

Before even beginning to submit an application, applicants must ensure that the appropriate preliminary work has been carried out. A literature review should have been done, and the applicant should know enough about the population to be studied to avoid elementary blunders. This point is a particularly important one where experimentalists are attempting to study a clinical population. Lack of experience with that population can result in the submission of an inappropriate project simply because of failure to appreciate the constraints imposed by the condition (e.g. examining higher visual processing in Alzheimer's disease without examining visual acuity first, etc.). At this early stage it is well worth discussing ideas and tentative proposals with as many colleagues as possible. This is the stage at which the clinician seeks the views of the theoretician and vice versa, and detailed and honest discussion here can prevent future disasters. As a result of these discussions it may become obvious that the first stage of the research is to carry out a small pilot study to identify problems and propose solutions. Pilot studies are seldom wasted, and many research referees expect to see evidence that methods and procedures have indeed been piloted.

Often during this early stage the researcher is not sure whether the research topic fits within the ambit of a particular grant awarding body. In addition, there may be problems in understanding exactly what is required in the application, and this is the stage at which to seek advice from the officers of the body awarding funds. A telephone call here may save hours of needless work in the future. The call may identify that the resources of the grant awarding body are too small for the project. It may indicate that the research area being proposed is one that the body does not wish to support, or alternatively, that it is one that has a high priority. It may result in helpful advice about 'marketing' a particular application. If in doubt, telephone.

Before considering detailed headings for the application, there are a number of other points to bear in mind in attempting to make the strongest application. Referees will need to know details about the applicants themselves, the institution from which they are working, and the justification for the timing of the application.

It goes without saying that applicants must state who they are and what their relevant qualifications are. However, applicants should go beyond this. They should be able to communicate to the referees a sense of why it is that the applicants and *only* those applicants are so uniquely well qualified to obtain the research award. Applicants should not hesitate to spell out details of particular qualifications or particular past or current experience that bear on the current application. In addition, they should identify any research collaborators. Many referees and many sources of research funding are keen to develop collaborative interdisciplinary research. Indeed, research that marries the skills of a theoretician and clinician can be particularly valuable, and conversely, failure of a theoretician to secure access to a clinical population can simply prevent research being carried out. Similarly, failure to secure access to a computer or to data processing expertise can equally prevent research succeeding. Access to high-quality enthusiastic help can tip the balance in favour of funding an application. The wise applicant chooses his/her collaborators with care.

Not only must applicants state who they are and with whom they are co-operating, but they will also need to spell out the nature of their institution. The referees will want to know where the research is to be based (university, clinical service department, etc.), and will need to be assured that the base is an ideal one for the proposed research. Relevant links with other institutions can with benefit be spelt out here, and letters of support from other institutions can always be included in an appendix. As a practical point, the awarding body will need to be assured that the host institution will administer financial aspects of the research (salaries, purchasing, etc.), and it is increasingly the case that institutions are charging for such a service. Does the host institution charge, and if so, will the grant awarding body meet such a charge?

There is a further point to bear in mind here. With performance indicators assuming ever greater importance in the public sector, government funding of universities will increasingly be based at least in part on the value of Research Council and similar peer-review funded awards obtained by researchers within the university. Indeed, some universities are already benefiting greatly from this, while others will suffer considerably. In a climate like this, the opportunity for individual negotiation within universities is obvious. The research worker who brings in a substantial grant is directly benefiting his or her university, and may reasonably expect the university to benefit them in turn. It is no longer enough for universities to tell enthusiastic researchers that equipment purchased or laboratory refurbishment or hiring of extra staff is simply not possible. One can envisage a major change in the process of accepting a major research award, with researchers who have obtained such an award delaying formal acceptance until bargains have been struck with the finance officer in the university.

There are two aspects of timing that are important. The first is the total amount of time for which the grant will be held, and the second is the amount of time that the applicant him/herself will be able to devote specifically to the project. Obviously the longer the project, the more expensive, so referees are particularly careful to scrutinize the justification for the length of time involved. If applicants are requesting funding for three years, but have not made a good case for this period, then referees are likely to advise that the research simply not be funded, or that funding be awarded for a 2- rather than 3-year period.

Referees will also be interested to know how much time the applicant will be able to devote specifically to the actual research, or to supervision of researchers employed on the award. Experienced referees are well aware that active researchers manage to find 25 hours in every 24, but if it is obvious that the nature of the applicant's other duties mean that he or she simply cannot spend the proposed amount of time on the grant, then this may well count against them in deciding on an award.

A thorny problem in deciding on the length of the award is the amount of time that should be devoted specifically and exclusively to data analysis and writing up the results. Grant awarding bodies differ in the extent to which they see these activities as crucial parts of the research, or as addenda which can be dealt with after funding has stopped. A careful reading of the guidelines for submission, and if necessary a telephone call to officers of the body awarding the money can be invaluable here.

Headings For The Application

Abstract

Many bodies demand a simple abstract of the research, and this is usually the first thing that referees read. It gives the applicant an early opportunity to communicate clear thinking and excitement at pursuing an interesting project. The abstract should be brief, it should not over-run the number of words allowed in the guidelines for submission. It should be clear and informative, and should give a flavour of what is intended and why. An example of such an abstract is given below:

'Although anecdotal evidence that ... exists, there is little empirical support for this. Our research proposes to investigate ... by means of ... in ... patients. Our results should provide evidence that....'

Background and purpose of research

This substantial section is where the applicant addresses the main conceptual and clinical issues, and communicates the sense of excitement and commitment which in its turn will excite referees. It incorporates the relevant literature review, and allows applicants to make the case that there is a crucial gap in knowledge that is important enough to be filled, and that only the applicant with his or her techniques and ideas can fill it. The background should be written with the knowledge that the application will be read by referees who may be as knowledgeable as the applicant, and will be able to detect major omissions, padding, incorrect citing of references, and inappropriate conclusions. Bearing this in mind, the background should be as brief as possible, consistent with the guidelines for applicants, and with the need to communicate effectively. There is often a temptation to stray into areas that are not relevant, but which signal some aspects of the applicant's knowledge. This can only detract from the main central case.

This section of the application is one which referees often find very difficult to read. Applicants in their enthusiasm may present a closely argued and densely written case which is difficult for referees to follow. Applicants should try to help referees as much as possible by using a clear and logical structure to this section, with headings and sub-headings, and a clear flow of ideas. At the end of the section, the applicant should be able to state a series of simple aims or questions or hypotheses, and ideally the background should have been so well structured that the knowledgeable referee should almost be able to complete the end of this section him/herself.

Plan of investigation

In this section, the applicant can spell out in detail the precise methods and procedures to be used, and the population of subjects or cases under investigation. Referees will expect the applicant to specify the exact procedures that are to be used, and to justify why these rather than other related and apparently equally appropriate procedures are not to be used. Applicants should try to be honest in identifying procedures that are up and running, and those that are being developed or have yet to be developed. If development work is required, then estimates of the likely time-scale of this development should be included. Inevitably and quite appropriately, the methods will often incorporate novel procedures which have not been used before, or not with the specific population to be studied. The fact that procedures are novel may be very positive, but it also means that problems such as reliability and validity of procedures become important. A procedure that is appropriate for a 4-year-old child may not be appropriate for a mentally handicapped adult. If very novel procedures are to be used, applicants must consider how reliable they are likely to be in the new population, and how accurately they are likely to measure the underlying processes being addressed in the application. When such novel procedures are being used, it is always worth including some conventional laboratory or clinical procedures which are known to work, and which would then act as 'marker variables' for the new procedures.

Precise details of the population under study should be given. Referees need to know how many subjects are to be studied, and will often expect a justification for the number chosen. Applicants, before writing this section, should ask themselves exactly how they arrived at the number of cases they proposed to study. Was it simply a convenient figure; a figure based on the size of the population; a figure based on statistical theory, etc.? Not only should numbers be given, but the defining features of the population must be described. Ages, volunteer status, diagnostic categories and criteria, chronicity, etc., are all important. Applicants should also spell out how often and over what duration the subjects will be seen, and by whom. For example, is the researcher him or herself going to carry out the studies, or will it be wholly or partly in the hands of a research assistant? If the latter, is the assistant already competent, or will specific training be given?

Finally, in clinical studies, the researcher often identifies clinical problems that have been missed in the routine clinical follow-up of patients. This faces the applicants with ethical and practical questions, and the wise applicant will have a policy for dealing with hitherto undetected clinical problems. If a decision is made to try to deal with the problems by the applicants themselves, then they must consider the extent to which this is ethically appropriate (is the applicant qualified, etc.?); practically appropriate (are there others able and willing and competent to undertake clinical management?); and conceptually appropriate (will intervention by the researchers compromise the research design?). As a general rule, it is unwise for the researchers themselves to take on the management of clinical problems, and at the outset they should open lines of communication with clinical colleagues to enable patients to receive appropriate management wherever necessary.

Data analysis   Whenever a research design involves very straightforward data analysis, this section can be dealt with very briefly. If, however, the researcher is going to generate a substantial database involving more than simple univariate analyses, applicants may have to spell out in some considerable detail how they propose to set up and manage the database. If statistical help is going to be needed, applicants have to show that this is available, and that it is either free of charge, or can be paid for out of the research grant. If the results are to be analysed by means of a mainframe computer, applicants should demonstrate that they have ready access to the machine, and will have to budget appropriately for the cost of computing time. Some grant-giving bodies are reluctant to pay for computing costs, and applicants should ascertain the policy of the body before preparing the computing budget.

Frequently, research applicants make a common error in this section of the application. The error is to deal very sweepingly with data analysis, saying rather grandly that 'data analysis will be by means of multivariate analysis'. Such a reference to multivariate analysis is unrevealing, and may raise suspicions in the minds of the referee that applicants have not in fact thought at all clearly about how they propose to handle the mass of data collected. It is rarely the case that multivariate analysis is the initial approach of choice, although with large data bases it will inevitably be *one* of the appropriate approaches to be employed.

Ethical and legal considerations

Any study carried out from a university or clinical base and involving patients will need to go through some form of ethical vetting. Clinically based submissions will need to have been cleared by the relevant hospital or unit ethical committee, and university and similar applications by the relevant departmental ethical committee. Such processes can take time, and ideally, ethical permission should be obtained in the very preliminary stages of the research application.

Although it is rare for experiments involving volunteer adults to pose ethical problems, problems do arise as soon as the researcher studies groups who cannot readily give informed consent (children, for example, those with mental disabilities, confused elderly). In these situations the researcher has to show that procedures are available to deal with ethical problems that may arise. Such procedures, together with approval from the relevant ethical committee, should always be appended with an application.

In the UK, a further problem has arisen, and this is the Data Protection Act (see Section 2.2.2) which is designed to protect personal data held in information repositories. Clinical data collected for research purposes comes within the restrictions imposed by the Act, and may demand two separate registrations (one from within the University, and one from within the Health Service). Institutions such as hospital and universities will almost certainly have a Data Protection Officer from whom advice can be sought, and if applicants have any doubts about the restrictions and obligations placed upon them by the Act, they should seek advice early in the research application. A formal statement of how applicants will deal with their obligations under the Act can only enhance an application.

Financial aspects

The application is designed to obtain money, and the money will be used mainly for hiring staff and purchasing equipment. Some bodies will only fund salaries; others only equipment. Some may have special schemes for purchasing a specific piece of equipment for a specific research project. Applicants should ascertain the policy of the body on funding. Both staff and equipment need to be justified in detail to show that without the exact staff and exact equipment proposed, the research could not be carried out. Applicants have to make a case for the type of staff they wish to employ (postgraduate or postdoctoral researchers, etc.), and also, the level within the particular salary scale. Applicants frequently try to save money by quoting a starting salary for research staff which is at the bottom of a scale. As soon as they interview staff they find that the ones they want to hire will have to be paid some increments up the scale, but the money is simply not available. A case for extra funding has to be made, and this takes time and may not always be successful. A realistic appraisal of the needs of the research (in terms of level of staff, etc.) at the outset can prevent problems of this type later on.

Obviously, applicants should aim to pare costs down as much as possible, but to do so without making the research impossible to carry out. For example, if medically qualified staff are to be hired, this may well need an extra justification, as such staff tend to be more expensive than non-clinical. In situations in which two or three staff are to be hired, it may be worth phasing their hiring over a period rather than hiring all at once. Often there is not enough work for all staff members at the beginning, and the volume of work increases steadily as the grant gets underway. In this situation, phased hiring of staff may be advantageous scientifically as well as financially prudent. Wherever it is possible to save money, applicants should do so, but *without* jeopardizing the scientific quality of the research.

Similarly with equipment, the aim is to cut costs as much as possible, while still allowing the research to take place. Equipment must be described and justified, and the case made to say why a specific piece of equipment is necessary rather than a cheaper alternative. In the UK there is a continuing decline in UGC funding for buildings and equipment (although see earlier comments about the block grant). This results in a temptation for applicants to use a research grant as an opportunity to re-equip a laboratory, or to buy top quality equipment when a simpler and cheaper version would do perfectly well. Referees invariably scrutinize equipment requests very carefully, and often suggest pruning in this area to allow applicants to buy equipment that is sufficient for the research, but no more than that.

DISCUSSION

Inevitably, many applicants will fail to obtain research funding, and often there is a very simple reason for this. The first reason is that the research was not good enough. The second is that although the research is fully up to standard, there was not enough money available. The third is that the research topic does not fall within the ambit of the grant awarding body, and the fourth is that the research, while good enough, cheap enough, and appropriate to the awarding body, was presented in such a way that it failed to communicate adequately.

While these may be concrete reasons for failure to receive a grant, rejected applicants may consider themselves hard done by, and console themselves with a variety of common defences. Two are particularly frequent. The first is that the referees simply did not take the trouble to read the research carefully enough. Obviously there are occasions when the referees have been incompetent; but usually referees take their job seriously, and referee applications with care. The second common defence is to say that referees had a personal bias against the applicant or his/her particular area of research. Only the foolish would deny that this never happens, but the system regarding the larger grant awarding bodies builds in a range of checks and balances. For example, in the UK the Medical Research Council uses both external and internal referees. The external referees are drawn from a very large panel, while the internal referees comprise members of the relevant Grants Committee, and membership of such Committees is public information which applicants should obtain. In this sort of situation of internal and external refereeing, personal or professional bias soon becomes obvious, and the biased referee is unlikely to be asked for an opinion in the future.

If an application has been submitted and rejected, it is obviously disappointing for the applicant, but the situation can be helped by means of feedback. Differing grant awarding bodies have very different policies about feedback, ranging from absolutely no information at all other than a statement of failure, to detailed summaries of referee's comments, or indeed copies of the comments themselves. There is a natural tendency for rejected applicants to argue against such comments, or to use them as a basis for a dialogue of the 'he said I did – I say I did not' variety, but this is likely to be counterproductive. If at all possible, applicants should read and listen to critical comments dispassionately and positively, and try to use such comments as a basis for a strategy for submission of a considerably strengthened application elsewhere.

SOURCES OF FUNDING

Major grant awarding bodies are well known. These include the British Research Councils (MRC, ESRC), the American Institutes (e.g. Health, Mental Health, etc.) various Government Departments or Government sponsored organizations (DoH, SHHD), and Charities and the like. The first two sources of money have clearly specified procedures, detailed application forms, officers who are informed and helpful, and an understanding of the problems in setting up and running a research study. The charities range enormously from medical charities, such as the Wellcome Trust, which functions in a manner very similar to the Medical Research Council, to those that may be disbursing small amounts of money on an irregular basis. It is impossible to give a detailed list of grant awarding bodies in a chapter like this but a very useful directory has been compiled by Villemur (1989). A further very helpful publication is by Burcham and Rutherfurd (1985) which discusses successful grant obtaining strategies, and gives examples of successful applications. This is highly recommended.

Despite problems with shrinking funds for research, it is important to be aware that psychological research is still being carried out, and successful applicants are being awarded substantial sums of money. A brief letter in *The Psychologist*, the *Bulletin of The British Psychological Society* asking researchers to supply details of research monies held resulted in replies from six researchers giving details about projects attracting support ranging from £2000 to £75,000. The sources of funding included the conventional Research Councils, the Wellcome Trust, the Mental Health Foundation, the Leverhume Trust, DoH, SHHD, the Parkinson's Disease Society, NATO, and Sainsburys. For the right projects directed to the right body, money is still available.

FURTHER READING

The Association of Medical Research Charities Handbook, Association of Medical Research Charities, Tavistock House South, Tavistock Square, London WC1H 9LG, UK.

Burcham, W. E. and Rutherford, R. J. D. (1985). *Writing Applications for Research Grants*. Educational Development Advisory Committee Occasional Publication, No. 3, University of Birmingham. (For further information contact the Advisory Service on Teaching Methods, University of Birmingham, Birmingham B15 2TT, UK.)

Villemur, A. (Ed.) *Directory of Grant-Making Trusts*, Charities Aid Foundation, 48 Pembury Road, Tonbridge TN9 2JD, UK.

4.5.2   WRITING A RESEARCH REPORT

Glenys Parry

IT is surprising how many people undertake a piece of research and carry it almost to completion, but fail to take the final steps of writing about it in a formal paper and seeing it through to publication. Many of us have some results lying in a drawer which we intend to write up – one day – or an idea for a paper which has not been written – yet. There are a number of reasons for this. Sometimes, having embarked on a project, one can become disillusioned with it, believing it not to be worth publishing. This may be true, but until you have written at least a draft of a possible paper, it is difficult to be sure. A much more common reason is that people lack confidence in writing and find it difficult. We sometimes forget that to write successfully needs practice, as with any skilled behaviour. Unfortunately it is a skill often neglected during clinical and research training, and many people do not have anyone to help them acquire it. This chapter aims to help the relatively inexperienced researcher at every stage of writing a research report. I shall focus on writing an empirical paper for publication in a journal, but many of the points apply equally to other forms of writing, such as a case report, a review article or a dissertation for examination.

HOW TO START

Getting Ready

Before you sit down to write, there is some important work to do in preparation. This time is well spent and will save a lot of problems later. The first question to mull over is 'What do I want to say?'. Writing is much easier if you have something you want to say. It is quite likely that there is no one clear idea in your mind. Perhaps your study addressed a range of questions which, in hindsight, are not closely related, or there may be some meaningless or negative results. These may be due to design flaws or measurement problems and cannot be interpreted. Despite this, I shall assume that you have some results which you find interesting and which are worth communicating. This is the purpose of the paper, to communicate your findings.

The same principle applies to writing a dissertation or a thesis. Here you have more room and more excuse to list your negative findings, but be careful. It has been remarked that there are many reasons for negative findings, but most of them are trivial. Do not spend pages over-interpreting the reasons why you did not find what you expected to; it is better to focus on what you did find. The quality of the dissertation will be enhanced by thinking carefully about what you found and presenting it as clearly as possible.

When writing up a case study or a piece of qualitative research, there are no numerical 'results' to present. The general importance of thinking through the purpose and the message of the paper is, if anything, even more important in language based research. In a case study, for example, it is easy for the reader to become lost in a mass of clinical detail. The case study is at its best when making a theoretical point. The clinical material, having previously been analysed by the author, can be used selectively to illustrate the argument, and, above all, presented in a logical sequence.

Having decided what it is you want to say, the next question, just as important, is 'Who wants to know about it?'. Even at this preliminary stage you should be thinking about the readers. The research paper is a communication from you to someone else. Imagine you were asked to give a talk about your work. You would find it disconcerting if the person who invited you refused to tell you who the audience was. American psychiatrists? Health visitors? Behaviour therapists? The same thing applies to writing a formal research report. You are not writing in a social vacuum, although it can feel like it sometimes. Think about which journal you are writing for, and what kind of readership it has. Study other articles published by the journal of your choice to get an idea of the style.

If you are writing with co-authors, you will need to allocate tasks and, just as important, decide in which order your names will appear. This can be a source of much bitterness to junior researchers who discover, when the paper reporting their research is nearly ready for submission, that a senior colleague expects to have his or her name first. Alphabetical ordering does not solve this problem, especially for people called Zug. There are, unfortunately, no hard and fast rules about author precedence. It seems fair that the person who did most work should be the senior author, but of course this is often not clear cut. Sometimes the person who planned the research or who wrote it up is not the one who carried it out or analysed the data. In any case, get the rules straight at the beginning, before starting to write – it will prevent acrimony later.

The next stage is to gather together all the ingredients for the paper. In empirical research, the results are the heart of the paper. Sort out all the findings you want to present and get them into a form you can work with. This means creating rough tables, graphs and figures rather than leaving it all on computer printout or scribbled on the backs of envelopes.

You will also need your notes on relevant articles. Ideally, you would have made notes on other papers at the time you first read them; a succinct but informative summary of each paper complete with a full reference. Alas, it is more likely that you have a few photocopies, a few references and several memories of interesting articles you read 6 months ago but cannot now remember – was it Bruddle and Dakey or Brobble and Daly? Was it 1985 or 1984? You can remember the journal had a green cover! Now is the time to spend some hours in the library searching out relevant articles. But beware! It is very easy to fall into the hands of the arch-enemy of academic writers – procrastination. This devious opponent can take many forms, and if you catch yourself, three weeks later, saying 'I can't possibly start to write my paper until I've managed to get hold of so-and-so's article', you must take this as an urgent signal to start writing, immediately.

The Right Conditions

By now you have some idea of what you want to say and to whom you wish to say it. You have gathered all your materials, or at least enough to be going on with. Now you must find the right conditions in which to work. This is a very individual thing. Different people have different strategies, from the well-known psychologist who is reputed to tackle the first draft walking along a towpath with a dictaphone, to a colleague who can only write at the kitchen table surrounded by the tea things with the radio on. You must find your own style, and this is one area where you can be entirely self-indulgent. If you like to write in 2B pencil on yellow paper and only in your garden shed – so be it.

There are some groundrules, though, which you ignore at your peril. The two most important are solitude and uninterrupted time. It's amazing how we expect to be able to dash off a quick paper between telephone calls, meetings and seeing patients, and then seem puzzled and disheartened when nothing happens. The single most common reason for failure to write is the lack of adequate clear time in which to do it. The longer you have the better, the more frequent and regular your sessions the better. You also need a refreshed, clear mind. Writing demands your highest cognitive functions, so it's a good idea to find your own best time of the day, when you have most energy. For many people that is first thing in the morning, so it seems a shame to waste this prime time opening the post or chatting to colleagues. Others like an evening session. Very few people can give their best at four-thirty in the afternoon at the end of a day in the clinic, or during the lunch hour. You also need support and encouragement.

Many would-be researchers working in health service jobs find their writing is not valued and can even be seen as an indulgence. You need to find someone, somewhere, who believes in you and will support you. This support can take many forms, for example shielding you from phone calls when you're writing, or reading and commenting on drafts. You are in the best position to know what kind of support you need and you should take yourself seriously enough to get it.

The final prerequisite for successful writing is having the right tools. A good dictionary is just as essential as pen and paper. Many people find word-processors invaluable as you can draft and re-draft, cut text or move it around on screen so easily. They are particularly liberating for those who are blocked by a perfectionist need to draft the perfect sentence on that blank sheet of paper.

So here you are, sitting in your locked room with the morning ahead of you, notes and results easily to hand and writing tools at the ready. It's time to start writing!

THE OUTLINE

The first thing to write is definitely not the introductory paragraph, but an outline, a plan of your paper (see *Example 1*). There are many excellent reasons for this. It is absolutely essential that the material you are presenting is organized so that there is a logical flow of ideas from beginning to end. There is nothing more frustrating for the reader than a muddled, formless paper which gets off to a few false starts, fails to explain why the study was undertaken, presents results in the method section and then describes previously unmentioned measures in the results. Taking the time to think through the content and structure is part of a genuine desire to communicate, since you are trying to help the reader. The outline is also a very good way of getting ideas down – you learn to tolerate partly formed ideas by sketching them in at an early stage under the appropriate heading. Gradually the structure of the paper takes shape without your getting bogged down in the minutiae of the method or results. A good outline also helps you to write the first draft.

The Main Headings

In an empirical paper, the standard headings are *Introduction, Method, Results* and *Discussion*. This format allows a logical and economic exposition of why you conducted the study, what you did, what you found and what it means. It is not meant to be a realistic account in chronological order of what you thought before you started, the whole story of

Example 1

What the chapter is about
People undertake a piece of research but do not report it in a formal paper.
People lack confidences in writing and find it difficult.
Chapter aims to help the inexperienced.
Focus is on writing an empirical paper for publication in a journal.
Mention case reports, review articles and dissertations for examination.

How to start
Getting ready
    What do you want to say? To whom do you want to say it?
    Gathering your results. Background reading and notes on other articles.
The right conditions
    Quiet solitude and uninterrupted time.
    A refreshed clear mind – support – the right tools.
What to do if you can't get started
    Why it is difficult.
    How to recognize procrastination.
    Getting into the habit.
    Some techniques to overcome a block.

The outline
Why bother?
    The supreme importance of a clear structure.
    If you can't write on outline the paper will be muddled.
    Good ways of getting ideas down – learning to tolerate partly formed ideas.
The main headings
Rough notes

The first draft
Using the outline.
What to write first – how much at a time.
The method – results – the introduction – the discussion.
Getting feedback.

Subsequent drafts
Redrafting and revising for major changes.
Re-analysing results.
Correcting for style.
Reading more articles – knowing when to stop.

Preparing the manuscript for submission
Tables and figures.
References.
The title and abstract.
Authors and addresses.
Acknowledgements.

The editorial process
The covering letter – packaging it.
Reviewers – how long to wait for the decision.
The decision and what to do about it.

the fieldwork, every piece of data you collected or how you changed the design twice in the middle. It is a formal, public account. It is scrupulously honest, but it is constructed. There may, for some purposes, be a better set of main headings, but convince someone else as well as yourself.

Under each main heading, sketch out subheadings. Don't worry if they are not all at the same level of detail. You may have quite a good idea of how your method and results will be written but be more hazy on the introduction and discussion. The aim is to have a working model of the paper, an overview of the whole thing. Under each subheading you can then sketch in rough notes of material you wish to include. There is no need to write in detail. An example might help – there is an initial outline of a paper in *Example 1*. This is as far as you need to take it before starting writing. The final paper will be rather different from the outline, but that is to be expected, since the paper develops in the process of being drafted and redrafted. The outline is your starting point. It is useful at this stage to make a list of all the tables and figures you want to present.

THE FIRST DRAFT

Now you are ready to write the first draft of the paper. It is best to do this quickly. Some authorities advise us to complete the first draft at one sitting, but I have always found this impossible. Getting started is the most difficult part, as a law of inertia seems to apply. The basic principle is to work intensively on the paper over a short period, so that you can be completely immersed in it. One or two hours a week are useless for this, since you have to begin painfully each time; much better to clear a day or two completely. This enables you to build up a momentum where you can become preoccupied with what you are writing. If you do this, you will be surprised and pleased by how much you achieve. When you do stop work, leave your draft at a point in the middle of a section or paragraph where you know exactly what you want to write next. It will be much easier to start writing at the next session than if you had to start thinking afresh about a new section.

The first draft can be written as an expansion of the outline, taking a section at a time. People sometimes wonder which section to write first. The books in the bibliography give a variety of opinion on this matter. Most authors are agreed, though, that it is unwise to start at the beginning and write through to the end. The introduction is often best left in outline form until the results and method sections are drafted. The method is often the easiest section to write, and on the principle that getting started is the most difficult thing, many people make life a little easier by beginning there. On the other hand, the whole reason for the paper is the findings, so it also makes sense to begin by examining these carefully and writing the results section first. Do not imagine that this will necessarily be the final set of results. In the course of writing a paper, gaps in the analysis are often revealed and extra analyses may be needed. The process is reiterative!

As you write the first draft, do not worry too much about niceties of style and grammar, just concentrate on getting it down. There will be ample time for revision later.

Method

In the method section you should aim to explain fully, but concisely, the procedures you used that yielded the data. There should be enough detail for a conscientious specialist to repeat your investigation. This would include the nature of the sample, how it was obtained, the context of the data collection, the procedures used, the measures used and the form of statistical analysis. Where measures are fully described elsewhere, a brief summary description should be given together with the reference. Never mention a measure without the reference, however familiar it may be. If you have included measures of your own devising, give fuller details, including some indication of the measure's psychometric properties (for example, internal consistency, test–retest or inter-rater reliability, validity estimates) and one or two sample items.

Results

The results section should also have a logical order. Methodological checks need to be reported first, for example you may expect certain measures to correlate highly with each other, whereas others should be unassociated. Other checks might include an analysis to determine whether one group within the sample differs systematically from another group (such as where the sample consists of patients from different sites), or you may wish to check that two equivalent groups are well matched on crucial variables.

As a general rule, descriptive statistics precede exploratory data analysis which precedes confirmatory data analysis. If you are discussing the results in a separate section, simply report them here. On the other hand, do not refrain from comment if it helps to organize and structure the section. When reporting significance levels, use two-tailed tests. Don't use a one-tailed test simply because you had a hypothesis which predicted a particular direction. It is really only safe to do so if a result in the other direction would have no meaning. Do not report a p value without the statistic from which it was derived. Give enough information for someone else to check it (for example, an F ratio needs both degrees of freedom). A golden rule is not to report any statistical procedures which you don't understand. This sounds obvious, but the rule is often violated. Ideally you will have analysed your own data. If someone else carried out the analyses, you must know exactly what was done and why. It is much better to report simple procedures clearly and appropriately than complex ones which are muddled or, worse still, non-sensical.

Do not repeat in the text what is already clear from the tables or figures. These should be thought through very carefully. Do not include too much material in any one table or clarity suffers. Often it is better to have two smaller tables than one massive one, unless there is a good reason why the results must be presented together. Always make sure that each table and figure makes sense on its own without the reader having to refer to the text. This means it should have an explanatory title. Make sure you don't call a table a figure or vice versa. Avoid abbreviations if you can, but if you must use them, make sure they are explained on the table (and if used in more than one, on each table) rather than in the text. In graphs, all axes must be clearly labelled. In general, editors prefer tables to figures because they convey more information in a smaller space. Reserve figures for results that need them. In *Example 2a*, the information in *Fig. 1.1* does not need a graphical presentation. It would be better presented as in *Table 1.1*. *Figure 1.2* (in *Example 2b*) is useful, however, because the crucial point is communicated better visually. Having said all this, don't worry about perfection at this stage, so long as you have a 'working version' of all your tables and figures.

Introduction

The introduction should 'set up' the paper. You are trying to explain as economically as possible why you undertook the investigation, and why you approached it in the way you did. There is no point in writing a 2000-word literature review simply to demonstrate that you have read a lot! One hallmark of a badly written paper is a verbose and muddled introduction. The literature reviewed should be apposite, enabling you to make a series of points. If you find this difficult, imagine you are having a conversation with an interested and intelligent colleague (this may be quite a feat of imagination but try it anyway). You are asked a series of questions, such as 'Why was it important to do this investigation? Have other people examined this in the past? How might your study add to existing knowledge? Why did you choose this design? Did you have any special reasons for using these particular measures?'. Answer the questions in normal conversational English and you have the basis for your first draft. When you do describe someone else's study, be specific about the major details without being verbose. For example, compare the two descriptions of the same study in *Example 3*. The second is only a few words longer than the first, but it is much more informative. It is essential to be accurate when describing other people's results. Misreported findings have a habit of slipping into future papers by authors who don't bother to check them. Remember the reviewers of your paper may be the authors of the papers you cite, or are likely to be familiar with them. Your notes will be helpful here; but if you are in any doubt, check.

Discussion

The discussion should not reiterate the results but should do what it says, discuss them. You are trying to explain what your results mean and to relate them to other people's work. Often you are pointing out the implications of the results. You can refer to material from the introduction in the light of your findings, but do not simply repeat it. You are taking it further now you have reported your results. It is appropriate in the discussion to take a sceptical view of your findings. If there are any design flaws (and there will be), this is the place to discuss how they might have affected your results. It is also the place to consider alternative explanations of your findings. If you are not able to think of these, wait until someone else has read and commented on the paper. Try to end the paper on a positive, interesting point. Do not finish it with any variant of the tedious cliche, 'more research is needed to investigate this further'. We can take that for granted!

SUBSEQUENT DRAFTS

Your first draft is a major achievement. The good news is that everything gets easier from now on. The bad news is that you are only half-way there. Many inexperienced researchers assume that the first draft needs only tinkering with before it is submitted. Not at all. Many authors go through two or three major revisions before they are satisfied with the paper. Some do more. The first draft is the basis of your paper, not the paper itself. You can do the first revision yourself by reading though carefully, putting yourself in the reader's shoes. Is it clear? Are there any parts which are particularly muddled or clumsy? Do you stay in the same tense or oscillate between past and present? Have you overused a particular word or phrase? Iron out the

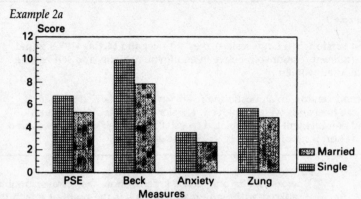

Fig. 1.1 Comparison between single and married mothers on measures of psychiatric symptoms and psychological distress.

TABLE 1.1

Single (n = 21) and married (n = 172) mothers: Comparison between groups on measures of psychiatric symptomatology and psychological distress

		PSE	*Beck*	*Anxiety*	*Zung*
Single	mean	6.76	9.95	3.50	5.67
n = 21	(SD)	(7.06)	(9.72)	(2.39)	(4.10)
Married	mean	5.32	7.81	2.63	4.84
	(SD)	(6.27)	(7.12)	(2.48)	(3.78)
t-value (191 df)		<1	1.25	1.48	<1
Significance		ns	ns	ns	ns

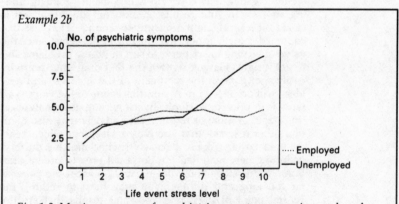

Fig. 1.2 Moving average of psychiatric symptom score in employed and unemployed groups across increasing life stress.

Example 3

First version In a large-scale survey, Kessler and McRae (1982) found a significant relationship between employment status and self-esteem in married women.

Second version In a questionnaire survey of 532 married women whose husbands were employed, Kessler and McRac (1982) found paid employment was correlated (p < 0.05) with self-esteem measured by a short form of Rosenberg's (1965) scale.

---

worst faults and get it typed – now, as always, double-spaced with wide margins. This is the point at which the word-processor comes into its own, since it is so easy to print out new drafts – as many as you want. Typists (including yourself) are neither so tireless nor uncomplaining.

Next, give the paper to at least one other person to read and comment on. Encourage them to write all over the draft. Tell them if there is something you particularly want them to do; for example, check that the results make sense, think of alternative explanations for the findings, spot unbuttressed assertions. One of these people could be a specialist who understands the field, but it is also useful for a non-specialist, even a layperson, to read the paper. They will be less tolerant of obscurities and the use of jargon. Remember that although your paper must be useful to the specialists, most of the journal's readers will not be specialists; be considerate of them.

Your 'reader' may come up with a major problem, finding an error in your results or showing your argument is based on a fundamental misunderstanding. Don't be discouraged, however negative the feedback seems, since the value of writing the paper is to sort out these problems and to get it right. Having written the first draft you can more easily spot gaps in the argument or the analysis, and new ideas will occur to you. Again, this is one of the ways your work is improved, so don't shy away from new analyses at this stage, or a major redraft. Your adviser may also mention other research that you have missed but which bears on your paper. Again, it is worth checking this out and including new material, but don't fall prey to procrastination. At this stage you will probably find that the paper is far too long and diffuse. You may have to rethink the central point of the paper and omit results that are not essential in order to provide a clear focus.

When you have redrafted the article to a point where you are happy with what it says, turn your attention to how you have said it; go through the paper carefully and correct the style. There are many useful guides to writing style, some are mentioned in the reference section at the end of this chapter, but the golden rule is to write as simply and clearly as you can. Ruthlessly cut out all the waffle, the redundant and circumlocutory phrases; fearlessly replace the passive verb forms with active ones, the cliches with fresh images, the 70-word, eight-clause sentences with two or more smaller ones (see *Example 4*). As well as trying your best to write in plain English, you must also observe the house-style of the journal. For example, the American Psychological Association publishes a guidebook on style (*The Publication Manual of the American Psychological Association*) which includes everything from whether to use single or double inverted commas to how to avoid sexist use of language.

PREPARING THE MANUSCRIPT FOR SUBMISSION

References, Acknowledgements, Abstract

You will find the reference list a time-consuming and frustrating job, but so does everyone else and there's no way round it. Write the references on cards or a word-processor so that the odd one càn be popped in the right place without having to re-write the lot. The references must be complete and accurate. This sounds easy but isn't and you will have to take trouble over it. Follow the style of the chosen journal obsessionally, down to the last full-stop. Check that every reference you cite is in the reference list and that every reference in the list is cited in the paper.

Example 4 – Correcting for style

First draft It is of interest to note that the approach employed by the present author is somewhat similar to that of Jones (1985) in terms of the assessment of individuals' conceptual structure, with the exception of the number of items included, where, in the present paper, ten is considered to be a sufficient number, as will be seen by examination of Table 3.

Second draft I used a ten item version of Jones' (1985) method to measure conceptual structure (see Table 3).

The acknowledgements should include those who gave substantial help in supporting you, collecting data, advising on statistics, reading and revising the manuscript. On the other hand, do not mention absolutely everyone with whom you had a coffee-time conversation about the research. Always tell someone if you intend to acknowledge their help.

The abstract should be a very brief summary of the paper, written with the non-specialist in mind. Try to include the main findings rather than the uninformative 'Results are reported of a comparison of two matched groups of outpatients'. It is better, for example, to say 'A group of depressed outpatients were found to have significantly smaller social networks than a matched group of anxious patients'. The journal will give a word limit for the abstract in the instructions to authors. Keep to it. You will have to draft and re-draft the abstract to whittle away every unnecessary word.

Tables and Figures

When preparing the final version of the tables and figures, always double check that every number is correct. An error that creeps in at this stage has every chance of remaining undetected until after publication – an embarrassment so intense it is not worth risking. Eventually, you should have the figures professionally produced by a graphic illustrator, who will produce high-quality glossy prints suitable for reproduction. It is safer to wait until the paper is accepted, and the definitive version of the figures is known, before committing yourself to the expense.

The Title Page

Now you have to worry about the title of the paper. You have probably been using a working title, but think about it again now. The title should be as concise as possible, but should accurately describe the paper's concerns. Your own and any co-authors' names and affiliations should also appear on the title page, but nowhere else. This enables the editor to send your manuscript for blind review.

The Final Manuscript

Take loving care over the final manuscript, so that it looks really professional. This means that if you do use a word-processor, learn to use it properly. The life of an editor or an examiner is made miserable by poorly formatted manuscripts littered with misspelt words, produced by misguided authors who have prematurely dispensed with the services of a professional typist. If you cannot find the time or take the trouble to get a really good result yourself, you could use the word-processor for all but the final draft, then get that properly typed. The typing should be perfect, double-spaced (that means everything, including the references), with wide margins. Show in the text where each table and figure belongs (*Fig. 1.3*). Make a final check that all the references in the text are in the reference list (and vice versa) and that the names and dates are identical in both places. Similarly, make sure that all the tables are referred to in the text and that any table you mention does indeed exist. Read the manuscript for typing errors, checking every word. Preferably, persuade someone else to proof-read it too, to pick up the mistakes you missed. The order in which the paper should be compiled is as follows:

1. Title page; includes title and authors' names and addresses. Some journals need index keywords here and a short title which will be used as a heading for subsequent pages (running head).
2. Abstract.
3. Text.
4. Acknowledgements.
5. References.
6. Tables (each on a fresh page).
7. Figure legends.
8. Figures.

When the sample was split into 'cases' and 'non-cases', all the measures showed a significant difference between the two groups (see Table 1).

TABLE ONE ABOUT HERE

The two self-esteem measures most clearly reflected differences between respondents. It is likely that even for these measures, there is considerable overlap between the distributions of scores of cases and non-cases. The breakdown of means of the two self esteem measures across the eight ID levels is presented graphically in Figure 1.

FIGURE ONE ABOUT HERE

There does appear to be a discontinuity in the linear relationship between ID level and self esteem, occurring at ID5.

Fig. 1.3 An example of typed manuscript

Before sending it off, check that all the pages are there, numbered and in the correct order. Send the top copy and two good photocopies, accompanied by a short, formal letter to the editor.

THE EDITORIAL PROCESS

The process of sending papers out for independent review does not only benefit the journal's editor, but gives you useful feedback on your paper and the research itself. The most frustrating thing is when you have no reply, save a postcard acknowledgement, for months on end. How long should you leave it before writing again to enquire about the decision? I think that three months is long enough, because if you have heard nothing by then your paper is probably sitting in the in-tray of one of the reviewers who needs to be reminded about it.

The decision you receive will be one of four – accept, accept subject to amendment, revise and re-submit, or reject. It is unusual to have a paper accepted outright, so please don't expect this. If it is accepted subject to amendment, you have done very well. After a celebratory night out, start the new version, so that the paper can be off your desk and back to the editor as soon as possible.

If you have been advised to revise and resubmit the paper, it will probably be sent to the reviewers again and there is no guarantee that it will be accepted. On the other hand, most revisions that are conscientiously undertaken do get accepted in the end. Don't think you can get away with a superficial readjustment of a few words; you must address the points raised by the reviewers and do everything you can to meet them. Read what they say carefully before deciding whether to attempt the revision or submit the paper as it stands to another journal. If you do revise the paper, an important part of the resubmission is the letter to the editor. Here you should list the points raised by reviewers, explaining how you have altered the paper, or what new analyses are included, corresponding to each point. A reviewer may suggest something with which you honestly disagree. If so, after the list of amendments you have made, explain why you have not made that particular change. Such a letter, if carefully written, can be very helpful to the editor and hence to your paper's chances of acceptance.

Rejection

The 'rejection' is a narcissistic blow and you will almost certainly feel bad about it. Read the reviewers' comments as objectively as possible and ask someone else to read them too.

If the editor advises you that the paper's subject matter is outside the scope of the journal, start to think where else you can resubmit it which would be more appropriate. Also submit it to another journal if the reviewers make a number of points which can be incorporated into the text, thus improving the paper and making it more likely to be accepted the second time. If the editor advises you that the results are unsound, do not submit it to another journal until you have thought how to improve the evidence in the paper.

If you are convinced that the editor's letter and the reviews are of poor quality, superficial, have missed the point or are just plain wrong, put the whole thing aside for a few days before reading them again. If you still feel unfairly treated, you are quite entitled to write to the editor explaining why and asking for the decision to be reconsidered. If you do this, take care that your letter is based on sound argument; avoid a shrill and acrimonious tone. Never telephone, and only write after thinking it over very carefully.

If you have taken care over the research and the earlier drafts of the paper, you should not be disheartened in the face of one rejection. Remember that there are very few academic writers, however distinguished, who have not had a paper rejected. Many good papers were rejected by the first journal to which they were submitted. Some journals are much more difficult to be published in than others, so you can patiently work your way down the hierarchy until you succeed. One important point though – always get the paper retyped in the style of the journal to which you are submitting. A dog-eared manuscript clearly intended for a different journal will be at a big disadvantage from the start.

COMMON PROBLEMS

You Can't Get Started

I have already said that the most difficult thing is beginning. For some people this is so difficult that they never do, putting off the fateful day for months on end. Procrastination is probably a response to anxiety about whether one is good enough; a fear of falling short of one's ideal, of failing, of being exposed, criticized, judged, vulnerable or lonely. It can sometimes feel as if something in you is actively blocking the work, rebelling against getting on with it. Successful avoidance (which includes a range of displacement behaviours like taking on too much clinical work, getting drunk, suddenly deciding the house needs redecorating) does have a pay-off because one's anxiety level goes down. Alas, this only serves to reinforce the procrastination, which has you ever more firmly in its grip. Eventually, if you have someone else policing a deadline, there is an anguished and undignified last-minute scuffle in which, amazingly, the paper gets written. Unfortunately, for most research papers intended for publication there is no deadline at all; it is entirely your own affair. Procrastination is so deadly to productivity and so painful for the sufferer (and I speak from personal experience) that one wonders why it is so hard to relinquish. Perhaps it is because, as well as reducing anxiety in the short term, it also provides a ready-made attribution, an insurance policy against failure or criticism: 'Well, I know it isn't much good, but I only had two days to write it in'. Thus one can keep unsullied the fantasy of the perfect paper one might have written, given enough time.

The first step is to recognize these processes in oneself. The way out is to get into the habit of writing, doing it regularly. It is often helpful to set up a plan of the week's work, setting realistic goals and building in rewards for when they are achieved. What seems like an enormous task can be tackled by slicing it into small pieces and doing one at a time. Simply to put an end to the avoidance is useful. Set the time aside, find the right conditions and sit there. If you really can't get on with the paper itself, write something else – rough notes, ideas, notes on other people's papers – anything. The important thing is to be in the habit of setting pen to paper (or fingers to keyboard), to get practice at forming sentences, working with words. Even if you sit for the whole of your designated session staring at the wall, you are breaking the pattern of avoidance, starting to face the anxiety that freezes you. Since procrastination depends on self-deception, the next session will not be so difficult.

Isolation

The other major problem you are likely to face is being a lone researcher, trying single handed to carry your project to completion. Do not struggle on alone if you are getting nowhere. Find someone else with whom you can share your work, on the basis that you give them the same kind of research support. This kind of reciprocal help can include a regular meeting to talk about research issues, how the writing progresses, to set deadlines. You can read and criticize each other's papers and help with boring jobs like checking the accuracy of references and proof-reading. You then also have someone with whom you can discuss the editor's letter, someone who will congratulate or commiserate as needed.

You will find more detailed guidance about the technical issues in writing a paper by reading the books in the reference section. I hope this chapter is a springboard to them and to achieving what is, in the end, a profoundly satisfying experience; seeing your own research paper published.

REFERENCES

BARZUN, J. and GRAFF, H. F. (1977). *The Modern Researcher*. New York: Harcourt Brace Jovanovich, Chapters 11, 12 and 13.

BAUSELL, R. B. (1986). Evaluating and communicating the results. In *A Practical Guide to Conducting Empirical Research*. New York: Harper and Row, Chapter 17.

DAY, R. A. (1979). *How to Write and Publish a Scientific Paper*. Philadelphia: ISI Press.

FOWLER, H. W. (1978). *A Dictionary of Modern English Usage*, 2nd edn. Oxford University Press.

GOWERS, E. (1986). *The Complete Plain Words*, 3rd edn. London: HMSO. (Also (1987) Harmondsworth: Penguin.)

O'CONNOR, M. and WOODFORD, F. P. (1978). *Writing Scientific Papers in English*. Tunbridge Wells: Pitman Medical Publishing.

4.6 EXAMINING: UNDERGRADUATE AND RESEARCH DEGREES

Ann Colley

SETTING EXAMS

THERE are a number of different types of examinations used in psychology degrees. The type of examination which is most appropriate varies according to the level of the course and its nature, that is, whether factual knowledge or understanding and critical awareness of the central issues in a particular area is being tested, or whether knowledge of research and theoretical approaches in an area of psychology or methodological and statistical competence is being examined. Increasingly, multiple choice questions are being used to assess factual knowledge in introductory courses, their advantage being that they offer an objective test of factual knowledge and are quick to mark. The marking may even be automated. Their disadvantage is that a large battery of questions must be prepared each year. Short note questions are also useful at an introductory level to test students' knowledge of basic concepts. More advanced methodological and statistical skills may be assessed using questions which require the student to undertake the design of a study to answer a particular research question, or to identify a suitable method of analysing a particular data set and undertake the analysis. For both short note answers and questions on methodology, it is a relatively straightforward task to prepare a marking rubric, identifying critical points and how marks will be allocated to them. However, the questions must be carefully checked for any possible ambiguities which might mislead candidates.

Essay questions are the most commonly used form of assessment at undergraduate level. They should reflect the level of the course for which they are being used, and hence the level of sophistication of the candidates in being able to draw upon skills of critical analysis. It is bad practice to allow candidates to answer several questions which overlap in the knowledge required to produce an adequate answer, because of the difficulties in marking answers which are clearly very similar. It is also important to consider the scope of the question: if it is too narrow, the candidate may reasonably not have sufficient material to produce a good answer; if it is too broad, producing an adequate answer may be difficult in the time allowed. Judging the relative difficulty of different questions on one paper may not be easy, and it is even more of a problem to attempt to set questions of similar difficulty on different topics. Nevertheless such issues should be taken into account when setting papers, so that students with preferences for particular topic areas are not disadvantaged relative to others. The best questions for more advanced students require them to impose a coherent structure on their answers, and to demonstrate background reading and careful thought.

EXTERNAL EXAMINING

Undergraduate and Taught Master's Courses

The role of the external examiner is to ensure comparability of standards across institutions and to ensure that the assessment of students for a particular degree is fair. All, or most, institutions should have a Code of Practice available which outlines the functions of the external examiner system. The normal period of appointment is for three years, and once an invitation has been issued, usually by the head of the Department responsible for the course in question, the appointment is recommended by the appropriate institutional academic committee, such as a Faculty Board. The external examiner may report to the Vice-Chancellor or perhaps to a board or committee of the institution. External examiners are selected for their experience, expertise and seniority and would not normally be from institutions at which a member of the inviting department is currently acting in a similar role. Because of the heavy workload at examination time it is inadvisable and undesirable to hold a number of such posts simultaneously. Some courses have more than one external examiner, usually justified by the scope of the course or the size of the student cohort.

The external examiner's role

There are three major aspects of the external examiner's role: taking part in the degree assessment and moderating marks where appropriate, adjudicating on the cases of problematic candidates, and making comments upon the structure and content of the degree and its assessment scheme. On appointment, an external examiner should expect to receive full documentation on the structure of the degree and the curriculum, course syllabuses, institutional Regulations and Code of Practice, the degree assessment scheme and the concluding report of the previous incumbent. A briefing visit may also be arranged.

The degree assessment

The degree assessment will usually include both examination papers and continuous assessment, and may also include *viva voce* examinations. The external examiner has a right to see all written work which contributes to the degree classification, but in practice may opt to sample from both examination scripts and continuously-assessed work. If only a sample is seen, the external examiner should specify the nature of the sample, for example, random sample within each degree class together with borderline scripts, first class scripts and failures. Not all departments hold *viva voce* examinations, and of those which do, most do not hold them for all candidates. The external examiner should expect to be involved in setting the criteria for selecting candidates, such as borderline cases, first class candidates and failures. The *viva voce* examination would normally explore the candidate's knowledge of selected aspects of the course and would be held by the external examiner in conjunction with one or more internal examiners, who would then together come to an agreed assessment of the candidate's performance and its implications for the degree assessment.

Approval of examination papers

The first point of participation in the assessment procedure comes when the first drafts of examination papers are prepared. The external examiner is asked to approve all papers for undergraduate degrees (that is, those which contribute to the final degree assessment, not usually those for examinations which are qualifying only) and all papers for Master's degrees. Some modifications to the scope or wording of individual questions may be suggested.

All, or a sample, of the continuously assessed work and examination scripts are sent to the external examiner when the internal examiners have completed their assessment. In modular degree courses which are based upon two semesters in each year, assessment normally takes place at the end of each semester. The external examiner may therefore be asked to moderate marks at the end of each semester. The marks of the internal examiners are also sent, which the external examiner may choose to ignore until his or her own assessment has been made. Where the external examiner feels that the standard of marking by the internal examiners is too high or too low, the marks may be moderated, normally by negotiation and discussion prior to or at the final examiners' meeting. In addition to looking at standards in general, candidates on borderlines, with first class marks, and with failures are usually looked at in more detail, and it is helpful for the external examiner to look at all of the work of these candidates in order to form a judgement and make a recommendation to the Board of Examiners.

Meetings of the Board of Examiners Although, as a member of the Board, the external examiner normally has the right to be present at all meetings of the Board of Examiners for a given degree, usually the only formal requirement is to attend the final examiners' meetings. The external examiner is briefed prior to the meeting on special cases involving disciplinary or medical matters which are then discussed at the meeting. *Viva voce* examinations, if held, normally immediately precede the final examiners' meeting. The role of the external examiner at this meeting is to offer general comments on assessment standards, adjudicate on special cases, and provide comments and recommendations concerning both the conduct of the assessment procedure and the structure of the degree and its syllabus. After the meeting a formal written annual report is made to the Vice-Chancellor or Principal of the institution, which is used by the institution as a basis for discussion of standards and possible improvements, and may also be sent to external funding or accrediting bodies. The examiner is also at liberty to report confidentially to the head of the institution on any matter which is felt to be both sensitive and serious.

Fees vary from course to course and are usually weighted by the number of students being examined.

RESEARCH DEGREES – MASTER'S AND DOCTORATES

Selection of the external examiner

The criteria for the selection of external examiners for research degrees are seniority, knowledge of the area of the thesis, and independence (that is, the examiner should not be compromised by a close working or other relationship with the candidate or supervisor). As with the appointment of undergraduate examiners, the appointment of an external examiner is confirmed by the institution on the recommendation of the department in which the candidate is registered. The normal practice is to have one external and one internal examiner for each candidate, although in special cases there may be more than one of either, and the internal examiner is not normally the supervisor. The role of the external examiner is to read the candidate's thesis and form an overview of the level of competence demonstrated, and to play the major role in the *viva voce* examination which takes place when both examiners have read and formed an opinion of the thesis. The research presented in psychology theses is usually empirical, and may consist, for example, of a series of studies using the same methodology, one large study with a sample from an unusual population (for example, in clinical psychology or neuropsychology) or one or more large studies using a large sample. Theoretical theses are sometimes submitted but are relatively rare. Research degrees reflect research training, and theses are assessed with this in mind. There may be aspects of empirical work contained in them which, in retrospect, could have been better executed, but assessment is made of the body of work as a whole. In order for the degree to be awarded however, the thesis should contain at least some work of a publishable standard. A Ph.D. or D.Phil. thesis is more substantial than a Master's thesis because it represents a longer period of training, and hence allows more work to be undertaken and a greater depth of enquiry.

The thesis & *viva*

The first significant duty of the external examiner is to read the thesis and prepare questions for the candidate. These may focus upon any aspect of the research or its background. Concerns about the methodology or analysis can be explored with the candidate at the *viva*. Typographic errors and other necessary corrections are also listed to give to the candidate. The *viva* is conducted in conjunction with the internal examiner(s) and the supervisor may be present at the discretion of the examiners, although it is appropriate to ascertain the candidate's wishes in this respect. The supervisor should not participate in the *viva*, but may answer questions from the examiners if appropriate. The way in which the *viva* is conducted is agreed beforehand by the examiners, who may also discuss their assessments of the thesis. After the *viva*, the candidate is usually asked to withdraw while the examiners confer, then called back in to receive the verdict. For a Ph.D. or D.Phil. the possible outcomes are: award of the degree, award subject to minor amendments which can usually be completed within a month (the internal examiner checks the thesis before it is lodged with the institution), referral for more major modifications (a time limit for resubmission is set by the institution, usually two years), award of a Master's, referral for major modifications for the award of a Master's, or fail. Similarly, a Master's degree may be awarded, awarded subject to minor modifications, referred or failed. Referral is used when substantial rewriting or additional data collection is required. The candidate is given feedback by the examiners on the nature of the modifications to be undertaken. After resubmission, a *viva* may be held or deemed unnecessary. Award of an M.Phil for a Ph.D submission may be recommended where the body of work is insufficiently substantial for the award of a doctorate. A joint report is prepared by the examiners for the academic committees of the institution, summarizing the nature of the thesis, their assessment of it and of the candidate's performance at the *viva*.

Examining fees vary from institution to institution, but the recommendation of the Association of University Teachers of a fee of £70 for a Master's and £100 for a Ph.D. is adopted by many.

FURTHER READING

Guidelines for External Examiners on Undergraduate Psychology Degrees. Leicester: The British Psychological Society.

NOTE

Ethical Principles

Students and examiners alike are reminded that all psychologists engaged in research with human participants are required to abide by the Society's *Ethical Principles for Conducting Research with Human Participants*, which supplement the Society's *Code of Conduct*. Violation could form a basis of disciplinary action, and it is essential that all members of the psychological profession abide by the principles if psychologists are to continue to retain the privilege of testing human participants in their research. Psychologists have legal as well as moral responsibilities for those who help them in their studies, and the reputation of the discipline in the long term depends in part on the first-hand experience of those taking part in psychological investigations. Copies of the *Ethical Principles* are available from the Society.

ESRC Studentships

The Economic and Social Research Council has asked the Society to bring the following information to the attention of our members.

We now make our general information on studentships available on the NISS Bulletin Board and this is updated on a monthly basis. Additionally the quarterly newsletter which we send to ESRC postgraduate training links in HEIs is posted on the Bulletin Board. We also now provide information about all current ESRC–funded Research students on the electronic NISSWAIS facility accessed through the NISS Gateway. These details include the student's name, academic address, supervisor, research topic and discipline under which it falls.The information is updated monthly. As with any database it can be searched by using key words.

The information is available to anyone who has access to JANET, and it is hoped that students, for example, will find the facility useful in identifying other ESRC–funded students at their own institutions, or ESRC–funded students with similar research topic areas. We hope, of course, that it will be useful in encouraging networking in the social science community as a whole.

Guidelines for External Examiners on Undergraduate Psychology Degrees

Published by The British Psychological Society in conjunction with the Association of Heads of Psychology Departments. Available free from the Society's office.

Contents:

- Background to the Guidelines
- CVCP and CNAA Guidelines
- The Appointment of External Examiners
- Vetting Exam Questions
- Balance of Assessment
- What Should External Examiners See?
- The External Examiners' Report
- Guidance and Training

- Psychological Considerations
- Role and Function of External Examiners
- Briefing of External Examiners
- Projects
- Marking of Exam Scripts
- The Examination Board
- Fees

Appendices:
CVCP Guidelines; CNAA Guidelines; An Attempted Synthesis of Marking Schemes; Project Report Form

Guidelines for Assessment of the PhD in Psychology and Related Disciplines

This document, issued as a statement by the Society, produced with assistance from the Economic and Social Research Council and the Association of Heads of Psychology Departments, and published by UCoSDA (The Universities' and Colleges' Staff Development Unit) is available at a cost of £4.00 to BPS and UCoSDA members (£12.00 for non-members) from: The Committee of Vice-Chancellors and Principals of the Universities of the United Kingdom, Universities' Staff Development Unit, Level 6, University House, Sheffield S10 2TN.

Contents:

- Introduction to the Guidelines
- The Selection of Examiners
- Assessing the Written Submission
- External Factors for Consideration
- Appeals by the Candidate against the Outcome of the Examination

- The Purpose of Assessment of the PhD
- Preparation for the Examination
- The Oral Examination of the Candidate
- Pay and Terms of Service of Examiners
- Assessment of Other Components of Research
- Training

Appendices:
Participants at Two Residential Workshops, March 1994; British Psychological Society's Code of Conduct for Psychologists; Criteria for Assessing PhD Theses in Psychology

SECTION V
INFORMATION AND RESOURCES

Contributors:

Nick Hammond
Reader, Department of Psychology, University of York

Annie Trapp
Manager, CTI Centre for Psychology, University of York

Ingrid Lunt
Senior Lecturer, Department of Educational Psychology and Special Educational Needs, University of London Institute of Education; Course Director of Professional Training for Educational Psychologists; Chair of the BPS Professional Affairs Board 1993–96; President of EFPPA

5.1 THE USE OF INFORMATION TECHNOLOGY IN PSYCHOLOGY

Nick Hammond and Annie Trapp

PSYCHOLOGY's involvement with the computer is almost as long-standing as the history of the computer itself. Initially, concern was not so much with actual use as with the notion of general purpose information processing and its relation to human intelligence. Indeed, the rise of cognitive psychology with its information-processing view of mental faculties owes a good deal to the computer metaphor (for example, Neisser, 1967). However, with the coming of the minicomputer, experimental psychologists were not slow to spot the computer's potential both in the control of laboratory instruments and as a replacement for mechanical equipment such as the memory drum and tachistoscope (Weiss, 1973). Hand-in-hand came the use of the computer for statistical analysis, not only increasing speed and reliability but making possible complex designs and techniques that it would have been unthinkable to analyse by hand.

Today the computer is ubiquitous in psychological research, and most psychology lecturers have at least a passing acquaintance with computer use. The great majority (88 per cent according to a recent survey, Trapp, Hammond and Lucas, 1994) have a microcomputer on their desk. This familiarity with computer technology, coupled with the changing pressures in the higher and further education sectors, is leading to a burgeoning use of educational technology within psychology. Outside education and research, the computer is also finding a growing role in vocational areas of psychology, whether for specialist applications such as the administration, analysis and reporting of assessments (for example, Dodd, Thomas and Macredie, 1993) or for more general usage such as record-keeping and word-processing.

This chapter summarizes some of the main uses of computers within psychology and lists sources of further information. Reaping the optimal benefit from information technology is not just a matter of choosing the right hardware and software; it is knowing what tasks can be effectively supported, and how this support can be achieved within appropriate organizational and social contexts. This is a common issue when introducing new technology into organizations. Technology provides opportunities for both short-term and long-term benefits, and while organizations may be quick to perceive the short-term gains, they often adopt a minimalist approach to new technology, placing it over existing organizational structures to cause as little disruption as possible (Blacker, 1988; Davenport and Short, 1990). This in turn imposes constraints on the way the application of the technology can be developed, particularly in innovative areas made possible by the power of the technology. Surveys of the take-up of educational technology in universities (Hammond *et al.*, 1991) provide an instance. While innovative use of educational technology is typically not discouraged, there is little advice or training on such matters available within institutions, and few explicitly reward teaching innovation. The point is that to make the most of what technology can offer may require a careful reorganization of the working context.

THE USE OF INFORMATION TECHNOLOGY IN PSYCHOLOGY

Our focus will be on microcomputer use by the individual in support of his or her work. The two common sorts of machines in this category are IBM Personal Computers and compatibles (hereafter referred to as PCs) and Apple Macintosh computers (Macs). In either case, a machine may be used on its own, or might be connected over a network to other computers, printers and other devices; it might also have access to national or international information networks.

In this section we will consider three areas of computer use: in education, in research and in vocational practice. General administrative use such as word processing and record keeping is not specific to psychology, and so is not covered in this chapter. New software for these applications emerges so frequently that any advice we could give here would be out of date before it is read; the reader is advised to consult local experts and, particularly, to learn from the experiences of others engaged in similar activities to themselves.

The subject matter of psychology often leads to personal information being stored electronically. You may therefore be under an obligation to register use of computers for holding personal data under the Data Protection Act (see Section 2.2.2). Often institutions register as a whole, but you may have to inform some institutional representative of your usage. In addition, individuals have the right to access stored information about themselves under some circumstances. If this is at issue, you should seek further advice.

Education

Given the familiarity of psychology lecturers with computers for research or word processing, one would expect the discipline to be in a good position to make use of educational technology. Certainly the two most common uses of computers in teaching, uses which occur in virtually all university psychology departments, reflect the two traditional research applications: to support statistical analysis, and to help run experiments (Hammond and Trapp, 1991). As in other disciplines (Darby, 1992), use of educational technology in psychology is predominantly tool-based, with relatively little use of tutorial, demonstration or teaching-support software. Where, one might ask, are the spin-offs of all that research into intelligent tutoring, exploratory environments, simulations and microworlds or more recently into hypermedia, mindtools or group learning? Psychologists are, after all, involved in all these research areas, and might reasonably be expected to be in a strong position to exploit the fruits of their labours within the teaching of their own discipline. Examples of the applications of these approaches to psychology teaching are rare, though they are growing; on the whole, the applications that have flourished are those that cause the least disruption to current teaching practice, both individually and organizationally.

We can categorize use of computers in education into three broad categories: as tools, to provide support for tasks carried out during learning, such as conducting statistical analysis or running an experiment; as a medium for course delivery, in much the same way as a textbook; and as tools to support the processes of learning, such as to enhance group communication. We will discuss each of these categories and then briefly consider some facilities to support the lecturer rather than the student.

Computers as tools

Using the computers to support learning tasks aims to enhance teaching and learning by adding to, or in part replacing, existing practice without changing fundamentally the way learning takes place. However, as we will illustrate, their effective use may often require careful thought about educational objectives, and this in turn may result in further developments.

We mentioned that two tool-based applications dominate computer-based methods in psychology teaching. These are statistical analysis and the control of experiments; all university psychology departments use computers in the teaching of statistics, and the great majority use computers in practical or laboratory classes (Trapp, Hammond and Lucas, 1994). For students, the effects of easing the burden of computation for statistical analyses are obvious enough, and the debate continues on just how much manual computation students should be required to perform to help them understand the concepts of statistics (three views can be seen in Monk, 1991; Simpson and Nicolson, 1991; and West, 1991). In addition to the use of conventional statistical packages, there are a number of more innovative approaches for helping the non-numerate psychology student come to grips with statistics. One is the use of tutorial texts based closely on specific analysis packages so as to enable students to develop concepts in close conjunction with carefully tailored practical work (Monk, 1991). A second innovative approach is the development and use of exploration-based tutorials for teaching statistical concepts and procedures; such a tutorial has been developed and evaluated with success at Sheffield University (Simpson and Nicolson, 1991), and allows students a variety of instructor-directed and self-directed learning. In both these cases, the tutorial development flowed from a considered view of the needs of learners, and both were iteratively tested with students during development. They are good instances of a shift from straightforward tool support to a more educationally-motivated tutorial approach.

Turning to the second major use, experimental control, we see a variety of applications in teaching. The most conventional is the use of the computer as a device to run a more or less fixed experiment – presenting materials to the student as subject, collecting data and generally controlling the experiment (a widely used package is Bushnell and Mullin, 1987). While automation of the laboratory practical class in this way can result in considerable savings in time by lecturers, care has to be taken not to degrade the extent and quality of teaching that the student receives (Halliday, 1991). For instance there is a danger that computerization eliminates some of the very experiences that are most instructive for students in the laboratory situation: moment-to-moment control of the experiment, creating and dealing with stimulus materials, getting a feel for experimental data and how to tabulate them, even what to do when things go wrong. Some materials, particularly from the US, may be packaged as a complete course, with a handbook for the graduate student assistant, workbook for the student and software complete in every detail (see reviews in Goolkasian, 1993, and Hornby and Anderson, 1990). A risk is that undiscriminating use of such packages reduces the face-to-face communication amongst students, and between students and staff, to the detriment of learning.

Packages for running experiments vary a good deal in the control they allow the student experimenter. The older software tends to run fixed experiments, whilst more recent packages such as MELLAB (St James and Schneider, 1991) tend to allow a variety of parameters to be altered (for example with a Müller-Lyer illusion experiment, the angle of the fins in different conditions, the number of trials and so forth). This allows students the possibility of exploring the effects of manipulating a range of independent variables on the measure in question, and tailoring their own experiments.

So-called 'experiment generators' (Chute, 1993; Cohen, MacWhinney, Flatt and Provost, 1993) allow even more flexibility for both teachers and students. A commonly used package is *SuperLab* (Eccleston, 1992; Haxby *et al.*, 1993). These systems provide a shell (effectively a constrained programming environment) within which a wide range of experimental paradigms can be defined. They have obvious application in the teaching of experimental design and allow students to recoup some of the lost ground in getting their hands dirty with experimental materials and experimental design. Experiment generators open up some intriguing educational possibilities. For instance, St James (1989) has proposed that psychology departments should combine to set up shared libraries of experimental materials, and even combine data from experiments using identical software in different institutions and report results of class studies with unprecedented numbers of subjects.

Use of these packages inevitably changes both the way practical courses are structured and the learning outcome for the student. Eckerman (1991) analyses laboratory courses in terms of five activities: collecting background information, generating ideas and questions, collecting data, analysing and interpreting data and reporting. Use of computer-based facilities changes the balance amongst these, and teachers have to be clear about what they want their students to learn, what impact changes will bring, and then to adapt the use of the facilities appropriately. The new opportunity afforded by software requires careful consideration to be given to educational objectives and how they are to be met.

There are many other uses of computers to support the activities required for learning, such as use of spreadsheets for various forms of analysis or modelling (for example, Hewett, 1991), or automated search of large datasets. The Oxford Psycholinguistic Database (Harley, 1993) is one example of a corpus of material that has a range of uses in teaching and research. Use by students of computerized bibliographic information, such as *Psychological Abstracts* on PsycLIT, is also increasingly common (Lewis, 1990; LeVoi, 1991). A recent development, not as yet impacting teaching, is access to very large amounts of information over international networks using standardized protocols such as World Wide Web or Gopher (Syllabus Press, 1993). Some authors predict that access to distributed information will have a profound influence on educational provision (Ehrmann, 1993).

Computers for course delivery and exploration

A small, but increasing, area of CAL in psychology is in the delivery of course materials, whether in a tutorial expository form, as demonstrations of psychological phenomena or as simulations of processes. Perhaps the most successful combine a judicious mix of these approaches; certainly a bland hypertext-based presentation of materials, with no additional guidance or incentives for engagement by the student, is unlikely on its own to lead to effective learning (Hammond, 1993). Systems such as *Neuroanatomy Foundations* – a hypertext tutorial on CNS anatomical structures – are therefore best used in conjunction with external assignments.

Many psychological phenomena, particularly in the areas of perception and cognition, can be well illustrated on computer; and since the human is the object of study, the student can experience phenomena from the perspective of the experimental subject. Some hypertext-based tutorial packages, such as *GRASP* (Thompson, 1989) and *Cochlear Anatomy* (Bailey, 1992), include demonstrations and problem-solving activities aimed at more active involvement of the learner with the materials. Other packages place the main focus on the use of the computer to demonstrate phenomena and provide perhaps only rudimentary tutorial information. The most comprehensive example is *The Active Eye* (Heard, 1991) which includes over 50 demonstrations covering a range of visual phenomena.

Use of simulations, where the computer is able to model some behaviour or process in an interactive fashion, is another fertile area for innovative learning. Often the computer allows exploration of situations which would be hard for students to experience for real, or permits a simpler or speeded-up representation. Examples include: simulated counselling interviews (Morton, 1991) to teach interviewing skills, simulated experiments on conditioning (Hall, 1993) to teach the rudiments of learning theory, the simulation of data for statistical analysis (Bradley, 1993) or the simulation of a range of behaviours using neural networks in order to understand the fundamentals of distributed processing (Orchard, 1990). A well-argued example of use of simulated experiments to teach experimental design can be seen in Simpson (1993).

Using these packages effectively is a challenge. Their use typically does not fall within the standard structure of lectures, tutorials and practicals encountered by psychology students, and it is tempting for departments to relegate software to distant computer rooms for students to use when and if they wish. However tutorial software will be much more effective if its use is integrated fully into courses.

Computers to support learning processes

One view has it that the true role of educational technology is to support learning not by substituting for the book or the tutor, but by providing tools which enhance the processes of learning themselves. For instance, the term *mindtool* has been used to refer to software which itself is content-free but helps the learner mobilize and focus appropriate analytical processes on the material to be mastered (Mayes, 1992). It is with these approaches that the traditional forms of learning, and their institutional support, can be most seriously challenged.

Since learning tools (as opposed to more general support tools such as word-processors) are only rarely used in psychology, we will not discuss them in any detail (see Kommers, Jonassen and Mayes, 1992, for more information). However, we will give a couple of illustrations of the use of these approaches within psychology. The first is the use of concept mapping tools (McAleese, in press). Concept mapping tools (such as *Learning Tool*, Kozma, 1992) support learning by requiring students to make explicit what they know and how their knowledge is structured by constructing 'maps' of their knowledge. The intention is to get students to think about and explore the materials in ways which will extend their understanding. Concept mapping tools have been shown to benefit learning as compared to use of a note-taking facility (Reader and Hammond, 1994). However, to reap the benefit, learners must have some understanding of the knowledge domain so that they can concentrate on defining conceptual links rather than solely on the material's surface form. Topics where the materials have some inherent, but not too simple, structure are best suited to concept map representation, and this is typical of many areas of psychology.

A second area where computers are starting to be used to support the processes of learning is in the use of computer networks. Even used locally, networks can bring advantages to the running of demonstrations in networked classrooms, either through the use of screen sharing software (Quigley, 1991) or through software which distributes control appropriately between instructor and students (Viera, 1989). Local networks can also support interaction amongst students, researchers and staff within a department (Crook, 1990), both through use of e-mail as a supportive role to other tutoring activities and through provision of general on-line information about courses and academic activities. Over more distributed networks, e-mail and electronic conferencing supports a growing number of distance learning courses in psychology, allowing learning communities to be built up across geographical barriers.

Computer support for the lecturer

The preparation and organization of teaching materials is increasingly computer-based, with word-processed handouts, computer-generated visual aids and computer-based materials written by the lecturer. Use of hardware facilities such as computer-controlled projectors, OHP display panels and 'electronic lecture theatres' is growing as a means of enhancing presentation and discussion of materials (Norman, 1990). Software to help lecturers create their own course materials, authoring systems, once the province of the technical wizards, is now both easier to use and more powerful than ever. This is a two-edged sword: mastery of the technology does not mean that developed courseware will be educationally effective; in addition there is a real danger of individual lecturers treading a well-worn path when it would be far more efficient to buy a package off the shelf or make use of materials developed down the road. There are tools to help lecturers plan courses, making explicit the objectives for the course and its components (Johnson, 1991; Petty, Lynch and Rosen, 1993), but we have yet to see such facilities in real use.

Computer-based assessment is another area of growing interest, whether to provide students with informal feedback as an integral component of learning or to gain more formal measures of student performance (Bull, 1993). The use of computers to administer or to make multiple-choice questions (MCQ) is becoming more widespread, and there is a range of software available. A number of introductory textbooks (for example, Wade and Tavris, 1993) include a large number of multiple-choice questions on disk, enabling lecturers to create their own tests from a subset of the questions.

Research

In this chapter we will not discuss specialized research applications, which often rely on the development of in-house software for experimental control, stimulus presentation or data analysis. Nor will we cover the technical area of computational modelling. However, just as lecturers should be aware of what's available so they don't waste time reinventing the wheel, so too should researchers be aware of general-purpose software tools which support a range of research applications, freeing researchers from much tedious software development. Some of these applications are similar to the educational packages discussed above, emphasizing the close ties between computer use in research and in educational practice. For example, the large datasets such as the ESRC Data Archive or the Oxford Psycholinguistic Database have applications in both teaching and research.

Perhaps the largest application is for experimental control, using the computer to present stimuli to the subject and to collect responses, either directly or via specialist devises for input and output interfaced to the computer. In many cases involving trial-based paradigms, general-purpose experiment generators such as *SuperLab* (Haxby *et al.*, 1993) provide the simplest solution, although for time-critical paradigms there is a continuing debate on the visual characteristics of computer displays and the accuracy of timing of response events (LeVoi, 1991; Schneider *et al.*, 1993; Ulrich and Giray, 1989). There are also a number of more specialized experiment generator packages, supporting experiments in areas such as visual search (Enns and Rensink, 1991), psychomusicology (Boltz *et al.*, 1991) and short-term memory (Cox *et al.*, 1992).

Where experiment generators cannot do the job, there are a number of programming languages designed specifically for experimental control (Gollub, 1991; Svartdal and Flaten, 1993). These languages are concerned more generally with the control and monitoring of external equipment (such as in an animal laboratory), and with event recording and data capture. There is also specialist software for use with particular devices or techniques, such as eye-movement recording (Nodine *et al.*, 1992), control of video players for event analysis (Macleod, Morse and Burford, 1993), or the presentation of 3D images via stereoscopic glasses.

There is a growing amount of more complex data acquisition and control equipment that involves specialized hardware and software used, for example, in computerized physiological monitoring. A list of suppliers can be found in *Appendix 1* to this chapter.

Turning to the second major research application, for data analysis, we see a similarly diverse range of facilities. As well as large numbers of quantitative statistical packages (many common in both teaching and research use), there is an increasing number of packages concerned with qualitative data analysis, supporting iterative segmentation and classification of observed behaviour (a number of such packages are discussed by Fielding, 1991). Related to qualitative analysis are packages to assist in the recording of events, such as *The Observer* (Lazarus, 1994) and *CAMERA* (van der Vlugt *et al.*, 1992). These are used to record and analyse time sequences of events in experiments involving direct observation of animals or humans.

Vocational practice

There are more software packages concerned with the administration and reporting of standard assessment tests – whether for appraising clinical, educational, personality, occupational or other individual characteristics – than with any other application in psychology. Most originate from the US, and are intended to assist in professional practice. Within this area we can distinguish four classes of software: for the administration of standardized tests for assessment purposes, for administration of exercises for rehabilitation, for generating reports based on test performance and for the management and analysis of client records. For further details of these packages and their use, the reader is advised to follow up the various sources of information listed later.

Computer-based presentations of tests, complete with initial instructions and appropriate feedback, may make for a more standard delivery and thus better control of confounding variables (West *et al.*, 1992) and recommendations for the design of software for computer-based assessment can be found in Bartram *et al.* (1986) and Bartram (1989). Some tests are particularly suitable for computer administration, perhaps where the presentation of items is contingent on previous responses, or where some form of computation is required on the fly, such as with repertory grid analysis.

There is also software available to assist in the construction of new psychometric tests, for example, *Testan*, or for adaptation of existing tests. *Screentest*, for example, automates test administration, scoring and interpretation with additional features that allow statistical operations. An increasing number of psychometric tests have been programmed to run under *Screentest* including: Gordon's Personal Profile and Inventory; Survey of Personal Values; Survey of Interpersonal Values; Cattell's 16 PF; and the Graduate and Management Assessment series. Computer-generated narratives tend to be rather rigid and it is important that inferences drawn should be treated more as hypotheses than definitive statements. Increasingly, these packages include an editing facility so that the practitioner can make changes, as, for example, with Quester report generator software.

Software is available for the treatment of cognitive deficits, such as memory, perceptual and speech disorders, and behavioural problems. These packages vary in flexibility with some packages allowing the user to create exercises tailored to the needs of an individual. Other software used in vocational practice include packages for career guidance, guiding managers through structured interviews (publishers include Sigma, Saville & Holdsworth) and various packages for decision support and for risk analysis. Finally, there is specialized software for the design and analysis of questionnaires and surveys, the analysis of data from psychometric test and questionnaires, including multidimensional scaling, factor analysis and item analysis.

Sources of information

Information can be sought from individuals and centres of expertise, through meetings and publications and, to an increasing extent, electronically through various on-line sources. Often the best information, though, can be obtained from colleagues who have already discovered the benefits and pitfalls for themselves.

It is inevitable that information on the use of technology becomes out of date quickly. We have made every effort to ensure the information was accurate at time of writing; however if you have difficulties, contact the CTI Centre for Psychology for the latest information (address at the end of this chapter).

Centres of expertise

Within the UK, the Higher Education Funding Councils support discipline-based CTI Centres (Computers in Teaching Initiative) to provide advice on the use of educational technologies. Each CTI Centre serves its own discipline area, and provides a range of information and support on the use of computers in education. All publish a regular newsletter or journal and a directory of resources (available software and other teaching materials). Addresses of the most relevant CTI Centres are listed in *Table 1*. (Contact the CTI Support Service for details of other Centres.)

A further source of information within the educational sector can be found in projects funded under the Funding Councils' Teaching and Learning Technology Programme (TLTP). These projects are charged with developing computer-based teaching materials. Details of some relevant projects are given in *Table 2*. The main projects developing psychology materials are the PsyCLE Project, led from the University of York, and the QUTAL project at Queen's University, Belfast.

Outside the UK, centres of expertise include ASK in Germany, with a general concern for academic software, iec ProGAMMA in The Netherlands, who are particularly concerned with the development of software and in research applications in psychology and the social sciences, and COMPsych, in the US, who disseminate a variety of infor-

Table 1   Addresses and contact details for selected CTI Centres

Address	Contact Details
CTI Centre for Psychology Department of Psychology, University of York, York YO1 5DD	Phone: 01904 433154 Email: CTIPsych@york
CTI Centre for Biology Donnan Laboratories, University of Liverpool, PO Box 147, Liverpool L69 3BX	Phone: 0151 794 5118 Email: CTIBiol@liv
CTI Centre for Computing Faculty of Informatics, University of Ulster at Jordanstown, Newtonabbey, County Antrim BT37 0QB	Phone: 01232 365131 Email: CTIComp@ulster.ujvax
CTI Centre for Human Services Department of Social Work Studies, University of Southampton, Southampton SO9 5NH	Phone: 01703 592779 Email: CTIHumServ@soton.ibm
CTI Centre for Library & Information Studies Department of Information & Library Studies Loughborough University of Technology Loughborough LE11 3TU	Phone: 01509 223057 Email: CTILIS@lut
CTI Centre for Mathematics & Statistics Department of Statistics, University of Glasgow, University Gardens, Glasgow G12 8QW	Phone: 0141 339 4873 Email: CTIStat@glasgow
CTI Centre for Medicine Royal Fort Annexe, University of Bristol, Tyndall Avenue, Bristol BS8 1UJ	Phone: 0117 930 3137 Email: CTICM@bristol
CTI Centre for Sociology & the Policy Sciences Department of Applied Social Sciences, University of Stirling, Stirling, FK9 4LA	Phone: 01786 467703 Email: CTISoc@stirling
CTI Support Service University of Oxford, 13 Banbury Road, Oxford OX2 6NN	Phone: 01865 273273 Email: CTISS@ox.vax

Table 2 Addresses and contact details for TLTP Projects

Address	Contact Details
Statistics Consortium Boyd Orr Building, University of Glasgow, University Avenue, Glasgow, G12 8QQ	Phone: 0141 330 4873 Email: susan@glasgow.statistics
Computer Aided Learning Tools in Statistics and Modelling Department of Statistics and Modelling Science, Strathclyde University, 26 Richmond Street, Glasgow G1 1XH	Phone: 0141 552 4400 Email: cais10@strath.vaxb
Biodiversity Consortium Department of Pure and Applied Biology, University of Leeds LS2 9JT	Phone: 0113 233 2862
BioNet: changing the patterns of teaching in biology Department of Biochemistry and Molecular Biology, University of Leeds LS2 9JT	Phone: 0113 233 2862 Email: bmb6agb@leeds.gps
PsyCLE: Psychology computer-based learning environment Department of Psychology, University of York, York YO1 5DD	Phone: 01904 433139 Email: jm25@york
Technology Based Learning in Medicine: beyond courseware Centre for Medical Education, Ninewells Hospital & Medical Schools, Dundee DD1 9SY	Phone: 01382 60111 x3433 Email: mn11@dundee.primeb
Fully Evaluated Problem Centred Practical and Tutorial Courseware for the Life Sciences Department of Physiology, Faculty of Basic Medical Sciences, Queen Mary and Westfield College, Mile End Road, London E1 4NS	Phone: 0171 982 6375 Email: m.j.george@qmw
QUTAL: Queen's University teaching and learning project Institute of Computer Based Learning. The Queen's University of Belfast, University Road, Belfast BT7 1NN	Phone: 01232 245133 x3767 Email: tltp@qub
Images for Teaching Education School of Education, University of Exeter, Heavitree Road, Exeter EX1 2LU	Phone: 01392 264727 Email: ne.davis@exeter
Applying Behavioural Sciences to the Teaching and Training of Health Professionals Department of Psychiatry, University of Nottingham, University Park, Nottingham NG7 2RD	Phone: 0115 948 4848 Email: mczpg@nott.vme
Pharma-CAL-ogy Department of Pharmacology, Worsley Medical Building, University of Leeds LS2 9JT	Phone: 0113 233 4313 Email: pha6ieh@leeds.novell.south01

mation on computer use in psychology, mainly via electronic means. Contact details are given in *Appendix 1*.

Conferences, meetings and publications

The US Society for Computers in Psychology (SCIP) holds an annual meeting, with proceedings published in the journal *Behavior Research Methods, Instruments, and Computers*. In the UK, the CTI Centre runs an equivalent conference series, entitled *Computers in Psychology*; selected proceedings from CIP 93 were published in the BPS journal *Psychology Teaching Review*. In addition, CTI Centres run workshops on a variety of topics, normally concerned with educational uses of technology.

Finally, iec ProGAMMA organizes a regular conference series, SSIT (Social Science and Information Technology Congress), with selected proceedings published in *Social Science Computer Review*.

Information on the use of computers in psychology can be found in a wide range of journals, newsletters and specialist publications. The three journals listed in the previous paragraph are a good starting point. The CTI Centre for Psychology publishes a newsletter (*Psychology Software News*, issued three times a year) which includes reviews of software together with articles on educational developments and good practice.

A number of directories of software for use in psychology are available. The CTI Centre for Psychology produces *The CTI Directory of Psychology Software* (Trapp and Hammond, 1994) which lists details of about 700 items, mostly of relevance to teaching. This publication can be purchased from the CTI Centre, and is also available electronically (see the following section). The American Psychological Association also produces a directory, with a stronger emphasis on software for professional applications (Stoloff and Couch, 1992). The Directory of Research into Automated Testing (DRAT) lists researchers in the field of automated testing together with software developed for automated testing. Finally, COMPSYCH, also in the US, produce a directory of software, together with news information, which is only available in electronic form. See the following section for details. The APA can be accessed via World Wide Web or Gopher on http://www.APA.ORG

All CTI Centres produce directories of software available within their disciplines. Directories of more general software are also readily available. The most relevant in the UK is produced by CHEST (Combined Higher Education Software Team), *The CHEST Software Directory*, published by Bath University Press). CHEST have negotiated special educational prices for much of the software. The directory can also be accessed electronically (see the following section).

There is a good deal of literature on software for testing

and assessment available from the main publishers in the field; contact details can be found in *Appendix 1*. *Appendix 1* also lists suppliers of hardware and software for data acquisition and experimental control.

Electronic sources of information

There is a wealth of information available on-line; the problem is finding it. Often such information provides a point of departure for contacting other experts or publishers. There are three main categories of on-line information: electronic versions of directories, newsletters and other documents; electronic discussion lists and bulletin boards, accessed via e-mail and to which you can contribute; and on-line copies of computer software, which can be copied onto your own machine. To make use of this information, you will need access to the academic network JANET. For information which is available from overseas, you will also have to access InterNet (Most JANET sites provide simple access to InterNet). Finally, to access information on World Wide Web or Gopher servers, you will need to access a 'client' machine which runs the appropriate software (such as Mosaic). Since the technical requirements for accessing these sources of information depend on local conditions and change frequently, you are advised to seek further details on access from local experts.

Electronic listings, databases and documents

The CTI Centre's *Software Directory*, together with other information such as software reviews, can be accessed from a World Wide Web or Gopher client. The URL address is: http://ctipsych.york.ac.uk/ctipsych.html

The COMPsych directory is also available via World Wide Web or Gopher. Connect to the State University of New York (SUNY)-Plattsburgh. Bulletins are located in the directory SUNY Plattsburgh Information/Compsych. (You can also connect to the COMPSYCH service through the CTI World Wide Web server.)

The *CHEST Software Directory* is available over the JANET network, accessed via the NISS Gateway. From most JANET sites, other sites are accessed via a PAD system. For the PAD> prompt, type: call niss.

Then select NISSPAC and CHEST Directory from the menu options.

Other databases of interest to psychologists include the following.

BIDS

The Bath ISI Data Service provides access to three multi-disciplinary citation indexes (science, social science and arts and humanities) containing details of articles drawn from over 7,000 journals worldwide. Your local library or Computer Centre will tell you how to register to access BIDS over the JANET network.

ERIC

The ERIC Clearinghouse on Assessment and Evaluation provides on-line information about educational and psychological testing. It currently includes:

- the Educational Testing Service Test File as a searchable database, with descriptions of 9,500 test instruments;
- the Buros and Pro-Ed Test Review Locators as searchable databases, providing an index to the *Mental Measurement Yearbooks* and *Tests in Print*;
- a comprehensive collection of full text articles about the latest in alternative assessment.

Information is available via a Gopher server with the address: GOPHER.CUA.EDU. Further enquiries can be addressed to: ERIC_AE@CUA.EDU

ESRC data archive

The archive acquires, stores and disseminates computer-readable copies of social science data from academic, commercial and governmental sources. There are over 3,000 datasets available, including, for example, surveys on crime, attitudes, employment and child development. For further details, contact the ESRC Data Archive (see *Appendix 1*).

HCIBIB

This is a database of over 5,000 bibliographic abstracts in the area of Human–Computer Interaction. The database can be searched over a standard e-mail connection. For further information on how to use the system send a blank message to: hcibib@rumpus.colorado.edu

OASIS

OASIS (Online Academic Software Information System) is a catalogue of microcomputer software for use in higher education; it has a psychology software category. Entries consist of a concise description, review citations, and machine and pricing information. For further details, send an e-mail to: oasis@ecncdc.bitnet

SIByl

SIByl is an extensive catalogue of existing (special purpose) software for the various research fields in the social and behavioural sciences. Currently SIByl contains over 300 of these descriptions. Information includes a functional description; technical and data requirements; price; test report; availability of manual and nature of user interface; literature references; and purchase addresses. A CD-ROM of the SIByl and SRM databases is available from iec Pro-GAMMA. The database can be accessed on-line using the Telnet protocol at the address: suniec.gamma.rug.nl

SISY

Software Information System of the Academic Software Corporation (ASK) in Karlsruhe, Germany. This databank contains information about more than 2,000 software applications for various research fields. Access can be via the SIByl catalogue detailed above.

SRM

The SRM database held in Rotterdam contains approximately 30,000 literature references providing a comprehensive overview of publications in social sciences research methodology since 1970. Access can be via the SIByl catalogue.

Electronic discussion lists and bulletin boards

When you join an electronic discussion list (or 'listserver'), any message you send to the list (via e-mail) will be forwarded to all members of the list. Their primary use is for sharing and discussing information around a particular topic. There are a very large number of lists both within the UK and internationally.

The CTI Centre of Psychology has set up two e-mail lists to help psychologists exchange information about computer use. The first is primarily for staff in university psychology departments to keep in contact with each other and with the CTI Centre, and to discuss ideas, information and problems on the use of computers in psychology teaching and research. To join this list, send an e-mail to: mailbase@mailbase

with the message: subscribe cti-psychology *firstname surname*

Once you are a member, you can send messages to: cti-psychology@mailbase

The second list, PEGG, is a discussion list for psychologists interested in the use of experiment-generating packages in their teaching or research. To join, follow the instructions above, sending the message:

subscribe psych-expts *firstname surname*

and, once joined, using the address: psych-expts@mailbase

Many of the relevant UK discussion lists are managed on the Mailbase system based at Newcastle. There are currently over 400 lists, and a listing of these can be obtained by sending the message: Lists full to: mailbase@mailbase

To join any list, send the command: JOIN *listname firstname lastname* to mailbase@mailbase.

There are also a number of US lists relevant to psychologists. These include the following.

Macpsych
An electronic mailing list for Mac users in academic psychology. Send your message to macpsych@stolaf.edu.

PSYCHGRAD
The purpose of this list is to provide a medium through which graduate students in the field of psychology communicate. To join, send the message:

sub psycgrad *firstname lastname* to: listserv@uottawa.bitnet

TIPS
A heavily used discussion list covering all aspects of teaching psychology. To join, send the message: subscribe tips *firstname lastname* to: listserv@fre.fsu.umd.edu.

INFO-LABVIEW
A list for LabVIEW users. LabView is a graphical programming system for the Macintosh used for data acquisition and instrument control. To join, send the message: sub info-labview *firstname lastname* to: info-labview-request@pica.army.mil

Bulletin boards differ from discussion lists in that readers access central information. Messages can be submitted to the bulletin board, and are usually moderated by an editor. The most relevant for psychology is:

PSYCOLOQUY
This is an electronic newsletter for psychologists. To subscribe, send the message: sub psyc *firstname lastname* to: listserv@pucc.bitnet.

Electronic software archives

A range of free, demonstration and 'shareware' software and teaching materials is available over networks. The CTI Centre's World Wide Web server contains a large amount of demonstration software relevant for the teaching of psychology.

The Macpsych facility also has an archive of psychology software for use on Macintosh computers. For further information, send a request to: macpsych-request@stolaf.edu.

A number of general software archives are also available. In the UK, the Higher Education National Software Archive (HENSA) contains a variety of software than can be downloaded onto your own machine via e-mail. HENSA is split into software for micros (PCs, Macs and other machines) and for Unix machines. To access the archive from a PAD terminal use the name hensa.micros or hensa.unix. Send queries to: archive-admin@hensa.micros (or unix).

A large archive of PC software is available on the ISAAC system (Information System for Advanced Academic Computing). ISAAC also contains discussion fora organized by academic discipline. To join, send a message to: ISAAC @uwaee, engr.washington.edu.

The authors of this section can be contacted at the CTI Centre for Psychology, Department of Psychology, University of York, Heslington, York YOI 5DD, UK. Tel: (+44) 01904 433154; Fax: (+44) 01904 433181; e-mail: CTIPsych@york.ac.uk

REFERENCES

BAILEY, P. (1992). Cochlear Anatomy: a review. *Psychology Software News, 3,* 58.

BARTRAM, D., BEAUMONT, J. G, CORNFORD, T., DANN, P. L. and WILSON, S. L. (1986) Recommendations for the design of software for computer based assessment. *Report prepared for the Scientific Affairs Board of the British Psychological Society.*

BARTRAM, D. (1989). Computer based assessment. In P. Herriott (Ed). *Handbook of Assessment in Organisations.* London: Wiley.

BLACKLER, F. (1988). Information technologies and organizations: lessons from the 1980s and issues for the 1990s. *Journal of Occupational Psychology, 61,* 113–127.

BOLTZ, M., KAPADIA, M. and JOYNER, R. (1991). Psychmuse: a Macintosh system for psychomusicology research. *Behavior Research Methods, Computers and Instrumentation, 23,* 409–414.

BRADLEY, D. R. (1993). Multivariate simulation with DATASIM: The Mihal and Barrett study. *Behavior Research Methods, Instruments and Computers, 25,* 148–163.

BULL, J. (Ed.) (1993). *TLTP Workshops on Assessment of Learning in Higher Education Working Papers.* CVCP Universities' Staff Development Unit: Sheffield.

BUSHNELL, W. R. and MULLIN, J. T. (1987). *Cognitive Psychology: a computerized laboratory course.* Lawrence Erlbaum Associates: London.

CHUTE, D. (1993). MacLaboratory for Psychology: successes, failures, economics, and outcomes over its decade of development. *Behavior Research Methods, Instruments, and Computers* 25, 180–188.

COHEN, J., MACWHINNEY, B., FLATT, M. and PROVOST, J. (1993). PsyScope: an interactive graphic system for designing and controlling experiments in the psychology laboratory using Macintosh computers. *Behavior Research Methods, Instruments, and Computers*, 25, 257–271.

COX, R., HULME, C. and BROWN, G. D. A. (1992). STM Experimenter: Using HyperCard and MacRecorder in short-term memory experiments. *Behavior Research Methods, Instruments and Computers*, 24, 575–580.

CROOK, C. (1990). Networks. *Psychology Software News*, 1, 22–23.

DARBY, J. (Ed.) (1992). U.K. Computers in Teaching Initiative special issue. *Computers and Education, 19(1/2)* (complete issue).

DAVENPORT, T. H. and SHORT, J. E. (1990). The new industrial engineering: Information technology and business process redesign. *Sloan Management Review*, Summer, 11–27.

DODD, J., THOMAS, P. and MACREDIE, R. (1993). The development of computer-based tools to support the analysis of individual capability. *Psychology Teaching Review*, 2, 106–114.

ECCLESTON, C. (1992). SuperLab: a review. *Psychology Software News*, 3, 51–52.

ECKERMAN, D. A. (1991). Microcomputers in undergraduate laboratory training in Psychology. *Behavior Research Methods, Instruments, and Computers*, 23, 91–100.

EHRMANN, S. C. (1993). US higher education in 1988: how it might use technologies for undergraduate education. *The CTISS File, 16*, 8–17.

ENNS, J. T. and RENSINK, R. A. (1991). VSearch Color: Full color visual search experiments on the Macintosh II. *Behavior Research Methods, Instruments and Computers*, 23, 265–273.

FIELDING, N. (1991). Qualitative data analysis packages in teaching. *Psychology Software News*, 2, 74–76.

GOLLUB, L. R. (1991). The use of computers in the control and recording of behavior. In I. H. Iversen and K. A. Lattal (Eds) *Experimental Analysis of Behavior, Vol II*, New York: Elsevier.

GOOLKASIAN, P. (1993). A review of Macintosh-based instructional software. *Behavior Research Methods, Instruments, and Computers* 25, 164–167.

HALL, G. (1993). Laboratory in Classical Conditioning: a review. *Psychology Software News*, 3, 93.

HALLIDAY, S. (1991). Practical Computing? *Psychology Software News*, 2, 36–37.

HAMMOND, N. V. (1993). Learning with hyptertext: problems, principles and prospects. In C. McKnight, A. Dillon and J. Richardson (Eds), *Hypertext: A Psychological Perspective*. Ellis Horwood: Chichester, pp 51–69.

HAMMOND, N., GARDNER, N., HEATH, S., KIBBY, M., MAYES, J., MCALEESE, R., MULLINGS, C. and TRAPP, A. (1991) Blocks to the effective use of information technology in higher education. *Computers and Education*, *18*, 155–162.

HAMMOND, N. V. and TRAPP, A. L. (1991). Computers in Psychology Teaching in the UK. *Behavior Research Methods, Instruments and Computers*, *23*, 118–120.

HARLEY, T. (1993). Oxford Psycholinguistic Database: a review. *Psychology Software News*, *3*, 95–96.

HAXBY, J. V., PARASURAMAN, R., LALONDE, F. and ABBOUD, H. (1993). SuperLab: General purpose Macintosh software for human experimental psychology and psychological testing. *Behavior Research Methods, Instruments and Computers*, *25*, 400–406.

HEARD, P. (1991). Active Eye: a review. *Psychology Software News*, *1*, 17–20.

HEWETT, T. (1991). A low-tech approach to instructional computing. *Psychology Software News*, *2*, 77–78.

HORNBY, P. and ANDERSON, M. (1990). A review of software for introductory psychology instruction. *Behavior Research Methods, Instruments, and Computers*, *22*, 184–194.

JOHNSON, J. F. (1991). Design Assistant: A Hypercard tool for courseware development. *Collegiate Microcomputer*, *9*, 103–106.

KOMMERS, P. A. M., JONASSEN, D. H. & MAYES, J. T. (Eds) (1992). *Cognitive Technologies for Learning*. Springer-Verlag: Berlin.

KOZMA, R. B. (1992). Constructing knowledge with Learning Tool. In P. A. M. Kommers, D. H. Jonassen and J. T. Mayes (Eds), *Mindtools: Cognitive Technologies for Modelling Knowledge*. Springer-Verlag: Berlin.

LAZARUS, J. (1994). The Observer: a review. *Psychology Software News*, *4*.

LEVOI, M. (1991). PsychLIT over a network. *Psychology Software News*, *2*, 6–7.

LEVOI, M. (1991). Reaction timing using personal computers. *Psychology Software News*, *2*, 38–40.

LEWIS, M. (1990). PsychLIT CD-Rom at the University of Sussex. *Psychology Software News*, *1*, 46–48.

MAYES, A. T. (1992). Mindtools: a suitable case for learning. In P. A. M. Kommers, D. H. Jonassen and J. T. Mayes (Eds.), *Cognitive Technologies for Learning*. Springer-Verlag: Berlin.

MCALEESE, R. (in press). A theoretical view on concept mapping. *Association for Learning Technology Journal*.

MACLEOD, H., MORSE, D. and BURFORD, B. (1993). Computer support for behavioural event recording and transcription. *Psychology Teaching Review*, 2, 120–128.

MONK, A. F. (1991). *Exploring Statistics with Minitab*. John Wiley and Sons: Chichester.

MORTON, H. (1991). Goal-focused Interviewing: a review. *Psychology Software News*, 2, 83–85.

NEISSER, U. (1967). *Cognitive Psychology*. Appleton-Century-Crofts: New York.

NODINE, C. F., KUNDEL, H. L., TOTO, L. C. and KRUPINSKI, E. A. (1992). Recording and analysing eye-position data using a microcomputer workstation. *Behavior Research Methods, Instruments and Computers*, 24, 475–486.

NORMAN, K. (1990). The electronic teaching theater: interactive hypermedia and mental models of the classroom. *Current Psychological Research and Reviews*.

ORCHARD, G. (1990). Teaching neural computation. *Psychology Software News*, 1, 26–28.

PETTY, L. C., LYNCH, E. A. and ROSEN, E. F. (1993). A ToolBook computer program to develop course objectives and assessment measures. *Behavior Research Methods, Instruments and Computers*, 25, 281–286.

QUIGLEY, P. (1991). Demonstrating Macintosh software. *Psychology Software News*, 2, 12–13.

READER, W. R. and HAMMOND, N. V. (1994). Supporting learning from hypertext: concept-mapping and beyond. *Computers and Education*, 22, 99–106.

SIMPSON, A. and NICOLSON, R. (1991). Creation and evaluation of a flexible learning package for statistics. *Psychology Software News*, 2, 44–47.

SIMPSON, A. (1993). Visual discrimination in the Snark: a practical encounter with hypotheses and refutations. *Psychology Software News*, 4, 7–10.

SCHNEIDER, W., ZUCCOLOTTO, A. and TIRONE, S. T. (1993). Time-stamping computer events to report. 1-msec accuracy of events in the Micro Experimental Laboratory. *Behavior Research Methods, Instruments and Computers*, 25, 276–81.

ST JAMES, J. D. (1989). The MEL library in the undergraduate research methods course. *Behaviour Research Methods, Instruments and Computers*, 21, 245–247.

ST JAMES, D. and SCHNEIDER, W. (1991). Student MEL software support for instructors and teaching assistants in research methods course. *Behavior Research Methods, Instruments and Computers*, 23, 149–154.

STOLOFF, M. L. and COUCH, J. V. (1992). *Computer Use In Psychology: a directory of software (3rd edition)*. American Psychological Association: Washington DC.

SVARDTAL, F. and FLATEN, M. A. (1993). Operant control programs in ASYST. *Psychology Teaching Review*, 2, 120–128.

SYLLABUS PRESS (1993). Getting started on the Internet. *Syllabus European edition*, 1, 16–17.

THOMPSON, P. (1989). Graphic Adventures in Sensory Physiology. *Psychology Software News*, 1, 10.

TRAPP, A. L. and HAMMOND, N. V. (1994). *The CTI Directory of Psychology Software (3rd edition)*. CTI Centre for Psychology: University of York.

TRAPP, A. L., HAMMOND, N. V. and LUCAS, L. (1994). The status of educational technology in psychology. *Psychology Software News*, 4.

ULRICH, R. and GIRAY, M. (1989). Time resolution of clocks: effects on reaction time measurement – good news for bad clocks. *British Journal of Mathematical and Statistical Psychology*, 42, 1–12.

VAN DER VLUGT, M. J., KRUK, M. R., ANNEMOON, M. M. and GEUZE, R. H. (1992). CAMERA: a system for fast and reliable acquisition of multiple ethological records. *Behavior Research Methods, Instruments and Computers*, 24, 147–149.

VIERA, A. (1989). Using MEL in a networked classroom. *Behavior Research Methods, Instruments and Computers*, 21, 248–249.

WADE, C. and TAVRIS, C. (1993). *Psychology*. Harper Collins: New York.

WEISS, B. (Ed.) (1973). *Digital Computers in the Behavioral Laboratory*. Appleton-Century-Crofts: New York.

WEST, R. (1991). *Computing for Psychologists: statistical analysis using SPSS and MINITAB*. Harwood Academic Publishers: London.

WEST, R., CHRISTIE, M. and WEINMAN, J. (1990). *Microcomputers, psychology and medicine*. Chichester: Wiley.

Appendix 1: Sources of equipment and expertise

Overseas centres of expertise

ASK, Universitat Karlsruhe, Englestr. 14, 7500 Karlsruhe 1, Germany

COMPSYCH, Department of Psychology, SUNY, Plattsburgh, NY 12901, USA Email: compsych@snyplava.bitnet

iec ProGAMMA, PO Box 841, 9700 AV Groningen, The Netherlands Phone: +050 636900; Email: gamma@rug.nl

Publishers of directories and databases

American Psychological Association, Order Department, PO Box 2710, Hyattsville, MD 20784, USA or c/o Eurospan Ltd., 3 Henrietta Street, Covent Garden, London WC2E 8LU, UK

CHEST and NISS Centre, Computing Services, University of Bath, Claverton Down, Bath BA2 7AY Phone: 01225 826282; Email: CHEST@bath

DRAT, Professor David Bartram, Department of Psychology, University of Hull, Hull HU6 7RX
ESRC Data Archive, University of Essex, Wivenhoe Park, Colchester CO4 3SQ
Phone: 012206 862286 ext 2242; Email: archive@essex

Publishers of testing and assessment software
AI Software Inc., PO Box 724, Wakefield, RI 02879, US
ASE, Division of NFER Nelson, Darville House, 2 Oxford Road East, Windsor, Berkshire SL4 1DF
Belbin Associates Ltd, The Burleigh Business Centre, 52 Burleigh Street, Cambridge CB1 1DJ
CoolSpring Software, 4 Moon Maiden Court, Walkersville, MD 21793, USA
Phone: +1 301 845 8719
Cybermetrics Testing Services, 7921 Ruxway Road, Baltimore, MD 21204–3515, USA
Harcourt Brace Jovanovich, PO Box 839954, San Antonio, TX 78283–3954, USA
Integrated Professional Systems, 5211 Mahoning Avenue, Suite 135, Youngstown, OH 44515, USA
Malibu Artifactual Intelligence Works, 25307 Malibu Road, Malibu, CA 90265, USA
Phone: +1 310 456 7787
Multi-Health System Inc. 908 Niagara Falls Boulevard, North Tonawanda, NY 14120–2060, USA
NFER-Nelson, Darville House, 2 Oxford Road East, Windsor, Berkshire SL4 1DF
Park Lodge Associates, 47 Four Oaks Road, Sutton Coldfield, Birmingham B74 2XU
Phone: 0121 323 2282
Precision People Inc, 3452 North Ride Cir S, Jacksonville, FL 32223, USA
Projected Learning Programs Inc, PO Box 3008, Paradise, CA 95967–3008, USA
Psychologistics Inc, PO Box 3896, Indialantic, FL 32903, USA
Quester Consulting, Thanet House, Sleap's Hyde, St. Albans, Herts AL4 0SE Phone: 01727 826183
Reason House, 204 East Joppa Road, Penthouse Suite 10, Towson, Maryland 21204, USA
Saville & Holdsworth Ltd, 3 AC Court, High Street, Surrey KT7 0SR
Selby MillSmith Ltd, Windmill House, Victoria Road, Mortimer, Reading RG7 3DF
The Psychological Corporation Ltd, Harcourt Brace Jovanovich, Foots Cray High Street, Sidcup, Kent DA14 5HP
The Test Agency, Cournswood House, North Dean, High Wycombe, Bucks HP14 4NW
Phone: 01494 563384
Towne Square Psychological Service, 14630 Eureka Road, Columbiana, OH 44408, USA
Western Psychological Services, 12031 Wilshire Boulevard, Los Angeles, CA 90025, USA
Phone: +1 310 478 2061

Suppliers of hardware and software for data acquisition and experimental control

Amplicon Liveline, Centenary Industrial Estate, Hollingdean Road, Brighton, East Sussex BN2 4AW
Phone: 01273 608331

Cambridge Research Systems, 80 Riverside Estate, Sir Thomas Longley Road, Rochester, Kent ME2 4BH
Phone: 01634 720707

Campden Instruments, King Street, Sileby, Loughborough LE12 7LZ
Phone: 01509 814790

Coulbourn Instruments, 7462 Penn Drive, Allentown, PA 18106, USA (UK distributor: Bilaney Consultants Ltd, St Julian's, SevenOaks, Kent TN15 0RX
Phone: 01732 450002

Sandown Scientific, 11 Copsem Drive, Esher, Surrey KT10 9HD
Phone: 01372 462561

Gebrands Corporation, 8 Beck Road, Arlington, MA 02174, USA

Harvard Apparatus, Fircroft Way, Edenbridge, Kent
Phone: 01732 864001

National Instruments, 21 Kingfisher Court, Hambridge Road, Newbury, Berks RG14 5SJ
Phone: 01635 523545

Paul Fray Control Systems, 4 Flint Lane, Ely Road, Waterbeach, Cambridge CB5 9QZ
Phone: 01223 441134

Stoelting Systems, 620 Wheat Lane, Wood Dale, Illinois 60191 USA
Phone: +1 708 860 9700

State Systems Inc., PO Box 2215, Kalamazoo, MI 49003, USA

Thought Technology, 2180 Belgrave Avenue, Montreal, Quebec, Canada
Phone: +1 514 489 8251

5.2 LINKS WITH OTHER COUNTRIES

Ingrid Lunt

ALTHOUGH psychology training and practice differ between countries, there are increasing numbers of contacts, interchanges, and international associations where psychologists may share information, develop research and other connections and learn from each other. Links with psychologists in other countries may be formal or informal and may be in the form of an organizational link or a link created through mutual interest, projects or research. Many universities foster links through research and student exchange, again either informally, or through programmes such as ERASMUS, TEMPUS, HELIOS, the British Council and so on.

There are a number of formal international organizations of psychology and psychologists across the world. These take the form of two types of organization. Firstly, those organizations which are 'umbrella' or federal organizations linking national organizations of psychology. The British Psychological Society is the member for the United Kingdom of one organization of this type, EFPPA (the European Federation of Professional Psychologists' Associations; see following and special arrangements covering the International Union of Psychological Science (IUPsyS)). Secondly, those organizations whose members are individual psychologists. The IAAP (The International Association of Applied Psychology) is an organization of this type (see following) as are many other smaller organizations concerned with branches of psychology.

International Psychology Organizations: Federal organizations

There are two 'umbrella' or federal organizations which link national psychology organizations. These are:

- the International Union of Psychological Science (IUPsyS)

- the European Federation of Professional Psychologists' Associations (EFPPA)

The International Union of Psychological Science (IUPsyS)

The IUPsyS is an international union with members from all over the world whose prime focus is psychology as a science. It was founded in 1951 and now has 53 member societies. The Royal Society is the member for the United Kingdom, but is advised by The British Psychological Society and the Experimental Psychology Society. Each country may be represented by only one member society, and in those countries where there are several psychology associations and societies, the member of IUPsyS will be the *scientific* psychological society of that country, hence the role of the Royal Society in the UK. The IUPsyS participates as a member organization in the International Council of Scientific Unions (ICSU), which is the main international scientific body, and in the International Social Science Council (ISSC). The IUPsyS aims to foster communication among its national members and to take up questions and problems raised by them. It sponsors an International Congress of Psychology every four years (hosted by a national member society) and publishes the *International Journal of Psychology* four times a year. It also produces the *International Directory of Psychologists* and *The IUPsyS Directory: Major Research Institutes and Departments of Psychology* and a number of other volumes.

The IUPsyS has a number of affiliated organizations. These are the International Association of Applied Psychology (IAAP) (see following), the Interamerican Society of Psychology (SIP), l'Association de Psychologie Scientifique de Langue Française (APSLF), the International Council of Psychologists (ICP), the International Association of Cross-Cultural Psychology (IACCP), the European Association of Experimental Social Psychology (EAESP), the International Society of Comparative Psychology (ISCP), the International Society for the Study of Behavioral Development (ISSBD), and the European Association of Personality Psychology (EAPP). This affiliation is intended to aid communication among organizations with mutual interests in the development and application of psychological science.

The Assembly of the IUPsyS meets every four years at the International Congress of Psychology, and each national member is entitled to send one or two delegates to the General Assembly. The day to day business of the Union is conducted by its Executive Committee which usually meets once a year. There are also a number of Working Groups and Standing Committees of IUPsyS.

IUPsyS Secretary General (to 1996)
Prof Géry d'Ydewalle
University of Leuven
Department of Psychology
B-3000 Leuven, Belgium
tel. 00 32 16 28 5964
Fax. 00 32 16 28 60 99

The European Federation of Professional Psychologists Associations (EFPPA)

The European Federation of Professional Psychologists Associations (EFPPA) was founded in 1981. At that time there was great enthusiasm for a forum which would bring together psychologists from different European countries. There was possibly a realization that European countries had matters in common which were different from America, Australia and other countries. Since that time EFPPA has held General Assemblies every two years, recently planning them to coincide with the biennial European Congress of Psychology which is organized under the auspices of EFPPA. EFPPA is the only European organization entitled to speak for European psychologists and provides a forum and mechanism for European co-operation in a wide range of fields in psychology practice and research. It now has 25 member associations representing about 100,000 psychologists.

*What does
EFPPA do?*

EFPPA is organized through its biennial General Assembly which is the ultimate decision-making body, and through an Executive Council of seven members which manages its affairs between meetings of the General Assembly. EFPPA carries out a range of activities which include the following:

● Collection and exchange of information
EFPPA has a unique potential for collecting and disseminating information on a wide range of areas such as ethical codes, training patterns, professional roles, regulations and legislation.

● Publications
EFPPA produces a number of publications: its magazine *News from EFPPA*, which is published four times a year; a number of information booklets and Task Force reports.

● Monitoring developments and lobbying in respect of developments, directives and legislation both within the European Community and outside.

● Development of common standards of training and common practices; work with EC Directives and the promotion of high standards of education, training and practice in psychology.

- Expert advice to governmental and non-governmental bodies and other organizations

- Links with other bodies
EFPPA has links with a variety of relevant international bodies including: WHO, EC, UNESCO, Council of Europe, SEPLIS, IUPsyS, IAAP, ASPPB, ISPA. These links exist to promote psychology as a discipline in practice and research across Europe.

- Conferences and meetings, in particular the European Congress of Psychology which is held every two years under its auspices.

- Task Forces
Much of the development work of EFPPA is carried out by Task Forces consisting of small groups of representatives from member associations. Task Forces are set up by the General Assembly, and each member association of EFPPA is entitled to send (at their own cost) a participant to join the Task Force. The Task Forces serve a useful function in collecting information from as many countries in Europe as possible on the topic area, and producing a report for publication and dissemination by EFPPA. At present there are Task Forces in the following areas: *Ethics; East West Relations; Evaluation of Psychology Curricula; Forensic Psychology; Health Psychology; European Legal Matters; Assessment; Traffic Psychology; Refugees, enforced migration, gender and ethnic issues; Psychologists in the Education System; Psychotherapy.*

- Communications and networking

EFPPA Secretary General (to 1997)
Birgit Hansson
Sveriges Psykolog Førbund
PO Box 3287
S-103 65 Stockholm, Sweden
tel. 00 46 8 6969760
fax. 00 46 8 24 78 55

INTERNATIONAL PSYCHOLOGY ORGANIZATIONS: ORGANIZATIONS OF INDIVIDUAL MEMBERS

International Association of Applied Psychology (IAAP)

The IAAP was established in 1920 and has individual members from more than 80 countries. Members are drawn from all over the world, with quite a number coming from the USA. It holds an International Congress every four years, alternating with the IUPsyS International Congress of Psychology, and publishes the journal *Applied Psychology:*

an International Review. The first Congress was held in Geneva in 1920, and since that time Congresses have been held every four years in major cities across the world. The major fields of activity of IAAP are reflected in its 11 Divisions: Organisational Psychology; Psychological Assessment; Psychology and National Development; Environmental Psychology; Educational, Instructional, and School Psychology; Clinical and Community Psychology; Applied Gerontology; Health Psychology; Economic Psychology; Psychology and Law; Political Psychology. IAAP also publishes a newsletter twice a year and provides a book service for discount purchase of selected books.

IAAP Secretary General (to 1996)
M. C. Knowles,
Graduate School of Management,
Monash University, Clayton,
Victoria 3168, Australia.

There are a number of other international and European psychology organizations of individual members. These usually focus on a specialist interest area within psychology, and include:

International Association for Cross-cultural Psychology (IACCP)
International Association of Organisational Psychology (IAOP)
International Association for Research in Economic Psychology
International Council of Psychologists (ICP)
International Neuropsychological Society
International Society of Comparative Psychologys
International Society for the Study of Behavioral Development (ISSBD)
International Society for the Study of Individual Differences
European Association of Behaviour and Cognitive Therapy (EABCT)
European Society for Developmental Psychology
European Association of Experimental and Social Psychology (EAESP)
European Association of Personality Psychology (EAPP)
European Association of Psychophysiology
European Association of Psychological Assessment
European Association for Research on Learning and Instruction (EARLI)
European Association for Work and Organisational Psychology (EAWOP)
European Health Psychology Society
European Mathematical Psychology Group
European Society for Cognitive Psychology

This list is not complete and there are a number of other

organizations; in fact, organizations are developing and forming the whole time.

WORKING AS A PSYCHOLOGIST IN OTHER COUNTRIES

The training of professional psychologists in the United Kingdom is different from the training in most other countries, particularly other countries in Europe. At present, each country has its own procedures for evaluating equivalence and comparability of training; this may be administered by the relevant national psychology organization, although the arrangements under the EC Directive are usually organized by a government department. Although the Directive EC 89/48/EEC provides for free movement of professionals within the European Union, countries have been slow to implement the Directive. In practice, it is still the case that a psychologist who wishes to work in another country should apply first to the national psychology organization (or to EFPPA) which will then provide the appropriate details and procedures for seeking recognition in that country. At the present time, these procedures are changing and developing rapidly.

Appendix: Member Associations of EFPPA

Austria
Berufsverband Österreichischer Psychologen
Kegelgasse 6/10, A-1030 Wien, Austria
tel. +43 222 712 86 90 fax +43 222 712 86 79

Belgium
Belgische Federatie van Psychologen-Fédération Belge des Psychologues
Kasteellan 42, 1652 Alsemberg, Belgium
tel. +32 2 380 69 17

Denmark
Dansk Psykologforening
Bjerregaards Sidevej 4, DK-2500 Valby, Denmark
tel. +45 31 16 33 55 fax +45 36 44 08 55

Estonia
Union of Estonian Psychologists
78 Tiigi St., Tartu 202400, Estonia
tel. +7 0142 448 538

Finland
Suomen Psykologiliitto ry
Akavatalo, Rautatielaisenkatu 6, 00520 Helsinki 52, Finland
tel. +358 0 1502312 fax +358 0 141716

France
Association Nationale des Organisations de Psychologues
62 Rue Liandier, 13008 Marseille, France
tel. +33 91 83 08 58 fax +33 91 25 73 33

Germany
Berufsverband Deutscher Psychologen E.V.
Heilsbachstrasse 22, D-5300 Bonn, Germany
tel. +49 228 64 10 54-56 fax +49 228 64 31 18

Greece
Association of Greek Psychologists
Avlidos 8, GR-115 27 Athens, Greece
tel. +30 1 77 11 449

Hungary
Magyar Pszichológiai Társaság
1067 Budapest, Erzebeth 13, 1536 Bp.Pf.220, Hungary
tel. +36 1 1426 178

Iceland
Association of Icelandic Psychology
Lagmula 7, IS-108 Reykjavik, Iceland
tel. +354 1 68 08 95

Ireland
Psychological Society of Ireland
13 Adelaide Road, Dublin 2, Ireland

Italy
Italian Network of Professional Psychologists Associations
Via in Publicolis 41, 00186 Roma, Italy
tel. +39 6 6873819 fax +39 6 68803822

Liechtenstein
Berufsverein der Psychologen Liechtensteins
Schulstrasse 18, FL-9485 Nendeln, Liechtenstein

Luxembourg
Association des Psychologues diplomés
60, Bd. Kennedy, L-4170, Esch sur Alzette, Luxembourg

Malta
Malta Union of Professional Psychologists
P.O. Box 341, Valletta, Malta

The Netherlands
Nederlands Instituut van Psychologen
Postbus 9921, 1006 AP Amsterdam, The Netherlands
tel. +31 20 610 95 96 fax +31 20 610 83 61

Norway
Norsk Psykologforening
Storgata 10A, 0155 Oslo 1, Norway
tel. +47 2 42 19 80 fax +47 2 42 42 92

Poland
Polskie Towarzystwo Psychologiczne
00–183 Warszawa, ul. Stawki 5/7, Poland
tel. + 31 13 68

Portugal
Sindicato Nacional dos Psicologos
R. Ferreira Lapa 2-B, 3-Dto., Lisbon 1100, Portugal

Slovenia
Drustvo Psihologov Slovenije
Prushnikova 74, 612 10 Ljubljana, Slovenia

Spain
Colegio Oficial Dos Psicologos
Claudio Coello 46–2 C, 28001 Madrid, Spain
tel. +34 1 4355212 fax +34 1 5779172

Sweden
Sveriges Psykologførbund
Box 30092, 10425 Stockholm, Sweden
tel. +46 8 130260 fax +46 8 137928

Switzerland
Föderation der Schweizer Psychologen
Cäcilienstrasse 26, 3000 Bern 14, Switzerland
tel. +41 31 460466 fax +41 31 460477

Turkey
Turkish Psychological Association
P.K. 117 Küçükesat, 06662 Ankara, Turkey
Fax 90 312 210 11 45

United Kingdom
The British Psychological Society
St Andrews House, 48 Princess Road East, Leicester LE1
7DR
tel. +44 116 254 9568 fax +44 116 247 0787

Other national psychology organizations
American Psychological Association
750 First Street, N.E., Washington D.C. 20002–4242,
U.S.A.
Tel. +1 202 336 5795; fax + 1 202 336 5630

Australian Psychological Society
1 Grattan Street, Carlton, Victoria 3053, Australia
Tel: +61 3 663 6166; fax +61 3 663 6177

Canadian Psychological Association
Rue Vincent R., Old Chelsea, Quebéc, Canada JOX 2NO

New Zealand Psychological Society
Dept. of Education, University of Auckland, Private Bag,
Auckland, New Zealand

Other addresses available from The British Psychological
Society.

5.3   PSYCHOLOGY BOOKS AND JOURNALS: Publishers and Sources

(This chapter originally appeared in
*Teaching Psychology: Information and
Resources*, 3rd edition)

THE aim of this section is simply stated: to help you, the
reader, to identify and locate all the useful books and
journals in your present sphere of psychological interest
and for any future searches. But a number of decisions
were involved: What should it cover? Which publishers
should be included? How should the information be presented? A short account of the methods used and of the
decisions underlying this database should help you to
make best use of the material.

THE SCOPE OF THE DATABASE

Mindful that the readership of this book includes psychologists and non-psychologists, academics and practitioners,
and teachers of psychology from school to university level,
we cast our net wide and assessed not only psychology lists
but also medical, nursing, paramedical, social work, management and many others. The twin criteria used were
'psychological relevance' and 'usefulness'. We included
therefore only English-language publishers in the UK, or
with a UK base. Most of the latter are American publishers
originating most of their titles in the States; we have tried to
indicate where this is the case. Other overseas publishers,
who quoted overseas addresses and non-sterling prices
only, were excluded. For journals, an exception was made
for the American Psychological Association, since many of
their journals are too important to omit.

Collecting the Information

The information for this chapter was collected by means of
questionnaires and requests for catalogues sent out to all

'significant' psychology publishers. ('Significance' was judged by the quality of the list rather than size, and for this reason we included a number of association and society publishers.) Some publishers returned both; others responded with a catalogue only or a questionnaire only. Some questionnaires gave full answers; others the briefest details. Where we were sent only the latest catalogue (perhaps covering only the last three months) some degree of subjectivity was involved in characterizing the publisher's activities. Where we had only the questionnaire, some degree of trust (and sometimes discretion) was necessary in adapting the information supplied. Within these constraints, we aimed to make the database as comprehensive as possible.

The Lists

The first section lists publishers in alphabetical order with a description of their scope and size, while the second section gives their addresses. If you write to a publisher for catalogues, don't forget to state which subject areas you are interested in.

GENERAL PROFILES OF PUBLISHERS

A B Academic

Publishers of a series dealing with social/psychological issues during adolescence and youth. Three journals for academics and professionals.

Academic Press

Now publish only in cognitive psychology, ergonomics, AI. An imprint of Harcourt Brace & Co. (q.v.). Also publisher of two psychology journals.

Addison-Wesley

A major publisher of books in psychology, originated both in the UK and the USA. Specialisms include computing and AI, cognition, linguistics and organizational psychology. The list caters for most readerships except schools.

Airlift Book Company

Distributor for mainly North American publishers, notably Inner City Books (Canada) and Spring Publications (US) as well as Daimon Publishers (Switzerland) who all specialize in Jungian psychology. Also a range of self-help titles.

Allyn & Bacon

See Harvester-Wheatsheaf.

American Psychological Assn

Publish in all fields, mainly for practitioners and professionals. Distributed by the Eurospan Group (q.v.). Publisher of 25 major journals.

Analytical Psychology Club
Publisher of the Journal for Jungian Studies, *Harvest*.

Ann Arbor Publishers Ltd
Publisher and distributor of educational tests and remedial materials (for use in schools) originated in the USA.

Anna Freud Centre
Publisher of the *Bulletin of the Anna Freud Centre*.

Aquarian Press
A HarperCollins imprint; popular psychology and sexuality.

Edward Arnold
A division of Hodder Headline PLC. List includes books in introductory and general psychology and in social and developmental psychology, mainly for a readership of academics and undergraduate students but with some overlap into A-level studies.

Artesian Books
Publisher of the *British Journal of Psychotherapy*.

Assn for Humanistic Psychology
Apart from *Self and Society: A Journal of Humanistic Psychology*, the AHP also publishes a few booklets in related fields, principally for practitioners.

Assn of Child Psychotherapists
Publisher of the *Journal of Child Psychotherapy*.

Assn of Educational Psychologists
Publisher (through Longman) of the journal *Educational Psychology in Practice*.

Avenue
Publisher of the *International Journal of Social Psychiatry*.

Bailliere Tindall
An imprint of Harcourt Brace & Co (q.v.).

BILD Publications (British Institute of Learning Disabilities)
A small and specialist list in the field of learning disability mainly for practitioners. Also have three journals (published by Multilingual Matters (q.v.)): *Mental Handicap, Mental Handicap Bulletin* and *Mental Handicap Research*.

Blackwell
Major publisher of psychology: books in most fields especially developmental, social and experimental psychology (but no clinical psychology and psychiatry, health or psychotherapy titles). Mainly for academics, practitioners and professionals. Some reference publishing in general, cognitive and educational psychology. Blackwell

also publish five psychology and psychology-related journals, including *Journal of Family Therapy*, *Mind and Language* and the *Journal of Research in Reading* (the latter aimed at teachers).

Blackwell Scientific

A substantial list in the fields of clinical psychology and psychiatry (with a degree of specialism in child psychiatry), and psychotherapy addressed mainly to a readership of practitioners.

BPS Books

This is the book publishing arm of The British Psychological Society (q.v.). A wide-ranging list is published with catalogues covering the subject areas of: personal and professional development, health and social care, education and schools, careers and psychometrics. Titles range from texts and academic monographs to self-help books. BPS Books caters for many different markets including social workers, health workers and managers, as well as for academic and applied psychologists.

British Assn for Counselling

A range of books (especially reference) and other materials for counsellors, including trainees and trainers. Publisher of *Counselling*, the journal of the BAC.

British Assn of Psychotherapists

Publisher of the *Journal of the British Association of Psychotherapists*.

The British Psychological Society

Publisher of nine major research journals, including the *British Journal of Psychology*. Also publish *Selection & Development Review* and *The Psychologist* (the monthly bulletin of the Society), plus the various newsletters from the Divisions, Sections and Special Groups of the Society. *See also* BPS Books.

British Society for Projective Psychology

Publisher of the *British Journal of Projective Psychology*.

W. C. Brown

US publisher of college-level psychology textbooks and ancillary materials; covering most fields especially introductory and developmental psychology.

Butterworth Heinemann Ltd

Emphasis on psychiatry but some psychotherapy and clinical psychology titles.

Cambridge University Press

One of the major UK publishers of psychology. Books in all areas of psychology and at all levels, with many titles for practitioners and professionals, but mainly for a readership of high-level research psychologists. CUP also distribute

MacKeith Press titles which include clinical psychology (with a special emphasis on childhood), psychiatry and neurology. CUP psychology journals (ten in all) include *Psychology of Women Quarterly* and *Behavioral and Brain Sciences*.

Carfax

Journals publisher, with ten psychology-related titles (mainly for practitioners), including *Addiction*, the *Journal of Mental Health* and the interdisciplinary journal, *AIDS Care*.

Cassell

An expanding psychology list with particular specialisms in educational psychology, and counselling and special needs. Aimed largely at undergraduates and practitioners in various applied fields.

Paul Chapman

A substantial education and educational psychology list, primarily for a readership of teachers and student teachers; also titles concerning management and organizational behaviour.

Chapman & Hall

Publish in clinical, health and other applied fields; directed towards nurses, therapists and health care workers.

The Children's Society

A range of books and other materials (covering such topics as child abuse, homelessness, leaving care) for childcare professionals including titles of interest to clinical and educational psychologists. The Children's Society is a voluntary society of the Church of England and the Church in Wales.

Churchill Livingstone

See Longman.

Community Psychiatric Nurses Assn

Publisher of the *Community Psychiatric Nursing Journal*.

Constable

A small psychology list dominated by titles in counselling and therapy (particularly the works of Carl Rogers).

Current Science

Publisher of *Current Opinion in Psychiatry*.

J. M. Dent

An imprint of Orion Publishing (*see also* Weidenfeld and Nicolson). Small but various psychology/sociology list (not easy to characterize here).

Duckworth

Small but eclectic list in psychology and psychiatry, with a bias towards the latter. Includes books for researchers and practitioners.

Element Books

Publisher and distributor of books on philosophy and religion, among other cognate subjects, with a focus on popular psychology, mainly originated in the USA.

Elsevier Science Ltd

Imprints of Elsevier are: Pergamon, North-Holland and Excerpta Medica. A major academic psychology publisher with a bias towards cognitive psychology, but most fields are covered in the extensive 'Advances in Psychology' series. Also a comprehensive 'Handbook of Neuropsychology' series. Publisher of some 14 psychology or psychology-related journals, including *Acta Psychologica, Artificial Intelligence* and *Cognition*.

Lawrence Erlbaum

One of the major UK publishers of books in psychology in all fields and (excepting school texts and general trade) at all levels. Sister company of LEA Inc. (USA), US-originated titles are a substantial part of the list. LEA Ltd also publish 12 psychology journals (including the *Quarterly Journal of Experimental Psychology*) and handle journals published by LEA Inc.

The Eurospan Group

Distributor of US publishers including the American Psychological Association, American Psychiatric Press (manuals, reference books and textbooks covering clinical practice and psychiatry), New York University Press (titles in a wide variety of areas but with a general bias towards psychoanalysis), Jason Aronson (psychotherapy), Praeger Publishers and Greenwood Press (wide range of academic monographs for social sciences), Haworth Press (academic and trade titles in psychology and medicine) and Teachers College Press (education and psychology).

Falmer Press

Part of the Taylor & Francis group. Specialist publisher of education books for teachers with a substantial list in educational psychology, as well as general psychology texts for undergraduate psychology students.

Fontana

Small list for the general reader with titles in child development, self-help and women's studies.

Fontana Press

A more academic market than Fontana, also focusing on child development, and psychology and philosophy.

Free Association Books

Independent psychology publisher, specializing in psychoanalysis and psychotherapy. Publisher of the journal *Free Associations*.

W. H. Freeman

Catalogues also contain publications from the imprints Scientific American Books and Scientific American Library. Also UK distributor of books published in the USA by Sinauer Associates Inc. The books in the life and behavioural sciences catalogue are mainly aimed at undergraduates, and include titles in social, developmental and abnormal psychology, learning and cognition, statistics, neuroscience, and general psychology.

Gaskell

Imprint of the Royal College of Psychiatrists (q.v.).

Gateway Books

Small publisher whose list includes some popular psychology, mainly self-help.

Guilford Press

US-based publisher with a substantial list of psychology titles ranging from clinical psychology, psychotherapy and psychoanalysis to organizational psychology and research. Publisher of several psychology journals.

Harcourt Brace & Co.

The American parent company includes the following imprints: Bailliere Tindall; The Psychological Corporation; W. B. Saunders; Holt, Rinehart & Winston; Grune & Stratton; and Academic Press. Publishers of large general introductory and child development texts; also some personality, physiological psychology and statistics. A few British authors. Also, high level education books and conference proceedings under Academic Press imprint.

HarperCollins

Psychology publishing is split between a variety of publishing divisions, depending on target audience. Textbooks are available from Collins Educational (GSCE and A-level/16+) and the College Division (16+ and undergraduate texts – US published). College Division also handles Basic Book's large psychotherapy list.

Harvester-Wheatsheaf

Catalogues also include titles from other publishers in the Simon & Schuster group (Allyn & Bacon, Prentice Hall). Publish in all areas of psychology but specialize in social and developmental psychology (notably the 'Developing Body and Mind' series). The sociology catalogue includes titles of interest (social work and social welfare, family and marriage, criminology), as does the economics catalogue (economic psychology and behavioural economics). Most readerships catered for, but no school texts.

Harwood Academic

An imprint of Gordon & Breach Science Publishers. Titles in health psychology and addiction research; also educational psychology and criminological and legal psychology. Readership mainly researchers, clinicians and health professionals. Harwood publish five psychology journals, including *Anxiety Research* and *Psychology and Health*.

Haverstock

Publisher of the *Journal of the Balint Society*, plus the occasional book in Balint-inspired medicine.

Hobsons

Publish a biennial psychology course guide and the *British Journal of Guidance and Counselling*.

Hodder & Stoughton

Specialize in textbooks for A-level and first year undergraduates. *See also* Edward Arnold.

Institute of Psychoanalysis

Publisher of *International Journal of Psychoanalysis*.

IPC Specialist Group

Publisher of *New Scientist*.

JAI

US publisher specializing in research annuals, with particular emphasis on management, cognitive science, educational and developmental psychology. Also six psychology journals.

Johns Hopkins University Press

US academic publisher with a list covering clinical and health psychology, cognition, and history and philosophy of psychology. Also specializing in psychoanalysis (including titles for practitioners).

Jossey-Bass

US-based publisher with catalogue which includes psychology-related titles in management and education, as well as a social and behavioural sciences list. Titles in the latter category are principally for practitioners. Distributed in the UK by Simon and Schuster IBD.

Karnac

Specialist publisher of books in psychoanalysis, psychotherapy and analytical psychology. Also publish the journal *Winnicott Studies*.

Jessica Kingsley

Emphasis on psychotherapy but also a significant social work list including titles of interest to psychologists and health professionals.

John Libby & Company Limited

Small list with specialized titles in clinical psychology and psychiatry.

Longman

Mainly introductory and general psychology books catering

for A-level and GCSE students. Specialized titles in clinical psychology and psychiatry are published through Churchill Livingstone.

McGraw-Hill

A substantial textbook list including introductory psychology, child development, personality theory, sexuality, feminist psychology, some clinical psychology and statistics/research methods. Most books originated in the USA.

Macmillan

Publishes an introductory psychology series for A-level, and a general focus on titles for applied fields (in particular, nursing, education, social work). Co-publishers (with the BPS) of the 'Psychology for Professional Groups' and 'Psychology Applied to Nursing' series.

Manchester University Press

A few titles in psychology for practitioners (education, working with the elderly) as well as a medical self-help series, 'Living With . . .'.

MCB University Press

The initials stand for Management Consultants Bradford. Publisher of more than 100 serials for professionals, including the *Journal of Managerial Psychology*.

MIND

Ten new titles per year in the field of mental health and cognate areas, including criminological and legal psychology. Also publisher of the bi-monthly journal *Openmind*.

MIT Press

US academic publisher (MIT stands for Massachusetts Institute of Technology) specializing in cognitive psychology but with titles in many fields, particularly neuroscience, AI and philosophy of mind. Three psychology-related journals including the *Journal of Cognitive Neuroscience*.

Multilingual Matters

Specialist publisher of psycholinguistics and education (also published under the Channel View imprint). Act as distributor for the British Institute of Learning Disabilities (BILD). Publish journals for BILD (q.v.).

National Extension College

Publisher of open learning materials for schools and FE colleges as well as for correspondence students and adult learners. GCSE and A-level psychology packages are available; some titles on health and social issues may also be of interest.

Thomas Nelson

Educational publisher whose sociology catalogue includes one introductory psychology textbook.

NFER-Nelson

Leading UK publisher and supplier of the full range of testing and assessment materials, from developmental and ability tests to selection and recruitment instruments for industry. For use by a wide variety of professionals including the caring professions, not least psychologists (clinical, occupational, educational) and counsellors. Also interdisciplinary training materials for practitioners and professionals. Many materials originate in the USA. ASE is a division of NFER-Nelson which focuses exclusively on tests for occupational use.

North-Holland

An imprint of Elsevier Science Ltd.

Norton

US-based publisher with a clear bias towards psychoanalysis and psychotherapy. Some undergraduate texts. Norton Professional Books covers titles for psychiatrists, counsellors and therapists.

Oneworld

Small publisher of general reader psychology, particularly therapy/psychoanalysis. Distributed by Element Books (q.v.).

Open University Press

A substantial psychology list, principally for students and teachers in higher education, and medical and health workers. Specialisms in social, developmental and health psychology as well as psychotherapy and counselling, but also a number of general/introductory texts.

Oxford University Press

Major international publisher in the life sciences. Specialisms in experimental psychology, clinical psychology and psychotherapy, but with titles in most fields. Most titles for academic/undergraduate or practitioner/professional readership. See also OUP's catalogues in medicine, neurosciences, psychiatry, and philosophy. OUP also publishes the *Journal of Psychopharmacology*.

Pan Macmillan

A dozen or so popular psychology titles, mainly general, health, and self-help; also some titles of psychological interest among the business management list. Pan Macmillan comprises Macmillan London, Pan Books, Picador and Sidgwick & Jackson.

Penguin

A large and expanding psychology list, with academic titles (especially undergraduate texts) in introductory; social and developmental; experimental and cognitive psychology; maths and stats/computing and AI; psychoanalysis (inc. the

Pelican Freud Library); organizational and management psychology; and history and philosophy of psychology.

Pergamon

An imprint of Elsevier Science Ltd. Major psychology publisher principally for undergraduate and graduate students, and practitioners. Titles in most fields, but especially strong in social and educational psychology, as well as in therapy, neuropsychology and other branches of clinical practice. Pergamon also publishes some 22 psychology journals, covering a wide range of research and applied fields.

Pinter Publishers

Pinter's social science catalogue includes titles in the series 'Communication in Artificial Intelligence'. The psychology list will be expanding with a new series in cognitive science. Some of the linguistics titles may also be of interest.

Pion

Publisher of the journal *Perception*.

Plenum

US-based publisher of high level monographs and conference proceedings for researchers and practitioners/professionals. Titles in a range of fields, but with a general bias towards behavioural psychology. Strong specialism in social and developmental psychology, also clinical psychology and neuroscience. The vast majority of Plenum's books originate in the USA. Plenum publishes some 20 high level psychology journals for researchers and practitioners.

Positive Productions

Specialist publisher of a range of materials dealing with teaching and classroom behaviour.

Prentice Hall

See Harvester-Wheatsheaf.

The Psychological Corporation

World's largest publisher of psychological tests for use in: clinical, educational and occupational practice; speech and language therapy; business, industry and government. American company, but since 1987 some of these materials have been designed and produced in the UK. Now an imprint of Harcourt Brace & Co. (q.v.).

Routledge

A major UK psychology publisher, with titles in most fields, principally for a readership of undergraduates, academics and practitioners/professionals. Particularly strong in psychoanalysis, psychotherapy and analytical psychology, but also separate education and health and social welfare lists. Routledge has co-published and distributed a number of titles with BPS Books (q.v.). Routledge also publishes two psychology journals.

Royal College of Psychiatrists
Publishes books under the Gaskell imprint. All publications are in psychiatry, for a practitioner/professional readership. Two journals including the *British Journal of Psychiatry*.

Royal Society

The *Proceedings of the Royal Society of London, Series B*, is a general biological research journal with occasional papers on animal psychology and behaviour. Likewise the *Philosophical Transactions, Series B*, which also occasionally publishes psychology-related conference reports.

Sage

A US-based social sciences publisher with a large London office. Books mainly for practitioners (and students) in various applied fields. Apart from psychology per se, the catalogue features psychology-related titles under categories such as: child abuse, counselling and psychotherapy, criminology, education, gender studies, gerontology, social work. UK-originated series include 'Counselling in Practice'. Major publisher of social science journals. Apart from their 30 psychology titles, there are many psychology-related journals under other heads (as above).

Sheldon Press

An imprint of the Society for Promoting Christian Knowledge. Mainly self-help and popular psychology books.

Souvenir

Some 35 psychology titles, with a focus on humanistic psychology. Most published under the Condor imprint, including the 'Human Horizons' series for people with disabilities.

Springer

International academic publisher with psychology titles in virtually every field. Also publisher of several English-language research journals in psychology, psychiatry and related fields.

Taylor & Francis Ltd
Major international scientific and educational publisher (also with an editorial and marketing office in the US). There is a growing psychology list with titles in health psychology, general psychology and social and developmental psychology. Aimed largely at undergraduates, A-level students and practitioners in various applied fields. Publisher of several psychology and related journals.

Thomson International
Distributor for US imprints Boyd & Fraser, Brooks/Cole, Van Nostrand Reinhold and Wadsworth which all publish a wide range of psychology texts for students.

Thorsons
Mainly for the general reader; popular psychology, personal development and self-help.

Transaction
US publishers, mainly of psychoanalysis, but also a recent volume on social psychiatry.

Transworld Publishers
Incorporates Bantam Press and Doubleday imprints. A small psychology list for the general reader, mostly originated in the US.

University Presses of California, Columbia & Princeton
All three publishers have lists of 60 to 80 psychology titles covering psychoanalysis/therapy and developmental, cognitive and legal psychology. Princeton has more academic titles (including a series on Jung), Columbia has a mainly practitioner market, including books for nurses, while California University Press includes titles aimed at the general reader. Distributed in the UK by John Wiley (q.v.).

Weidenfeld & Nicolson
An imprint of Orion Publishing (see also J. M. Dent). A dozen or so miscellaneous psychology titles, including some general/introductory textbooks for schools.

Whiting and Birch
Focuses on childhood and health, also titles for social workers. Publisher of three psychology-related journals including *Children and Society*.

Whurr Publishers Ltd
Titles in psychology and psychiatry, but focus on psychotherapy and counselling. Publish three psychology-related journals.

John Wiley
A subsidiary of John Wiley & Sons Inc., New York. Major international publisher in psychology, especially for practitioners and professionals but also many academic and reference titles. Books in many fields, but in particular clinical, psychotherapy, organizational and developmental. Also 17 psychology journals, including the *European Journal of Personality*.

Williams & Wilkins
US medical publisher. A range of titles (some 39) in clinical psychiatry, textbooks as well as books for practitioners. UK distributors for Igaku-Shoin and F. A. Davies (also US medical and health sciences publishers). W & W also publish five psychiatric journals for practitioners.

Winslow
Some psychology books among a range of multi-media therapy/rehabilitation materials for various professional

groups, including teachers, nurses, occupational therapists, geriatricians and social workers; also a range of special-needs materials for childcare professionals.

Women's Press

Titles in educational, health, and general psychology; also in psychotherapy. Some of interest to practitioners and professionals, and some to teachers of women's studies, but mostly addressed to general readers.

Yale University Press

US publisher with clear specialisms in psychiatry, psychoanalysis and child development. Readership: primarily academics, psychoanalysts and other practitioners.

Publishers' Addresses

A B Academic Publishers
PO Box 42
Bicester
Oxon OX6 7NW

Academic Press
see Harcourt Brace & Co.

Addison-Wesley Publishers Ltd
Finchampstead Road
Wokingham
Berks RG11 2NZ

Airlift Book Company
26/28 Eden Grove
London N7 8EF

Allyn & Bacon
see Harvester-Wheatsheaf

American Psychological Association
750 First Street, NE
Washington DC 20002–4242
USA

Analytical Psychology Club
37 York Street Chambers
London W1H 1DE

Ann Arbor Publishers Ltd
PO Box 1
Belford
Northumberland NE70 7JX

Anna Freud Centre
21 Maresfield Gardens
London NW3 5SH

Aquarian Press
see HarperCollins

Edward Arnold
see Hodder & Stoughton

Artesian Books
18 Artesian Road
London W2 5AR

Association for Humanistic
Psychology in Britain
BM Box 3582
London WC1N 3XX

Association of Child
Psychotherapists
Burgh House
New End Square
London NW3 1LT

Association of Educational
Psychologists
3 Sunderland Road
Durham DH1 2LH

Avenue Publishing Co
55 Woodstock Avenue
London NW11 9RG

Bailliere Tindall
see Harcourt Brace & Co.

BILD Publications
see Multilingual Matters

Blackwell Publishers
108 Cowley Road
Oxford OX4 1JF

Blackwell Scientific Publications Ltd
Osney Mead
Oxford OX2 0EL

BPS Books
see The British Psychological Society

British Association for Counselling
1 Regent Place
Rugby
Warks. CV21 2PJ

British Association of
Psychotherapists
21 Cantelowes Road
London NW1 9XR

The British Psychological Society
St Andrews House
48 Princess Road East
Leicester LE1 7DR

British Society for Projective
Psychology
Tavistock Centre
120 Belsize Lane
London NW3 5BA

W. C. Brown Publishers
Holywell House
Osney Mead
Oxford OX2 0ES

Butterworth Heinemann
Linacre House
Jordan Hill
Oxford OX2 8DP

Cambridge University Press
The Edinburgh Building
Shaftesbury Road
Cambridge CB2 2RU

Carfax Publishing Co.
PO Box 25
Abingdon
Oxon OX14 3UE

Cassell plc
Wellington House
125 Strand
London WC2R 0BB

Paul Chapman Publishing
144 Liverpool Road
London N1 1LA

Chapman & Hall
2–6 Boundary Row
London SE1 8HN

The Children's Society
Edward Rudolph House
Margery Street
London WC1X 0JL

Churchill Livingstone
Robert Stevenson House
1–3 Baxter's Place
Leith Walk
Edinburgh EH1 3AF

Community Psychiatric Nurses
Association
44 Dartford Road
Sevenoaks
Kent TN13 3TQ

Constable Publishers
3 The Lanchesters
162 Fulham Palace Road
London W6 9ER

Current Science
34–42 Cleveland Street
London W1P 5FP

J. M. Dent & Sons Ltd
see Weidenfeld & Nicolson

Duckworth
48 Hoxton Square
London N1 6PB

Element Books
Longmead
Shaftesbury
Dorset SP7 8PL

Elsevier Science Ltd
The Boulevard
Langford Lane
Kidlington
Oxford
OX5 1GB

Lawrence Erlbaum Associates Ltd
27 Church Road
Hove
East Sussex BN3 2FA

The Eurospan Group
3 Henrietta Street
Covent Garden
London WC2E 8LU

Falmer Press
Rankine Road
Basingstoke
Hants RG 23 0PR

Fontana
see HarperCollins

Fontana Press
see HarperCollins

Free Association Books
26 Freegrove Road
London N7 9RQ

W. H. Freeman & Co. Ltd
20 Beaumont Street
Oxford OX1 2NQ

Gaskell
see Royal College of Psychiatrists

Gateway Books
The Hollies
Mill Hill
Wellow
Bath BA2 8QJ

Guilford Press
UK distribution:
27 Palmeira Mansions
Church Road
Hove
East Sussex BN3 2FA

Harcourt Brace & Co.
24–28 Oval Road
London NW1 7DX

HarperCollins Publishers
77–85 Fulham Palace Road
Hammersmith
London W6 8JB

Harvester-Wheatsheaf
Simon & Schuster International
Group
Campus 400
Maylands Avenue
Hemel Hempstead
Herts HP2 7EZ

Harwood Academic Publishers
PO Box 90
Reading
Berks RG1 8JL

Haverstock Publications
249 Haverstock Hill
London NW3 4PS

Hobsons Publishing plc
Bateman Street
Cambridge CB2 1LZ

Hodder & Stoughton Publishers
Mill Road
Dunton Green
Sevenoaks
Kent TN13 2YA

Institute of Psychoanalysis
63 New Cavendish Street
London W1M 7RD

IPC Specialist Group
King's Reach Tower
Stamford Street
London SE1 9LS

JAI Press Ltd
The Courtyard
28 High Street
Hampton Hill
Middx TW12 1PD

Johns Hopkins University Press
101 Beckett House
14 Billing Road
Northampton NN1 5AW

Jossey-Bass Publishers
see Simon and Schuster IBD

Karnac Books
58 Gloucester Road
London SW7 4QY

Jessica Kingsley Publishers
116 Pentonville Road
London N1 9JB

John Libby & Company Limited
13 Smiths Yard
Summerley Street
London SW18 4HR

Longman
Longman House
Burnt Mill
Harlow
Essex CM20 2JE

McGraw-Hill Book Company
Europe
Shoppenhangers Road
Maidenhead
Berks SL6 2QL

Macmillan Press
Houndmills
Basingstoke
Hants RG21 2XS

Manchester University Press
Oxford Road
Manchester M13 9PL

MCB University Press
60–62 Toller Lane
Bradford BD8 9BY

MIND Publications
Kemp House, 1st Floor
152–160 City Road
London EC1V 2NP

The MIT Press
14 Bloomsbury Square
London WC1A 2LP

Multilingual Matters
Frankfurt Lodge
Clevedon Hall
Victoria Road
Clevedon
Avon BS21 7SJ

National Extension College
18 Brooklands Avenue
Cambridge CB2 2HN

Thomas Nelson & Sons Ltd
Nelson House
Mayfield Road
Walston-on-Thames
Surrey KT12 5PL

NFER-Nelson
Darville House
2 Oxford Road East
Windsor
Berks SL4 1DF

North-Holland Publishing Co.
see Elsevier Science Ltd

W. W. Norton & Company
10 Coptic Street
London WC1A 1PU

Oneworld Publications
185 Banbury Road
Oxford OX2 7AR

Open University Press
Celtic Court
22 Ball Moor
Buckingham MK18 1XW

Oxford University Press
Walton Street
Oxford OX2 6DP

Pan Macmillan Ltd
18–21 Cavaye Place
London SW10 9PG

Penguin Books
27 Wrights Lane
London W8 5TZ

Pergamon Press Ltd
see Elsevier Science Ltd

Pinter Publishers
Wellington House
125 Strand
London WC2R 0BB

Pion Ltd
207 Brondesbury Park
London NW2 5JN

Plenum Publishing Co. Ltd
88/90 Middlesex Street
London E1 7EZ

Positive Products
PO Box 45
Cheltenham GL52 3BX

Prentice Hall
see Harvester-Wheatsheaf

The Psychological Corporation
Foots Cray High Street
Sidcup
Kent DA14 5HP

Routledge
11 New Fetter Lane
London EC4P 4EE

The Royal College of Psychiatrists
17 Belgrave Square
London SW1X 8PG

The Royal Society
6 Carlton House Terrace
London SW1Y 5AG

Sage Publications
6 Bonhill Street
London EC2A 4PU

Sheldon Press
Holy Trinity Church
Marylebone Road
London NW1 4DU

Simon and Schuster International
International Book Distributors
Campus 400
Maylands Avenue
Hemel Hempstead HP2 7EZ

Souvenir Press Ltd
43 Great Russell Street
London WC1B 3PA

Springer-Verlag London Ltd
8 Alexander Road
London SW19 7JZ

Taylor & Francis Ltd
Rankine Road
Basingstoke
Hants RG24 0PR

Thomson International Publishing
2–6 Boundary Row
London SEI 8HN

Thorsons
see HarperCollins

Transaction Publishers UK
c/o Plymbridge Distributors Ltd
Estover
Plymouth PL6 7PZ

Transworld Publishers
61–63 Uxbridge Road
London W5 5SA

University Presses of California,
Columbia and Princeton Ltd
1 Oldlands Way
Bognor Regis
West Sussex PO22 9SA

Weidenfeld & Nicolson
Orion Publishing Group
5 Upper St Martins Lane
London WC2H 9EA

Whiting & Birch Ltd
PO Box 872
London SE23 3HL

Whurr Publishers Ltd
19b Compton Terrace
London N1 2UN

John Wiley & Sons Ltd
Baffins Lane
Chichester
West Sussex PO19 1UD

Williams & Wilkins Ltd
Broadway House
2–6 Fulham Broadway
London SW6 1AA

Winslow Press
Telford Road
Bicester
Oxon OX6 0TS

The Women's Press Ltd
34 Great Sutton Street
London EC1V 0DX

Yale University Press
23 Pond Street
London NW3 2PN

5.4 USEFUL ADDRESSES

This list does not aim to be comprehensive; its starting point was the list held by the Society's Helpdesk, and it was expanded by sending it to the Training Committees of the Divisions and to various Society members and office personnel who all suggested additions from their areas of practice. The end result can therefore be said to be eclectic, and, we hope, useful.

ASSOCIATION OF BLIND AND PARTIALLY SIGHTED
TEACHERS AND STUDENTS
5 Gravel Hill, Tile Hill, Coventry,
Warks. CV4 9JD
Tel: 01203 468899

ASSOCIATION OF CAREERS ADVISERS IN COLLEGES
OF HIGHER EDUCATION (ACACHE)
Liverpool Institute of Higher Education,
Woolton Road,
Liverpool L16 8ND
Tel: 0151 722 7331 ext 292

ASSOCIATION OF CHARTERED CLINICAL
PSYCHOLOGISTS IN PRIVATE PRACTICE (ACCPPP)
PO Box 2EB, London
W1A 2EB
Tel: 0171 323 2370

ASSOCIATION FOR CHILD PSYCHOLOGY AND
PSYCHIATRY (ACPP)
70 Borough High Street,
London SE1 1XF
Tel: 0171 403 7458

ASSOCIATION OF CHILD PSYCHOTHERAPISTS
Burgh House, New End Square,
London NW3 1LT
Tel: 0171 794 8881

ASSOCIATION FOR DATABASE SERVICES IN
EDUCATION AND TRAINING (ADSET)
Chancery House, Dalkeith Place, Kettering,
Northamptonshire NN16 0BS
Tel: 01536 410500

ASSOCIATION OF DIRECTORS OF SOCIAL SERVICES
(ADSS)
Social Services Division, Stockport MBC, Town Hall,
Stockport SK1 3XE
Tel: 0161 474 7896

ASSOCIATION OF DISABLED PROFESSIONALS (ADP)
170 Benton Hill, Horbury, W. Yorks WF4 5HW
Tel: 01924 270335 (voice and text)

ASSOCIATION OF EDUCATIONAL PSYCHOLOGISTS
(AEP)
3 Sunderland Road, Durham DH1 2LH
Tel: 0191 384 9512

ASSOCIATION FOR FAMILY THERAPY (AFT)
6 Heol Seddon, Danescourt, Llandaff, Cardiff CF5 2QX
Tel: 01222 554595

ASSOCIATION OF GRADUATE CAREERS ADVISORY
SERVICES (AGCAS)
c/o Eveline Nicholls, Loughborough University of
Technology, Ashby Road, Loughborough, Leicestershire
LE11 3TU
Tel: 01509 263 171

ASSOCIATION OF HEADS OF PSYCHOLOGY
DEPARTMENTS
Chair: Ray Bull: Portsmouth University, King Charles St,
Portsmouth PO1 2ER

ASSOCIATION FOR HUMANISTIC PSYCHOLOGY
(AHP)
27 Rodgers Close, Elstree, Herts WD6 3HN
Tel: 0181 953 5834

ASSOCIATION FOR MANAGEMENT, EDUCATION
AND DEVELOPMENT (AMED)
21 Catherine St, London WC2B 5JS
Tel: 0171 497 3264

ASSOCIATION OF PROFESSIONS FOR THE MENTALLY
HANDICAPPED (APMH)
Greytree Lodge, 2nd Avenue, Ross-on-Wye, Hereford &
Worcester HR9 7HT
Tel: 01989 81297

ASSOCIATION FOR THE PSYCHIATRIC STUDY OF
ADOLESCENTS
13 Bonaly Drive, Edinburgh EH13 0EJ
Tel: 0131 441 1049

ASSOCIATION OF PSYCHOLOGICAL COUNSELLING
AND TRAINING (APCT)
33 Marlborough Rd, Swindon SN3 1PH
Tel: 01793 538586

ASSOCIATION OF PSYCHOLOGY TECHNICIANS
Secretary: Mrs Westley, Department of Psychology, Royal
Holloway University of London, Egham Hill, Egham,
Surrey TW20 0EX
Tel: 01784 443526

ASSOCIATION FOR SCIENCE EDUCATION
College Lane, Hatfield, Herts AL10 9AA
Tel: 0170 267 411

ASSOCIATION OF SCOTTISH PRINCIPAL
EDUCATIONAL PSYCHOLOGISTS (ASPEP)
Psychological Service, 7 Merchiston Park, Edinburgh
EH10 4PR

ASSOCIATION FOR STUDENT COUNSELLING (ASC)
c/o The British Association for Counselling

ASSOCIATION FOR THE STUDY OF ANIMAL
BEHAVIOUR (ASAB)
Dept of Biology, Royal Holloway & New Bedford College,
Egham, Surrey, TW20 0EX
Tel: 01784 434455

ASSOCIATION FOR THE TEACHING OF PSYCHOLOGY
c/o The British Psychological Society

ASSOCIATION OF UNIVERSITY AND COLLEGE
LECTURERS (AUCL)
104 Albert Road, Southsea, Hants PO5 2SN
Tel: 01705 818625

ASSOCIATION OF UNIVERSITY TEACHERS (AUT)
United House, 1 Pembridge Road, London W11 3JY
Tel: 0171 221 4370

ASSOCIATION OF UNIVERSITY TEACHERS
(SCOTLAND) (AUT(S))
6 Castle Street, Edinburgh EH2 3AT
Tel: 0131 226 6694

ASSOCIATION OF WORKERS FOR CHILDREN WITH
EMOTIONAL AND BEHAVIOURAL DIFFICULTIES
Red Hill School, East Sutton, Maidstone, Kent ME17 3DQ
Tel: 01622 843104

BIOTECHNOLOGY AND BIOLOGICAL SCIENCES
RESEARCH COUNCIL (BBSRC)
(Formerly the AFRC)
Polaris House, North Star Avenue, Swindon, Wilts
SN2 1UH
Tel: 01793 413200

BRITISH ASSOCIATION FOR THE ADVANCEMENT OF
SCIENCE
Fortress House, 23 Savile Row, London W1X 1AB
Tel: 0171 494 3326

BRITISH ASSOCIATION FOR BEHAVIOURAL AND
COGNITIVE PSYCHOTHERAPIES (BABCP)
59 Revelstoke Road, London SW18D 5NJ
Tel: 0181 715 1725

BRITISH ASSOCIATION OF COUNSELLING (BAC)
1 Regent Place, Rugby, Warks CV21 2PJ
Tel: 01788 550899

BRITISH ASSOCIATION OF PSYCHOTHERAPISTS
37 Mapesbury Road, London NW2 4HJ
Tel: 0181 346 1747

BRITISH ASSOCIATION FOR SEXUAL AND MARITAL
THERAPY (BASMT)
PO Box 62, Sheffield, Yorkshire S10 3TS

BRITISH ASSOCIATION OF SOCIAL WORKERS (BASW)
16 Kent Street, Birmingham B5 6RD
Tel: 0121 622 3911

BRITISH ASSOCIATION OF SPORTS SCIENCES (BASS)
c/o Sarah Rowell, Sports Science Education Programme,
4 College Close, Beckett Park, Leeds LS6 3QH
Tel: 0113 2784113

THE BRITISH COUNCIL
10 Spring Gardens, London SW1A 2BN
Tel: 0171 930 8466
or
Medlock Street, Manchester M15 4AA
Tel: 0161 957 7000

BRITISH DENTAL ASSOCIATION
63/64 Wimpole Street, London W1M 8AL
Tel: 0171 935 0875

BRITISH INSTITUTE OF LEARNING DISABILITIES
(BILD)
The Crescent, Wolverhampton Road, Kidderminster,
Worcestershire DY10 3PP
Tel: 01562 850251

BRITISH INSTITUTE OF TRANSACTIONAL ANALYSIS
(ITA)
BM Box 4104, Old Gloucester St, London WC1N 3XX
Tel: 0171 404 5011

BRITISH MEDICAL ASSOCIATION (BMA)
BMA House, Tavistock Square, London WC1H 9JP
Tel: 0171 387 4499

THE BRITISH PSYCHOLOGICAL SOCIETY (BPS)
St Andrews House, 48 Princess Road East, Leicester
LE1 7DR
Tel: 0116 254 9568

BRITISH PSYCHO-ANALYTICAL SOCIETY
63 New Cavendish St, London W1M 7RD
Tel: 0171 580 4952

BRITISH SOCIETY OF GERONTOLOGY (BSG)
Age Concern Institute of Gerontology (Kings College),
552 Kings Road, London SW10 0UA

BRITISH SOCIETY OF HYPNOTHERAPISTS (BSH)
37 Orbain Rd, London SW6 7JZ
Tel: 0171 385 1166

BRITISH SOCIETY FOR MUSIC THERAPY (BSMT)
69 Avondale Avenue, East Barnet, Herts EN4 8NB
Tel: 0181 368 8879

CAREERS RESEARCH AND ADVISORY CENTRE
(CRAC)
Sheridan House, Castle Park, Cambridge CB3 0AX
Tel: 01223 460277

COMMITTEE ON THE PUBLIC UNDERSTANDING OF
SCIENCE (COPUS)
c/o The Royal Society

COMMITTEE OF VICE-CHANCELLORS AND
PRINCIPALS OF THE UNIVERSITIES OF THE UNITED
KINGDOM (CVCP)
29 Tavistock Square, London WC1H 9EZ
Tel: 0171 387 9231

DEPARTMENT FOR EDUCATION (DFE)
Sanctuary Buildings, Great Smith Street, London
SW1P 3BT
Tel: 0171 925 5000

ECONOMIC AND SOCIAL RESEARCH COUNCIL
(ESRC)
Polaris House, North Star Avenue, Swindon, Wilts
SN2 1UJ
Tel: 01793 413000

EDUCATIONAL INSTITUTE OF SCOTLAND (EIS)
46 Moray Place, Edinburgh EH3 6BH
Tel: 0131 225 6244

ENGINEERING AND PHYSICAL SCIENCES RESEARCH
COUNCIL (EPSRC)
(Replaces some of the activities of SERC)
Polaris House, North Star Avenue, Swindon, Wilts
SN2 1ET

THE ERGONOMICS SOCIETY
Devonshire House, Devonshire Square, Loughborough,
Leics LE11 3DW
Tel: 01509 234904

EUROPEAN FEDERATION OF PROFESSIONAL
PSYCHOLOGISTS ASSOCIATIONS (EFPPA)
c/o Ingrid Lunt, Editor *News From EFPPA*,
University of London, Institute of Education, 20 Bedford
Way, London WC1H 0AL
Tel: 0171 612 6281

EXPERIMENTAL PSYCHOLOGY SOCIETY (EPS)
c/o Dr Elaine Funnell, Department of Psychology, Royal
Holloway and Bedford New College, University of
London, Egham Hill, Egham, Surrey TW20 0EX

FACULTY OF OCCUPATIONAL MEDICINE (ROYAL
COLLEGE OF PHYSICIANS OF LONDON)
6 St Andrews Place, London NW1 4LE
Tel: 0171 487 3414

FACULTY OF PUBLIC HEALTH MEDICINE
4 St Andrews Place, London NW1 4LB
Tel: 0171 935 0243

FAMILY INSTITUTE
105 Cathedral Road, Cardiff CF1 9PH
Tel: 01222 226532/3

HIGHER EDUCATION FUNDING COUNCIL FOR
ENGLAND (HEFCW)
Northavon House, Coldharbour Lane, Bristol BS16 1QD
Tel: 0117 931 7317

HIGHER EDUCATION FUNDING COUNCIL FOR
WALES (HEFCW)
Lambourne House, Cardiff Business Park, Llanishen,
Cardiff CF4 5GL
Tel: 01222 761861

INSTITUTE OF GROUP ANALYSIS, GROUP ANALYTIC
SOCIETY (LONDON)
1 Daleham Gardens, London NW3 5BY
Tel: 0171 431 2693

INSTITUTE OF MANAGEMENT CONSULTANTS LTD
(IMC)
32 Hatton Gardens, London EC1N 8DJ
Tel: 0171 584 7285/6 & 0171 242 2140

INSTITUTE OF PERSONNEL AND DEVELOPMENT
(IPD)
35 Camp Road, London SW19 4UX
Tel: 0181 946 9100

INSTITUTION OF PROFESSIONALS, MANAGERS AND
SPECIALISTS (IPMS)
75–79 York Rd, London SE1 7AQ
Tel: 0171 928 9951

INTERNATIONAL SCHOOL PSYCHOLOGY
ASSOCIATION
Dr R L Burden, University of Exeter School of Education,
St Luke's, Heavitree Road, Exeter EX1 2LU

INTERNATIONAL UNION OF PSYCHOLOGICAL
SCIENCE (IUPsyS)
c/o The British Psychological Society

LINCOLN CLINIC AND INSTITUTE FOR
PSYCHOTHERAPY
19 Abbeville Mews, 88 Clapham Park Road, London
SW4 7BX
Tel: 0171 978 1545

MANCHESTER SCHOOL OF MANAGEMENT (run CPD
courses of interest for Occupational Psychologists)
Continuing Education Department, UMIST, P.O. Box 88,
Sackville Street, Manchester M60 1QD

MEDICAL FOUNDATION FOR THE CARE OF VICTIMS
OF TORTURE

96 Grafton Road, London NW5 3EJ
Tel: 0171 284 4321

MEDICAL RESEARCH COUNCIL (MRC)
20 Park Crescent, London W1N 4AL
Tel: 0171 636 5422

MENCAP – ROYAL SOCIETY FOR MENTALLY
HANDICAPPED CHILDREN AND ADULTS
MENCAP National Centre, 123 Golden Lane, London
EC1Y 0RT
Tel: 0171–253 0454

MENTAL AFTER CARE ASSOCIATION (MACA)
Bainbridge House, Bainbridge St, London WC1A 1HP
Tel: 0171 436 6194

MENTAL HEALTH MEDIA COUNCIL
380–384 Harrow Road, London W9 2HU
Tel: 0171–286 2346

METANOIA – GROUP AND PSYCHOTHERAPY
TRAINING INSTITUTE
13 North Common Road, London W5 2QB
Tel: 0181 579 2505

MIND – NATIONAL ASSOCIATION FOR MENTAL
HEALTH
22 Harley St, London W1N 2ED
Tel: 0171 637 0741

NATIONAL ASSOCIATION OF PRINCIPAL
EDUCATIONAL PSYCHOLOGISTS (NAPEP)
The City of Birmingham Education Department, Child
Advisory and Psychological Services, Council House
Annexe, Margaret Street, Birmingham B3 3BU
Tel: 0121 235 2199

NATIONAL ASSOCIATION FOR SPECIAL
EDUCATIONAL NEEDS (NASEN)
2 Lichfield Rd, Stafford, Staffs ST17 4JX
Tel: 01785 46872

NATIONAL ASSOCIATION OF TEACHERS IN
FURTHER AND HIGHER EDUCATION (NATFHE)
27 Britannia St, London WC1X 9JP
Tel: 0171 837 3636

NATIONAL BUREAU FOR STUDENTS WITH
DISABILITIES
336 Brixton Road, London SW9 7AA
Tel: 0171 737 7166

NATIONAL CHILDREN'S BUREAU
8 Wakley St, London EC1V 7QE
Tel: 0171 278 9441

NATIONAL COUNCIL FOR VOLUNTARY
ORGANIZATIONS (NCVO)
Regents Wharf, 8 All Saints Street, London N1 9RL
Tel: 0171 713 6161

NATIONAL GRADUATE PSYCHOLOGISTS' GROUP
c/o The British Psychological Society

NORTHERN IRELAND DEPARTMENT OF EDUCATION
(DENI)
Rathgael House, Balloo Road, Bangor, County Down,
BT19 2PR
Tel: 01247 466311

OXFORD CENTRE FOR STAFF DEVELOPMENT
Oxford Brookes University, Gipsy Lane, Headington,
Oxford OX3 0PB

PERSONAL CONSTRUCT THEORY GROUP
c/o Dr Fay Fransella, The Sail Loft, Mulberry Quay,
Market Strand, Falmouth, Cornwall TR11 3HD
Tel: 01326 314 871

RELATE – NATIONAL MARRIAGE GUIDANCE
COUNCIL
Herbert Gray College, Little Church Street, Rugby,
Warwickshire CV21 3AP
Tel: 01788 73241

RESEARCH DEFENCE SOCIETY (RDS)
58 Gt Marlborough St, London W1V 1DD
Tel: 0171 287 2818

ROYAL COLLEGE OF GENERAL PRACTITIONERS
14 Prince's Gate, Hyde Park, London SW7 1PU
Tel: 0171 581 3232

ROYAL COLLEGE OF NURSING OF THE UNITED
KINGDOM
20 Cavendish Square, London W1M 0AB
Tel: 0171 409 3333

ROYAL COLLEGE OF PSYCHIATRISTS
17 Belgrave Square, London SW1X 8PG
Tel: 0171 235 2351

THE ROYAL SOCIETY
6 Carlton House Terrace, London SW1Y 5AG
Tel: 0171 839 5561

ROYAL SOCIETY FOR THE PROMOTION OF HEALTH
(RSH)
38a St George's Drive, London SW1V 4BH
Tel: 0171 630 0121

THE RUNNYMEDE TRUST
11 Princelet St, London E1 6QH
Tel: 0171 375 1496

SAINSBURY CENTRE FOR MENTAL HEALTH
134–138 Borough High Street, London SE1 1LB
Tel: 0171 403 8790

SANE
199–205 Old Marylebone Road, London NW1 5QP
Tel: 0171 724 6570

SCOTTISH ASSOCIATION OF FAMILY CONCILIATION
SERVICES (FAMILY CONCILIATION SCOTLAND)
(SAFCOS)
127 Rose Street South Lane, Edinburgh EH2 4BB
Tel: 0131 220 1610

SCOTTISH ASSOCIATION FOR MENTAL HEALTH
(SAMH)
38 Gardner's Crescent, Edinburgh EH3 8DQ
Tel: 0131 229 9687

SCOTTISH COUNCIL FOR RESEARCH IN EDUCATION
15 St John St, Edinburgh EH8 8JR
Tel: 0131 557 2944

SCOTTISH COUNCIL FOR VOLUNTARY
ORGANISATIONS (SCVO)
18–19 Claremont Crescent, Edinburgh EH7 4QD
Tel: 0131 556 3882

SCOTTISH EDUCATION DEPARTMENT
Room 4/25, New St Andrew's House, St James Centre,
Edinburgh EH1 3SY

SCOTTISH HIGHER EDUCATION FUNDING COUNCIL
(SHEFC)
Donaldson House, 97 Haymarket Terrace, Edinburgh
EH12 5HD
Tel: 0131 313 6500

SCOTTISH INSTITUTE OF HUMAN RELATIONS
56 Albany St, Edinburgh EH1 3QR
Tel: 0131 556 0924

SOCIETY OF ANALYTICAL PSYCHOLOGY LTD
1 Daleham Gardens, London NW3 5BY
Tel: 0171 435 7696

SOCIETY OF HEALTH EDUCATION AND PROMOTION
SPECIALISTS
c/o Sheffield Health Authority, Westbrook House,
Sharrow Vale Road, Sheffield S11 5EU
Tel: 0114 2670333 Fax: 0114 2660498

SOCIETY FOR RESEARCH IN THE PSYCHOLOGY OF
MUSIC AND MUSIC EDUCATION
38 Westfield Rd, Horbury, Wakefield WF4 6EA
Tel: 01924 260302

SOCIETY FOR REPRODUCTIVE AND INFANT
PSYCHOLOGY
c/o Pamela Warner, Department of Public Health Sciences,
Edinburgh University Medical School, Teviot Place,
Edinburgh EH8 9AG

SOCIETY FOR RESEARCH INTO HIGHER EDUCATION
(SRHE)
344–354 Gray's Inn Road, London WC1X 8BP
Tel: 0171 837 7880

STAFF AND EDUCATIONAL DEVELOPMENT
ASSOCIATION (SEDA)
Gala House, 3 Raglan Road, Edgbaston, Birmingham
B5 7RA

STANDING CONFERENCE ON PUBLIC HEALTH
55 North Wharf Road, London W2 1LA
Tel: 0171 402 2555

STEPFAMLY (National Stepfamily Association)
72 Willesden Lane, London NW6 7TA

THE TAVISTOCK CLINIC
Tavistock Centre, 120 Belsize Lane, London NW3 5BA
Tel: 0171 435 7111

TRUST FOR THE STUDY OF ADOLESCENCE
23 New Road, Brighton BN1 1W2
Tel: 01273 693311

UNITED KINGDOM COUNCIL FOR PSYCHOTHERAPY
Regent's College, Inner Circle, Regent's Park, London
NW1 4NS
Tel: 0171 487 7554

UNITED STATES–UNITED KINGDOM EDUCATIONAL
COMMISSION
6 Porter Street, London W1M 2HR
Tel: 0171 486 7697

UNIVERSITIES' AND COLLEGES' STAFF
DEVELOPMENT AGENCY (UCoSDA)
Level 6, University House, Sheffield S10 2TN
Tel: 0114 282 4211

WELSH EDUCATION DEPARTMENT
Government Buildings, Ty-Glas Road, Llanishen, Cardiff
CG4 5WE
Tel: 01222 761456

WORLD ASSOCIATION FOR EDUCATIONAL
RESEARCH
Secretary General: Prof. Dr. M.-L. van Herreweghe,
Rijksuniversiteit Gent, Pedagogish Laboratorium, Henri
Dunantlaan 1, B-9000 Gent, Belgium

YOUNG MINDS
22a Boston Place, London NW1 6ER
Tel: 0171 724 7262

5.5 USEFUL PUBLICATIONS

This is by no means a comprehensive list, and suggestions for titles which should be included will be welcomed.

APA Membership Register
American Psychological Association, c/o Eurospan, 3 Henrietta Street, Covent Garden, London WC2E 8LU, UK
Provides a record of the American Psychological Association's membership, with details of mailing addresses and membership status.

The Association of Medical Research Charities Handbook
Association of Medical Research Charities, Tavistock House South, Tavistock Square, London WCIH 9LG, UK
Provides information on charities, their objectives and interests, types of awards available, and the criteria for these awards.

British Universities, Guide to Graduate Study
Association of Commonwealth Universities, John Foster House, 36 Gordon Square, London WC1H 0PF, UK

The Charities Address Book – UK
Aurelian Information Ltd, 129 Leighton Gardens, London NW10 3P3, UK

Charities by Counties and Regions
Will to Charity, Equus House, 48a High Street, Walton-on-Thames, Surrey KT12 1BY, UK

Charities Digest
The Family Welfare Association, 501–505 Kingsland Road, London E8 4AU, UK

CNAA Directory of First Degree and Undergraduate Courses
Council for National Academic Awards, 344–354 Grays Inn Road, London WC1X 8BP, UK

Compendium of Postgraduate Studies in Psychology in the UK and Ireland
BPS Books, The British Psychological Society, St Andrews House, 48 Princess Road East, Leicester LEI 7DR, UK. Guide to all UK and Irish academic departments and research institutes offering postgraduate education in psychology.

Croners Reference Book for Employers
Croner Publications Ltd, Croner House, London Road, Kingston-upon-Thames, Surrey KT2 6SR, UK
Loose-leaf employment law guide.

Directory of British Associations
CBD Research Ltd, 15 Wickham Road, Beckenham, Kent BR3 2JS, UK

Directory of Chartered Psychologists
The British Psychological Society, St Andrews House, 48 Princess Road East, Leicester LE1 7DR, UK
A 'yellow pages' of services offered by psychologists in the UK.

Directory of Education–Industry Organisations
Resources Plus, 4 Medway, Thatcham, Berks RG13 3AU
Guide to education–industry link activities and organizations.

Directory of Further Education
Hobsons Publishing PLC, Bateman Street, Cambridge CB2 1LZ, UK

Directory of Grant-Making Trusts
Charities Aid Foundation, 48 Pembury Road, Tonbridge TN9 2JD, UK

Directory of Hospitals
Longman Group UK Ltd, Longman House, Burnt Mill, Harlow, Essex CM20 2JE, UK

Directory of Independent Hospitals and Health Services
Longman Group UK Ltd, Longman House, Burnt Mill, Harlow, Essex CM20 2JE, UK

Directory of Mental Health Services (published in association with MIND)
Longman Group UK Ltd, Longman House, Burnt Mill, Harlow, Essex CM20 2JE, UK

Directory of Opportunities for Graduates
Newpoint Publishing Co. Ltd, Windsor Court, East

Grinstead House, East Grinstead, W. Sussex RH19 1XA, UK

Directory of Services for Elderly People
Longman Group UK Ltd, Longman House, Burnt Mill, Harlow, Essex CM20 2JE, UK

Directory of Youth Services in the UK
Longman Group UK Ltd, Longman House, Burnt Mill, Harlow, Essex CM20 2JE, UK

Disability Rights Handbook
Disability Alliance, Educational and Research Association, Universal House, 88–94 Wentworth Street, London E1 7SA, UK
Guide to Social Security benefits for people with disabilities and their families.

DOD's Parliamentary Companion
DOD's Parliamentary Companion Ltd, Hurst Green, E. Sussex TN19 7PX, UK

DOG Guide to Postgraduate Study
Newpoint Publishing Co. Ltd, Windsor Court, East Grinstead House, East Grinstead, W. Sussex RH19 1XA, UK
Guide to full and part-time postgraduate taught courses and research opportunities in the UK.

Education A to Z
Advisory Centre for Education (ACE) Ltd, 1B Aberdeen Studios, 22–24 Highbury Grove, London N5 2EA
A reference guide to sources of information in education, listing major topics and organizations.

Education Authorities Directory and Annual
School Government Publishing Company Ltd, Darby House, Bletchingley Road, Merstham, Redhill RH1 3DN, UK

Guide to Libraries and Information Units in Government Departments and Other Organisations
British Library, Science Reference and Information Service, 25 Southampton Buildings, Chancery Lane, London WC2A 1AW, UK

Hospitals and Health Services Year Book
Institute of Health Services Management, 75 Portland Place, London W1N 4AN, UK

Independent Schools in the UK
Ed J. Barrow and Co., Publicity House, Streatham Hill, London SW2 4TR, UK

International Directory of Psychologists (exclusive of the USA)
Publication of the International Union of Psychological Science, published by Elsevier Science BV, PO Box 211, 1000 AE Amsterdam, The Netherlands

The International Who's Who
Europa Publications, 18 Bedford Square, London WC1B 3JN, UK

Journals in Psychology: A resource listing for authors
American Psychological Association, c/o Eurospan, 3 Henrietta Street, Covent Garden, London WC2E 8LU, UK
A selective guide to several hundred English-language publications, which aims to help authors determine which journal to consider submitting papers to.

Libraries Directory
James Clarke and Co. Ltd, PO Box 60, Cambridge CB1 2NT, UK

Public Authorities Directory
LGC Communications, 122 Minories, London EC3N 1NT, UK
Details on all local authorities.

The Register of Chartered Psychologists
The British Psychological Society, St Andrews House, 48 Princess Road East, Leicester LE1 7DR, UK

Social Services Year Book
Longman Group UK Ltd, Longman House, Burnt Mill, Harlow, Essex CM20 2JE, UK

The Training Directory
Kogan Page Ltd, 120 Pentonville Road, London N1 9JN, UK
Explains how government initiatives affect current UK training policy, and lists training providers, consultants, suppliers of training materials.

The Voluntary Agencies Directory
NCVO Publications, Regents Wharf, 8 All Saints Street, London N1 9RL, UK

The World of Learning
Europa Publications, 18 Bedford Square, London WC1B 3JN, UK
Directory of educational, cultural and scientific institutions worldwide.

Appendix A: BROAD AREAS IN WHICH CHARTERED PSYCHOLOGISTS OFFER SERVICES

(Reproduced from *The Directory of Chartered Psychologists*, by kind permission.)

1 CLINICAL PSYCHOLOGY SERVICES

CLINICAL psychology is the application of psychology to health and community care. Clinical psychologists work in specialities. The most common specialities are adult mental health acute services, including a range of psychological therapy services, adult mental health rehabilitation and resettlement services, child health care (including paediatric and child and family mental health services), services for people with learning disabilities, care of elderly people (including geriatric and psychogeriatric services), primary care services, management (including advising purchasers, and consultancy on health care systems), general hospital acute services (including acute medical and surgical specialities), neuropsychology (including neurological and neurosurgical services and neuropsychological rehabilitation), services concerned with substance abuse (including those for people with alcohol and drugs problems), forensic services, services for people with physical and sensory disabilities (including young disabled people and those described as 'the chronic sick') and HIV/AIDS services. Clinical psychologists also work in educational and social service settings. Clinical psychologists are problem solvers, formulating problems and questions in psychological terms and drawing creatively on a wealth of psychological theories and techniques from the discipline of psychology to support the finding of ways forward. Clinical psychologists work directly with complex problems involving individuals, couples, families, groups and service systems. Consultancy and training is provided to carers and health-care professionals in order to maximize the use of their psychological skills.

Organizational consultancy is carried out with provider and purchaser organizations with respect to the psychological aspects of health and community care.

2 CLINICAL NEUROPSYCHOLOGY SERVICES

Clinical neuropsychologists are concerned with the changes which occur following damage to, or disease of, the nervous system. Their skills lie in the measurement of changes in intelligence, thinking, memory, personality and other aspects of behaviour so that neurological conditions may be more accurately detected, diagnosed and treated. They may be able to accurately determine the degree to which the client is affected psychologically, and to make prognoses about the likely course of the disorder. Clinical neuropsychologists play a central role in the management of disorders resulting from brain damage or disease, and in the planning and conduct of programmes of treatment and rehabilitation.

3 COUNSELLING PSYCHOLOGY SERVICES

Counselling psychologists work with individuals and groups helping them to improve their sense of well-being, alleviate their distress, resolve their crises and increase their ability to solve problems and make decisions. Counselling psychologists are concerned to help people to cope more effectively with normal life cycle developmental issues, such as relationship breakdown, career change, redundancy, loss and bereavement, and illness.

Counselling psychologists apply systematic research-based approaches to help themselves and others to understand problems and to develop potential solutions to them. Counselling psychologists use a range of approaches and skills including humanistic, psycho-dynamic and cognitive-behavioural, and may also employ skills of assessment and testing.

Counselling psychologists work in a range of settings including health centres, G.P. practices, industry and commerce, student counselling services and private practice.

4 EDUCATIONAL PSYCHOLOGY SERVICES

Educational psychologists are applied psychologists working both within the school system and in the community. They are concerned with children's learning and development. They have skills in a range of psychological and educational assessment techniques and in different methods of helping children and young people who are experiencing difficulties in learning or social adjustment. They are involved in trying to prevent children's learning difficulties where this is possible and ameliorating them where it is not. They have a central role in the assessment of children's difficulties from an early stage and a statutory role in the 1981 Education (Scotland) Act and the 1993 Education Act multi-professional assessment. Under Scottish legislation, educational psychologists have a statutory role with respect to the Children's Hearing Systems. They also have a role and function in improving or optimizing the learning of all children. Much of the work of educational psychologists is with children and young people from 0 to 19 years, both in ordinary and in special schools, though they also work extensively with parents, teachers and other professionals. They also offer a service to young people and adults in further and higher education.

Educational psychologists thus work at different levels within a system applying different knowledge and skills as appropriate. Some of their work will be with children; other work is with adults and with institutions and organizations. Most educational psychologists in the UK work within Local Authority Psychological Services and every parent and child and all state maintained schools are therefore entitled to this service. There are also a number of educational psychologists working in private practice who take referrals from parents, schools, doctors and others. These educational psychologists usually work outside the school system either as sole practitioners or as members of a private service. Although much of their work is with individual clients and families, educational psychologists also offer consultancy and research to groups and institutions, particularly schools. This includes staff training, systems analysis and evaluation.

5 FORENSIC PSYCHOLOGY SERVICES

Psychologists contribute to criminological and legal services (often referred to generically as forensic psychology) in many ways. They might be interested in the behaviour of people within legal systems; they might study offenders, offending behaviour and crime detection, the administration of justice including the giving of evidence, or the management of individuals following sentencing. Psychologists interested in criminological and legal matters are often called upon to give evidence to the courts, to tribunals and committees of enquiry as expert witnesses; sometimes they will have skills in other branches of psychology, for example clinical or educational psychology. Psychologists with an interest in the 'forensic' area can be found working in prisons, in special hospitals and secure psychiatric units, in university departments, and probation and social services departments amongst others.

6 OCCUPATIONAL PSYCHOLOGY SERVICES

Occupational psychologists are concerned with people in relation to work – in the widest sense, both paid employment and other constructive and co-operative activities.

Their concern is how work tasks and conditions of work can affect people – developing them or constraining and stressing them; but also with how people and their characteristics determine what and how work is done. In consequence, they are concerned with:

• selection, training and personal development to ensure effectiveness;
• the modification and basic design of equipment, work procedures and the structures of an organization; and
• above all, with solutions which enable people in the work situation to participate in the process of modifying the work situation for greater effectiveness and satisfaction.

The main areas of occupational psychology are:

• Job and Work Environment (including ergonomics, health and safety at work and environmental psychology);
• Assessment and Development (including competency analysis, selection, assessment appraisal, counselling, and systems for personal development);
• Organizational Development (including motivation in the work place and employee relations, team building, the study of organization 'cultures', the management of change in organizations and the development and modification of reward systems);
• Training (including training needs analysis, the design, conduct and evaluation of training, open and distance learning, computer based training, and the training of trainers).

All occupational psychologists will have a knowledge of the concepts and findings in all of the above areas; each will usually, however, have developed a specialized expertise within one or two of the above areas.

7 PSYCHOLOGICAL SERVICES IN SOCIAL SERVICES SETTINGS

Chartered Psychologists offer a wide range of services to Social Services Departments (SSDs) and Social Work Departments in Scotland (SWDs). Services offered are predominantly in the areas of child care and child health, people with long term mental illness, care of the elderly, and learning disabilities (mental handicap). The changing nature of the profession and its training has led to more interventions for the clients of Social Services, and their professional staff involved. SSDs and SWDs are major users of Chartered Psychologists' time, but traditionally have not been direct employers. As their client-populations are similar, SSDs and SWDs are provided with psychological services, in the majority, by clinical psychologists employed by NHS provider units, or by educational psychologists employed by a Local Education Authority. A small number of Chartered Occupational Psychologists have contracts with SSDs and SWDs.

8 SERVICES BY TEACHERS OF PSYCHOLOGY

Teaching psychologist are concerned with the psychological aspects of teaching and learning – in other words, how to make both teaching and learning more effective. In doing so, they look at all aspects of the teaching and learning situation, such as the social psychology of the classroom; revision and examination management; the skills which are needed for educational achievement; and how different methods of teaching can help people to learn. Teaching psychologists are usually based in colleges or universities rather than schools, and tend to be mainly concerned with teaching and learning for those who are in further, higher, or adult education. They may also be concerned with vocational training and they will, of course, also teach psychology themselves.

9 OTHER PSYCHOLOGICAL SERVICES

No classification system describing the services offered by psychologists can take account of every area in which the application of psychological knowledge has been found to have practical benefits. However, in this section a number of additional areas in which some Chartered Psychologists offer services are described. Some of these areas have their origins almost directly in developing areas of applied research (e.g. health psychology, and market, social and consumer research, sports psychology), or are research services themselves.

Psychotherapy is not listed as a separate category as psychotherapy represents an area in which Chartered Psychologists who have qualified in a variety of other areas offer a range of psychological and therapeutic series which are also offered by members of other professions (e.g. psychiatry).

9.1 Health Psychology

Health psychologists are concerned primarily with the relationship between psychological factors and physical health. Health psychology has a strong academic and applied base within the UK. Academic health psychologists are concerned, amongst other issues with: (i) the relationship between psychological factors and health-related behaviours such as smoking and exercise, (ii) identifying factors likely to promote the uptake of health-related behaviours either in preventive or treatment settings, and (iii) examining the impact of illness and of the health care system on patient well-being and behaviour.

Applied health psychologists are primarily involved with the implementation of treatment interventions, their evaluation, or the development of health care services. Most applied health psychologists have a strong background in research and frequently advise on, or establish, research programmes in health service settings.

Health psychologists work in a variety of settings, including university departments of psychology, health promotion, acute medical wards, and rehabilitation programmes, and public health departments. They may be involved in direct work with individual clients, community interventions, and in a consultative capacity with other health professionals.

9.2 Sport and Exercise Psychology

Sport psychologists apply psychology as a science in:
(a) sport, both competitive and non-competitive, at individual and team level;
(b) the exercise domain, encompassing individual and group training for health, fitness and enjoyment; and
(c) the field of motor skill research and human performance.

Sport psychologists may be involved in scientific research or practical, applied work into psychological aspects of sport, exercise and human performance.

The science of psychology can be applied to a whole range of sporting activities including educational, information and research services to teachers, coaches, trainers, clubs, groups and individual participants in sport and exercise.

9.3 Market, Social and Consumer Research

Psychologists working to provide and use commercial research services are employed in a research executive capacity by market and social research agencies and as research advisers 'in-house' by manufacturing and service companies, government departments and other organizations. They are concerned to:

• Provide advice and consultancy on the application of psychological techniques to research problems concerned with the attitudes and behaviour of individuals as consumers and users of products and services;

- Design and use *ad hoc* psychometric survey instruments in response to specific needs of client companies and other client organizations, in both the private and public sectors;
- Design and carry out programmes of qualitative research to investigate the motivational and psychodynamic factors that influence individuals' responses to the marketing and promotional activities of private and public sector companies and organizations.

9.4 Psychological Research

All applications of psychology have their bases in fundamental scientific research. Some Chartered Psychologists (many of whom may be employed in academic posts within the universities) offer their services as research psychologists to help clients solve practical problems, often within their particular area of expertise. For instance, a motor manufacturer or a Government Department may commission a research psychologist to investigate and then advise on aspects of vehicle safety.

Appendix B: SPECIALIST SERVICES OFFERED BY CHARTERED PSYCHOLOGISTS

(Reproduced from *The Directory of Chartered Psychologists*, by kind permission.)

1 CLINICAL PSYCHOLOGY SERVICES

1.1 Adult Mental Health – General

Psychologists in this specialty provide services to clients and staff working with adult clients across a broad spectrum. The precise boundary of the specialty in any one locality will be defined by other available specialties. Presenting difficulties include the consequences of problems in living such as anxiety, depression, phobias, obsessions, ruminations, anger control, alcohol-related problems, eating disorders and sexual and marital problems. Clinical psychologists working in Adult Mental Health may also deal with more enduring personality or skill problems, and the psychological elements of psychotic illnesses. The specialty may be designed as a primary care service and/or secondary referral service.

1.2 Adult Mental Health – Rehabilitation

Severe mental illness and the psychological and social consequences of long-term illness are the key concerns of this specialty. Clients are most usually suffering from schizophrenia or severe affective disorder. Psychological assistance is offered with goal planning and skill training. Support is provided for clients and carers. Staff training and consultation with respect to resettlement and development of community services are available. Psychologists will usually be making a major contribution to the Care Programme Approach.

1.3 Child Clinical Psychology

Clinical psychologists working with children and young people offer specialist consultation, assessment, management, treatment and training for individuals, families and groups, as well as for professional staff and organizations responsible for the care and welfare of young people. Presenting difficulties include anxiety, phobias, aggressive behaviour, hyperactivity, learning difficulties, sleep and eating problems, problems relating to chronic physical illness and its effects, school attendance problems, and the effects of disability. By virtue of their generic training, clinical psychologists will have had training and experiencing in working with adults as well as with children and can therefore meet a wide spectrum of needs. In addition, individuals will have specialist skills: for example, the neuropsychological assessment and rehabilitation of children suffering from acute and chronic neurological problems; assessment for child protection where children have been abused; dealing with language disorders, anxiety or sensory impairments, and audit and monitoring of the quality of care of children in hospital. Where problems co-exist, the intervention may occur at a number of different levels, for example individual behaviour management of a child, plus marital therapy with parents and advice to Social Services. Clinical psychologists in this specialty will work in a range of settings including health, social services, education and the voluntary sector. The Children Act has had a major impact on these services.

1.4 Learning Disabilities (Mental Handicap)

Clinical psychologists working with people with learning difficulties can help clients and carers to identify strengths and needs, and to incorporate appropriate goals into individual programme plans. They will also be able to plan, implement and evaluate training programmes to develop skills and to reduce behaviour problems. Clinical psychologists in this specialty can help alleviate difficulties in social skills, communication, developmental delay, anxiety and sensory impairments, and will be able to deal with issues around resettlement from hospital and the development of community services. They offer support to carers, including families and staff in the NHS, Social Services and Voluntary agencies. They will also be involved in staff training and consultancy work. The Community Care Act has increased the role of psychologists in the assessment of needs.

1.5 Elderly People

One of the major functions of the clinical psychologist working in this specialty is the assessment and management of changes in psychological function arising from, for example, memory problems, confusion and dementia. Clinical psychologists will also be involved in dealing with emotional problems such as depression, grief and reactions to bereavement and other losses. They will also be involved in the provision of support for families and other carers, staff training, assisting staff with goal planning, intervention and evaluation, and other consultancy work. Much of the work is directed by the Care Programme Approach and Community Care Act.

1.6 Health and Psychology (including HIV/AIDS)

Clinical psychologists working in this specialty can deal with psychological reactions to physical illness, and in developing improvements to medical and surgical procedures to take account of psychological factors, such as providing increased levels of information, reassurance and counselling and improving compliance with treatment. They may also be involved in psychological aspects of terminal care including work with relatives; support, guidance and rehabilitation of clients with HIV/AIDS and their families and carers; and health promotion, including advice in respect of risk behaviours.

1.7 Neuropsychology

See Section 2 – Clinical Neuropsychology.

1.8 Addictive Behaviours

Clinical psychologists in this specialty will deal with individuals who have drug or alcohol-related problems, their families and carers and any other relevant organizations. Such work may involve designing, implementing and evaluating programmes to reduce or eliminate the use of these substances, or rehabilitation. Psychologists dealing with assessment and intervention into addictive behaviours (including gambling) may be involved in educational and other preventive work.

1.9 Forensic Services

See Section 5 – Forensic Psychology Services.

1.10 Sensory and Physical Disabilities

Psychologists in this specialty will be involved in assessing the type and severity of problems and the psychological implications of these. They will be able to plan, implement and assess training and rehabilitation programmes with family, carers and other staff. They can also be involved in providing counselling support to individuals and their carers, and consultancy services to other staff.

1.11 Research

All clinical psychologists have received training in the conduct of psychological research. This may take the form of, for example, individual process-outcome treatment research, studies of the effects of interventions on groups of clients, large scale longitudinal studies, and research into the effects of aspects of institutionalization. While all of this research will be based on theoretical knowledge, the vast majority of the research done by clinical psychologists is of an applied nature, with real implications for the treatment and management of psychological problems.

1.12 Teaching

One of the major strengths of the science of psychology is that there are a large number of theoretical frameworks which can be brought to bear on a range of problems or situations. Clinical psychologists are uniquely equipped to teach psychological principles and practice to carers, members of other caring professions, and staff involved in planning and providing a service to any of the client groups mentioned previously.

1.13 Management and Planning

Clinical psychologists can make useful contributions to all aspects of service planning in which psychological processes are a factor. This can mean the drawing up of community care programmes for any of the client groups mentioned above; devising, implementing and evaluating the effects of transfer of resources; researching and reporting on the most appropriate forms of need assessment and audit; or creating effective and efficient business plans.

2 CLINICAL NEUROPSYCHOLOGY SERVICES

2.1 Head Injury (Adults) – Assessment
2.2 Head Injury (Adults) – Treatment & Rehabilitation

Head injuries result from a variety of causes: road traffic accidents, occupational and sports injuries, domestic accidents and personal assault. They may range from mild injuries involving no loss of consciousness to severe states associated with coma for a prolonged period. Psychological changes, with social and occupational effects, occur very commonly in more serious cases, but can also follow relatively minor head injury.

2.3 Neurological Disease (Adults) – Assessment
2.4 Neurological Disease (Adults) – Treatment & Rehabilitation

Most diseases of the brain have psychological consequences. The most common are cerebrovascular accidents (strokes and cerebral haemorrhage) and tumours (cancer) of the brain, but there are also degenerating conditions of the nervous system (e.g. MS). Neuropsychologists are concerned not only with the psychological effects of the disease, but also with the side-effects of drug treatment, neurosurgery or radiotherapy, which may save the patient's life but have other psychological consequences for the patient.

2.5 Childhood Disorders (Developmental and Acquired) – Assessment
2.6 Childhood Disorders (Developmental and Acquired) – Treatment & Rehabilitation

Disorders of childhood are a relatively specialized field within neuropsychology because of the developing nature of the growing brain. Children suffer both head injuries and diseases of the nervous system (see 2.3 and 2.4) but the effects may be different from those seen in adults. In addition, certain developmental disorders which affect specific abilities (e.g. dyslexia, spelling difficulties) may become apparent during childhood, as may the syndrome of autism.

2.7 Congenital Disorders – Assessment
2.8 Congenital Disorders – Treatment & Rehabilitation

Congenital disorders are strictly those present from conception, but may include others acquired before and during birth. A number of forms of mental handicap result from congenital conditions of the brain, as do cerebral palsy and spasticity.

2.9 Disorders of the Elderly – Assessment
2.10 Disorders of the Elderly – Treatment & Rehabilitation

A serious problem which affects many elderly people is cerebral dementia: loss of mental faculties in advanced age. Other neurological disorders, such as Parkinson's Disease are also more common in older age groups. The diagnosis and management of these conditions, together with the effects of head injury and neurological disease is a specialized field within neuropsychology.

Each of the preceding are subdivided into:
Assessment
The use of psychological tests and other assessment procedures to determine the current level of intellectual functioning of an individual, or the present state of an individual's personality or life skills. Clinical neuropsychologists offering services for assessment of any of the categories of disorder mentioned should be able to report the likelihood that a given disorder is present, the degree to which psychological functions have been affected, the likely course of the disorder, and to make preliminary recommendations about psychological management and treatment of the disorder.

Treatment and Rehabilitation
Neuropsychologists who offer treatment or rehabilitation services for any of the above categories of disorder will be able to undertake procedures which will improve the psychological condition and functioning of a given client (or relieve the advance of progressive illnesses). They may treat not only the direct effects of the injury or disease, but also anxiety, depression, sexual dysfunction, low self-esteem, anger, or instability arising out of the condition.

They may recommend other treatments and forms of management which can be expected to benefit the patient.

2.11 Medico-legal Services

Certain neuropsychologists have the relevant expertise to offer advice in relation to legal proceedings (civil or criminal) which involve brain damage or disease. Civil proceedings often arise out of road accidents, but may also follow personal, medical or occupational injury. Such neuropsychologists will assess psychological issues, and give opinion on their relationship to behaviour abilities, disablement and treatment in a written report. If necessary they will act as expert witness in a court of law.

2.12 Behavioural Disorders

Some forms of brain damage and disease produce very drastic changes in the sufferer's personal and social behaviour. In certain cases the individual may become untypically aggressive, or may develop personal habits or forms of behaviour which make caring for the individual within the family, with any degree of normal social life, impossible. The care of clients with severe abnormalities of behaviour, and the treatment of these conditions, is the speciality of certain neuropsychologists.

3 COUNSELLING PSYCHOLOGY SERVICES

3.1 Adults

Counselling psychologists offer to adult clients a combination of counselling experience and formal research-based knowledge. They seek to alleviate the psychological distress and suffering that can accompany life transitions and experiences such as parenting, relationship breakdown, sexuality, mid-life changes and infertility. In one-to-one sessions, clients are encouraged to confront and clarify the realities of their lives, including the painful aspects, and to express feelings and concerns, so as to move towards living more resourcefully.

3.2 Students and Young People

The issues and difficulties experienced by young people are assisted by counselling psychologists through student counselling services and career evaluation, psychometric assessment and educational guidance.

3.3 Family and Couples

An understanding of the dynamics involved in human relationships and family systems and alternative strategies for communication and human interaction are offered to those meeting difficulties in these areas of life.

3.4 Elderly

The issues of the elderly, including retirement, bereavement, chronic illness, and loss are a speciality of counselling psychologists. The emphasis is on increased self-empowerment and the creative use of all available resources.

3.5 Health/Medical

Through their employment in GP surgeries, alongside other NHS colleagues or in specialist agencies, counselling psychologists work to assist those challenged with life threatening diseases, such as cancer and AIDS, or disabling conditions. They also counsel those experiencing medical interventions such as pregnancy termination and surgery.

3.6 Groupwork

Exploration of life issues and needs can be effectively explored in a group setting facilitated by a counselling psychologist.

3.7 Organizational

Work place counselling focuses upon issues such as redundancy, management, job satisfaction, organizational stress and creativity.

3.8 Community/Social

Those challenged with issues of social diversity (ethnicity/gender/disability/sexual orientation) are supported and encouraged by counselling psychologists to explore both self-empowerment and changes in community relations through individual and group experience.

4 EDUCATIONAL PSYCHOLOGY SERVICES

4.1 Adolescent Counselling

Adolescence can be a period when some young people encounter emotional or social difficulties. Occasionally they may become involved in different forms of addiction. They may experience other problems such as eating disorders or school refusal. Educational psychologists have skills in counselling and may offer a one-to-one service to adolescents who are in need. This serviced may be either through the school or outside the school, with a referral from parents, the young person or another professional.

4.2 Adults

The great majority of educational psychologists' work is with young people from 0 to 19 years. However, they also offer a service to adults who have educational difficulties, for example students in Further Education, Adult Education and Higher Education considered to have specific learning difficulties. They may be involved in assessing on Adult Literacy programmes and advising on the teaching arrangements necessary. Educational psychologists also work with adults who are parents of children or teenagers causing concern.

4.3 Consultancy

Educational psychologists are able to offer a consultancy services to professionals who are working with children and young people. This service involves helping the adult to define and analyse the area of concern, presenting and evaluating alternative approaches, formulating a strategy and evaluating its effectiveness. Educational psychologists offer consultation or consultancy services to institutions, both schools and other organizations, working with staff in these institutions on an area of concern identified by the organization, for example staff training and research into aspects of the system's functioning, including the demand for certain provision and evaluation of its effectiveness.

4.4 Counselling

Educational psychologists have counselling skills which they use with children and young people of all ages, though more so with older children, and also with adults, particularly parents who are concerned about their children's learning, behaviour or general progress.

4.5 Disability and Handicap

Educational psychologists work with children and young people who have a disability or a handicapping condition. They have expertise in a range of disabilities: sensory handicap, communication disorders, physical disability, moderate and severe learning disability. Their work may involve assessment of the child or young person for educational placement, for planning learning or developmental programmes or to assess resources required or to review progress. They also work with parents and teachers of such children, organizing support groups, counselling sessions on inservice training.

4.6 Dyslexia and Specific Learning Difficulties

Educational psychologists have extensive skills in the assessment of literacy or numeracy difficulties and in planning instructional programmes. Assessment will involve an evaluation of the child's strengths and weaknesses and also an assessment of the learning context in which the child is experiencing difficulties. Educational psychologists give advice about educational placement and a child's needs for additional help and resources. They may also be involved in giving advice to schools or helping to formulate LEA policy in this area. They also advise examination boards on the needs of young people and adults who may require dispensation on account of their specific learning difficulties.

4.7 Family Focused Work

Educational psychologists work with families and some psychologists are qualified to offer family therapy. They will always consult the family when they are working with a child or young person. Sometimes family focused work is what is needed to help the child with the difficulties. This may take place at the school, at the psychologist's own base, a clinic or a health centre.

4.8 Group Work

Educational psychologists have skills in group work and social skills training. They are able to offer groupwork sessions to schools and other organizations working with young people. Such work can help a group of young people to work together more constructively to address their difficulties. Groupwork sessions will take place regularly over a period of time. This work may have either a preventive or a therapeutic function and focus. They may also offer groupwork to teachers and other professionals, including stress management.

4.9 Individual Assessment

Educational psychologists are skilled in a range of educational and psychological assessment techniques. These include psychometric and curriculum related tests, observational checklists and structural clinical interviews. Individual children who are given cause for concern may be referred to educational psychologists in order that they may investigate the concern and suggest ways in which this may be resolved. Most psychological assessment will include an evaluation both of the strengths and weaknesses of the child and of the context in which the child is developing.

4.10 Individual Therapy

Some educational psychologists are qualified to offer individual therapy to children and young people. Children and young people may be referred for therapy because of their emotional or social problems, general anxiety, eating disorders, family or relationship problems, learning difficulties or for some other reason. The context of the referral will often be the school. Educational psychologists may be qualified to offer psychotherapy, hypnotherapy, behavioural therapies or family therapy.

4.11 In-service Training

Educational psychologists offer in-service training to teachers, schools, local authority, voluntary, community agencies and other organizations. They will usually offer a range of specified topics. These might include: assessing learning difficulties, behaviour management, stress management, classroom management, effective learning, improving study skills, bereavement and assessment methods. In-service training will differ in length according to the course and the needs of the audience. Most psychological services and teams will have a list of a range of courses on offer which can be tailored to meet the needs of educational and other establishments.

4.12 Management of Behaviour Problems

Educational psychologists have skills in managing behaviour problems. They may work either with the individual child or young person whose behaviour is causing concern, or with the teacher(s) or with the parents in order to help to reduce or eliminate the behaviour problems. They will first assess the child and the context and then use a range of techniques. These may include behavioural contracts, behaviour therapy, social skills work and instructional programmes, provide help to the school, the parent or from another professional.

4.13 Education Act

Educational psychologists provide psychological advice to local educational authorities who are carrying out a formal assessment of a child's special educational needs under the 1981 Education (Scotland) Act or the 1993 Education Act. They will also reassess these young people who have a statement of special educational needs as necessary and they are involved in the annual review of children and young people with statements.

4.14 Organizational Work

Many educational psychologists have knowledge and skills in the area of organizational development and use these to offer a consultancy service to organizations both within the education service and outside it. They may become involved in issues of staffing, communication, appraisal, management and the functioning of the organization.

4.15 Pre-school Work

Educational psychologists work with under-fives in nursery classes and schools, in day nurseries and in the home. Their work includes assessment for educational placement and developmental programmes. They work with parents both in programmes such as Portage and in less formal settings such as parent groups.

4.16 Research and Evaluation

Educational psychologists have a training and background in research methods. They maybe involved in evaluating the effectiveness of programmes, carrying out surveys to determine needs, planning research and evaluation activities in relation to the education service in general and provision for children with special educational needs in particular. Educational psychologists are familiar with a range of qualitative and quantitative research and evaluation methods including case study, questionnaire and survey methods and relevant statistical and other tools for data analysis.

5 FORENSIC PSYCHOLOGY SERVICES

5.1 The Assessment of Offenders

Concentrates upon issues of offending behaviour and explanations for its commission. Offences might include violent and sexual crime, arson, theft, terrorism, vandalism, and drug misuse. Offenders might include those with mental health problems or learning difficulties, juvenile and adult offenders.

5.2 The Management of Individuals prior to Sentencing

The focus here includes advocacy, alternatives to custody, assessment, the detection of crime, evidence, eye-witness testimony, expert witness skills, informed consent, inquiry, lie detection, offender profiling, remand, witness reliability, false confessions and rights.

5.3 The Management of Offenders following Sentencing

Concentrates upon the rehabilitation of offenders (including sentence planning, anger management, capital punishment, correctional treatment, ethical issues, probation, risk assessment, sex therapy and offender treatment). Issues particular to settings such as persons, young offender institutions, special hospitals, regional and interim secure units, bail and probation hostels.

5.4 The Victims of Crime

Attention here is paid to compensation, including disaster and head injury compensation; malpractice, prevention, third parties, and post-traumatic stress.

5.5 Family/Domestic Issues and Children

Including child abuse, child offenders, children and the law, child witnesses, divorce conciliation, family law, family therapy, incest, juvenile justice, matrimonial law, moral development.

5.6 Policy Issues

Alternatives to custody, clinical criminology, Court of Protection, criminal justice, criminal responsibility/diminished responsibility, ethical issues, guardianship, Home Office affairs, hostage taking, Judiciary, Law Commission, legal frameworks, legislation, Mental Health Act, Mental Health Act Commission, Mental Health Act tribunals, mentally abnormal offenders, Parole Board, Police, Magistrates, and socio-legal studies, reform.

6 OCCUPATIONAL PSYCHOLOGY SERVICES

6.1 Counselling and Personal Development

Counselling can help people to cope with stressful events – change and uncertainty, relocation or redundancy, organizational change, new demands on workers, upheavals in their private lives. Happy events, such as promotion or the decision to make a career change, are also stressful. Occupational psychologists use their wide knowledge and understanding of work to help their clients gain control of their work and to manage their careers.

6.2 Design of Environments and of Work

The right conditions can improve productivity, increase job satisfaction and protect the health of workers. Important factors include such things as lighting, noise and temperature, shift work and fatigue, and the effects of drugs (including medicines and social drugs such as alcohol – not just illegal substances).

6.3 Employee Relations and Motivation

The relationship between an organization and the individuals of whom it is composed is of great importance. Motivation may be difficult to measure but no-one could doubt its significance. Reward, recognition, respect, leadership, loyalty – these key concepts are all psychological in nature.

6.4 Human–machine Interaction

People cannot give their best if they are struggling with the tools they use in their job. Human-centred design and installation of equipment can enhance every aspect of performance. This is true in all spheres, but computer systems in particular need good design, careful selection and thoughtful introduction into the workplace if they are to produce real benefits. And software is as important as hardware.

6.5 Organizational Development

Some organizations are planned, some are haphazard, quite a few are planned yet are *still* haphazard! Occupational psychologists help to plan and manage systematic change in organizational structures, relationships and work procedures in response to changes in the organization's external environment or, for example, to accommodate the introduction of new technology. They do this through many techniques (e.g. team building) and use various tools to assess the organization's culture.

6.6 Performance Appraisal and Career Development

Organizations need to know how their members are performing. They need this information to identify and to rectify conditions which are causing inefficiency, but organizations also need this information for the proper development of their members. Management development is well-established but development is not just for managers.

6.7 Personnel Selection and Assessment

Selecting the right person for the job is the first crucial step in achieving good results for employer and employee alike. Modern systems of assessment, which include the use of psychometrics, computerized selection, assessment centres, biographical information ('biodata') and structured interviews, can ensure that the best decisions are made.

6.8 Training

Maintaining and improving efficiency depends on training and developing staff. Choosing or designing the right programme depends on a proper understanding of the task and an understanding of the learning process. Occupational psychologists have expertise in analysing tasks, in designing and using modern training systems (including Computer-Based Training), and in evaluating the effectiveness of training outcomes.

7 PSYCHOLOGICAL SERVICES IN SOCIAL SERVICES SETTINGS

7.1 Adoption and Fostering

Risk analysis, breakdown, children's reports, parental guidance, BAAF guidelines, abuse in adoption and fostering, broken families, place of safety orders.

7.2 Care of the Elderly in the Community

Residential care, HEPs, dementia, confusion, old age, dependent parents, stimulation, staff training, neurological testing, skill maintenance, terminal care, carer training.

7.3 Child Protection

Child sexual abuse, incest, risk analysis, assessment of trauma, treatment for victim/perpetrator, court reports, consequences of physical abuse, violence with the family, neglect, Children Act (1989), training, prostitution.

7.4 Counselling and Direct Psychological Intervention with Clients

Cognitive behavioural methods, interpretational methods, harm limitation, self control, anger management, stress management, temptation control, assertion, covert sensitization, befriending, post traumatic stress disorder, bereavement counselling, programming, self assessment, sexual counselling.

7.5 Ethnicity Issues

Cultural factors, language factors, religious factors, inner-city problems, hostility to authority, under-valuing, black psychology, racism, under-privilege, housing, uptake of services, anti-discriminatory practice.

7.6 Gender Issues

Sexuality, power politics, rape, sexual discrimination, familial roles, devaluing, stereotyping, abuse, harassment, transsexualism and transvestism, homosexuality, AIDS, HIV.

7.7 Implications of Legislation (Children Act, Care, Access, Adoption and Fostering, Mental Health Act, etc.)

Care and control, Children Act, Education Act, Disabled Persons Act, Care in the Community, Griffiths 2, NHS reform, working for patients, court reports, forensic evidence, giving evidence, child sexual abuse, risk analysis, interviewing victims, interviewing perpetrators, probation, police, solicitors, barristers, juvenile justice, expert testimony, care assistant training.

7.8 Managerial Advice (including service uptake by the community) Offending

Problem solving, communication, decision-making arbitration, personnel, occupational health, stress management, anger management, assertion.

7.9 Personnel Selection

Interviewing, questionnaires, objective methods, projective methods, informal interviews.

7.10 Psychological Aspects of Disasters

Debrief, post traumatic stress disorder, bereavement, counselling, flashbacks, hyper-vigilance, rehabilitation, management of disasters, planning, psychological sequelae of burns, psychological consequences of war, over-protection, crisis psychology, guilt, anger, stress management, re-employment.

7.11 Services to People with Learning Difficulties

Mental handicap, Down's Syndrome, skill acquisition, training, ATCs, SECs, residential care, challenging behaviours, severe brain damage, community support, rehabilitation, normalization, parent and carer training, Portage, secure accommodation, programming, shared action plans, care assistant training.

7.12 Teaching Psychological Skills and Counselling

Psychology, psychiatry, mental health, child development, learning theory, programmes, report writing, observation, data collection objectivity, empathy, statistics, interpretation, normalization, rehabilitation, multi-disciplinary work, mental health, substance use.

8 SERVICES BY TEACHERS OF PSYCHOLOGY

8.1 Assessment

Assessment is about judging how well learning is progressing, either formally or informally, so it includes examinations, marking and giving students informal help. Teaching psychology is concerned with identifying what help students need to deal with different kinds of assessment, including improving learning or performance skills, or coping with academic and emotional pressures.

8.2 Curriculum

The curriculum represents the sum and progress of what students learn when undertaking a course. Planning the curriculum needs to take into account the skills which the students have at the beginning and will have at the end; the psychological aspects of their educational experience and the assessments used; and the way in which educational development will happen as the student follows the course.

8.3 Educational Resources

Students can learn using a wide variety of materials. Educational resources vary in how appropriate they are for any given form of learning; and the construction of effective educational resources may also require psychological expertise.

8.4 Skill-Based Education

Success in education generally involves using many different skills. Some syllabuses, like GCSE, make these very clear; for others the skills are less apparent, although they are still there (for example, the skill of putting together a good essay).

8.5 Teaching Style

Teaching style concerns the way in which students are helped to learn by a tutor or lecturer, since different styles are appropriate for the various types of materials and also for students' needs.

9 Other Psychological Services

Please refer back to pages 356–358.

Appendix C: PROFESSIONAL LIABILITY INSURANCE

The following policy statement is published by the Professional Affairs Board to draw attention to the moral obligation of all Chartered Psychologists to ensure they are covered for third party liability for their actions as psychologists. It should be read by all Society Members and acted on as necessary. First published in The Psychologist, The Bulletin of The British Psychological Society, *Vol. 8, No. 2, 1995.*

WHEN the Professional Affairs Board (PAB) addressed the question of professional indemnity insurance for psychologists in 1987 it considered various proposals put to it as a result of the recommendations of the Board's Working Party on legal protection for psychologists. It authorized the establishment of, and endorsed, a voluntary insurance facility for members which was launched in January 1988 by insurance brokers Bartlett & Co. Ltd.

The Society has already taken a significant step towards the better protection of the public by establishing the *Register of Chartered Psychologists*. The PAB now considers that a further step is necessary to try to ensure that funds are available for redress where a member of the public is harmed in any way by the actions of psychologists. The Working Party recommended that, to ensure that such funds are available, all individual practising psychologists should carry insurance.

The Board recognizes that, until now, the Society has done no more than to draw attention to the desirability of psychologists having personal professional insurance and to make available an approved facility. The Board is, however, aware that the climate in all professions is changing. Other chartered bodies, and some of the registration councils, make it mandatory for professionals to carry third party insurance so that, if they are successfully sued by a client for damages, the professional will not simply go bankrupt leaving the client with no recompense.

RECOMMENDATION

The PAB recognizes that it is probably too early to move to a mandatory requirement for insurance although it would consider such a step if the majority of practising members had voluntarily taken out their own insurance cover.

However, it now considers that, for the protection of the public, there is a moral obligation on every Chartered Psychologist to ensure that, in one way or another, they are covered for third party liability for their activities as a psychologist. In other words, they have a moral duty to protect their client's interests by ensuring that either they have personal third party liability cover for their work or written assurance from their employers that they are so indemnified by insurance policies (or Crown indemnity) held by their employers. The PAB therefore:

- is of the view that it is the responsibility of every Chartered Psychologist to ensure that they have this form of cover and, where their employers do not provide it, to effect such cover themselves;
- also recommends that other practising members should follow this advice;
- reminds all members that, as amplified below, there can be advantages to the individual employed psychologist in having their own personal cover, to look after their own interests, even where an employer provides the necessary indemnity.

The Society does not, at this stage, wish to make the carrying of professional liability insurance compulsory as a prerequisite of registration, but contents itself with the preceding strong recommendations. Similarly, the Society does not suggest that there is only one insurance policy that members should consider, although it has endorsed one scheme which, in its view, meets the requirements set out by the original Working Party.

As substantive guidance on this topic has not been issued since the summary published by the members of the Working Party in 1987, the Board has prepared the following guidance notes.

WHAT ARE THE RISKS?

On what grounds might a psychologist be sued? The grounds are many and diverse. As a way of introduction a few examples (some drawn from actual claims on the scheme) may serve to illustrate the diversity of the problems which may lead the psychologist to the courts:

- a participant in a psychological experiment complains of experiencing considerable distress and of developing undue agitation following a social psychology experiment;
- a clinical psychology trainee is attacked and injured by a patient referred by the supervisor;

- a male counselling psychologist is accused of sexual impropriety with a female client (N.B. The scheme policy is unique in covering such allegations but will only meet the costs of a *successful* defence of an allegation of sexual impropriety);
- an educational psychologist gives schooling and career advice to a teenage child and his or her parents. The child subsequently complains that, by following the advice, he or she did not attend university and has substantially damaged his or her future career (and earning) prospects;
- a company sustains a loss by following the recommendation of a psychologist that they should employ a top executive who subsequently proves to be inadequate;
- on the advice of occupational psychologists a company does not employ a particular candidate. The rejected candidate sues the employer, the psychologists and their firm and complains about the unprofessional conduct of the psychologists to the Society.
- a parent injures their child while carrying out restraint procedures following a talk on child management.

Most of the claims against insured members have proved to be ill-founded, but not until after legal costs (and, in some cases, substantial legal costs) have been incurred on their behalf by the insurers.

TYPES OF LIABILITY

The Society's scheme policy has undergone several metamorphoses since its original conception. In its early days, it was built up from a composite of several different types of insurance cover. The scheme brokers have now coined the term 'professional liability insurance' to identify the modern policy which provides cover for any civil liability devolving on the member arising out of their activities as a psychologist. The cover is all-embracing subject to defined exclusions (such as motor insurance and employers' liability risks). The cover therefore includes, but is not limited to, the following insurance classes:

- Professional indemnity
- Public liability
- Product liability
- Libel and slander.

The *professional indemnity* area of the cover represents the principal area of exposure for psychologists being concerned with a breach of professional duty. This breach can arise in diverse ways:

- through injury to a patient who follows faulty advice;

- through loss to a company which acts on inadequate advice;
- even in the case of an acquaintance who has been given informal, yet faulty, advice without a fee being charged.

Liability for death of or injury to persons other than employees or for loss or damage to third party property is termed *'public liability'*. This liability can arise from the ownership of premises, the defective state of equipment used in consulting rooms or can be something as simple as burning down a client's premises by carelessly discarding a cigarette end. The record award of damages to one person in the UK stood at £1,700,000 until early 1994, for a medical negligence claim. The record now stands at £3,400,000 for a paraplegic injury resulting from a motor accident. If figures of this magnitude can be awarded to *one* person, it emphasizes that psychologists should look very carefully indeed at the level of indemnity protection they carry.

Product liability arises where any items are supplied and these items lead to injury, loss or damage. Thus if a psychologist supplies a client with a faulty enuresis apparatus, faulty biofeedback equipment or even faulty stress management tapes then the psychologist could be liable for any resultant injury or damage.

There have been several interesting claims on the scheme for *libel and slander*. In one case , a psychologist prepared a report for a Social Services department which criticized a child's grandparents. The child's mother saw the report and used the allegations in a family row with her parents. The grandparents sued the psychologist. In another instance, a clinical psychologist's patient asked for a relaxation tape. Unfortunately, the psychologist recorded the tape on the second side of a cassette tape which contained the record of conversations between the psychologist and the patient's psychiatrist which were not particularly flattering to the patient. The patient sued the psychologist.

The Society, in its briefings to the scheme insurance brokers, has tried to ensure that as many as possible of the liabilities which may devolve on members are covered in one policy at a competitive premium. The Society is aware of the difficulties which members have in the past experienced in trying to purchase the individual covers separately, often at very high minimum premiums.

EMPLOYMENT STATUS

The psychologist's risks of litigation are determined by two principal factors – by their employment status and by the domain of psychology in which they operate. Thus the risk for a psychologist who is employed is different from the risk of one who is in private practice or, indeed, from one who gives guidance on a voluntary basis. The risks experienced by academic psychologists are different from those experienced by applied psychologists. If an individual psychologist has several modes of employment, gaining income from employed work and private work, liability depends on the role occupied at the time when the negligent act occurred. The majority of psychologists are employed for most or all of their professional activities. We will start, therefore, by considering the liability of employees.

Employment and the principle of vicarious liability

The liability of employed psychologists is immutably linked to the principle of vicarious liability (Hall, 1983; MacPherson, 1983) which is a legal principle under which the employer of an individual who commits a negligent act bears an obligation in law. If a negligent act occurs in the course of employment, the employer is liable to pay compensation or redress.

However, the employee also remains personally liable for the consequences of their own acts. While this is the strict legal position, in practice claims are usually made against employers because they are more likely to have the funds to meet any damages awarded. If monetary gain is the motivating factor, all may be well for the employed psychologist. As MacPherson (1983) indicated, however, a vindictive claimant may pursue a claim, not (only) in the hope of gaining financial reward but in the hope of generating the greatest degree of distress or the greatest amount of adverse publicity. Thus, the principle of vicarious liability does not necessarily protect the psychologist from litigation.

The risks of the employed psychologist

While, when negligence is alleged, it is usual for the claimant to sue the employer, the litigant also has the option of suing the psychologist. Even when it is the employer alone who is litigated against, there are potential dangers for the individual psychologist.

As a general rule, when an employer pays damages these can be recovered from the negligent employee. Psychologists employed by government agencies may benefit from Crown Indemnity. Other public bodies have a convention that they will not seek to recover from negligent employees. While most private forms would take the same view, it would be prudent for the employed psychologist to seek guidance on this point before any claim is made.

There may be further dangers. MacPherson (1983) noted

it may be '. . . hazardous for a psychologist to depend solely on an NHS lawyer and not be personally represented'. The employer's goal may be to limit their damages as far as possible and, to this end, they may settle out of Court or, indeed, they may defend another employee at the expense of the psychologist. If the psychologist is not independently represented there may be no opportunity to defend their professional reputation which may be impugned in the Courts and in subsequent newspaper articles.

Whilst this paragraph has concentrated on the risks associated with professional negligence claims, the remarks are true, with minor differences, in the area of public and product liability and defamation.

The risks of the psychologist in private practice

Such psychologists need to carry their own protection for all of the areas of professional negligence, public liability, product liability and libel and slander. In addition, if they have employees they must, by law, carry employers' liability insurance.

If they trade as a partnership or a limited liability company then the company itself needs to carry cover. The company's cover should indemnify not only the company/partnership but also the directors/partners and employees for their own negligence and also for any liability those parties might have for the acts of one another. The policy should also provide cover for the acts of self-employed consultants. The company (or indeed, an individual psychologist who employs sub-contractors) is responsible for the acts of consultants carried out in the name of or on behalf of the company. The scheme policy does not provide an indemnity directly to the consultants themselves – as self-employed consultants they should carry their own insurance to protect their own personal liability. However, as noted above, the first port of call for any claimant is almost certain to be the company whether the liability emanates from the acts of an employee or from the acts of a consultant.

A further aspect of private practice relates to academic psychologists. Three types of 'private work' are common:

a) Where an academic institution is awarded a contract and asks a psychologist to perform additional duties for which a specific fee is payable;

b) where an individual psychologist is approached by an outside body to undertake duties outwith normal academic duties. The institution charges a fee and remits an agreed proportion to the individual psychologist;

c) where an individual psychologist is approached by an

outside body and carries out the duties from home, using their own notepaper and not using any facilities belonging to their institution.

Professional indemnity insurance carried by the academic institution will normally only cover private work of the type described in a) or b). Academics engaged in activities similar to those in c) *may* be able to obtain cover under the institution's professional indemnity policy. However, not all institutions carry professional indemnity insurance and only a minority cover all types of private work. Individual psychologists should clarify their own position with their institution.

Similarly, an increasing number of firms of psychologists are effecting professional indemnity/professional liability insurance cover. If such policies are effected through the scheme broker, the policies will automatically indemnify employees, but only 'at the request of the employer'. Employed psychologists should check what cover is carried by their employers and, as importantly, obtain confirmation from the employer that it should be the employer's intention to invoke the protection of the policy for an employed psychologist who was either sued individually or joined in an action with the employer. Even with this confirmation, many employed psychologists are happier to maintain their own individual cover to ensure that their interests will be protected where those interests conflict with those of the employer for a quick and expedient settlement of any claim. (However, this advice must not be read as being alarmist; in most cases the interests of both parties will be identical.)

The risks of the psychologist involved in voluntary activities

Even where services and advice are given on a voluntary basis, a psychologist is still open to litigation on matters relating to professional behaviour. Even in the absence of payment, if psychologists give advice they have a liability if that advice leads to loss or injury. Thus, if voluntary counsellors, trained by a volunteer psychologist, cause harm through the inappropriate use of psychological techniques or if a member of a self-help agoraphobic group falls in front of a bus while carrying out graded exposure exercises which were described by a psychologist, then the psychologist is open to litigation. Even a casual conversation, in which a psychological opinion is sought and acted upon, can lead to litigation.

FINANCIAL AND MORAL VIEWPOINTS

Much of the preceding summary has been concerned with the impact on the individual psychologist. It is not incumbent on the Society to insist that members take out insurance to protect their own interests. However, the PAB is now concerned with the moral obligation psychologists have to ensure that their clients' interests are protected in the event of their being damaged by some action on the part of a psychologist.

The Society's approved insurance scheme

The individual members' policy provides cover for:

- legal costs (both the psychologist's own costs and any other side's costs which may be awarded against the psychologist);
- awards of damages;
- the legal costs involved in representing the psychologist at disciplinary hearings of the Society (the Society elected to include this cover as it was deemed vital to ensure that a member was not denied proper representation purely because of lack of funds; the Society willingly accepts the additional costs in which this decision may involve the Society);
- legal advice on any personal or business matter (it is important to stress that this legal advice helpline is provided by a totally separate organization from that which provides the insurance cover). The premium for this advice helpline is £2 for each insured psychologist. Members will therefore appreciate that this facility is not in any way designed to replace the normal legal advice which every business requires at some time. (It does, however, have the advantage of being available 365 days a year on a 24 hour a day basis.)

It is stressed that, if a member becomes aware of an incident which they think might give rise to a claim against them, they must notify the scheme brokers formally so that the insurers can be notified. Advice taken from the legal helplines does *not* constitute such a notification as advice given by the legal helpline is totally confidential from the insurers and the brokers.

The other cautionary note is a reminder to members that the insurance policy is designed to be reactive rather than proactive. It is designed to respond to claims for damages made against the psychologist. It is not a legal expenses policy and is therefore not designed to allow the psychologist to take action against other persons. The most usual instance of a proactive claim would be where the psychologist thinks that he/she has been defamed; the insurance is not designed to provide funds for psychologists to take action to clear their good name.

The scheme brokers have asked the PAB to remind those members who work from home of the necessity of advising their household buildings and contents insurers of that fact; as well as the fact that it is most unlikely that members' business equipment will be covered by their household contents policy (even where the insurer is aware that the member is conducting a business from home).

Firms and companies

The members' scheme is designed for individual members only. Members who trade as partnerships or who are directors of limited liability companies need a 'firms' policy which gives additional cover and is more expensive. However, the scheme brokers have, over the years of operating the scheme, managed to 'educate' a small panel of insurers into what it is that psychologists do, so have gradually succeeded in obtaining cover for firms at much more realistic levels of premium than used to be the case when insurers assumed that the risks associated with psychology were akin to those associated with accountancy, the law or surveying.

Scheme insurance brokers

In 1987 the Society appointed Dr R. A. Litton AFBPsS to be scheme administrator and his employer, Bartlett & Co. Ltd, as insurance broker. Following Dr Litton's recent appointment as a director of Smithson Mason Ltd, the Society has reconfirmed his appointment as scheme administrator and, with effect from 1 December 1994, has appointed Smithson Mason as insurance brokers to the professional liability insurance scheme.

A revised insurance scheme brochure is available for Chartered Psychologists in the UK and Republic of Ireland from the Society's office. The leaflet also breaks the news to members that, like all insurance premiums, the scheme insurance premium must bear Insurance Premium Tax at 2.5 per cent for all policies incepted or renewable after 1 October 1994.

SUMMARY

For the seven years of the insurance scheme's existence the Society has merely recommended that psychologists should carry such insurance. The PAB now points out that it is very cognizant of the moral responsibility of Chartered Psychologists to protect the interests of the general public and that it now expects Chartered Psychologists to ensure that they either carry insurance or have a promise of indem-